VAN
HALEN
RISING

VAN HALEN RISING

HOW A SOUTHERN CALIFORNIA BACKYARD PARTY BAND SAVED HEAVY METAL

GREG RENOFF

=ecw press=

To Denise and our two little rockers

ACKNOWLEDGMENTS

Many people contributed to the researching and writing of this book. Along with my extended family, I owe a special thanks to my wife, Denise Dutton, who kept the home fires burning as I worked to finish *Van Halen Rising*. I am fortunate that key participants in the rise of Van Halen saw the merit in this project and took the time to speak to me: thank you to Pete Angelus, Michael Anthony, Marshall Berle, Donn Landee, Ted Templeman, and Neil Zlozower. Michael Kelley generously shared his knowledge of the L.A. rock scene in the '70s and has been an unwavering supporter of this project. Roger Renick and Janice Pirre Francis offered me their time and their trust, and they helped me make many essential connections with key interview subjects. Debbie Imler McDermott and Kim Miller shared their priceless memories of their adventures with Van Halen. David Konow introduced me to my fantastic agent, Bob Diforio. Matt Wardlaw helped me secure an essential interview, while Nathan Hodge and D.X. Ferris helped me keep my eyes on the prize. Thanks as well to Jack David, Erin

Creasey, Michael Holmes, Laura Pastore, Susannah Ames, and everyone else at ECW Press. You guys are the best.

Other individuals generously gave their time and energy to the nuts-and-bolts aspects of producing and marketing this book. Andy Harris and Gita Varaprasathan graciously housed me on my Los Angeles research trips. Jesse Fink connected me to many individuals who helped me spread the word about the book. Ruth Blatt, BJ Kramp, Marshall Poe, and Rich Zeoli gave me platforms to discuss this book long before its release. Vain Eudes provided his graphic artistry for my websites and this book's cover. Jeremy Entin built my fantastic website, vanhalenrising.com. Bill Flanagan and Robert J. Stoltz fact-checked and helped edit the manuscript, saving me from many errors. Rob Heinrich patiently labored through many early drafts of my chapters. The talented Jeremy Steffen color corrected and lovingly repaired many of the images that appear in this book. Tom Broderick, Nik Browning, Douglas Guenther, Steven Rosen, and Mike Wolf shared some key source material. Doug Anderson gave me a tour of his fantastic Van Halen Museum. Lou Capoferri offered legal counsel at a key juncture. Thank you all.

I was also fortunate to have a number Van Halen fans as friends, whose emails and messages reminded me that there were many people eager to read this book. Thank you to Gibson Archer, Aaron Cutler, Kevin Dodds, Scott Faranello, Jeff Fiorentino, Allen Garber, Jeff Hausman, Cully Hamner, Heath McCoy, Josh Peters, Mark Prado, Mark Reep, Grant Richards, Cary Schiffman, and David Schnittger. Rock on, all.

A number of individuals shared their rare photographs and memorabilia and, in doing so, greatly enriched this book. My deepest thanks to Lorraine Anderson, Tom Bonawitz, Brian Box, Patti Fujii Carberry, Mary Garson, Dan Hernandez, Mike Kassis, Lynn Larson Kershner, Miles Komora, Jan Velasco Kosharek,

Julian Pollack, Leslie Ward-Speers, Steve Tortomasi, Cheri Whitaker, and Elizabeth Wiley.

While conducting research for *Van Halen Rising*, I interviewed more than two hundred people. Those who went above and beyond the call of duty in helping me include Mark Algorri, Rusty Anderson, Vincent Carberry, Dennis Catron, George Courville, Martha Davis, John Driscoll, Bruce Fernandez, Jackie Fox, Kevin Gallagher, Tommy Girvin, Lisa Christine Glave, Tracy "G." Grijalva, Carl Haasis, Leonard Haze, Eric Hensel, Bill Hermes, Terry Kilgore, Chris Koenig, Jonathan Laidig, Greg Leon, Larry Logsdon, Debbie Hannaford Lorenz, George Lynch, Matt Marquisee, Rafael Marti, William Maxwell, Mike McCarthy, Dana MacDuff, Mario Miranda, Gary Nissley, Valerie Evans Noel, Nicky Panicci, George Perez, Maria Parkinson, Jim Pewsey, Gary Putman, Joe Ramsey (RIP), Randy Rand, Janet Ross, Donny Simmons, Emmitt Siniard, Dana Spoonerow, Nancy Stout, Steve Sturgis, David Swantek, Dan Sullivan, Dennis Travis, Jack Van Furche', Terry Vilsack, and Peter Wilson. To each of you, my sincere thanks.

Most of all, I owe a thank you to those most responsible for sparking this project: Michael Anthony, David Lee Roth, Alex Van Halen, and Edward Van Halen. Van Halen fans hope to see you in the future, not in the pasture.

INTRODUCTION

In light of heavy metal's perennial popularity, it's easy to forget that the abrasive musical form was on the ropes by 1978. Bands that had packed coliseums just years earlier, such as Mountain, Deep Purple, and Grand Funk, had splintered and disappeared. Hugely successful acts like KISS and Black Sabbath saw their album sales soften at a time when the industry enjoyed its greatest profits ever.[1] Even Led Zeppelin, one of the genre's originators, hadn't released an album since the spring of 1976.

As metal declined, other genres exploded. Punk rock, with its aggressive sound and nihilistic lyrics, took root in New York City and London. The growing movement, which was spearheaded in America by Television and the Ramones and in the UK by the Clash and the Sex Pistols, had conquered England and seemed poised to do the same in the States. As the trendsetting Seymour Stein of Sire Records predicted in late 1977, "Boston, New York, San Francisco, and Los Angeles are all into punk now . . . by February and March of next year, I expect punk to explode in America."[2]

While punk had yet to prove its mass appeal, light rock had become a commercial colossus. Starting in the early 1970s, West Coast–based singer-songwriters, country-folk artists, and soft rockers filled stadiums and dominated airplay. By 1977, its appeal showed no sign of subsiding. In fact, the latest releases from Los Angeles's two leading rock groups, Fleetwood Mac and the Eagles, each sold four million copies within twelve months of release.

Then there was the throbbing beat of disco. What had begun in the early '70s as an underground urban phenomenon had become a national dance sensation.[3] Radio stations of all stripes switched to the format, and the music-industry revenues derived from disco totaled something like four billion dollars annually in the late 1970s.[4] The *Billboard* charts, naturally, reflected disco's ability to turn vinyl into gold. For example, the *Saturday Night Fever* soundtrack, driven by the seemingly limitless appeal of the Bee Gees, sold an astounding twenty million copies in 1978 *alone*.[5] And in perhaps the most powerful statement of the genre's chart power, rock acts like the Rolling Stones and Rod Stewart recorded their own disco-flavored singles.

This three-pronged attack further corroded heavy metal's popularity. Punk's ferocious assault on metal's conventions rendered the once mighty Led Zeppelin and Black Sabbath dinosaurs in the eyes of many rock fans. High school kids who came of age hearing hard rock from Ted Nugent and Aerosmith blasting out of their radios encountered the easy listening sounds of Peter Frampton and Jackson Browne on their FM dials by the time they were old enough to vote. Other young people traded leather for polyester and found their musical release on lighted dance floors rather than smoke-filled arenas.

These trends led many industry observers to declare that metal's days were numbered. *Creem*, which had come to embrace punk, asked, "Is Heavy Metal Dead?"[6] *Circus*, which covered hard rock, queried, "Will Heavy Metal Survive the Seventies?" and "Why Are Rockers Going Disco?"[7]

Even rock critics who'd previously flown the metal flag stopped saluting by 1978. Sylvie Simmons gave the Motor City Madman a kick in the balls by writing: "Ted Nugent plays about the best powerhouse rock around, but that's not to say he isn't getting stale. Heavy metal music *per se* is getting stale."[8] Lester Bangs, who was once known as America's greatest rock critic, concluded, "We might as well forget about heavy metal making a comeback, ever."[9]

These trends and appraisals help explain why Van Halen remained unsigned in Los Angeles for years before Warner Bros. Records snatched them up in early 1977. Record industry executives who had encountered Van Halen, a quartet consisting of singer David Lee Roth, guitarist Edward Van Halen, drummer Alex Van Halen, and bassist Michael Anthony, had little use for the group. The conventional wisdom was that the singer, who didn't have the greatest chops, came off like a cheap imitation of the outdated Jim "Dandy" Mangrum of boogie-rockers Black Oak Arkansas. Likewise, the guitarist's playing was too uncontrolled to find a niche on commercial radio. In short, label executives thought the band was an anachronism.

Moreover, Van Halen was too intense and aggressive even for A&R (artists and repertoire) men drawn to riff-based hard rock. Van Halen didn't sound much like the studio-crafted, melodic Boston, the platinum act that in 1976 had produced the bestselling debut of all time. Van Halen sounded even less like Foreigner, the smooth, radio-friendly band that had broken through in 1977. An authority no less powerful than KISS's manager, Bill Aucoin, told the band in late 1976 that they had "no commercial potential" — this more than three years after the Van Halen brothers had joined forces with David Lee Roth.

In the face of this seemingly intractable opposition, Van Halen didn't spend their time trying to drum up label support. Instead, they filled their calendar with bookings and gigged their asses off. Long before anyone outside of the San Gabriel Valley had heard of

Van Halen, they played huge backyard parties, ones that saw sedate suburban streets play host to mini-Woodstocks, and cemented their reputation as Pasadena's most outrageous and notorious local band. They performed at sticky-floor dives, providing the soundtrack for Los Angeles's first wet T-shirt contests. When the city's leading nightclubs wouldn't hire them, they put on their own concerts. And when an unsigned Van Halen opened for the powerful UFO in May 1976, they bulldozed the headliner, leaving no doubt that the quartet was ready for the big leagues.

Van Halen's years in the wilderness also helped the band build a repertoire of amazing original material. While the band had cut their teeth as a cover band, they penned great songs as an unsigned act.[10] Indeed, the band had written future Van Halen classics like "On Fire," "Runnin' with the Devil," "I'm the One," "House of Pain," "Feel Your Love Tonight," and "Little Dreamer" long before they recorded their debut album with producer Ted Templeman.

Their constant gigging and outstanding originals helped the band build a large local following. Because Van Halen didn't have a record deal, their wide popularity surprised even veteran observers. Hollywood DJ and scene-maker Rodney Bingenheimer was stunned by what he encountered when he went to Pasadena Civic Auditorium in April 1976 to watch Van Halen perform in front of their hometown fans. As he told the *Los Angeles Times,* "When I got there, they had something like two thousand kids in the place. They had put the show together themselves. Amazing."[11]

Generating this kind of impassioned support was the band's game plan from the get-go. "We campaigned hard to get a following when we started," Roth later explained. "All the time we were playing we were drawing larger and larger crowds."[12]

In the spring of 1977, the band finally got a contract, and in February 1978, their debut dropped. *Van Halen,* an eleven-track LP featuring a cover of the Kinks' megahit "You Really Got Me," seemed to have a decent shot at charting, especially because it

One of the thousands of flyers distributed by the band and show promoters for one of Van Halen's Pasadena Civic shows. MARY GARSON / HOT SHOTZ

came with the backing of Warner Bros. Records and hit-making producer Ted Templeman.

But industry tastemakers on both sides of the Atlantic took one quick listen to the adrenalized material on *Van Halen* and forecast that the quartet would meet the same fate as metal's moribund giants. Outlets like *Hit Parader* and the *New Musical Express* panned the album, suggesting that Van Halen had just recycled the heavy metal sound of years past. The influential Robert Christgau piled on by writing, "For some reason Warners wants us to know that this is the biggest bar band in the San Fernando Valley."[13] But *Creem* drew the most blood. Seeing Van Halen as the last of a dying species of metallic dinosaurs, the publication predicted that the quartet would "find their evolutionary fulfillment in a quick extinction."[14]

In retrospect, it's clear that metal-averse critics didn't listen dispassionately to *Van Halen*. When they heard the ass-shaking swing of "Ice Cream Man," they grouped Van Halen with boogie-rockers like Foghat. When they heard the bottom-end stomp and monster riff of "Runnin' with the Devil," they labeled Van Halen as a born-again Black Sabbath. When they heard the virtuosity of "Eruption," they pigeonholed the band's guitarist as just another self-indulgent Ritchie Blackmore clone. They thought they'd heard it all before, and what they heard from Van Halen, they hated.[15]

In spite of the critical opposition, *Van Halen* started to sell. Driven by the first single, "You Really Got Me," which topped out at No. 36 on the *Billboard* singles chart, a buzz built about the band and their album.[16] In early March, *Van Halen* cracked *Billboard*'s Top 200 albums chart and would eventually peak at No. 19.[17]

In the meantime, Van Halen toured the world and performed like their lives depended on it. After years of gigging in Los Angeles, they were a tight and powerful band. In the spring, Van Halen pummeled melodic rockers Journey and monster guitarist Ronnie Montrose, who kept them on the bill largely because they'd become a draw. Soon after, Van Halen left that tour for greener pastures as the Pasadena quartet's album went gold in America by selling a half a million copies.

In the months that followed, Van Halen stole the show everywhere they played. The band's creative consultant Pete Angelus, who saw every date of the tour, remarks, "As the success grew — and it grew *very* quickly — at every venue and with every act that they played over or opened for, the response from the audience was just overwhelming." Van Halen was a hurricane of power and energy that devastated audiences and bands alike.

By selling over two million albums worldwide and thrilling hundreds of thousands of fans in 1978, Van Halen kept heavy metal from slipping beneath the waves. Don't believe me? Consider the *Billboard* chart and sales performances of some other potential saviors, young hard rock/metal bands that would become *massive* in the decade that followed. AC/DC's *Powerage*, which was released on May 5, 1978, stalled at No. 133, and wouldn't achieve platinum status until 1981.[18] Judas Priest's *Stained Class*, also a 1978 release, peaked at No. 173 and wouldn't go gold until 1989.[19] The Scorpions' *Taken by Force*, released in December 1977, failed to chart and has sold less than half a million copies to date.[20] These talented acts, despite recording great records for major labels, were still some years away from their commercial breakthroughs. Van Halen, in contrast, broke big right out of the gate.

It's always a rare feat when a brand-new band tops the charts and becomes an in-demand live attraction.[21] But Van Halen had accomplished something even more remarkable. They'd transformed the staid sound of metal into something that sounded fresh and vibrant, an undertaking that many observers would have deemed impossible before *Van Halen*'s street date.

They pulled this off by performing an alchemical miracle on the album. They started by retaining metal's essential elements: the swagger and screams, the monster power chords and over-the-top guitar acrobatics, and the jackhammer rhythms. At the same time, they removed the abrasive impurities — the meandering song structures, fantastical lyrical themes, and doomy sound — that had made metal unpalatable to many late-'70s consumers. They then added hooks so big they could land a whale and choruses so sweet they could rot teeth. With Roth's otherworldly screams and Edward Van Halen's groundbreaking guitar pyrotechnics dominating each of the album's eleven tracks, Van Halen had distilled heavy metal down to its essential elements.

So when rock fans dropped the needle on *Van Halen*, they didn't hear lengthy, self-indulgent jams or lumbering, doomy dirges. On the contrary, they heard what Roth would later term "Big Rock": a streamlined sonic assault that combined metal's power, energy, and virtuosity with shimmering pop sensibility. In doing so, they invented pop metal — radio-friendly hard rock catchy enough that it could sell millions in a musical climate that was flat-out hostile to the genre.

In the end, Van Halen's success proved the theory of musical evolution and made it difficult for critics and cynics to make the case that in 1978 heavy metal was doomed to extinction. By drawing up the lasting blueprint for pop-friendly hard rock — and heavy metal guitar prowess — Van Halen redefined and reinvigorated hard rock at the very moment when it seemed destined for musical obsolescence and cultural irrelevance. Van Halen, in other words, saved heavy metal from the scrap heap.

Remarkably, the way that Van Halen evolved into a band great enough to sell millions of records and skilled enough to electrify stadium crowds has been shrouded in mystery and supposition since Van Halen became famous. That's a pity, because before anyone outside of Los Angeles knew about the greatness of Van Halen, everything that has made the best episodes of *Behind the Music* must-see TV had already happened to the band. Van Halen's road to success wasn't smooth and it wasn't short, but it was a dizzying, white-knuckle ride.

BEGINNINGS

It's rare that something so loud comes to life in someplace so quiet, but that's exactly how it happened with America's greatest rock band. In the 1970s, Van Halen evolved into a musical force in Pasadena, a Los Angeles suburb of white picket fences, tree-lined streets, and good schools. David Lee Roth reminisced about those environs on the band's 2007 reunion tour. "The suburbs, I come from the suburbs," Roth told a packed house at the Staples Center in Los Angeles. "You know, where they tear out the trees and name streets after them. I live on Orange Grove — there's no orange grove there; it's just me . . . we used to play the backyard parties there. I remember it like it was yesterday."[22]

But years before Van Halen ever disturbed the peace in Pasadena, the group's future members laid the foundation for a partnership that would make rock history. Soon after arriving in America in 1962, the Van Halen brothers resolved to become top-flight rock musicians. Likewise, David Lee Roth set his sights on becoming a rock singer — a rock star, as he'd put it — before he and his family even made it to the San Gabriel Valley in 1963. Van Halen didn't come to life until the early 1970s, but the band's true genesis dates back a decade prior.

= =

Before the Van Halen family made music in California, they made it in Holland. Jan van Halen (Jan would begin capitalizing his surname's first letter after he arrived in America) was born in Holland on January 18, 1920, to Herman van Halen and Jannie Berg.[23] When the Netherlands fell to the Nazis in 1940, a young Jan joined the Dutch resistance, only to become a prisoner of war. After his Nazi captors discovered that he had an aptitude with the saxophone and clarinet, they placed him in an orchestra that toured German-occupied Europe.[24]

When the conflict ended, he played in jazz acts, hit the road as part of a circus orchestra, and later performed on live radio shows in Holland.[25] He then relocated to Indonesia, where he met and married Eugenia van Beers. "Our pop went over to Indonesia on a six-week radio contract, which turned into six years," Alex recalled. After the fall of the Dutch-backed Indonesian government, the couple moved to Amsterdam, where they welcomed two new additions to their family: Alexander Arthur van Halen, born on May 8, 1953, and Edward Lodwijk van Halen, born on January 26, 1955.[26]

The boys had their musical baptism almost at birth. In Holland, they started taking piano lessons when Edward was about five years old.[27] They also traveled with their parents as their father toured with jazz and big band acts during the late 1950s. "We were taken all over the place," Alex explained to the *Los Angeles Times*. "If my dad was going somewhere, we'd all go to the gig and hang out. My mom couldn't afford a babysitter."[28] Edward added, "Growing up in Holland when me and Alex were seven years old, we used to go across the border to Germany to clubs where he played. That was just normal to me . . . staying up to two, three in the morning, hanging in the club."[29]

By 1960, Jan's career was on the ascent. His talents had earned him a spot in the elite Ton Wijkamp Quintet, which won honors at Holland's Loosdrecht Jazz Festival that year.[30] Edward, reminiscing about his father's musical career in Europe, said, "My dad was one of the baddest clarinet players of his time. He was so hot — unbelievably."[31]

Despite Jan's success, the van Halen family began to consider relocating. Some of Eugenia's relatives, who lived in Southern California, had written to Jan and Eugenia and told them about the promise of American life. "We had some family that had moved to L.A.," Alex said, "and they were always writing letters about the beautiful weather, the ample opportunities, and whatnot."[32]

Convinced that Jan could find greater success in America, the van Halen family departed Holland on February 22, 1962, by steamship. They carried with them a few suitcases, a Rippen piano, and about seventy-five guilders. To subsidize the cost of their passage, the family entertained their fellow passengers during the nine-day trip. "Alex and I actually played on the boat while we were coming to America," Edward recalled. "We played piano, and we were like the kid freak-show on the boat."[33]

After arriving in New York, the family took a cross-country train trip to Southern California and settled in the prosperous Los Angeles suburb of Pasadena, having spent most of their savings to pay their way to America.[34] As Edward would later summarize, "My father was forty-two years old when he left Holland and came to Pasadena with fifteen dollars and a piano."[35]

= =

Despite the city's advantages, the family's dream of a better life did not initially come to pass. Instead of finding themselves in a suburban dream home, the Van Halen family rented a cramped apartment at 486 South Oakland Avenue. Their new home was so modest that all three families in the building shared the same bathroom.[36] Over the next four years, the family would relocate in Pasadena at least two more times.[37]

During their first months in America, the Van Halen clan had bigger problems than housing. "My dad couldn't speak the language . . . and he didn't even know how to drive a car, 'cause in Holland you ride bicycles, at least back then," Edward said, as he recalled his father's first American job as a dishwasher at Arcadia Methodist Hospital.[38] Because his father didn't even own a bicycle, he walked six miles each way to work,[39] and his mother pitched in by working as a maid.[40] These difficulties led their youngest to call the "American Dream" that had brought them to America "a crock of shit."[41]

Of course, Jan had hoped to support his family through music. "For my dad, America was the land of opportunity," Alex remembered. "Then he found out differently, of course. The big band thing wasn't happening here either."[42] In fact, when it came time to provide the city of Pasadena with information for the 1962 city directory, Jan listed his occupation as a "machinist."[43] Nevertheless, Jan did find some part-time work as a musician.[44]

For the brothers, the language and cultural barriers that initially separated them from their peers drew the two together. Alex explained, "The only friends we had were each other. That's part of the reason we're so close. We knew no English whatsoever. It had a lasting effect on us in terms of [being able to accept] traveling and touring and not being sure what the next day brings."[45] Edward agreed, adding, "We were two outcasts that didn't speak the language and didn't know what was going on. So we became best friends and learned to stick together."[46] Still, in the months that followed, the brothers began to build friendships with kids they'd met in school and in their neighborhood.

As the brothers acculturated, their parents' hard work began to pay off. On April 27, 1966, they purchased an 896-square-foot home located at 1881 Las Lunas Street in Pasadena.[47] Still, the Van Halens remained far from prosperous. George Courville, who lived nearby and has known the Van Halens since he was seven years old, remembers, "They had the smallest house on the block. These were all Pasadena bungalow homes. There were two bedrooms. The kids had one room and the parents had the other. There was a single bathroom, a living room, a dining room, and what they called a galley kitchen."

Ross Velasco, who was a close friend of the brothers, recalls an incident that highlights life in the Van Halen household in the 1960s. "Alex and I had been down to the beach to bodysurf. Someone broke into my van when we were in the water and stole all of our clothes, even our shoes. So we drove back to Pasadena in our wet swimsuits. When we pulled up to Alex's house his mother was at the door. She was such a sweet woman. He told her what happened, and she got very upset. I think at that time she might have been sewing and making the clothes he wore. She was most upset that he had lost his shoes."

This hand-to-mouth existence prompted Jan and Eugenia to ponder their sons' futures. In their minds, music offered the best prospects, and so music lessons remained a staple in the brothers' lives. Alex and Edward took violin lessons while in elementary and junior high school, with Alex progressing well enough on the instrument to make the Los Angeles All City Orchestra.[48] But their parents had one particular hope for their children. "Mom had this grandiose idea of us becoming concert pianists," Alex told the *Los Angeles Times*. "We kept it up about ten years. It made for a great foundation in music. You learned all the theory, and it forced you to listen to different kinds of music."[49]

While Edward's and Alex's years of piano lessons are a well-known component of the Van Halen story, less is known about *who* gave them lessons. Soon after settling in Pasadena, Jan and Eugenia hired an elderly Lithuanian pianist named Stanley Kalvaitis. He'd teach the boys for a stretch of years during the 1960s. From their first lesson onward, the brothers learned that Kalvaitis was nothing if not demanding and harsh. "I had this Russian teacher who couldn't speak a word of English," Edward told *Guitar Player*, "and he would just sit there with a ruler ready to slap my face if I made a mistake."[50]

Despite the family's meager resources, Jan and Eugenia had not employed a run-of-the-mill teacher. Kalvaitis was a seasoned professional pianist and a 1914 graduate of the elite Imperial Conservatory in St. Petersburg, Russia, an academy that trained, among other musical greats, Pyotr Tchaikovsky. While at the Conservatory, Kalvaitis studied under some of the giants of Russian classical music, including composer, pianist, and conductor Nikolai Tcherepnin and violinist Leopold Auer. He also shared classrooms with luminaries like composer Sergei Prokofiev and violinist Jascha Heifetz.[51] Edward and Alex, it turns out, learned piano from a musician who'd studied and played with world-class talent.

In the case of Edward, these revelations cast his later guitar mastery in a new light. While he never took guitar lessons, his musical foundations came from formal study with an elite musician.

Kalvaitis, who recognized his young pupils' gifts, entered them in the Southwestern Youth Music Festival in Long Beach between 1964 and 1967.[52] As a contestant, Edward enjoyed success. "I was good," he told journalist Steven Rosen. "You sit there and practice one tune for the whole year, and they put you in a category and judge you. I think I won first place twice and second place the last time."[53]

Despite Edward's achievements, neither Edward nor his brother enjoyed these lessons or thought much of their under-girding philosophy. Alex remembered, "We used to go to these contests, where you were given a certain piece of music, and they tell you to play it, and if you don't play it the way they interpret it, then you lose points. Well I don't think music should be that way."[54] Edward rebelled by memorizing the compositions rather than learning how to read music.

Still, Jan and Eugenia indulged their children by letting them play other kinds of music with friends. Dana MacDuff, who went to school with Edward and Alex, remembers one of these kiddie acts: "I was a third grade student at Hamilton Elementary School. We'd have lunch outside near the pergola and there'd be performances for the student body. One day there was a band playing; it was Ed and Al, and their band was called the Broken Combs. I was totally unaware that they were budding musicians." The pint-sized group, which featured Edward on piano and Alex on tenor saxophone, was rounded out by Don Ferris on alto saxophone and the Hill brothers on drums and guitar.[55] "They were just kids at our school. Ed played the piano. He was a year ahead of me. I remember the guy who was the leader of the group said, 'And now — your favorite and ours — Boogie Woogie!' They played that kind of music."

For young boys who loved music but were less than enthusiastic about violin and piano, guitar-driven rock music had become a potent distraction by the mid-1960s. Edward noted that the brothers had been "kind of sheltered" from rock prior to their arrival in America.[56] As Alex recalled, "Edward and I were seriously going to train to be concert pianists, but then the Beatles and the Dave Clark Five came along, and so it was goodbye, piano."[57] Alex, who'd begun taking flamenco lessons, now wanted an electric guitar, while his brother coveted a drum set.

To pay for these instruments, the brothers became paperboys. Edward's childhood friend Rafael Marti remembers, "Alex had a double paper route. Hmm, I think both of them had double paper routes come to think of it. They used the money to buy equipment. It was beg, borrow, and steal with those guys."

Before long, friction arose in the Van Halen household over Alex's and Edward's declining commitment to the piano and violin. Alex, who struggled to make progress on the guitar, saw his interest shift to drums, which he played with gusto when his brother wasn't around. Edward, in turn, took to guitar as he continued to play drums. Despite their parents' wishes, it became clear that the brothers' other instruments wouldn't be central to their aspirations.

Within a short period of time, both brothers realized that they had an affinity for each other's instruments, which led them to make their legendary swap. As Alex explained, "I could play all the chords and do whatever, but for some reason, my fingers could just not move fast enough. I knew that I was limited. I mean, you can practice all you want; if it isn't there, it isn't there. It's not going to grow. But I noticed when Ed picked up the guitar, he could play better than guys who'd been playing for years. So when he was gone, I got on the drums and just started playing them."[58]

For Edward, the switch made sense not only because he had a talent for guitar, but also because the instrument inspired him in a way that drums didn't. "The first song I ever learned was 'Pipeline,' by the Surfaris, and 'Wipe Out.' Then I hear this song on the radio — it was the 'Blues Theme' on the soundtrack to [*The Wild Angels*]," he told *Spinner*. "It was the first time I heard a distorted guitar, and I'm going, 'God, what is that?' I didn't really have an amp then. I went to Dow Radio in Pasadena, and I jury-rigged this plug to plug into the stereo. I just turned the damn thing all the way up, and it distorted. So every amp I've ever used, I just turn it all the way up."[59]

Rob Broderick, who was friends with the brothers, remembers when Edward had taken up guitar full-time and had gotten his hands on an amp. "When I first met Eddie, he was going into sixth grade and I was going into seventh, and he had this little Fender twin amp. He was playing something like 'Day Tripper' and I was like, *Wow, this kid is playing this song well and he is in elementary school!*"

Edward's and Alex's interest in rock only grew after they formed a band with a friend. Jim Wright, who met Edward at Pasadena's Jefferson Elementary School after Edward transferred from Hamilton Elementary, recalls, "My last name is Wright, so they stuck the new kid with the last name Van Halen by me. We got to talking and we got along. Ed said, 'Do you want to come over my house and have lunch?' I said sure. So I went over to the house on Las Lunas. I see this guitar and drum kit in the back room."

That day, Edward strapped on a Sears Silvertone guitar plugged into a Fender Deluxe Reverb. "Ed played something and I said, 'Wow, you can really play!' Well one thing led to another and we became close friends. This was in sixth, seventh, and eighth grade. Ed said, 'We've got these paper routes. Why don't you save your money, buy a guitar, and I'll teach you how to play.'" After throwing papers for some weeks, Wright had an instrument of his own.

Wright remembers that soft-spoken Edward was eager to teach him. "I played bass guitar on a regular guitar, so I wasn't much of a bass player." Wright, who isn't a natural musician, says that his friend did his best to improve his chops. "I took guitar lessons from Eddie Van Halen," he laughs. "He was very patient. He never got mad. I'd never tell people I took lessons from him, because today all I can do is barre chords. Ed taught me everything I knew how to play, and Al would get frustrated because I played it so poorly!"

Regardless of Wright's struggles, a new band was born. "Our band was first called 'The Sounds of Las Vegas,' and then just 'The Sounds.' Al took this piece of white cardboard and wrote 'The Sounds' on it and stuck it in his bass drum."

The brothers then set out to teach Wright the songs they knew and learn some new ones together. This meant that at first the Sounds' repertoire consisted largely of surf music. "Mostly we played things like 'Wipeout,' 'Pipeline,' and instrumentals like that. They liked the Ventures." Edward later recalled that one of the first songs he learned on guitar was "Walk, Don't Run" by the Ventures, suggesting that the Sounds played this tune as well.⁶⁰ Later, the band added pop songs by the Beatles and the Monkees, including "Steppin' Stone." Wright remembers, however, that they played them without vocals. "None of us liked to sing. Ed didn't really sing during my time with him."

By 1967, the brothers had discovered Cream, the English blues-rock power trio that had broken big in America after the release of their *Fresh Cream* and *Disraeli Gears* albums. Wright says, "They were both Cream fanatics. Alex was really into [drummer] Ginger Baker."

Edward, in turn, went wild for Eric Clapton. At that moment, Clapton was arguably the most famous electric guitarist in the world, and his exceptional playing would prompt rock fans to dub him a "guitar hero." But, tellingly, Edward's initial attraction to Clapton stemmed more from his musical upbringing than anything "Slowhand" had recorded. "I was just turned on by the sound and feel he got," Edward explained. "To me, a guitar sounds like a saxophone. My father plays sax and clarinet, and I guess that's part of it. But Clapton reminded me of a tenor sax."⁶¹

Wright says that the brothers' musical obsession meant that practices involved hard work and significant stress. "We'd learn songs. Ed and Al played their albums. They'd listen to a part. They'd pick up the needle, and then they'd practice it. Al worked on the arrangements. In the beginning of learning a song, he'd say things to Ed like 'You need to pick up the tempo.' But mostly he left him alone." Instead, the intense, hardheaded Alex rode Wright, who always felt one step behind the brothers and was intimidated by the elder Van Halen child. "I thought we duplicated songs pretty well, but I never sounded good enough for Alex, who was the boss. I was afraid of Alex more than anyone else. Alex was not too nice to me."

Eventually, the Sounds started gigging. "The Van Halens played at Marshall Junior High School," Dana Anderson remembers. "It was an assembly where kids could show off their talents . . . I don't know if Ed would remember this. I was sitting in the audience with a girl named Sandy, and we were going, 'Oh man, these guys are good!' Alex played drums and Ed played guitar, and they had another guy on guitar."

Rudy Leiren, who later served as Edward's guitar tech, saw the same show. He recalled, "I was way up in the balcony of Marshall Junior High School here in Pasadena. Down on stage there were these three guys in jeans and white T-shirts standing there, playing Top 40, all the top hard rock songs back then. I was just spellbound. They were playing all the songs I knew off the radio."[62]

Along with learning songs on their own, Edward and Alex also received a musical education at the hands of their father during the mid to late 1960s. Jan, who didn't love his sons' tastes but was thrilled that they'd taken to music, gave Alex, Edward, and Wright the chance to warm up his audiences. "Ed and Al's dad was a clarinet player, and we also played at a nightclub when he played. We'd be the intermission act for his polka band. Ed and Al and I would play our Monkees music. That was our heyday," Wright laughs.

In the years that followed, the brothers tagged along with their father when he gigged. Edward recalled that Jan played "weddings, bar mitzvahs, polkas, and all that other shit . . . My dad would play at the Continental Club every Sunday night, and we would sit in with him. He'd play at a place called the Alpine Haus off of San Fernando Road in the Valley, and we'd wear the lederhosen."[63] When Jan let thirteen-year-old Alex sit in on drums, he'd tell him "just duck your head down," in the hopes no one would notice he wasn't even old enough to drive.[64]

These opportunities increased as the brothers grew up. Rob Broderick remembers, "We were down playing football at Victory Park, and their dad shows up and says, 'Kom hier' to Alex. He wanted him to substitute as a drummer that night. This had happened before, but I didn't know it. But then Jan decided to drag Ed and me along to be the 'baby band' and open the show."

They all repaired to a large German-American club on Hollywood Boulevard. Broderick recalls Jan wearing his leder hosen as he helped the boys set up onstage in front of a "very festive, all-German" crowd. That night, Broderick played drums while Edward played guitar. "It was the very first time we got to hear Eddie sing" in front of an audience, he says. "We were doing 'Day Tripper' and all this Beatles stuff." At the end of the night, Broderick says Jan "passed the hat" so the boys could be paid for their performance. Edward later recalled that on a night just like this one, Jan collected twenty-two dollars. He counted the money and then handed Alex and Edward each five dollars before telling them, "Welcome to the music business, boys."[65]

= =

In 1963, Nathan and Sibyl Roth and their two children, David and Lisa, moved from Massachusetts to Altadena, a community that abutted Pasadena. Nathan, who was training to be an oph-thalmologist, hoped to start a medical practice to support his family. David, who was born on October 10, 1954, in Bloomington, Indiana, would describe his new environs as "the middle of the lower-middle-class multicultural hodgepodge."[66] A few years later, Nathan and Sibyl would have another child, Allison.

In elementary school, Roth became enamored with music and began soaking up the influences that would give shape to the classic Van Halen sound. But unlike the Van Halen brothers, who were instrumentalists, Roth focused on vocals.

His interest in singing took root early. When he was barely in elementary school, Roth got his first phonograph records, which were Al Jolson recordings. As he told *Rolling Stone*, "I had a collec-tion of the old breakable [Jolson] 78s. I learned every song, and then the moves, which I saw in the movies."[67] Roth explained to *Musician* what drew him to the long-dead singer, actor, and comedian. Jolson, Roth said, "was doing something completely off the wall. He had a great voice, a lot of conviction, determination, a show that shook the world." Roth had "learned all his greatest hits by the time I was seven. And ever since, I've known that I would make music onstage."[68]

While Jolson's influence would never fade, Roth had arrived in California at the same moment that the British Invasion hit American shores.[69] He embraced the Beatles, the Kinks, and the Rolling Stones.[70] Roth explained, "Music got cool. At the same time, it was revved so hot that you would watch *The Ed Sullivan Show* and one week see the Beatles and the next week see the Rolling Stones. Now, the Beatles had matching suits without lapels, the boots with the pointy toes."[71]

He also came to love soul music. Roth, who'd received a radio as a gift from his Uncle Manny, remembered the life-changing moment when he first switched it on: "I put it on, and there was Ray Charles singing 'Crying Time,' and I just knew I had to be on the radio."[72] Roth sang along with Motown artists like Martha and the Vandellas, the Four Tops, the Temptations, and other black singers like Major Lance, whose 1964 smash "Um, Um, Um, Um, Um, Um" was the first record Roth ever bought.[73]

By the time Roth matriculated to Eliot Junior High School in Altadena in the fall of 1966, his love for music had already shaped his aspirations. He'd tell his younger sister Lisa, "I'm going to be a rock star." As Lisa observed to her friend Maria Parkinson (who'd later appear in Roth's "Yankee Rose" video), Roth wouldn't say, "I *want to be* a rock star." Instead, he'd tell his sister, "I'm *going to be* a rock star."

He soon started sharing this vision with his friends. George Perez, who met Roth in seventh grade at Eliot, remembers that one day he and Roth struck up a conversation about the future. Perez told Roth that he wanted to be a ballplayer, and then asked,

"What do you want to be when you grow up?" Without missing a beat, Roth replied, "A rock and roll star." Perez says, "I looked at him and went, 'Yeah, right, sure. Whatever. You've got to be kidding. You? Come on! You're a little punk kid! What are you talking about?'" Bill Maxwell, who later played in a garage band with the Van Halen brothers, recollects having similar exchanges with Roth. "Way before that guy met anyone in Red Ball Jet [Roth's first band], that guy wanted to be a rock star. He did. We used to laugh at him. 'You're *never* going to be a rock star!' You know how kids can be so mean." But as Perez explains, regardless of what he, Maxwell, or anyone else thought, Roth "was determined. *Determined.*"

Still, Vincent Carberry, a friend of Roth's who also attended Eliot, insists that Roth was no one-trick pony. Carberry met him in ninth grade, sometime after Roth had departed and then returned to Eliot after a less than stellar semester at the private Webb School. "I think we probably just met walking home from Eliot Youth Club or something. Now I do remember him often talking about music, but he also talked about other things. That's kind of how we got started being friends; we were both interested in stuff maybe most other kids our age weren't interested in, like new books and books that were cool, like *Catch-22* . . . We could talk about jazz music or Lenny Bruce or something, things most guys our age didn't have a clue about. Most of the guys we knew either liked that kind of stuff or white hot-rodder, hard rock type of stuff. There were very few people we knew [who] liked both. Dave had a very wide-ranging cultural knowledge."

Part of that knowledge involved horses. In his early teens, Roth took up horseback riding, a pursuit that his mother loved as well. Dennis Neugebauer met Roth at the Arroyo Seco Stables, where Roth's mother boarded her horse. "I had to work out at the stables, because my grandmother owned them," he says. "He was a very good rider. His younger sister, Lisa, and his mom, Sibyl, also rode."

Roth would take a job at the stables around 1967 and would

work alongside Neugebauer and Bill Maxwell. Maxwell explains, "We worked there and walked horses and got kicked or bit or whatever for two bucks an hour."

Roth's life was profoundly changed when his mother had a riding accident at the stables. At the time, Roth was in the ninth or tenth grade.[74] Sybil, it turned out, had suffered a significant head injury and spent a year in the hospital, leaving Dave, his two sisters, and his father to hope and pray for the best as she convalesced.

Sybil's fall and the subsequent dissolution of his parents' marriage affected Roth in another way. It somehow unshackled him. Perez observes, "In middle school he was pretty straight. His dad had a lot of influence over him, a lot of control. Dave couldn't really do a lot back then. He went to youth club dances back in seventh and eighth grade and his parents picked him up. They pretty much had control over him during those early years. I think the change came when his mother had an accident on a horse. After that his freedom exploded."

In 2013, Roth explained to the *Brisbane Times* that the aftereffects of his mother's injury made his parents' already strained marriage unworkable. "When she came out [of the hospital]," Roth said, "she was a different person, and that added fuel to an already smoldering antagonism in her marriage with my dad. I learned when it's over, it's over."[75]

Over, in the interim, meant that Nathan Roth, whose new medical practice was doing well, would move out of the family's home in Altadena. Carberry recalls, "I don't know what happened, but it was after that things all went downhill between the parents. Dr. Roth moved out to this big, cold, modern house in San Marino, which is a very wealthy suburb right by Pasadena." Roth's parents would eventually divorce, prompting Roth to move in with his father while he was in high school.

= =

Meanwhile, tensions grew in the Van Halen household about the boys' waning interest in piano. Broderick recounts the family dynamic that developed around this point of conflict in the late 1960s: "We played in their house all the time. It was a small house, smaller than you even think. Their mom really couldn't hide from the noise of the drums and the guitar. We'd be playing and I'd ask, 'Where's your mom?' They'd say, 'Oh, she's taking a nap.'" With a laugh, Broderick recalls that he'd incredulously reply, "She's taking a *nap?*"

But, as Broderick observes, "The drums and guitar and the amp were the carrot. They got the carrot, but they *had* to practice piano or they'd get the stick. We'd be goofing off in the back playing guitars and his mom would pop in and say, 'Edvahd! *You must practice piano!*' He'd give her some crap, sigh, and say no. But he *had* to practice at least thirty minutes every day. It was, 'If you want to play guitar, you have to play piano.'"

Jim Wright has a different take. He remembers that Jan and Eugenia always put the piano first, which, at least in Edward's case, actually served to make him a better pianist. "Before they played drums and guitar they had to practice the piano for the allotted time that the teacher had assigned. Ed could not pick up the guitar until he finished that time. I think that's why he learned to play the piano so well. They had to finish their piano practice *before* they played the other instruments and they *really* wanted to play the guitar and drums."

Regardless, Jan and Eugenia remained focused on piano instruction for their sons, especially after Kalvaitis made a very generous gesture. "We were taking lessons in San Pedro," Alex recalled. "It was quite a schlep, and we couldn't do it anymore. [Our] folks were working. Then he says to us, 'If you come down here on the weekends, I will teach you for free.' So now you [feel] obligated. It creates a very strange guilt-kind-of-a-trip. He's doing it for free, so we better do it."[76]

Still, Wright says that perhaps the clearest demonstration of Edward's guitar-first mentality took place *at* their piano competitions. "Eddie and Alex would compete in these talent contests. We'd all go, and Eddie would bring his guitar. In between the sessions of piano we'd play guitars that we brought along."

This kind of dedication allowed Edward to progress rapidly on the instrument. Dana Anderson remembers the fall of 1967: "I met Ed on the first day of seventh grade. I think I had been playing for two-and-a-half years and he had just started playing guitar. We got together and played a few times. He was learning very quickly."

In the months that followed, Anderson would discover that his friend had a musical ear that was unparalleled. "I recall going down to a local music store and picking up Cream's *Wheels of Fire* when it first came out [in August 1968]. We'd heard a couple of songs on the radio. So we took it back to his house with my guitar and amp to figure out 'Crossroads.' He listened to it the first time through, diddling here and there. By the second time he was basically playing along with it."

By the fall of 1968, other musical changes were afoot at 1881 Las Lunas Street. Wright decided suddenly to end his partnership with the Van Halen brothers. By this point, Edward and Alex both smoked and drank and hung around kids who didn't make school a priority. Wright says, "Eventually I could see that the lifestyle of a musician would lead me down the wrong path. I was not doing well in school. I had stopped playing baseball. I was smoking cigarettes. There was dope around. So I just stopped hanging around. Ed was just like, 'What happened?' I never had the chance to explain things to him because I didn't want him to feel responsible. I still feel badly about that, because it wasn't his fault."

Despite this bump in the road, the brothers didn't let their lack of a bass player stop them from playing. Brian Box, a harmonica-playing friend of the brothers, remembers, "They practiced at my house a few times. A lot of those days it was just Alex and Edward.

Nobody else. They were just learning how to play, basically. They knew some cover songs. One song we used to play all the time was 'Sitting on Top of the World.' Other than Cream, the other one we played was 'Stormy Monday.' But they didn't have a bass player, and they didn't even have a vocal mike. That's why they were always looking for somebody who had other equipment."

Even without a bassist, they still played plenty loud. Box says, "One funny thing happened when they were really young and practicing at my house. The cops showed up. They come inside the house, saying, 'This neighbor behind you is complaining.'" Box and the brothers agreed to turn it down, and the police left, only to return two more times in the next hour. "So finally this cop comes and says, '*If I hear one more note, somebody's going to jail.*' Right then Alex just hit the snare drum." Box left the house in handcuffs.

= =

Across town, David Lee Roth started high school at a moment of racial upheaval in greater Pasadena. In the fall of 1969, Roth — along with Carberry and Perez — entered John Muir High School as tenth graders just months before a Federal district court held that Pasadena Unified School District had failed to integrate its schools.[77] As a result, students of different races would be bussed around Pasadena in order to promote racial balance in each school. Roth later explained with a bit of poetic license, "See I went to the school where they first started bussing, in Pasadena, California, and I was there on the first bus."[78]

At the time, Muir had a primarily black student body but also had a significant number of Hispanic and Asian students. Unlike many white students at Muir, Roth came to embrace and internalize this racial landscape. "I started to see myself as a black person," Roth asserted in his autobiography.[79] He later explained that his love of all things black led his white friends to come up with a nickname for him: "I picked up all kinds of dancing, dress, and musical styles from the black and Hispanic kids there. My pals from the all-white school across town would look at me in wonderment and say, 'There goes Diamond Dave. Very shiny. Very colorful kid.'"[80]

Roth underwent other transformations. Carberry says, "In junior high school, he had kind of an old-fashioned English boy hairstyle like Malcolm McDowell in O Lucky Man! He had his hair parted on one side and one wave in front of his eyes. Then right around ninth grade he started growing his hair long."

Roth's build was also changing. Perez, who'd long had a reputation as a fighter, had "watched David's back all through junior high and early high school." But as time went on, Perez noticed that Roth was getting ripped. "David told me he was working out and doing stuff like that. He took martial arts. He was getting bigger and stronger, and I noticed he wasn't a skinny weakling like he was earlier. He was filling out."

At the same time, Roth developed the persona that would help make him a rock superstar. Perez says, "I remember in high school, I realized he had surpassed me. I had been ahead of him in popularity and all of a sudden he passes me up, with the coolness and the popularity and so forth. He blows right by me and I go, 'Damn. This guy's special. He's really something special.'"

Roth's charms — and perhaps his own sense of himself as a black man trapped in a white body — also made him a favorite of Muir's black female students. Perez recalls, "Black chicks definitely did go crazy over him. Oh hell yeah. There were a couple of them that he liked. I think there was one that he really, truly loved. I can't remember her name but she was very attractive. You've got to remember that back in that era this was not common. You saw black guys with white girls, but you didn't see white guys with black girls very often."

Roth's popularity with African-American girls gave him some significant street cred, even at other high schools. "David was definitely a *cool* white guy back then," Perez observes. "I remember David and I went to a dance over at Pasadena High School (PHS). We met these black guys. I thought we were going to have trouble with them. Then we started talking and this one guy goes, 'Hey, I know you — you're that white guy who goes with black women!' David looks at them and starts laughing out loud. Later he and I started talking about how his reputation had expanded to the east side of Pasadena."

All of these changes made it clear that Roth was going places. Carberry says, "Pretty much everybody, well our friends in common, anyway, figured that he was going to be successful at something. A lot of people didn't think he was a good enough musician to be successful at music, but they thought he'd be successful at something. He certainly had star quality and showmanship and God knows the gift of gab and self-confidence."

Long before he fronted Van Halen, Roth had the chance to show off that self-confidence onstage at Muir. Juliana Gondek, who took a drama course with Roth, recalls, "In drama class he was a real cutup and he was a real class clown. It was hard to nail his feet to the floor to get him to do what you wanted him to do. But he was always bigger than life. Always. He had long blond hair and this huge personality. The David Lee Roth that came to prominence in Van Halen? He was that in high school."

Gondek is quick to note that Roth did more than tell jokes in drama class. "My most vivid memory of him is in a play by [Polish dramatist] Slawomir Mrożek. He wrote *The Martyrdom of Peter Ohey*. It's a theater-of-the-absurd play about a normal family man living in a small apartment who suddenly has a tiger appear in his bathtub. The whole play is about what he's to do about this tiger. It's a big protest play about communism. David was cast as a maharaja who comes from India to hunt this tiger. So we all put together our own costumes. He found himself a pair of tight jodhpurs, and nothing — nothing — was left to the imagination. And he had on a big pair of black riding boots pulled over his tight jodhpurs. He was shirtless and very tan. He had this great set of pecs and no hair on his body anywhere. He looked like a Chippendales dancer. In retrospect, of course, it makes complete sense that he would dress like that because he was David Lee Roth."

= =

The Van Halen brothers remained without a stable bass player into the middle of 1969. Still, they loved to play, and so one day they lugged their equipment over to Bill Maxwell's house. Some of Maxwell's other friends, who played in a blues band, showed up, and before long, a jam session was underway. Edward and Alex eyed the blues band's bass player, an older teen named Dennis Travis. Travis says, "I guess my bass playing impressed them, as I was very into not playing bass fast with a lot of notes . . . like your typical bass player of the day. That fit in with their love for Cream, as Jack Bruce was one good bass player."[81]

Over the weeks that followed, Travis saw Alex and Edward play a couple more times. The first time, he saw them performing with a bassist and figured they'd finally solved their lineup problem. But a few weeks later, Travis was walking past Marshall Junior High School "and heard the unmistakable playing of Eddie and Alex." He entered the gym and saw the brothers with their equipment set up on the basketball court. Between songs, Travis asked, "Where is your bass player?"

Shaking his head, Edward replied, "We got rid of him, because he was more interested in his girlfriend than the band."

"You need another bassist?"

"Yes! Let's go get your equipment."

With that, the trio went around the corner to Travis's house. "We all went over," Travis says, "and grabbed my bass and amp and carried them to the gym, and I had my first jam with them. If I remember correctly, this was the beginning of the summer of 1969."[82]

In the weeks that followed, Travis practiced with the brothers. They also settled on a name: Trojan Rubber Company, a cheeky moniker that Edward came up with.[83] They toyed with the idea of adding a keyboard player, a local prodigy named Jim Pewsey. But after two jams with him, they decided not to invite the serious, somewhat uptight keyboardist to join. Still, Edward and Alex wouldn't forget about Pewsey.

The band soon developed a repertoire. Bill Maxwell, who often played with them, remembers, "Trojan Rubber Company played Hendrix's 'Foxey Lady' and 'Purple Haze' and a lot of stuff off Cream's *Disraeli Gears*. We played 'Badge.' We played 'White Room.'"

Edward and Travis also taught each other songs. Most notably, Travis turned his friend on to *Undead*, a live album by the English blues-rock band Ten Years After, which contained a song that would later become Edward's backyard party signature piece. "One day I showed Eddie some of the licks from Ten Years After's 'I'm Going Home,'" Travis recalls. "He learned them so fast my head spun. All you had to do is show him one time, and he had it down."[84] Ten Years After, much like Cream, stretched out their songs live, with Alvin Lee's guitar gymnastics serving as the centerpiece for their jazz-like improvisations.

While in later years Edward would emphasize Clapton's influence on him, it was Ten Years After's guitarist Lee's performance on "I'm Going Home" that established a new benchmark in Edward's mind for lead guitar virtuosity. While Clapton's tasteful playing profoundly inspired Edward, Lee's manic, fiery runs opened Edward's eyes to the possibilities of pure speed. Indeed, it would be Edward's note-for-note performances of "I'm Going Home" that cemented his local reputation as a prodigy during the early 1970s.

Travis also secured a place for them to practice and play: the St. James United Methodist Church. After reserving the space, they'd pass the word to their friends that they'd be performing live. Gary Taylor, who later played with Roth in Red Ball Jet, says, "I used to go see those guys at the church. It was the Van Halen brothers with Bill Maxwell on guitar and vocals and Travis on bass. They were a half-assed junior high school group that actually played incredibly good. They used to change instruments when they were playing. They'd play three or four songs and switch out." Dana Anderson says, "They did a few gigs there. It was in a youth center. It had a little basement where they were allowed to do a little rehearsal, and I remember it turned into kind of a party. I think this was their first real gig."

While things were going swimmingly with Trojan Rubber Company, a traumatic event would shake the Van Halen household sometime that summer. One night, a screaming Jan staggered into the house with his right hand covered in blood. Larry Abajian, who owned the local liquor store that Jan patronized, recalls, "Jan was coming home from a job and he went to pull into his garage. The guy who lived right next door was the guy who delivered magazines, *Hustler*, *Playboy*, all the porn magazines basically. He had his trailer out there and it was blocking Jan's garage. So Mr. Van Halen went to lift up the tongue and move it, and it fell off the stand and came down and cut his finger off." Jan had lost half of his right middle finger, a devastating injury for a working musician.[85]

As Jan attempted to adjust to this harsh new reality, he and Eugenia began to reconcile themselves to another fact: their sons wanted to be rock musicians. So on August 15, 1969, Jan took Alex and Edward, one of Edward's guitars (perhaps a Lafayette-branded Japanese knockoff of a Gibson ES-335), and a Bundy Flute to a local music store called Music for Everyone.[86] Jan then traded in the two instruments and purchased — on eighteen percent APR credit with a twenty-dollar down payment — a new Gibson Les Paul Goldtop and a case for Edward and a new drum set for Alex, for a total cost of $805.10, a small fortune for a family of modest means. Despite their dislike of rock music, and their own financial limitations, Jan and Eugenia supported their sons' aspirations by purchasing instruments for them — in Edward's case, his first professional-quality guitar.[87]

The brothers put them to good use. "We did a gig for a dance at John Marshall during the summer," Travis says. Edward, who loved the way that Travis played Hendrix songs, encouraged a mid-set instrument switch. "The one night I did take Ed up on his offer to have me play guitar, I did two Hendrix songs — I believe 'Purple Haze' and 'Foxey Lady.' Ed grabbed my bass and played so well without one lesson, it almost floored me! He was that good."[88]

Sometime later, Trojan Rubber Company signed up for a battle of the bands at the Altadena Country Club. Travis recalls that they had rented a PA and amps, because their own hodge-podge of amplifiers looked "tacky." They'd also talked a neighborhood kid, Gary Booth, into singing that night.

When they showed up, they discovered that they were the youngest musicians in the contest. Regardless, Travis says, "We made the best of it and did our set."[89] Along with a Led Zeppelin song, they played an original called "Ball Blues," which featured a bass solo by Travis. They also performed two Cream songs: "I'm So Glad," the only song that Booth sang that night, and "Toad," Ginger Baker's drum extravaganza from *Wheels of Fire.* Travis remembers, "We did 'Toad,' the full twenty-minute version, and I do not remember one mistake on his drum solo. [Alex] was amazing even at sixteen."[90]

One of the other bands that competed that night — and won the contest — was a Pasadena group called Colonel Savage. Don

Ross, the band's drummer, recalls, "Even though we won, we were blown away by how good Alex and Eddie were. At the time, our sister Janet was going out with Alex and he would come over to see Janet and hear us practice in our Sierra Madre garage. Janet mentioned that Alex was in a band that was also going to play at the Altadena battle, so [we] were anxious to see his fledgling group. We were stunned at how easily they mastered Led Zeppelin, but we thought at that time their vocals and [lack of] stage presentation hurt them."[91]

Over the subsequent months, Edward and Alex upgraded their equipment. Edward purchased a wah-wah pedal and his legendary late-'60s Marshall 100-watt Super Lead amplifier. The amp, which would become the foundation of his guitar sound on Van Halen's early albums, had been the house amplifier at the nearby Rose Palace. Much to the chagrin of residents all over Pasadena, it was ear-piercingly loud. When Edward turned it up, as he always did, his guitar playing could be heard blocks away.

His brother, too, acquired a Ludwig double-kick drum set, one that he likely purchased with funds he'd earned as a machine operator. This job, however, almost cost Alex his future as a drummer. John Nyman, who played drums for Eulogy, a band that gigged with Van Halen in later years, remembers what Alex had told him: "He was working in some sort of a machine shop and he cut his hand really badly, right across the web of his hand, to where it would have cut his whole thumb off if it had gone all the way through. It was some sort of a deep cut." Luckily, Alex avoided permanent injury, and now both brothers, who were just teenagers, had professional grade instruments to make great music with.

They used this gear in Trojan Rubber Company, which had evolved into a three-piece with Travis on bass. Bill Maxwell recalls, "There was a power trio, just those three guys, for a long time. They just practiced and practiced and practiced and learned. That's basically what they did."

Edward, Alex, and Travis continued to seek out new music. During the late summer of 1970, they discovered Cactus, a hard rock quartet featuring drummer Carmine Appice and bassist Tim Bogert, the former rhythm section of Vanilla Fudge. When they dropped the needle on *Cactus*'s first track, an absolutely manic cover of Mose Allison's "Parchman Farm," the hair stood up on their necks. It was heavy and fast; an electrifying shuffle played at breakneck pace. It was Cream on steroids. It was Ten Years After on amphetamines. It was the blueprint for Van Halen boogie-shuffles like "I'm the One," "Ice Cream Man," and "The Full Bug."

In later years, Appice explained what sparked the song's avalanche of momentum and power. "We did a lot of speed," said Appice. "At the time 'Parchman Farm' was one of the fastest songs ever recorded. And that's what we wanted it to be. We were trying to outdo Ten Years After. They had a this really fast song called 'I'm Going Home,' so we said, 'Let's make ours even faster.'"[92]

This new benchmark for speed and power attracted the Van Halen brothers. To be sure, "I'm Going Home" was an up-tempo blues-rocker that demanded superior musicianship. But "Parchman Farm" took things to the next level. The Van Halen brothers, at their cores, wanted to play speedy, intense, and *heavy* rock, and Cactus's supersonic boogie-rock fit that bill.

In seemingly no time at all, Edward, Alex, and Travis had worked up the song. When Trojan Rubber Company, with fifteen-year-old Edward on guitar, debuted it for friends, jaws dropped. Maxwell recalls, "He was playing at [a friend's] house. I think it was 1970, halfway through the [fall] semester. He was playing 'Parchman Farm.' I remember it was the first time I ever heard it. I can close my eyes and still see myself standing there watching him play this. They *just tore it up*. That's the best I've ever seen him play."

= =

Edward and Alex Van Halen were teenage musicians who played better than any other kids in Pasadena, and better than many professional musicians. But once again, they lost their bass player when Travis moved away with his family sometime in late 1970. Regardless, their legend would only continue to grow.

David Lee Roth encountered the Van Halen brothers around this time. Neugebauer, who now saw Roth less frequently, remembers, "Dave and I first saw the Van Halen brothers perform at a Jewish temple when Dave and I belonged to this Jewish youth club called AZA. We were amazed."

Afterwards, Roth and his friend went over to Neugebauer's grandmother's house and sat in the big tree house in her backyard. The pair talked about what they'd seen and heard and then out of the blue, Roth told his friend that he intended to be a rock star. Neugebauer says, "I recall him asking questions like, 'Man, where did the Beatles get the idea for Sgt. Pepper?' For 'Lucy in the Sky with Diamonds'? He really wanted to be a songwriter." The fuse had been lit.

THE GENESIS
OF MAMMOTH

Around 1971, Genesis, a power-trio comprised of Edward on guitar and vocals, Alex on drums, and fellow Pasadena teenager Mark Stone on bass, was performing in the basement of a Jewish temple in Whittier. A group of Genesis backers had turned out for the gig, including the brothers' friends Ross Velasco, future Van Halen drum tech Gregg Emerson, and Brian Box. The audience also included other kids who'd turned out to support the other bands on the bill.

Genesis's fans, who loved to party, came prepared. Box remembers, "I had a bottle of Jack Daniel's I had taken to that thing. I was drinking that, but I wasn't shitfaced." As Genesis played some Black Sabbath and Cream covers, the Pasadena crowd danced and watched the band perform as Box and his friends passed the bottle. "But all of a sudden," Box recalls, "one of the other guys there bumped into us and knocked all these girls down. I was picking them up and I said, 'Apologize.'" The other kid answered

Box's request with a shove. Immediately, Emerson and Velasco slammed him to the floor, which ended the confrontation. Red-faced and angry, the aggressor stormed off.

Box and the others turned their attention back to Genesis. But within a few minutes, some of Whittier's finest burst into the room, nightsticks in hand. The way Box remembers it, "I was sitting down, watching the band. Then the next thing I knew all these cops came walking in and all these kids pointed right at me. These cops grabbed me by the back of the hair and were dragging me out of this place."

Velasco and Emerson were having none of it. They jumped on the cops in an effort to free Box. Box says that this was a "really bad move" on the part of his friends, because along with swinging their nightsticks, the cops Maced everyone. Once that happened, Alex brought Genesis's set to a halt and threw himself into the fray.

By now, Box had been hustled into a police cruiser. He watched as the disturbance spilled into the street. Backup units arrived around the same time that he saw his "bottle of Jack Daniel's come flying out of the crowd and hit a police car." At that point, the police had started arresting everyone, including Alex and his friends. Box says, "Those cops were really out of line. That really pissed me off," but regardless, they still needed Jan Van Halen to come bail them out of jail. Box says with a laugh, "Fortunately I got that taken off my record."

In later years, Alex and Edward remembered that their "pre–Van Halen" band (first named Genesis, later Mammoth) had a reputation for causing trouble. Edward explained in 1985, "It seems that since Dave has been in the band we got this rowdy and crazy brown cloud hanging over us. But we had it way before Dave was even in the band. Schools wouldn't hire us, [and] nobody wanted anything to do with us."[93]

To be sure, Edward's correct when he suggests that folks like school administrators, youth club directors, and parents hated

Genesis and Mammoth for playing abrasive blues-rock and heavy metal at ear-piercing volumes.

But of course, beer-drinking and hell-raising teenagers loved them for the same reasons. The Van Halen brothers' bands played loud, but more importantly, they played great. Years before "Eruption," local kids knew Edward, then a teen, was a special talent, the kind of guitarist who could replicate any solo. They also knew that teenagers who could play entire sides of records by the Who and Black Sabbath without missing a note possessed astounding musical ability. Long before anyone had ever heard of a tribute band, the Van Halen brothers filled backyards and parks with young people who knew there was something remarkable about three high school kids who played this well and always aspired to get better.

═ ═

In the spring of 1971, Mark Stone got to hear Genesis play at a wedding with a bass player named Kevin Ford. Ford had a reputation as a solid player, but Stone didn't think much of his chops. So the next time Stone bumped into Alex Van Halen at PHS, he told him that he could outplay Ford and said that he'd like to jam with Alex and Edward. Soon after, Ford was out and Mark Stone was in.

Stone and the brothers got to work. They shared a love for proto-metal and blues-rock bands like Cream, Mountain, Black Sabbath, Deep Purple, Cactus, and the Who. They'd rehearse in the Van Halens' living room, filling the small space with their equipment to the point that it was hard to get in the front door of the house. When the boys got hungry, Mrs. Van Halen would make them big egg rolls, which she called *lumpia*.[94]

By the summertime, Genesis started looking for more places to play. Two plum gigs for teenage bands were the summertime concerts sponsored by the Pasadena parks and recreation department, which were held at two parks, Hamilton Park and Victory Park. These outdoor gigs, despite their informality, went far in spreading the word about Genesis's talents.

On summer nights, Genesis, along with some other long-forgotten bands, would set up on an expanse of blacktop. Stone and the Van Halen brothers would hook up a small, rented PA system. But while their PA was underpowered, the rest of their equipment was professional quality. Alex would set up his silver Ludwig double-kick kit. Edward tuned up his Les Paul Goldtop, and Mark did the same with his Lucite Dan Armstrong Bass. They plugged their instruments into their powerful amps. Stone played through an Acoustic 360 while Edward used his 100-watt Marshall amp, which stood tall on top of two Marshall cabinets. Before any of the three were old enough to vote, they all had equipment used by rock's leading musicians.

A teenage bassist from Pasadena named Lee Gutenberg remembers when he first saw Genesis. He says, "When I was fifteen, I used to see Genesis on Sundays at Victory Park. The city had funded it, and they'd book the Van Halens. I don't know if they got paid for it, but they'd be up there on a tennis court or a volleyball court. There'd be two or three dozen people, and it was just a place to meet girls and stuff. I had just seen the *Woodstock* movie with Alvin Lee, and Eddie did Ten Years After's 'I'm Goin' Home' note for note. It was just unbelievable. And Alex had a double bass — two kick drums. On them, it said 'Genesis.' It was written in black, kind of in hippie-art style."

Sigificantly, Edward's rising local fame as a guitarist coincided with the cultural ascent of the Guitar Hero. Since the late 1960s, rock fans who loved blues-rock had come to embrace guitarists who'd mastered their instruments, making the riff-rock of British Invasion bands like the Dave Clark Five and the Kinks seem like child's play. These innovators played solos faster, cleaner, and with more verve than their peers. By 1970, the leading players included

Eric Clapton, Jeff Beck, Jimmy Page, and the American innovator Jimi Hendrix. Then there were the rising stars: Paul Kossoff of Free, Leslie West of Mountain, and Alvin Lee of Ten Years After.

Even though players like Clapton, Beck, and Page would ultimately overshadow Lee's playing, when Lee unleashed a nine-plus minute version of "I'm Going Home" at the Woodstock festival, it signaled that he'd arrived as a player. In fact, Lee's speedy, intense lead work, which would be featured in the *Woodstock* feature film, built his reputation as the fastest guitarist in the world.

So when a skinny fifteen-year-old kid with a cigarette smoldering between his lips shredded his way through the song's nearly ten minutes of leads, Pasadena teenagers were in disbelief. It was simply astounding to see a local player — with a band that didn't miss a beat backing him — perform at this level. It would have been no different if a gangly teenager had turned out for a pickup football game at a Pasadena park and started unleashing Joe Namath–esque passes all over the gridiron — frozen ropes fired across the field, tight spirals that arced like rainbows before landing in the hands of sprinting receivers fifty yards away, play after play, game after game. Fifteen-year-olds didn't play like professionals. Except when they did, because Edward Van Halen had the chops of a pro guitarist before he'd started shaving.

Guitarist Eric Hensel discovered Genesis around the same time as Lee Gutenberg did. "When I first saw the Van Halen brothers, it was right around the summer of 1971. A friend and I knew there was going to be a battle of the bands at Hamilton Park. There were about five bands there. We didn't know who the hell was going to be playing so we just went."

Because the bill was crowded, Genesis only performed a couple of songs. Hensel says, "Ed was better than anyone I had ever seen in town by about a mile. It wasn't just that he could duplicate these songs note for note. He took them and expanded upon what was already there."

Alex and Edward Van Halen perform at a dance at the all-girls Alverno
High School in Sierra Madre, California, early 1973. LYNN L. KERSHNER

Hensel also emphasizes that even in 1971, the brothers had a musical connection that was deep and powerful. "I don't want to discount [Alex's] contribution, because when you saw them it was the combination of the two of them. It was a two-man show. They had a synergy between them that was just unbelievable. It was like they could read each other's minds. It was never just about Ed. It was the Ed and Al thing."

When Genesis finished, Hensel and his friends turned to each other, asking the names of these musicians. "That was before I had any idea who these guys were. I didn't find out until a couple of weeks later. It wasn't like there was a whole bunch of guys standing around in the audience, nodding and going: *Yep, oh yeah, these guys are great.* We're all standing there with our jaws open, wondering, *Who in the hell are these kids?*"

As teenagers are wont to do, they gossiped about how these guys got *so* good. Gutenberg recollects, "There were all sorts of rumors that they used to shoot up heroin underneath their tongues so that no one would know. This was just high school innuendo and rumor. It was also because people were jealous of them. Alex was a great drummer and Eddie was a great guitarist. It was really amazing. Eddie had not developed his own style, but he could emulate anyone. Carlos Santana. Alvin Lee. He emulated their styles note for note."

But Hensel, who'd started catching every Genesis performance he could, ascertained that Edward was more than a gifted mimic. "Up to that point," he says, "I'd seen almost everybody who was anybody already. Page, Clapton, Beck, I'd seen them all. I'm going, *Man I paid money to see guys who weren't as good as this kid.* He had that great-sounding Marshall stack on ten, and he'd plug straight in with that Les Paul. The combination of the two was just stunning. He was either singing and playing or just playing. He'd just barely move. He just stood there and played better than ninety percent of the people I'd already paid to see. I felt so lucky to be able to stand ten feet away from somebody who was that unbelievably good."

Musicians who saw Genesis evangelized about the band. Guitarist Rodney Davey, who played in a local cover band called Uncle Sam, explains, "There was a park in Sierra Madre where bands used to play. That was the first time I saw Genesis. They played the second side of the first Black Sabbath album perfectly — every note."

When Davey went to his band's rehearsal space, he cornered bassist Jonathan Laidig. "Rodney came into a practice ranting and raving. He said, 'Wow, man, you've got to see these guys. He's got a Marshall stack. They played Black Sabbath!' Then he kind of stopped and lowered his voice. 'And they played "I'm Going Home"!'"

Laidig then caught them at a Pasadena house party. He recollects, "The first time I saw them was in somebody's living room. The living room wasn't even twenty-by-twenty; it was this tiny room. Eddie's got this big old Marshall stack. Eddie was fifteen or sixteen, so they're just a bunch of kids, and that's why it was mind-blowing."

Guitarist Gary Putman and his friends also saw them at a Pasadena party. "When I first saw them I was enraptured," he explains. "I saw Ed in a room, in an old Pasadena house with hardwood floors, do 'I'm Going Home.' We saw that and thought, *That's unbelievable. That's tighter and more intense than the original.* He'd take these little avenues and add a little lick here and there, and I'd think, *I don't even know if Alvin Lee could do that lick.* It was almost superhuman [compared to] what had come before. Now I think there are better sweep pickers today and stuff like that, but the shift — the paradigm shift with him — it's hard to equate it with anything. All the stories you hear? They're absolutely true."

Still, there was little fortune for the band members during those days. Cheri Whitaker, who was dating Edward at the time, says, "Genesis played around at really little parties. They'd make, literally, thirty or forty dollars to play these gigs." At this point, no one in Genesis was getting rich from playing music.

Regardless, they rehearsed for hours. According to Stone, during their years together as a trio they had a repertoire that included songs from the Who's *Live at Leeds* and *Tommy* such as "My Generation," and "See Me, Feel Me, Touch Me." They played Cream's "Spoonful," "Politician," "Sitting on Top of the World," "Tales of Brave Ulysses," "White Room," and "Crossroads." And they also performed Black Sabbath's "Paranoid," "Iron Man," and "Fairies Wear Boots."[95]

When Edward and Alex's parents tired of amps in their living room, Genesis practiced at the home of Edward and Alex's friends Ross and Bill Velasco. Ross says, "They were always short on practice space. They'd move from house to house to practice and occasionally they ended up at our house." Bill adds, "They played at our house three or four times. My parents were cool enough to let them practice in the living room, and then we'd have parties at night. They played in the living room. We'd charge three dollars at the door. This was before Dave. They had a harmonica player, Brian Box, who sat in with them sometimes."

Ross and Bill's then ten-year-old sister Jan remembers that her parents were particularly accommodating when it came to Genesis. She explains, "I remember watching them practice in our living room before a gig or before they played a party at our house. They'd come by that afternoon and they'd practice. I can picture Edward singing [Alice Cooper's] 'I'm Eighteen.' I wasn't allowed to go to the parties, so my father would take me down to the local bowling alley and shoot pool with me until we were allowed to come back. Then I'd walk around the perimeter of the house and look in all the windows if the party was still going on. It was all very decadent to a ten year old!"

= =

Around late 1971, Edward and Alex received an unwelcome surprise at a local record store. Edward pulled an LP called *Nursery Cryme* out of a bin. The band's name? Genesis. Edward turned to his brother and said with a chuckle, "Hey, we've got a record out, Alex."[96]

Whitaker recalls the brainstorming sessions that followed. "I remember Edward saying, 'Oh, there's another band called Genesis. We've got to change our name.' Of course, this was before any of us had ever heard of Genesis. I remember them thinking of names, and they thought through all kinds of things before they came up with Mammoth."

This change didn't dampen their popularity. When parents left town, PHS kids planned parties and hired Mammoth. Dana MacDuff says, "These backyard and house parties were what we did on weekends. These parties would all happen by word of mouth. You'd be at school and someone would say, 'Hey there's a party

Mammoth, a power trio comprised of the Van Halen brothers and bassist Mark Stone, work their way through their set in Sierra Madre, California, early 1973. LYNN L. KERSHNER

tonight at so-and-so's house. Mammoth's playing.' In fact, it seemed like literally every party we went to, Mammoth was playing. We saw them *all* the time. They were the party soundtrack, and we always knew it would be a good party if Mammoth was playing. You'd pay a buck or two to get in to pay for beer. There would be a hundred, two hundred, or three hundred people there."

Over time, these parties grew larger. Debbie Hannaford Lorenz remembers that when the Van Halen brothers first hit the scene, there'd be "room in the backyards" when they performed at modest suburban homes in neighboring Altadena. "You could walk in and walk around," she says. "But within a short time those parties became so widespread. They were putting those flyers out at so many schools. It was just amazing how many people would be inside these small houses up in Altadena. Those houses weren't big, and their backyards were small. And the whole backyard right up to where they were playing was solid people. Sometimes there was no way to get into the house or to get into the back-yard. And the whole front yard would be full. Then there'd be people walking up and down the street, because they could hear the music since it was so loud."

= =

Despite the band's reputation, Edward refused to rest on his laurels. The introverted teen practiced incessantly and passed up almost all social opportunities in order to do so. Taylor Freeland says, "Edward was a really nice, very mellow guy. He was not a partier. Now this was the age of drug experimentation, so people would leave school and dash over to somebody's house to party. We'd have plans, so we'd go, 'Hey Edward, come with us.' He'd say, 'Nah. I gotta go home and *practice, man.*' I can hear him saying it to this day. Those were his famous words, and that's all he'd do. He's the classic tale of the guy who liked to do one thing. They had a mission." George Courville, who in later years repaired Edward's amps, agrees and adds, "Ed never liked pot, because he would forget the licks and words to songs. He drank a few beers but not the whole six-pack. Ed would stay at home and not leave his room. A lot of people think it came natural for Ed to play. No, he practiced his ass off. We would leave him sitting on the end of his bed. We'd come back four or five hours later and he would be in the same spot still playing." Whitaker remembers that Edward even brought his guitar with him when he came to her home: "He'd always practice at my par-ents' house. Every day he'd have his guitar there. He'd leave it there during school. He'd always play me 'Can't Find My Way Home' by Blind Faith, because I loved it so much."

Along with practicing, Edward was always learning new songs. In an age before guitar tablature books and YouTube guitar tuto-rials, Edward's amazing ear gave him the ability to listen to a song once and then start playing along. Michael McCarthy, who grew up in Pasadena, says, "I'd seen Eddie play at Hamilton Park, but I didn't know him. A friend of mine later told me he knew Eddie. This is when Eddie's about sixteen. But he said I had to be a better guitarist before he'd bring me to meet Eddie. So I practiced for eight hours a day for a spell, and then my friend said, 'Okay, we can go.' We went over there, and Eddie and Alex were sharing this tiny room. The whole room smelled like an amp, because there was a Marshall cabinet and head that took up like half the room. There was a picture of Ginger Baker on one wall and Eric Clapton on the other. Eddie put on Yes's *Fragile* on this little cheap Silvertone turntable. The motor was exposed, so it looked like Eddie had taken it apart to fix it or something. He started playing along to 'Roundabout' note for note, and then played along with the whole album, note for note. That really blew me out of the water, because that stuff was not easy to play. He had an incredible ear."

For a further challenge, Mammoth soon made performing whole album sides — rather than individual songs from different albums — its trademark. Freeland observes, "When I listen to something like Black Sabbath's *Master of Reality* that gives me chills because it reminds me of Edward and Alex. I didn't even know it was Black Sabbath at the time. They'd do medleys of Black Sabbath, same with Cactus, and the same with Captain Beyond."

Still, Mammoth's commitment to playing songs exactly like they'd been performed on vinyl occasionally produced problems. Brent Pettit recalls with a laugh, "I went to a party and Mammoth was playing. They started playing a Captain Beyond song called 'Dancing Madly Backwards.' I used to jam to that album and that song all the time with headphones. So I'm watching and all of a sudden there was this jarring moment during the long riff in the middle of the song. I thought, *Wait a minute — that's not right!* . . . Later I asked Mark what the hell went wrong there and he told me the record they owned and learned the song from had a skip so they had to do the wrong part to fill in what they couldn't hear."

Skips aside, by 1972, Mammoth was the best backyard party-band in Pasadena. But there was solid competition in the form of Uncle Sam, a three-guitar band that featured the three Pettit brothers and a great Robert Plant–sounding singer, Chris Legg. Edward's old friend Rafael Marti remembers, "Uncle Sam were Mammoth's rivals. The Pettits *hated* the Van Halens. They'd always cut them down and make little comments before and after they performed. Like Mammoth, Uncle Sam did really pristine cover versions; they played songs exactly like the records. They'd play Alice Cooper, Led Zeppelin, and Rolling Stones stuff like, 'Can't You Hear Me Knocking' from *Sticky Fingers*. Chris, the lead singer, played sax on that one."

Around June 1972, the two bands faced off at a battle of the bands. In the weeks leading up to the gig, Uncle Sam's drummer, Brent Pettit, mentioned to his drum teacher, Roger Liston, that Uncle Sam would be competing against Mammoth. Pettit, who knew that Liston didn't like Mammoth either, had an idea. Would Liston be willing to sit in for a song? Pettit's teacher, who was a seasoned professional musician, quickly agreed.

That night, Mammoth performed first and received a rousing ovation. Uncle Sam followed, and just as they'd planned, halfway through the set Pettit handed his sticks to Liston. Laidig recalls, "So Liston had learned the song, and it had this drum solo that Brent normally played. When we did it at the battle of the bands he just did this one killer drum solo. I'm not saying he was a better drummer than Alex, but man, he kicked ass on that drum solo." Pettit says, "He brought the house down. He was a standout drummer."

After Uncle Sam finished, the judges announced the winner: Uncle Sam. The room exploded with Mammoth fans jumping out of their seats, booing and yelling. Laidig chuckles, "Of course all the Mammoth fans and even other kids in the room were angry. They said, 'That's cheating! How could you do that? That's not fair!'"

Pettit, for his part, concedes, "That was mean to do to the guys in Mammoth, but they were our rivals and Roger did not like them."

Despite the setback, Mammoth sought more competition. Sometime in 1972, Mammoth signed up for another battle of the bands at Altadena Country Club, a venue that they'd competed at previously as Trojan Rubber Company. Perhaps recalling that they'd used a singer named Gary Booth when they'd gigged there back in 1969, Alex and Edward called on Booth again. But, in a harbinger of things to come, this time Alex wanted Booth to sing because he felt that his brother, who was shy and of limited vocal talent, "was not cutting it as our frontman." Booth, who initially agreed to do the gig, backed out at the last minute. So "Ed sang," Alex told Steven Rosen. "It was cool, but we didn't win."[97]

= =

In the fall of 1972, Edward and Alex got a call from a Pasadena City College (PCC) student named Paul Fry. Fry, who sometimes rented his PA system to the band, had a proposition. As the school's student events director, Fry had organized a concert that Manna, a brand-new folk-rock band that was signed to Columbia Records, would headline.[98] The show would be held on October 28 at the college's Sexson Auditorium, which featured a capacity of nearly two thousand people. Would Mammoth be willing to open the show? Fry's thinking was that Mammoth's local popularity would help sell tickets, since Manna, a largely unknown band, would not be a heavy draw. Edward and Alex said yes.

Fry then prevailed upon Mammoth to make some upgrades to their stage show. Fry says that he thought the band's "lack of image" would hurt them within the spacious confines of Sexson.

While the band played through great gear, the trio put little emphasis on their stage garb and show. Jeff Burkhardt, a local

Edward Van Halen strikes a chord on his Les Paul, late 1972. JULIAN POLLACK

guitarist who hauled gear for Van Halen before the band became famous, recalls, "They wore Pendleton shirts — flannels — and jeans. They wore Levi's jackets and boots, like they got off work at the gas station and came to play. Stone would, literally, look like he was a lumberjack." Guitarist John Driscoll, who gigged alongside Genesis, adds that the band didn't interact with their audiences and offered onlookers almost nothing in terms of showmanship.[99] When you saw Genesis, there was no flashy clothing, wild choreography, or impressive stage show. Their musicianship *was* the show.

The band agreed to make some changes. Fry encouraged Edward to wear a T-shirt, suspenders, and a blazer rather than a Pendleton. He also told him that a little showmanship was in order, in light of the fact that the venue had a large stage and an elaborate lighting system, complete with spotlights.

The night of the concert, Edward stood in the darkness next to his Marshall. As he played the first notes of Johnny Winter's "Rock

Edward Van Halen lost in the music, late 1972. JULIAN POLLACK

and Roll, Hoochie Koo," the spotlight illuminated him. Moving forward with purpose, Edward strutted to the front of the stage and stood behind his microphone, a sequence that Fry says made the crowd go wild, since they'd never seen Edward move in that manner. But right before that first song's solo, disaster appeared to strike when Edward broke his D string. Fry watched, amazed, as Edward played right through. He remembers, "Eddie was so friggin' good that no one even realized he had broken it!"[100]

Meanwhile, audience members were mightily impressed. Box says, "That was a great concert. I remember it was the first time I'd seen Edward dressed like that. He had on this blue suit jacket that was just really professional looking. We'd kept trying to talk him into moving, because he'd never move on the stage. He used to have this Clapton 'I'm just going to stand here and rip' approach. Finally at this show he started moving around. He appeared like he was enjoying the music because he finally started moving. "

Rudy Leiren, in later years, would remember that Mammoth won over the audience that night. "Manna was very professional. They had very good sound effects with the rain and the lightning and all that. But I'll tell you what. The crowd didn't want anything to do with them, and they ended up walking off the stage."[101]

= =

Despite Mammoth's triumph at PCC, the truth was that nothing had really changed for the band, at least in the minds of their fans. Nancy Stout, who was a fixture on the Pasadena party scene, remembers, "Nobody in Pasadena was looking at Mammoth as making it. We knew they were good, but it was just fun for us. They were playing cover tunes, like James Gang stuff, so it was just entertainment at parties. Some of the parties they played at were free, and some we paid fifty cents to get in and we could drink all the beer we wanted." Of course in the months that followed, the band's ambitions and purpose would change, but that would come after the addition of a new member with a different kind of vision for the band's future prospects.

THE ADVENTURES
OF RED BALL JET

On Las Lunas, the din never seemed to cease. Bill Matsumoto, a Van Halen neighbor, remembers, "I used to get on my Schwinn Sting-Ray bike and ride to [Rob] Broderick's house and pedal right by the Van Halen home. I'd hear this noise blaring out of the house. I used to hear them practicing *every single day*."

With the crack of his snare ringing in his ears, Alex initially didn't hear the doorbell one day in the spring of 1971. But when he yanked it open, this guy named Dave was standing on the stoop. He'd recently chatted them up after a party, telling them that he thought their band was *bad*. He said he was a singer — a great one, in fact. Alex thought he at least looked the part. His light brown hair hung to his shoulders and his clothes were more outlandish than anything that anyone in Genesis's circle would ever don.

Roth immediately got to the point. He told the trio that he "wanted to sing" for Genesis, and in fact, he was *the* singer they needed.[102] The brothers looked at each other, reading each other's minds. To Edward, singing was a chore. *Maybe this guy can sing*, he

Edward and Alex Van Halen confer backstage, late 1972. JULIAN POLLACK

thought. After a bit of back and forth, Alex said that Roth could audition.

Edward explained to *Rolling Stone* in 1995 what happened next. "I'll never forget, we asked him to learn a few songs like 'Crossroads,' by Cream, and something by Grand Funk Railroad, then come back and see us the next week. And he came back the next week, and it was terrible. He couldn't sing. So, of course, I put my guitar down and said, 'Al, I'll be right back.'"[103] Alex recalled, "I was completely and thoroughly appalled. Ed and Mark left the room, and I had to tell Dave this was no good. I gave him another shot; I gave him songs to work on" and told him to "come back in a week."[104]

A week later Roth came back again. Genesis played and Roth sang, dreadfully. "He came back, and it sounded like pure hell," Alex said. "The intonation was completely out of whack, the timing was completely off, and it was an abysmal failure."[105] After Alex told him that he'd failed again, Roth begged for another chance. Dana Anderson later heard from the brothers that Alex then gave Roth one final test. Alex sat at the family's piano, and "hit a note." He then "told Dave to sing it and when he couldn't, they immediately told him no way."[106] Roth, humiliated and angry, stormed out of the house in a "huff and a puff," Alex recalled, "and that was it."[107]

For however long Roth had angled to join Genesis, his disastrous audition made clear that he wasn't going to sing for that band anytime soon. Since Genesis didn't want him, he'd start his own band, one that would emphasize entertainment over musicianship.[108] His group would bring flashy costumes, fancy dance moves, and infectious beats to the Pasadena backyard party scene. When his band fired on all cylinders, they'd rev up audiences and get everyone on their feet to dance and groove. At the center of this carnival would be Roth, Pasadena's homegrown version of a classic song-and-dance man.

And most importantly, he'd prove Edward and Alex dead wrong in their estimation of him. His musical ambitions, he later explained in the pages of *Musician*, were "primarily motivated by fear and revenge . . . My songs, my interviews, the way I dress . . . every time we go out and play, yeah, I'm having a great time, but I'm also dancing somebody else into the dirt."[109] If Dave had his way, the Van Halen brothers would be trampled underfoot.

= =

Some weeks after Dave's botched audition, the Van Halen brothers and Stone arrived at Hamilton Park, equipment in tow, on a Thursday afternoon in June 1971. Genesis, along with a couple of other teenage bands, would play a short set as part of the Pasadena parks and recreation department's free summer concert series.

As the sun descended, the three members of Genesis bullshitted, smoked, and snuck gulps of warm beer with their friends.

After the first group finished, an unfamiliar band set up. Forty years later, no one seems to remember the name of this quintet. But before they'd played a note, fifty to a hundred kids — most of them Genesis fans — had assembled to hear them play.

Finally, the drummer bashed out a tom roll and clanked an insistent beat on his cowbell. The guitars and bass entered, playing a familiar song. Kristopher Doe, who was looking on, remembers that all of a sudden, he then "witnessed a most ridiculous entry of one Dave Roth leaping from behind an amplifier to the strains of [Santana's] 'Evil Ways' and going down on his knees to sing the opening lines."[110] Edward, eyes bulging, looked on with the others and thought, *Holy shit. Roth has his own group!*

As the first song proceeded, it was clear that Roth was cut from a different cloth. While nearly every other musician who played that night would stand nearly stock-still, Roth roamed the stage, mugging for the crowd, shaking his hips, and pointing at girls.

Out in the crowd, disbelief reigned. Edward and Alex's friend Peter Burke remembers that Roth's band didn't play anything "super-aggressive. But Dave was wearing his jeans and strutting around up there and doing his thing." By the time "Evil Ways" gave way to the Stones' "Little Queenie," audience members guffawed and shook their heads. "The Stones were the biggest band in the world in 1971," Rafael Marti observes. "Roth thought he was Mick Jagger. They were trying to be the Stones. Roth would pout his lips and strut like a rooster." As Edward told *Circus* in 1979, "I remember playing a gig with David's band once and I hate to say it, but we were the band everyone liked. They threw beer cans and shit at Dave's band. So he hated us and we hated him because he hated us."[111] By the time the last song, "Brown Sugar," began, the heckling had become unmerciful.

Still, at least one kid in the audience disagreed. Miles Komora, an aspiring bassist, had just returned to Pasadena after spending time in northern California, only to have his brother Mark tell him that he was playing guitar in a band with this singer named Dave Roth. Miles says that while Roth's "dancing around like Mick Jagger" was off-putting, "the awkwardness was that not too many other singers would do that. They might move around a little bit but not to the degree that he did." On balance, Miles thought that this singer was "kind of cool" because "he was different from anybody else" he'd ever seen in a garage band. After Genesis played, he resolved to talk to his brother about playing together.

= =

Before the summer was out, Roth's bassist quit and Miles entered the band, which now included Roth, the Komora brothers, guitarist Gary Taylor, and drummer David Hill.[112] Miles immediately suggested a new band name: PF Higher and the Red Ball Jet, which combined the names of two popular sneaker models with "Higher" serving as a teenage stoner pun on "Flyer." After chopping the moniker in half, Red Ball Jet came into being.[113]

Miles recalls that from the beginning, it was clear that the "brilliant" Roth had a vision. He "knew what he wanted and he went for it, and he was going to do it come hell or high water. He had this insight." Band meetings involved Roth telling them "I need to do this. I need to do that" when they performed. Most importantly, Red Ball Jet needed to *practice*. Miles says that Roth's desire to rehearse showed that for all of his bluster, he knew he wasn't ready for Carnegie Hall. "There's natural talent there, but David would be the first one to admit 'I don't have very good range.'" Collectively, they'd go to work in a new rehearsal space, the basement of Roth's father's ophthalmological office in tony San Marino.

After Dr. Roth closed up shop for the day, Red Ball Jet would descend into the basement. While Roth wanted to work up some Motown and James Brown songs, they initially played tunes by Chuck Berry, Bill Haley, the Rolling Stones, Ten Years After, B.B.

King, the Beatles, Jimi Hendrix, Led Zeppelin, and even Jethro Tull. Taylor says, "Of all things, can you imagine Dave Roth singing *Sitting on a park bench*? We thought we could play anything. We were all full of ourselves."

After rehearsing four or five nights a week for a few weeks, Red Ball Jet invited their friends to watch their practice. Vincent Carberry says, "Red Ball Jet would rehearse whole sets and put on a show in the basement. That was a blast." Frivolity aside, it was clear that for at least one band member, these rehearsals represented a serious pursuit. "Roth was driving the aesthetics of the band," Miles Komora's friend, Ron Morgan, observes. "He had a lot of ambition even then. Everyone else was there just to get together and jam." After practice, Roth bragged about his band's greatness and announced Red Ball Jet's upcoming performances, including a Friday noontime assembly at Muir.

That Friday, freshman Paul Blomeyer sat in the Muir auditorium. Surrounding him was a true rainbow coalition of a student body, including many black students. With the weekend in sight and an assembly taking students out of class, the mood in the room was boisterous.

Blomeyer, like many in the room, may not have heard of Red Ball Jet, but he knew of Dave Roth. "Roth was a senior when I was a freshman," Blomeyer says. "We were all in awe. He looked exactly like he does now, only with more hair. He was tall, he was thin, and he had long hair. The school system had just gotten rid of the dress code as a reaction to the '60s, so he'd walk around with a vest with no shirt underneath. We'd always watch him go to the parking lot at lunch, and it seemed like he always had at least two women with him. We were a bunch of geeks and we'd just look at him and go, *Wow, that's amazing that anyone can do that.*"

At noon, a few hoots and cheers rang out. Finally, the curtain parted, and the assembled students, including future Van Halen keyboardist Jim Pewsey and Roth's friends — Carberry, Perez, and

David Swantek — watched as Red Ball Jet played its first song. To get off to a fast start, Roth strutted to the edge of the stage and drop-kicked a red ball into the audience. Red Ball Jet had arrived.[114]

Audience members who knew Roth immediately took note of the differences between Roth's and his bandmates' approach to the stage. Pewsey recalls that in those days, "Roth would come out in his tights and with a sock down in his crotch. I'm as serious as a heart attack about that." The other four musicians, however, didn't join him in such rock excess. Perez remembers at this time the other "guys would wear corduroys or jeans and flannel shirts, with the long hair parted in the middle. They were more like Neil Young or Crosby, Stills, and Nash. Even though they had long hair, it just didn't match."[115]

After the first song, Red Ball Jet's singer addressed the audience. Blomeyer says, "I remember him saying something to the effect of, 'Oh you guys, it's Friday! You're all looking at each other, and you're all really *horny!*' I remember thinking, *Wow, he said horny on campus? Excellent!*"

This stage rap, however, represented the show's apex. As the performance continued, black students started jeering. David Swantek says, "I remember Red Ball Jet playing in front of a largely black audience. They were laughing as they played the Beatles, making fun of the band."

Despite this debacle, Red Ball Jet soon had a chance for redemption, this time at the City of Sierra Madre's new recreation center. Unfortunately, it didn't happen. "I remember seeing David Lee Roth there for the first time," says Mel Serrano. "He put on a show with his band, Red Ball Jet. It was terrible. He mostly just screamed a lot." Also there was drummer Harry Conway. He says that while it was clear that Roth "had 'the gift,'" the band as a whole was "God awful." And once again, Roth's effort to leave a lasting impression worked in all the wrong ways. Indeed, Serrano says that this performance was "memorable because [Roth] got up on one of the Ping-Pong tables, and it collapsed and he fell on his ass! Hilarious!"[116]

= =

Afterwards, Roth dusted himself off and went right back to work. He brought his Vox Rio Grande acoustic guitar to school so he could practice more often.[117] Roth informed *Hit Parader*, "I used to love to take my guitar to school and just sit under a tree and play. I'd always forget what time it was, and I'd always miss class, but I found out very quickly that you could meet a lot more girls sitting under a tree with a guitar than you could in chemistry class."[118] Summing up Roth's outlook on formal education, a Muir music teacher, Marvin Neuman, told *Circus* in 1981 that "nothing else seemed to interest" Roth in those days other than music.[119]

At lunch, he'd tell Carberry and Perez what his band needed to succeed, including a more powerful PA system. Perez remembers, "He told me, 'We *need* to get a PA system.' I remember him going on and on at lunchtime all the time, 'We've *got* to get this. We've *got* to get that.'"

Slowly, Roth's efforts gained traction. Roth convinced his father to front him the money for a better PA system, an Acoustic 850 PA. Once deployed, it paid immediate dividends according to Perez. "Sure enough, when he got the [new] PA, it made a big difference," particularly in allowing Roth's vocals to be heard over the rest of the band.

Roth also worked to shift the band's repertoire and identity. Initially, he had waged a one-man war to bring some soul to Red Ball Jet, but when the band's drummer quit and Roth recruited his funkiest friend, Dan Hernandez, he gained a welcome ally.

Hernandez says that he and Dave had simpatico musical tastes. "Dave and I went to the same high school. I was playing jazz music with these guys at somebody's house, and I seem to recall Dave hanging out or something. I'm pretty sure he would sing with us. We were doing jazz and blues." When they weren't jamming, they'd listen to Janis Joplin, Jimi Hendrix, and the Beatles, along with lots of Motown records and the Los Angeles jazz station, KBCA-FM.

But more than music, Hernandez says, what connected them was a shared desire to "get our soul on." While PHS largely drew students from the side of town "where all the rich white people lived," Muir was more of "a mixed ethnic bag." This atmosphere helped produce a like-minded approach to culture and identity in them. "Dave wanted to hang around with all the brothers, as did I," he explains. "We were basically white dudes who wanted to be black . . . I think this was a big reason why Dave and I got along."

When the rail-thin drummer first set up his battered drums in the basement, the others doubted that Hernandez could fit the bill, but after just a couple of practices, it was clear that he was the group's missing ingredient. Taylor remembers, "Danny made all the difference in the band."

With Hernandez behind the kit, Red Ball Jet began to swing. The band's growing funkiness, Hernandez says, "came from me and Dave. We wanted to funkify stuff. We wanted it to be greasy. We wanted to be like James Brown, and Dave wanted to sing like James Brown, and I wanted to play like his drummer. We wanted to be versatile. That's what we were trying to do. We were trying to show people that we had more than [Bill Haley's] 'Shake, Rattle, and Roll.'"

Despite these changes, Red Ball Jet still had a tough time getting audiences to see things their way. In late 1971, Taylor remembers, "We played a high school or junior high school in Arcadia, and they threw cookies at us. They didn't like us." While the temperamental guitarist remained angry about this humiliating incident for days, Hernandez could only laugh when two weeks later he shook out the pillow he used to muffle his bass drum and stale pieces of cookie flew across the room.

David Lee Roth and Red Ball Jet get their groove on outside a police station in downtown Los Angeles, late 1972. From left to right: Gary "Hurricane" Taylor, David Lee Roth, Dan Hernandez, Miles Komora, and Mark Komora. LORRAINE B. ANDERSON

School administrators also found reasons to dislike Red Ball Jet, sometimes before the band had even played a note. "We were supposed to play at St. Francis High School," Hernandez remembers. "Dave was wearing — literally — a little boy's sweater, so it was really tight and small. The sleeves only went up to his elbows and exposed half of his midriff, because it was so tiny. And the girl [Elizabeth Wiley] who used to make clothes for Dave had sewed a bunch of shiny sequins all over it."

As Roth got ready, a stern nun told him that he needed to don a shirt more suitable for an audience of Catholic schoolgirls — *or else*. "So he's wearing that when we go to play. She told us we couldn't play unless he changed." After a tense exchange, Roth told his bandmates to pack up. "He wouldn't change," Hernandez says, "so we didn't play."

Roth's costumes and antics also caught the eye of some other religious-minded folks in Los Angeles. Lorraine Anderson, who dated Hernandez, recalls that a friend at school had told the band that a local church wanted to hire Red Ball Jet, and so the band took the gig. The show, she says, "was in the basement of a church on Wilshire Boulevard." The band set up and started "doing their whole thing" in front an audience comprised of church members.

After playing a few songs, the group took a break. While Dave held court, one of the band members burst into the dressing room and announced that an audience member just told him that the band had been hired to serve as an "example" of the evils of the Devil's work.

Anderson remembers that Roth and the others soon started grinning. "Dave said, 'Oh, I'll show them an example!' So they all took their shirts off. Dave unzipped his pants. Now he left everything in there, just got them as low as possible, but you could see some follicles."

Once they started playing again, "Things got pretty blue in there," Anderson says. "They were playing the most suggestive songs. Dave was probably humping the floor. It was a delight, but it was also terrifying, because a lot of the audience members were real dyed-in-the-wool Christians who were sure they were seeing the end of the world."

After the last song, the musicians quickly broke down their gear. She recalls, "We went back into the dressing room with the equipment and everything and basically barricaded the door. I don't know how that was accomplished, but it was. They had a fairly big window in there and we left through the window. Everybody."

 ═ ═

In early 1972, Red Ball Jet finally began to see some light at the end of their tunnel. Perez explains that he hired Red Ball Jet to play a family party for his cousin. Only after agreeing did it occur to anyone in the band to ask for the address. The house, it turned out, stood in a gritty barrio near the Rose Bowl, a part of town that white folks didn't frequent.

That day, kids descended on the home. Perez says, "It was kind of funny because the neighborhood was shocked to see all these white kids coming in from all over the place into the barrio. Then you had the Mexican kids from [Pasadena's] Blair [High School] and John Muir there. It cracked me up, because everybody was there." This mixing of whites and Latinos outside of school, he says, "didn't occur very often."

As the small backyard filled, Red Ball Jet swaggered through its set. "Dave came out like a junior Mick Jagger," Perez remembers. Once the band got cooking, "these Mexican kids were sitting there and all these white kids were there. They all kind of looked at each other and went, *Oh. Okay!*" As the party raged, even the authority figures enjoyed themselves. "There are five adults there and the party's going on. My aunt's there and my dad's there. Kids are coming up to the house, and we've got a keg."

Eventually, though, neighbors called police. "The cops came," Perez says, and "they are like, in shock. They go, 'This is the barrio. What are all these white kids doing here?' They're looking around. They see all the food, the booze, and the beer, and they can't believe it. And then they take off. Days later, of course, we realized that my aunt could have got in trouble for giving beer to kids, but in those days, they let it slide."

Afterwards, Perez, who is of Mexican descent, wasn't surprised that Roth had been able to facilitate this meeting of the tribes. "Lots of kids who tried to make it in bands," he explains, "didn't have that background of [knowing about] the ghetto or the barrio, which David had. David could even speak Spanish back then." According to Perez, Roth's social circle at Muir, like his choice of friends, reflected "an understanding of minority groups. He appreciated and saw the value in what blacks and Mexicans brought" to the city's broader culture. As a result, Roth and Red Ball Jet brought together, at least for one night, some very different groups of people.

= =

As school let out for the summer, Roth was determined to outdo the Van Halen brothers on the backyard party scene. Roth, in his autobiography, wrote that "playing at those parties got competitive fast," and as a result "conflict and rumor mongering" set the. tone for the rivalry.[120]

That summer, Roth and the rest of his band took a strategic approach to this feud. Understanding that they'd never match Mammoth's virtuosity, they upped the ante when it came to staging. Roth declared in *Crazy from the Heat* that Red Ball Jet made "the impossibly forward-thinking move of *renting* a little stage from Abbey Rents. It was about nine inches tall, with little risers."[121] With a stage underfoot — and Roth's Acoustic PA system to better project his vocals — Red Ball Jet set out to dethrone Mammoth.

The battle took place all over Pasadena neighborhoods. Taylor points to "the best gig we probably ever had." The home itself was built at the base of a gentle rise. Taylor remembers, "This backyard had a flat patio and it sloped at a thirty degree angle up to a pool," which made for a natural amphitheater for partygoers.

After Red Ball Jet started playing that night, all eyes were on Roth. Perez says Roth drew attention because he "dressed like an entertainer. He'd wear the leather pants and the vests and so forth, and the long hair and everything. The girls, man they would line up. They'd wet their panties going to look at this guy." In his autobiography, Roth recounted his techniques: "Halfway through singing at a party, I'd take my suspenders down and let 'em hang around my butt, and that really showed I was workin'."[122] Perez notes, "That showmanship was the show. That's what people wanted to see. They didn't go to see Red Ball Jet; they went to see David. That was the game. Whether they came to mock or to appreciate him, he would get a crowd." Leiren felt the same way, saying, "All the girls would go down and see Dave, and all the guys would go down there and hate Dave!"[123]

At another party that summer, there were a couple of observers who took a particular interest in Roth and his band. Paul Fry remembers, "I went with Eddie and Alex one night to see Red Ball Jet play. They were checking out the competition, so to speak."

The fact that the Van Halen brothers went to see Red Ball Jet, a band they hated, suggests that they may have seen the gap between the two bands beginning to narrow. Hernandez remembers, "What I always used to say about the two bands was that we were actually cross-town rivals; the Van Halens could play, but we had Dave! They were the 'musician' band and we were the 'entertainment' band." Despite their superior musicianship, the brothers seemed to appreciate Fry yelling over the noise, "This is *not* competition to you guys! Are you guys nuts?"

Even if Roth's group wasn't a serious musical threat, Edward would, albeit contemptuously, credit Roth for achieving his goal, saying in 1979 that Red Ball Jet were "totally into showmanship, except that they . . . couldn't play a note."[124]

= =

Sometime in July, Roth began bringing an older friend to the band's practices, a fast-talking karate instructor–*cum*–Hollywood stuntman named Sonny Hughes. Perhaps a year earlier, Roth had shared his rock star dream with Hughes after one of Roth's training sessions at Pasadena's storied Ed Parker Kenpo karate studio. Hughes had experience in these matters, he informed Roth, because his mother had sung background vocals on some Sinatra records and on Elvis's 1968 comeback special. Roth urged him to watch Red Ball Jet practice, something that Hughes quickly made a habit of doing.[125]

After Roth and Hughes got to talking, they drew up plans for a show that would set a new standard for a high school gig. With Hughes at his side, Roth then presented the idea to the band. Rather than playing in a backyard, Red Ball Jet would rent the football stadium at Eliot Junior High School. In fact, Hughes and Roth had already reserved the venue through the Altadena parks and recreation department and the board of education.[126]

To top it all off, Dr. Roth had offered to help the band in two ways. First, he agreed to pay for radio advertisements. Second, he promised to rent a helicopter to fly the band from a nearby helipad to the Eliot grounds, landing in plain view of everyone, just like the Stones had done at Altamont. Once they touched down, they'd duck their heads, run through the rotor wash, and head into the stadium and onto the stage, while the delirious crowd looked on in amazement. Roth and Hughes had no doubt it would be the most outrageous local concert in Pasadena history.

Within days, Roth set out to design a gig flyer. He'd seen enough of them around town to know that most didn't warrant a second glance. That just wasn't going to cut it this time around.

Taylor recalls Roth's suggestion: "David wanted us all naked and covering up with guitars." Miles Komora adds, "It was a thing of how to catch people's attention through publicity," so "we said, 'Let's get naked and take a picture.'" In Roth's father's backyard, the band posed for a photo in the midst of some high grass and thick brush, giving the impression that they'd just emerged from some primeval forest. The Komora brothers and Taylor squatted down in a semicircle with their guitars strategically concealing their private parts. Hernandez used a large cowbell for the same purpose as he kneeled amidst them. And in the middle stood Roth, his body turned to the side, his bare left leg bent at the knee and his hands covering his crotch, wearing some patterned socks and

The infamous Red Ball Jet "naked" flyer, summer 1972. MILES R. KOMORA

flashy Cuban-heeled shoes. For a finishing touch, they all sported colorful ties, which only served to reinforce the fact that the members of Red Ball Jet weren't wearing clothes.[127]

After a trip to the print shop, they discussed how to distribute the three thousand copies of the racy flyer before the August 25 gig. Although Miles questioned the wisdom of posting them all over the San Gabriel Valley, he was outvoted. The others grabbed stacks of the flyers and hit the streets. Hernandez says, "The flyers were tacked up all over the city, on telephone poles; these things were plastered all over the place."

The day before the show, the head of the Altadena parks and recreation department returned to the office after a relaxing two-week vacation. His assistant, with a short knock, burst into the office and handed him the flyer, saying, "Look at this! These are all over town. They're up and down Lake Avenue and across Colorado Boulevard." The director took one look at the picture of the five hairy, nude young men and told his assistant to get the person behind this upcoming event on the phone. Now.[128]

Soon after, Hughes took his call and explained that he'd spoken to *someone* in the office about the concert. After a bit more back and forth, Hughes said, "Well, once I fly them in by helicopter —"[129] With that, the director's eyes got wide. Taylor recalls that the city administrator "thought he had a *naked* rock and roll band that was going to helicopter into this gig at Eliot Junior High School" and then perform wearing nothing more than funny ties and their guitars. He cut Hughes off, told him the show was canceled, and slammed down the receiver. Soon after, however, he realized that he had another problem.

The next day, Hernandez picked up the Pasadena *Star-News*. Inside the front page was an article with the headline, "Altadena Rock Fest Canceled." It informed the concerned citizens of the San Gabriel Valley that the scheduled concert at Eliot had been the product of a "misunderstanding between parties." Hernandez thinks that Altadena officials called the newspaper "because of the anticipation of how many people were going to show up. They knew it was likely there were going to be a lot of people."[130]

In the wake of this affair, Taylor remembers that even though the fallout was significant, the whole caper had served a larger purpose. "People got all pissed off. But looking back at it, it's the old adage in show business. Any publicity is good publicity."

= =

As the summer ended, Roth maximized the band's backyard-party opportunities. In September, Roth's friend Bobby Hatch hired Red Ball Jet to play at his parents' home, which was situated right down Michigan Avenue from Roth's close friend Stanley Swantek's house. "I met Dave Roth through Stanley," Hatch remembers. "He fit in with us because we had a boys club. We had thirteen or fourteen [boys] growing up on our own block. We used to hang out in front of my parents' house. We used to call it 'the wall.' Basically if you didn't have a date that night you'd hang out at the wall and upset the neighbors with loud music, just having fun."[131]

During these days, one key component of the Michigan Avenue party scene was an ice cream truck. As Roth often told audiences on Van Halen's 2007 tour, "We'd park the ice cream truck in the backyard and take all the ice cream out and put beer in it for the party."[132] Although Roth recalled Stanley Swantek having driven it, Stanley's brother David sets the record straight: "This guy named Tommy Lake bought an ice cream truck and did it as a business at least for one full summer. We used to party [at our house] and the Hatch's house, which is right down the street. Tommy used to bring his ice cream truck over there, and sometimes we'd go out and sell ice cream with him and drink beer because we had beer in the ice chest." During one of these boozy summer rides around the city, Lake told the Swantek brothers about an old John Brim record he had with a song called "Ice Cream Man." David Swantek says that his brother then "borrowed the record and played it for Dave. Anyway that is where the [Van Halen] song came from."

With both the ice cream truck and Red Ball Jet situated at Hatch's, the party got underway and soon got out of control. Hernandez recollects playing in the "absurdly crowded" backyard with the police helicopter hovering overhead, shining a high-powered spotlight down on the band. Roth followed the light around the stage, mugging for the revelers before the cops shut things down.

= =

On another front, Roth's and Hernandez's efforts to bring some soul to Red Ball Jet had paid off by the fall of 1972. The band started playing some James Brown, like "Cold Sweat," and more

Motown, like Jr. Walker & the All Stars' "Shotgun," and some selections from Edgar Winter's *White Trash*.

Along with these covers came a handful of originals, including one swinging number that was inspired by the 1958 hit "Tequila." On it, Roth played saxophone and said the song's title and sole lyric — "Lotion!" — during breaks in the song's instrumental sections. What tied all of these songs together, at least in Roth's mind, was crystal clear. "Dave kept saying, 'It has to have danceabilty! You *have* to be able to dance to it,'" Taylor recalls.

Roth had also talked others into donning funkier stage clothes. Miles and the others drove into Hollywood and picked out some vibrant shirts, flared pants, and gaudy shoes to add some flash to the Red Ball Jet show. Roth, too, pushed his look in new directions. By this time he started taking cues from the burgeoning glam-rock movement, which had hit nearby Hollywood in a big way. Hernandez recalls that Roth had gotten turned on to David Bowie and glitter rock, and as a result he "was wearing platform shoes in Red Ball Jet." Elizabeth Wiley, a close friend of Roth's who worked with and supported him through his stints with Red Ball Jet and Van Halen, remembers decorating an "amazing leather jacket with studs and rhinestones" and sewing a lamé tuxedo for Roth, just two of a number of outfits she and her sister, Linda, created for him. She says, "Dave got these ideas, and it was our job to make them reality."[133]

≡ ≡

At the end of 1972, Roth pursued another avenue in his effort to transform the band. Dr. Roth — with the encouragement of his son — decided to interject himself into the affairs of Red Ball Jet. He and Dave had a number of ideas, not the least of which involved auditioning at some Hollywood clubs, like the Sunset

Strip landmark Gazzarri's. Dr. Roth argued, however, that before they took that step they needed some professional guidance, so he hired a sixty-dollar-an-hour consultant to help the band craft its show.[134]

This guidance would come from Carlton Johnson, a veteran tap dancer and Hollywood choreographer. Before he walked into Red Ball Jet's rehearsal space, he had masterminded the dance routines for blockbuster movies like *It's a Mad, Mad, Mad, Mad World* and successful television shows such as *The Danny Kaye Show, The Sammy Davis Jr. Show*, and *The Carol Burnett Show*.[135]

Over the next few weeks, Johnson would teach Red Ball Jet a dance routine. Hernandez remembers that all of them except Dave "hated" the whole idea of choreographing their show to this degree. Hernandez states, "I was a drummer so I wasn't involved in that, but Carlton was trying to teach them what they used to refer to as Motown step. As you know, this was a rock and roll band." Taylor says it was futile to try to turn three awkward guys into Fred Astaire: "Teaching a bunch of white boys to dance like that? Dave's the only one who had any chance, because he was into it and we were white boys listening to white rock and blues."

Observers had similar reactions. Ron Morgan says, "Miles was telling me about this professional choreographer, and I was just chortling. 'You've got to be kidding. Some guy from Motown is going to come out and teach you white boys how to dance?'" Morgan then headed to the basement and watched "Miles, who had a football player type of physique, tiptoeing around while he's trying to play bass at the same time." Kevin Gallagher says that this made Red Ball Jet "the laughingstock of the band scene." Morgan adds that all of this just reinforced his sense that "Roth was kind of nutty, really off the wall, compared to the other people I was hanging around who played music."

But to Roth, none of this was nutty. Adding black-influenced choreography to Red Ball Jet made perfect sense to a kid who'd grown up imitating the latest dance steps on *American Bandstand*, aping the dance moves of Al Jolson and James Brown, and singing along to Louis Armstrong records. Indeed, when Roth later told interviewers that he'd taken more musical cues from the Ohio Players than Deep Purple, he wasn't kidding.[136] As Roth wrote in his autobiography, he tried to soak in black culture "in all of [its] finery, whether that's the Afro, the bell-bottoms, the platforms. Their cars, their slang, their ordinance."[137]

Hernandez says that Roth consumed these components of black popular culture in crafting his own sense of showmanship. "It's just how he was," he explains. "It wasn't calculated or manipulated personally. If anything was calculated or manipulated, it was because of entertainment. It's who he is. He'd say, 'I'm an entertainer.'" So one day when Roth told Hernandez over a mac-and-cheese lunch that one of his "big dreams" was "to go to Vegas and stand on the stage and tell killer jokes and dance like a fool" just like Sammy Davis Jr. had at the Sands, Hernandez just nodded and went back to eating.

Roth's Vegas fantasies aside, the band secured a Gazzarri's audition. Joining them that day were Carlton and Dr. Roth. But when Red Ball Jet stepped on the stage, they realized that two of its features — a pole at its center and a spiral staircase off to the side — would make their dance routine, to be done to B.B. King's "Rock Me Baby," impossible to perform. Komora says that Johnson had planned for Taylor, his brother Mark, and him to walk "around in circles or behind David. You know how you get lower by bending your knees and then go up? We were doing something like that." After an impromptu meeting, the band decided that the three instrumentalists wouldn't dance.

Things went from bad to worse once they started playing. Taylor's pants were so tight that they split, producing chuckles from onlookers. And even though Roth danced his ass off, the entire audition fell flat. Miles Komora recollects that after he came offstage he "actually felt pretty badly, because Carlton was there and watching. Carlton said, 'Oh, you guys sounded good.' I thought, *Oh yeah, right. This is the last time we'll ever see him,* and it was!"

= =

Even though the band was sputtering after the Gazzarri's disaster, the well-connected Dr. Roth got the band some gigs. "He got us into a few places just by mentioning the fact that he was *Dr. Roth*," Miles Komora says. "I remember he got us gigs at the police station in downtown L.A., a USO gig or two . . . and one at a girls' prison in L.A." Taylor recalls, "He was talking to ABC Television, trying to get us in a 'nightclub scene' in those made-for-TV movies back then. The man was genuinely trying to put us in the right places to get noticed. [Dave's] dad was basically trying to represent us."

Nathan Roth's interest in the band, however, would ultimately hurt more than it helped. One day, Dave and his father announced that Dr. Roth deserved a band vote since he was paying the bills. The others weren't having it and proceeded to quit. In the end, Red Ball Jet went out with a whimper.

Hernandez thinks that Dave knew the writing was on the wall. "He was very ambitious," Hernandez observes. "So he's in Red Ball Jet. I think he's frustrated. He knows what he wants to do and what he wants to be around. I think he understands that the Van Halen brothers are much better players than we are. He wants to be associated with that kind of quality, and so there was a struggle for him as an artist."

Still, Roth had to have known that at that moment, his chances of joining Mammoth were only slightly better than his chances of joining the Rolling Stones. "The Van Halen brothers didn't like him," Leiren explained. "They thought he was a jerk."[138] But that didn't seem to bother Roth.

= =

In 1984, Roth provided insight into why he was able to shake off episodes like his failed auditions and his fractured band. "I've always been very self-motivated," he told the *London Sunday Times*. "It's always irritated me that people say, 'Where's the action? Oh wow, there's no action here; let's go somewhere else.' These people will *never* find the action. There's [*sic*] three kinds of folks on this planet. There's people who *make* things happen; there's people who *watch* things happen; and there's people who wonder, what happened?"[139]

Roth gave Hernandez a taste of how seriously the singer took the power of positive thinking in early 1973. The drummer had recently joined his first professional group. "I remember a day when he came to my house, and I had just started playing in this western swing band. This is after Red Ball Jet, but we were still hanging out a little bit. This is before Van Halen."

Hernandez, sitting with sheet music in front of him, expressed his anxieties to Roth. "I was kind of freaked out as a nineteen-year-old drummer in rehearsal sessions with these way big-time studio musicians. I had the charts at my house, and I showed them to Dave. I remember telling him, 'The charts kind of freak me out.' They were kind of challenging at my skill level."

Roth cut Hernandez off, saying, "Don't you have any confidence?" Hernandez says, "I'll never forget that. He was saying 'Get your shit together . . . and kick everybody's ass, and it will all be good.'" To Roth, these weren't empty words. Within the next few months, he'd take his own advice.

DAVID LEE ROTH
JOINS VAN HALEN

Red Ball Jet's demise should have gutted Roth. His Sunset Strip dreams were dashed after his band blew its Gazzarri's audition. His father, who'd invested his time and money in his son's band, only to see it break up, no longer supported his musical dreams. For his troubles, all that Dave was left with in early 1973 was the small PA system that his father had bought for him.

Despite these setbacks, Roth was undeterred. To be sure, finding himself without a band was problematic. But for a young man of just eighteen who'd resolved to be an entertainer long before he smoked or shaved, and later was so determined to become a vocalist that it "never" occurred to him to assess whether he was even a good singer, this was hardly a dealbreaker.[140] He would now set out to join a local band.

While there were a few talented groups in town, including Uncle Sam, Roth's ideal landing spot was Mammoth. That band, now a quartet after the addition of a keyboardist, had built its reputation by playing precise covers of songs by the era's leading hard rock groups.

Even though Edward, who remained Mammoth's lead vocalist, didn't like to sing, the Van Halen brothers had no interest in Roth. Why would they? They and their friends saw Roth as a spoiled rich kid from San Marino. Class envy aside, Roth had shown no evidence that he was a competent singer during his 1971 audition.[141] Edward and Alex didn't think he'd improved when they saw him with Red Ball Jet, a band they hated. "Ed and I couldn't stand the motherfucker," Alex declared to Steven Rosen. "We couldn't stand the band. We couldn't stand the music."[142]

Nonetheless, Roth was undeterred. Back in 1970, Roth had seen the Van Halen brothers play at a Jewish temple, and sometime later, Roth watched them play at a party. Roth told the *New York Post*, "I still remember the first time I saw [Edward] playing in a backyard party in Pasadena in high school. He was great."[143]

This singular talent is what drew Roth to the Van Halen brothers. And despite the disdain of Mammoth and its fans, Roth remained self-assured. He had a plan. Somehow, some way, he would convince Edward and Alex to invite him to join Mammoth.

═ ═

Without a band, Roth sought other ways to pursue his musical dreams. Before long, an unexpected opportunity materialized. "I knew Dave before he joined Van Halen," Debbie Imler McDermott remembers. "We worked together at this store called London Britches in Pasadena that sold these super tight, low-low cut, below your navel bell-bottoms." At some point during his stint at the store, Roth approached the store's ownership with an idea he had for an advertising campaign.

Roth's pitch succeeded. Miles Komora recalls, "I remember the first time he was on the radio was for London Britches. He actually wrote a little tune and they played it on the radio." David Roth, with his acoustic guitar and his songwriting skills, had debuted on the airwaves.

After work, Roth spent time at the Swantek residence on Michigan Avenue. As David Swantek recounts, "Roth was my brother Stanley's closest friend in high school. They used to go out chasing girls together." Before a night on the town, Roth would hang out with the brothers. David Swantek says, "David Roth used to come over to my mom's house all the time. We'd sit out on the front porch and smoke a J, and Dave would tell us about his plans for the future."

Roth's short-term plans didn't include waiting for a call from the Van Halen brothers. With his radio jingle under his belt, Roth looked for troubadour work. "After Red Ball Jet broke up and before he joined Van Halen," David Swantek says, "he decided, *Well, I'm going to go play clubs.*" Perhaps inspired by singer-songwriters like Cat Stevens and Jackson Browne, Roth would practice guitar in front of the others. "Since he partied there on the front porch, he'd say, 'Hey let me play a couple of songs for you guys, and you can tell me what you think.' He had 'Ice Cream Man' and he had a song called 'Honolulu Baby.'"

Roth, it turns out, had worked hard on his playing. Hernandez observes, "Dave didn't do acoustic stuff in Red Ball Jet, but he loved to play. He and I would play acoustic guitars and jam. We'd play blues together and make up words. I remember one day going to his house in San Marino, and he was playing [the Eagles'] 'Peaceful Easy Feeling,' and it was beautiful. He played and sang well."

After winning plaudits from his friends, Dave auditioned at the Ice House in Pasadena. When he tried out, though, Roth got an earful. As he explained to a reporter in 1994, "Sunday night was the audition night for the club, and if you veered towards cliché the

David Lee Roth strums his Vox acoustic at his father's home in
San Marino, California, circa November 1972. ELIZABETH WILEY

owner would interrupt with a mocking voice that boomed over the
PA system." This high-pressure atmosphere, Roth remarked, "built
character."[144] Edward later affirmed the value of these experiences

for Roth when he told Steven Rosen that Dave did "solo stuff before. That's where 'Ice Cream Man' came from; he used to play that acoustic at the Ice House all the time."[145] More recently, however, Roth conceded that he'd never actually made the club's roster of performers. "Audition night was as far as I ever got."[146]

= =

Meanwhile, Mammoth had two problems. First, Edward, a self-conscious teenager who had never felt comfortable singing, began to dislike his dual role as guitarist and lead singer. With his hair hanging in his face and a lit cigarette stuck in his Les Paul's headstock, he'd scream over Mammoth's wall of sound until his throat was raw. "I never technically learned how to sing," he observed in 1996. "So, I would kind of do a Kurt Cobain — after five songs and three beers my voice would be gone. You know, I would just scream it out and kind of waste my voice."[147] This double duty also detracted from his playing. As he told *Guitar Player*, "I couldn't stand that shit! I'd rather just play."[148]

Second, the band didn't own a PA. From 1971 onward, Edward and Alex rented PA equipment from various people. They rented one from Paul Fry, who'd gotten them the gig at PCC, and later, they rented a system from Greg Pettit, who played in Uncle Sam, Mammoth's main rival.

During one of their visits to pick up Pettit's PA, they had an unexpected encounter. Guitarist Nicky Panicci, who as young teen watched Uncle Sam practice, says that one afternoon in early 1973, Edward and Alex bumped into Roth at Uncle Sam's rehearsal space. Roth wasted no time in lobbying the Van Halen brothers to let him join Mammoth. Panicci recollects that Alex and Edward turned him down flat as they left with Pettit's PA.[149]

By the early summer of 1973, Edward and Alex had run out of patience and money. One day Alex showed up to rent Pettit's

Alex Van Halen at a Mammoth band practice at the Pewsey
Dance Studio in Altadena, California, early 1973. ELIZABETH WILEY

equipment only to hear that the fee had increased. Alex, who had
a notoriously short fuse, accused Pettit of trying to overcharge
Mammoth and left after telling him "to fuck off."[150]

A few days later, Miles Komora answered a knock at the door and found the brothers on the doorstep. "They came over to my house and said, 'Hey do you have Dave's phone number? We want to rent his PA.' So I said, 'Yeah, sure.'" Alex then contacted Roth, who agreed to rent it to them.[151]

As the *David Lee Roth Joins Van Halen* story has been told, after a "few months" of renting Roth's system, Alex sat his brother down and observed, "Look, you're not really capable of being the frontman and singing . . . Why not just get [Roth] in the band, and [then] we won't have to pay him."[152] Edward later explained why this made a lot of sense: "We were renting his PA every weekend for thirty-five dollars and getting fifty dollars for the gigs. So it was cheaper to get him in the band."[153] Soon after, Mammoth became a quintet.

In the weeks between Roth agreeing to rent his equipment and the brothers inviting him to join are the details of one of the great rock and roll power plays of all time. With his Acoustic 850 PA as leverage and his persistence as means of entry, David Lee Roth would persuade the Van Halen brothers to reconsider their refusal to let him join Mammoth.

= =

In early 1973, Jim Pewsey was Mammoth's newest member. He explains, "There were so many keyboards on all of the Top 40 then that they needed a keyboardist." Rodney Davey of Uncle Sam adds that Edward's love for one of the great hard rock groups of the '70s also made a keyboard player seem like a necessity: "Ed got on a Deep Purple kick. Jim was really the guy for them to go to. He could do all that Purple stuff with a lot of flair." Mammoth, with Pewsey on Farfisa organ and Wurlitzer electric piano, played Purple's "Bloodsucker," "Into the Fire," "Smoke on the Water," and "Highway Star."[154] Pewsey says, "We played a *lot* of Deep Purple, especially before Dave got in the band."

Bassist Mark Stone and keyboardist Jim Pewsey of Mammoth perform in the San Gabriel Valley, August 1973. ELIZABETH WILEY

Deep Purple aside, the band broadened its horizons now that it had a keyboard player. Along with their heavy rock standbys, Mammoth played the Allman Brothers' "Ramblin' Man," Sugarloaf's

"Green-Eyed Lady," the Zombies' "Time of the Season," and Santana's "Hope You're Feeling Better"[155] and "Soul Sacrifice."[156] In fact, Edward would later say that out of all the keyboard material the band did during this era, this last Santana track was his favorite because "on that song the keyboard cooked."[157]

Pewsey says that after the brothers rented Roth's system for the first time, Roth started hanging around Mammoth, irritating at least half of the band. Wearing hip huggers, platforms, and flashy shirts, Roth looked out of place when set against Mammoth's torn blue jeans, white T-shirts, and faded flannels. "You know, I was a lot more conservative than Dave," Pewsey says. "He was a punk. His daddy had money. At first we didn't want anything to do with him." Mark Stone, for his part, says he "didn't like Dave," because he "found his personality difficult and weird."[158]

So how did a guy who rubbed the members of Mammoth the wrong way become a part of the band? Pewsey contends that the Van Halen brothers didn't just decide one day to let him join. Instead, Roth "literally snuck his way in" to Mammoth. "I don't know how else to put it," he declares. While it's true that "he would rent us his old Acoustic PA," this was merely Roth's opening gambit as he worked to ingratiate himself with the Van Halen brothers.

Some weeks after Roth and Mammoth started doing business, Roth changed the rules of the game. Pewsey says that on the day of a gig, Roth said to the band, "If you let me in to the party for free, you can use my PA." In this way, he got to hang out with the brothers and spend time with them in between sets, drinking beers and smoking cigarettes.

As the Pasadena backyard party season got into full swing, Roth played his trump card. Pewsey remembers that just hours before a big gig, Roth declared that Mammoth wasn't "going to be able to use [his PA] anymore unless he could start singing a couple of songs with us." Roth had put Mammoth in an impossible situation. Even

David Lee Roth, the new lead singer of Mammoth, August 1973. ELIZABETH WILEY

as Alex's temper flared, the brothers knew they had nowhere else to turn. Pewsey says they had no choice, and "so we let him do that." By the time that night was over, David Roth had sung for Mammoth.

Pewsey recalls that Roth soon found another way to close ranks with Mammoth. At the time, the band rehearsed at the keyboardist's family's dance studio in Altadena. On early summer evenings when they'd be working, he'd "just show up at the dance studio with" his PA, a gesture that allowed him to hang out with the band some more.

During these visits and everywhere else he encountered them, Roth made his case to the brothers about what he could bring to Mammoth, other than a working PA. With Camels crammed between their lips and beers in their hands, Edward and Alex stood nonplussed in front of an animated Roth as he diagnosed Mammoth's weaknesses and laid out his vision for the band's future. First, the brothers needed to think and dream about bigger things than local keg parties and high school dances. There were bars and nightclubs all over the sprawling City of Angels, *hundreds* of them in fact, where working bands could ply their trade on any given night of the week.

When the brothers replied that they'd had little luck with nightclub bookings, Roth asserted that people went to nightspots to *get down*, not relive Woodstock. "It's because you play all twenty minutes of 'I'm So Glad' by Cream, complete with drum solo, live, note for note, and it's very impressive, but you can't dance to it."[159] Mammoth had the players and the chops. It was the musical mindset, and most importantly the songs, that had to change. "I will personally check every song for danceability," Roth guaranteed. "And we'll play rock tunes, but ones that you can *dance* to." The more Roth talked, the more the brothers nodded.[160]

In the summer of 1973, with Edward sick of singing and the band tired of seeing its profits disappear into Roth's pocket, the Van Halen brothers debated whether to invite him to join their band. As Alex revealed to Steven Rosen, the brothers concluded that Roth's swagger and charisma outweighed his shortcomings as a vocalist.

"He couldn't sing for shit, but he was a very cocky guy. He had long blond hair, and he walked around with a certain confidence. He compensated for his lousy voice by being the outspoken loudmouth who looked different. We just figured his singing would improve with time."[161] And with that calculus, the brothers decided to invite Roth to become a member of Mammoth.

Surprisingly, this time around there was no tryout for Roth. Stone recalls, "One day Al and Ed said, 'Dave's officially in the band now.'"[162]

In light of the hazing Roth had endured from Mammoth and their fans during his Red Ball Jet days, this was undoubtedly a sweet moment for him. The Van Halen brothers had let him join their band.

Still, there was at least one other singer whom Edward and Alex had considered. About two weeks before Roth joined Mammoth, Edward sought out Rafael Marti. He recalls, "Eddie came to my house. He said, 'We've got to get a singer. Can you get me that guy's number? . . . Legg, the singer from Uncle Sam, can you get me his phone number?'"

Marti says, "I could see what Eddie was trying to do. They needed a frontman. Legg was a very good singer. He sounded like Robert Plant, actually. He could hit those high notes. So I said yes, and I started asking around and tried to get Legg's number, but before I got back to Eddie I had heard that Roth had joined [the band]."[163] It's unlikely Roth knew about Edward's last-ditch effort to find someone else to sing, but regardless, he was now in Mammoth.[164]

= =

Not surprisingly, this lineup change generated strong reactions. Jonathan Laidig observes, "Everybody who heard that Eddie had hired Roth was like, 'You did *what*?'" Marti remembers that when

Roth joined, all of Mammoth's followers "seriously thought [the Van Halen brothers] had ruined Mammoth," telling Edward, "'Wow. I can't believe you did this. This guy sucks.' Eddie was apologetic, but he'd say to us, 'Be nice to him. He's okay.'"[165]

Despite the negativity, Edward never wavered in his support for his new singer. A few weeks after Roth joined, Marti pulled Edward aside in between sets at a beach party in Corona Del Mar, asking — with Roth within earshot — "How long are you going to keep this guy?" Edward stood up for Roth, telling Marti, "We *need* this guy."[166]

While Roth's limited vocal ability certainly fed these reactions, it wasn't as if Roth's vocals were worse than Edward's. To be clear, *no one* paid money to hear Edward sing. Marti highlights this by saying, "They'd do a whole side of *Live at Leeds*, note for note. The playing was so amazing no one cared about vocals." While Edward had soldiered through in his dual role, he wasn't a better singer than Roth. Clearly, vocal talent wasn't driving the opposition to Roth.

In fact, it was Roth's cultural style and musical taste, rather than his singing, that rubbed everyone the wrong way. In Red Ball Jet, Roth had worn outrageous stage costumes.[167] In addition, Roth's musical stew took most of its flavor from genres like R&B and glam rock rather than hard rock.[168]

Mammoth's musical sensibility could not have been more different. Mammoth's sets emphasized the darker and doomier sounds of the early '70s: boogie-rock merchants Cactus, heavy metal pioneers Black Sabbath, and blues-rock stalwarts Grand Funk Railroad. Even Santana, with its Latin-influenced sound, ranged outside of Mammoth's comfort zone. "The brothers and Mark really liked a lot harder rock than I did," Pewsey observes. "I always wanted to do more Santana, but they didn't want to." Edward, in *Rolling Stone*, explained that at that time he had no interest in the kind of music that Roth preferred, saying that if "Cream and Led Zeppelin are white, then, yeah, I was very white."[169]

Edward's outlook, in one sense, reflected his band's fan base. PHS, which had birthed Mammoth, remained predominantly white in the early 1970s, despite the court ordered integration of the city's public schools.[170] In the PHS parking lot, Mammoth fans smoked grass in Chevelles and custom vans as their 8-track players blasted Black Sabbath's *Vol. 4*, Alice Cooper's *School's Out*, and Deep Purple's *Machine Head*. This was *Dazed and Confused*, Pasadena-style. David Swantek, who attended PHS while his brothers were bussed to John Muir High School, summarizes: "A lot of my friends were blacks as well as whites. All of the guys at PHS couldn't handle that. PHS was a lily-white school . . . the football-jock-types and cheerleaders thought Mammoth was the only way to fly."

Roth, of course, had developed a different musical and cultural identity, which made for a rough transition for him once he joined Mammoth. Edward said that Dave "probably got a lot more flack, because he used to be into David Bowie, wear platform shoes, and [have] funny haircuts."[171] David Swantek explains, "Mammoth's fans already didn't like David, because he was the enemy. He had always been the enemy in the past, so it was pretty ballsy to take David on, to be honest with you." Roth, to his credit, dismissed his detractors and took his lumps like a man.

= =

With Roth at the helm, Mammoth moved forward. Pasadena native Jose Hurtado recalls that one of the first parties, if not the first party, the five-piece Mammoth played was at a local tract home. "My friend knew Steve Whitaker. Steve's sister dated Eddie, so that's how we hired Mammoth."

With five kegs on ice and no parents in sight, the party got off to a great start. "They had a small space to play in," Hurtado remembers. "It was not a big backyard. They did [Beck, Bogert & Appice's] 'Superstition' and stuff like that. Roth was pretty standoffish. He'd say hi or whatever, but his father had money. He was a doctor, right? So Roth acted like a superstar. The police busted it around ten o'clock, so it lasted awhile. I know a lot of people liked the old Mammoth or Genesis and didn't like it with the singer and the keyboards; they didn't like it as much as before, but everyone seemed to enjoy themselves."[172]

Roth's recollection of his first gig is less upbeat. He conceded in his autobiography that "the first time" he performed "with the band in a backyard party the audience hated it!"[173] One problem Roth faced was that he had no experience singing the tunes that Mammoth had made its bones performing. "When I first joined the band," Roth recalled, I "tried to sing some of the songs — there was Grand Funk Railroad, as well as Black Sabbath. The music was pretty alien to me. I didn't even own those records. I had to go to the Thrifty Drugstore to buy them. Did my best, which was awful."[174]

The next day, Edward, Alex, and Roth all reflected on their performance. Roth remembered that when the Van Halen brothers took stock, they "were shocked and horrified" by Roth's shortcomings. Roth, on the other hand, now apprehended how seriously Mammoth's fans took the band. "It was the first time," Roth observed, "I really became aware of how possessive an audience could really be about a given artist or a given band. Way beyond 'this is great music,' it was almost as if it were football-team time. 'Hey, this is our band, they represent *us*.' I came from another side of town, so to speak."[175]

As the band's newest member, Roth had little luck convincing the Van Halen brothers to alter their musical approach. Unsurprisingly, he suggested that Mammoth play more pop songs. "Dave was more entertainer than musician," Edward said in 1980. "As a result, he had a better eye for the commercial thing. He was into short-format stuff because people's attention spans are only so long."[176]

Roth eventually made headway. Pewsey says, "Dave brought 'The Jean Genie' by Bowie. He liked that glitter stuff." Bowie's song, along with Edgar Winter's "Free Ride," "Hangin' Around," and the instrumental "Frankenstein" soon became staples for the band.[177] Pewsey remembers, "We did 'Frankenstein,' but since I didn't have a Moog, we cut that part out. Instead Dave imitated the Moog by humming." Pewsey summarizes, "The truth is that Dave musically changed the Van Halens and the Van Halens changed Dave."

Roth also pressed the band to take on more of a soul, funk, and blues feel. With Pewsey's support, he proposed Billy Preston's 1973 hit, "Will It Go Round in Circles." The others agreed to play it. Brent Pettit says that even though it was different from Mammoth's usual fare, "they did that song *great*. They put their own spin on it." Roth had less luck when it came to the Godfather of Soul. Pewsey recalls, "Dave liked James Brown. He pushed for us to do 'Cold Sweat.' Tell you the truth, I didn't know what to think when he suggested that." The brothers, however, did know what they thought about it. They told Roth no.

= =

In the midst of these musical changes, they took on more gigs: backyard parties, high school dances, and youth club events. As the summer progressed, Roth remained a target for the ire of disgruntled Mammoth fans. Patti Smith Sutlick recalls, "When David Lee Roth was new in the band, I remember going to a party up in Altadena . . . There were all of these car [club] guys that we knew. They were just *so* disgusted that David Lee Roth was in the band. David Lee Roth was wearing platform shoes and they were throwing their beer cans at him, yelling, 'Go home Hollywood! Go Home! Hollywood go home!'" Debbie Imler McDermott felt much the same way: "When he first joined the band, I didn't like him as their lead singer. I didn't know that he had any musical talent. It took me a while to warm up to him. Here's this guy strutting around the stage like a rooster. He was very cocky onstage."

Paying no attention to his critics, Roth wore increasingly out-landish outfits, even though the others in the band didn't share his fashion sense. Pewsey reveals, "When he first got into Van Halen, he dressed in a more low-key fashion. He knew the brothers didn't like the way he dressed. Dave started out wearing jeans when he joined the band, but then his pants started to get tighter and tighter, and the clothes got brighter and brighter. He eventually got more and more extravagant."

This shift from denim to lamé offered visual evidence that Pasadena's favorite hard rock cover band was evolving into some-thing new. Patti Smith Sutlick explains, "This was really a change for the people who were seeing Van Halen at the time when David Lee Roth first came onboard. Mammoth and Genesis, they were more of a dark band, focused on guitar, on the other instruments. They all looked like these long-haired, dark-haired people. David Lee Roth just kind of brought a new kind of spirit to the group, as an entertainer, a frontman. I think it turned off a lot of people at the beginning, but then through the months they changed their tune."

But for those not emotionally invested in the old Mammoth, these changes had an undeniable appeal. Gary Putman remem-bers, "I thought it was great when Roth joined. I think I liked it better. All of a sudden you heard that he was in the band. Although we were all obsessed with electric guitar, we'd talk about Roth and all the unique aspects he added to Van Halen, beyond the music. We loved it. We got a kick out of it, Roth's fucking around with the girls and all that stuff."

Putman's comment highlights the fact that Roth did help expand the band's female fan base. Patti Smith Sutlick explains that even as her male friends flung beer cans at Roth, she embraced the new lineup. "I loved him from the beginning," she remembers. Debbie Imler McDermott explains, "As they got more popular in Pasadena, my girlfriends would coo, 'Oooh, you — you *know* him?' Girls would be pressuring me to introduce them to Dave. They

Edward and Alex Van Halen lock in during an instrumental break while
David Lee Roth performs for the crowd, August 1973. ELIZABETH WILEY

were *so* excited to meet him. It got to the point where you almost
had to surgically remove girls from his body. They'd just hang all
over him."

In the meantime, Roth eventually got the band to bend to his will when it came to "Cold Sweat." Pewsey recalls, "We rocked it out. Dave used it as our song to introduce the band members and say everyone's name. He'd say, 'Master James Pewsey on the keyboards!'" The addition of this song, however, had a larger symbolic importance. "Once we started to do 'Cold Sweat' live," Pewsey contends, it showed that Roth "had been accepted into the band." After weeks of lobbying, Roth had succeeded in bringing soul and funk to Mammoth.[178]

= =

On balance, Roth's addition and the band's changing sound didn't slow the growth of Mammoth's popularity. Tom Broderick, who later did live sound for the band, says that a Mammoth party was "*the* place to be . . . you had to find out where it was."[179] But many of these parties didn't last long. Leiren recalled that once the band started playing, "the cops were going to be there in ten minutes and bust the party. I think it was very rare that a party went to ten o'clock let alone past ten o'clock."[180]

Art Agajanian, whose family lived in a sprawling home with a big backyard, decided to hire Mammoth and throw a spectacular party that he hoped would last late into the night. Roth, in *Crazy from the Heat*, credited Agajanian for taking the backyard party scene to the next level. He wrote, "Backyard parties developed into an art form. J.C. Agajanian, the famous auto-racing promoter, had a nephew who lived in a house with five bedrooms and a big pool and lots of space. So when his folks would split, two, three times a year, there'd be a massive party."[181]

By sundown, the gathering at the Agajanian home was in full swing, with something like eight hundred people filling the backyard. The members of Mammoth, who'd rented their own spotlight, had set up by the pool. Agajanian's neighbor Jeff Touchie recalls, "At that party a lot of people went swimming. They had an outbuilding back there, almost like a barn. They'd have spotlights up there in the window shining on the band." Agajanian says he knew he'd thrown a great party when he saw that "there were girls everywhere." Pewsey says, "We'd play by the pool, and there'd be girls skinny-dipping right in front of us!"

As the band sweated through their first set, many in the crowd expected the police to arrive. But the celebration proceeded without interruption, and the band sounded better than ever. In a reflection of Roth's efforts to give the band a more pop-friendly sound, Mammoth had improved their vocals. Marti observes, "Their harmonies got much better. They had no harmonies before Roth joined. I remember going to the Agajanians' and they did 'Wildfire' by Spooky Tooth. That was the first time that Mammoth ever did harmonies."

By the time the second set began, the party had reached a fever pitch. Agajanian remembers, "There were people dancing on top of the pool house, partying on the roof of the house, standing on top of the slide, they were jumping off the balcony of the house into the pool. Things went well and nobody got hurt." Nor did the police ever arrive. In the end, "It was a damn good time. Mammoth got to play two complete sets, maybe more, so they were happy, because they got to perform a lot of songs."

= =

Despite Mammoth's dominance on the backyard party circuit, Roth knew that they needed to aspire to bigger things. The first step in that process would be to find Mammoth a steady nightclub gig. To be sure, the three-piece Mammoth had played a handful of gigs at tiny clubs like Glendale's Under the Ice House and Pasadena's Gas Company, but these shows had involved the band slamming through its usual set of hard rock cover songs in front of its teenage fans.

What Roth had in mind was something wholly different: a Top 40 gig, which would mean playing radio-friendly material to a more mature crowd. To find a suitable place to play, Mammoth struck a deal with a teenage San Gabriel Valley promoter named Angelo Roman, Jr. Roman recalls that he "was trying to book them into rock/top-40 clubs as well as local gigs, such as concerts in local parks, which was a popular activity in the early- to mid-'70s. I also tried to promote them for high school and college dances." He also "got them benefit gigs, little parks and rec gigs, and local homecoming concerts that paid something like $125 for a four-hour gig."[182]

Because the band wanted to play nightclubs, they needed to make a demo tape that could be shared with club owners. On July 30, Mammoth entered a small studio in La Puente with Roman and made what was perhaps the band's first demo recording. The resulting five-song tape opened with Spooky Tooth's "Wildfire." Next came Preston's "Will It Go Round in Circles" followed by Beck, Bogert & Appice's "Superstition." Rounding out the recording was B.B. King's "Three O'Clock Blues" (a song that Roth had done with Red Ball Jet) and a final song, perhaps a James Gang cover, that Roman listed on the tape box as "Woman."[183]

After working the phones, Roman finally found them a gig at a Covina club called Posh. This booking, however, presented a stiff challenge. The contract called for five sets of music, which translated into something like forty songs. Edward explained, "At the gig you had to play five 45-minute sets, but most pop songs are three or four minutes long, so that's a lot of tunes to learn!"[184] Roman underscores this by noting, "When I worked with them, they were a *pseudo* Top 40 band" made up of musicians who much preferred to crank up their amps and play heavy rock than play pop songs. This limited ability with Top 40 material was, in Roman's view, "the reason why club owners . . . didn't want to hire them."[185]

When the band rehearsed, Edward and Alex told Roth they were almost certainly going to have trouble fulfilling their

Van Halen, formerly Mammoth, makes an early attempt to make it as a nightclub act, October 1973. ELIZABETH WILEY

contract. As Edward recalled, "It was real hard for us to get into the clubs . . . you'd have to play five sets of Top 40 stuff, and we'd only have one set."[186] Of course, to the relentlessly optimistic Roth, this was no problem. Edward remembers that the band then came up with a plan: "We figured we could play our own stuff and no one would care as long as the beat was there."[187]

They put that theory to the test. Pewsey recollects that Posh "was a tiny place. Alex's set took up half the stage. Mark kind of stood behind him. I was off to the side of the stage. Dave and Eddie were out front." The first set, and even the second set, went tolerably well, but by eleven the band had run out of suitable material.

Now Mammoth started performing hard rock hits like "Smoke on the Water." Since it was too early to start repeating songs, Roth called for the band's few original songs, which once completed, segued into an intense Black Sabbath, James Gang, and Captain Beyond blitzkrieg, all played at an insane volume. Pewsey explains,

"Eddie used to keep his full stack onstage for a club show but only plug in the top cabinet so he could get his feedback." Still, "he turned everything up to eleven. It was hard for me to be heard a lot of the time, even when we miked me through the PA. That's how loud Eddie's amp was."

Between the volume and the songs, Posh's owner had had enough. Edward told *Guitar World* what happened next: "The owner of the club walks up to us while we were playing a song and goes, 'Stop! I hired you to play Top 40. What is this shit?'"[188]

The band, however, refused to quit. Pewsey explains, "I remember the owner cut the power because he was so mad. All of sudden we were all cut off, but then Alex just played a solo, because the drums weren't miked! The owner couldn't have been too mad because the people were going crazy for us and buying drinks."

When Alex finally relented, Posh's proprietor unloaded. "He told us to get the fuck out of there, and he wouldn't let us take our equipment," Edward said. "We had to come back the next week and pick up our equipment. It was always that way. It was either 'the guitarist is too loud' or 'plays too psychedelic.' They always complained about me."[189] Pewsey adds, "We got fired after one night," but "we didn't give a shit, because we knew we would keep getting gigs." Those gigs, however, would have to come from promoters other than Roman, who parted ways with the band after a few months' time.

= =

Sometime in the late summer or fall of 1973, the band received some unwelcome news in the form of a cease-and-desist notice from another band that demanded that Edward and the others stop using their band name.[190] Michael Kelley, who haunted the Strip during these years, explains, "The 'other' Mammoth was from the

San Fernando Valley; they had a great Cozy Powellesque drummer named Rick Poindexter, and I saw them once at the Starwood."[191]

The band held a meeting to hash out a new moniker. The brothers, still thinking of their band as a cover act, wanted to use the name Rat Salad, after the Black Sabbath song.[192] Roth countered with Van Halen, which "had power to it" and reminded him of "the name Santana."[193] Alex later told Steven Rosen that he and Edward initially objected "because we didn't want to appear conceited."[194] Pewsey remembers that once the brothers came around to the idea of using their surname, they asserted, "It's our name. No one can steal that." Mammoth now had a new name, which, to Edward, sounded "huge, like an atomic bomb."[195]

= =

With Roman out of the picture, Roth took the lead in trying to get club gigs. As he created his wish list of venues, one logistical challenge involved hauling their equipment, which wouldn't all fit into their cars. Thus, Roth enlisted the help of his friend Bobby Hatch. According to Roth, he'd call Hatch, who owned a pickup truck, "whenever we would borrow extra guitar amps" for important gigs.[196]

Hatch remembers that they convoyed to nightspots all over the city, including a Glendale club called the Sopwith Camel, which by October 1973 was featuring a local band called Steely Dan. He describes how he'd "be one of the one or two people in the audience" when Van Halen auditioned. "They sounded great," but they didn't get these gigs.

Roth was undeterred. Hatch explains that Roth "was the go-getter. He got everybody amped up. He was relentless. He did not stop." Regardless of the pitfalls, he always seemed like he had a plan. "He had *mucho huevos*," Hatch asserts. "Nothing scared him."

Roth and the rest of the band decamped to his father's home in the fall of 1973 to record some original material. "We did do a demo at Dave's house," Pewsey remembers. At least two solid hard rock songs ended up on tape, one called "Gentleman of Leisure," which featured a Johnny Winter–influenced riff that played cat-and-mouse with Alex's cowbells. The other, "Glitter," paid lyrical tribute to the era's hottest rock trend and was propelled by an angular proto-metal riff that would have been at home on any early Iron Maiden record.

With a new demo tape in the can, Roth steered Van Halen towards Gazzarri's, the club that Red Ball Jet had auditioned at back in mid-1972. For the Sunday night audition, Roth dressed for success. Pewsey relates, "I remember he wore platform shoes at Gazzarri's. He was towering with those shoes on . . . all of us except Dave were in jeans." Fashion aside, Edward later explained that at this initial audition, Van Halen played "a couple of our own tunes" and some "rock and roll."[197]

Along with not playing the Top 40 songs that the club's management desired, Edward played at an ear-piercing level, which drove a club employee to interrupt Van Halen's tryout by yelling, "You're too loud, turn down!"[198] Apart from the volume issues, Hatch says he was at a loss to explain their lack of success. "I don't know why" they didn't get those gigs. "I heard them enough. I started thinking, *God, these guys are great.* They had a nice beat and everybody sounded good together."

As the setbacks mounted, Roth reiterated to the others that one key thing that was holding them back was their rejection of onstage fashion. Roth was, according to Hatch, "a rock star *before* he was a rock star. I swear to God. You *knew* he was going to be a rock star, honestly." When they loaded in and out for these gigs, Roth would tell the other four guys in the band, "You've got to play the part." Hatch says, "He's the one that actually got Eddie and Alex to start dressing right, because when I used to drive them

Edward Van Halen, wearing some new stage clothes, takes a smoke
break while his brother looks on, October 1973. ELIZABETH WILEY

to the Sopwith Camel and other clubs they'd dress like old hippies
still. It was kind of a joke. Dave Roth was going, 'Come on, guys,
you've got to do this. You've got to act like this.'"

Edward and Alex had come to a crossroads. They could blend in with their friends, or they could follow Roth's lead by building a band image that would set them apart. Bill Maxwell says, "We were all wearing Levi's and white shirts and desert boots. You didn't get caught wearing anything else. But Dave did."

Still, the idea of donning gaudy stage clothes was galling for the brothers. Debbie Imler McDermott explains, "After Dave joined, their image began to change. That was all Dave with the image stuff. He was the flashier one. When they started wearing lamé and platforms, it must have been hard for Edward and Alex to put those clothes on. When they were younger, all they would wear were Levi's, T-shirts, and tennis shoes, because that's all they could afford."

In effect, Roth wanted them to dress like rock stars, but Edward never aspired to that kind of stardom. He confessed to *Esquire* in 2012 that as a young person "I certainly never would have wanted to be in the business that I'm in, meaning the fame and the glory, the glitter, the rock star, the famous part."[199] He'd touched on this same issue years earlier, saying, "I had an English class where I had to do an essay on what my future plans were — what I wanted to do in life. I said I wanted to be a professional rock guitarist — not a rock star."[200]

Regardless, Roth tried to instill confidence in his shy guitarist. David Swantek remembers, "One night Dave comes up in his little Opal wagon that his dad bought him. He says, 'Hey, Eddie's coming up. Compliment him on his hair. I got him to get his hair done professionally instead of cutting it in front of the bedroom mirror. He got it done by a hair stylist.' This was a *huge* event. He says, 'Tell him his hair looks good.'"

Hatch was there as well and remembers that when the guitarist arrived, he could tell that "Eddie felt so bad, like, *This isn't me, I look like a woman or something.*" Still, Hatch and the others chimed in with, "Oh man, Ed! That looks *great!*" Swantek explains, "This kind of tells you how Dave worked. He comes up and preps the whole thing, then Eddie comes up and we say, 'Yeah, looks good man! Come on, let's smoke one!'"

Along with a new haircut for his guitar player, Roth pressed for more stage presence from the band members. Swantek says, "I do remember him working on the idea that the band had to move around. One of the things he did early on is that he introduced each member of the band and had them do a solo, trying to build identity for each member of the band." Still, Roth had to move cautiously as he "leaned on them a bit" to shift their approach: "He had to be careful about it, because these guys were really set in their ways."

By October 1973, these changes began to take hold, and guitarist David Perry was there to witness them at an Arcadia High School dance. He recalls, "I was in my sophomore year. I didn't know this band. There was lots of excitement as they set their amps and drums up. Before they went on, it was dark onstage. Out of the darkness, Eddie started doing this little pull-off riff. It absolutely scorched the place. I was like, *Wow, listen to that!* The light came on as they started the song. They had a 'Vanhalen' banner with their old-school logo. Dave was in a drab trench coat, and he suddenly ripped it off as he started moving around. He had these striped black-and-white pants on. Eddie wore a blue crushed velvet suit and played a Les Paul. They played some originals. I remember they also played [ZZ Top's] 'La Grange.'"

Carl Haasis, an Arcadia guitar player, also saw this gig. He remembers that despite Roth's best efforts to get his guitarist in motion, Edward's stage presence remained limited. "The first time I ever heard of Van Halen, they played a high school dance at Arcadia High School. They played [Elton John's] 'Saturday Night's Alright for Fighting.' They played 'Free Ride' by Edgar Winter. I thought they sounded great, but I remember Ed just kind of stood there. He just kind of looked down and played. He didn't really move around a lot."

David Lee Roth, wearing a pair of gag glasses, poses outside
Caesars Palace in Las Vegas, 1973. PATTI FUJII CARBERRY

Even if Roth hadn't gotten Edward moving, he had his own
ideas about how to create a spectacle onstage. Back in May 1973,
Vincent Carberry, his girlfriend Patti, and Roth had taken a road
trip to Sin City. Right before they returned home, Roth did some
shopping. Carberry explains, "You know those plastic glasses with
a rubber nose attached? He bought one. It had plastic glasses, but
instead of having a rubber nose it had a dick! He got it in a novelty
place and he was wearing it in the car." As they drove out of Vegas,
Roth looked "out the back window at other cars going by with
kids and old ladies and stuff, getting people all shocked and pissed
off and everything."

Months later, Van Halen played a Halloween party at Glendale
High School. The first set transpired without incident, but then
Roth put Edward up to doing a sight gag to start the second set.
"After a break," Pewsey says, "Eddie came out with a Groucho
Marx hat and glasses with a penis for a nose." While the assembled

students laughed and pointed, Roth set out to further shock the audience. Perhaps inspired by the way that David Bowie had simulated fellatio on Mick Ronson's guitar during the *Spiders from Mars* tour, Roth, to Pewsey's disgust, "fondled the nose with his mouth while Eddie was wearing it."

However long it took the audience to recover, it had an immediate effect on Van Halen itself. Pewsey says he took serious offense at Roth's actions and, after months of barely tolerating Roth's antics and personality, he exited the band.

For Edward, losing his keyboardist was a relief. "We used to have a keyboard player," he told *Guitar Player* in 1978. "I hated it because I had to play everything exactly the same with him. I couldn't noodle in between the vocal lines, because he was doing something to fill it up."[201] Other moments of tension followed: "My guitar kept going out of tune and he got so pissed," Edward remembered. Pewsey, who has perfect pitch, would shout to Edward, "Tune, Goddamn!" The guitarist would yell back, "Fuck you! Tune to *me!*"[202] Ultimately, "I was writing songs then and the keyboards just didn't fit," Edward explained. Thus, once Van Halen became a quartet, they would remain so for the duration of the band's thirty-year career.[203]

= =

Apart from the fact that the band now could split its earnings four ways instead of five, it probably mattered little to Roth whether or not Van Halen featured a keyboard player. Roth knew that the essential members of the band were Alex and Edward, and to the amazement of nearly every observer in Pasadena, Roth had built a musical partnership with them. In the months that followed, this union would provide the foundation for Van Halen's growth outside of greater Pasadena, but not before they made the case that they were the city's most disruptive and talented rock band.

BREAKTHROUGH

Mark Algorri and Mario Miranda had a problem with Van Halen. The two young music entrepreneurs had just heard the results of Pasadena City College's December 1973 battle of the bands, and Van Halen had eliminated the two bands they managed. Gary Putman, who played guitar in one of them, recalls that Van Halen won by playing a killer version of the glam rock hit "All the Way from Memphis" by Mott the Hoople. Putman observes that even though it's a piano-based song, "Eddie would go, *I'll figure out a way to fuckin' do that riff — Dah Da Da Da Dah Da Da Da! — on guitar.*"[204] Thanks to Roth's song selection and Edward's creativity, they'd come out on top.

As Van Halen broke down its equipment, Miranda walked onto the stage. Roth immediately stopped him.

"Hey man! What do you need? What are you doing?"

Miranda introduced himself. "Hey, you guys are really, really good. We've got some connections." As Miranda talked to Roth about how he and his partner could help Van Halen with club bookings, Edward and Alex stood off to the side, paying little attention to the conversation.

Roth listened impatiently. "No, I do everything. We don't need anybody. I take care of business. Thank you. We'll take your card and let you know if we need any help."

Miranda handed Roth a business card and said goodbye.

It's hard to believe that Roth and the others felt confident about their nightclub gig prospects; after weeks of effort, the band still hadn't landed steady work. In fact, Roth later revealed that during his first months in the band, Van Halen had been rejected by *nineteen* clubs.[205] But the next few months proved to be momentous for Van Halen as they worked to become more than just the biggest backyard party band in Pasadena.

When the Swantek brothers heard from a neighbor that he planned to have a late December party, they knew just who to call. David Swantek explains, "Rod Heublein lived down from us on Mountain Street in a really big house. His dad was a judge and his parents were out of town. Well, he'd never done a party before. But he knew us, Dave Roth, and the Van Halen brothers."

That's all it took. Scores of teenagers arrived at the Heublein residence before Van Halen even began playing. And once the group's songs started reverberating through the neighborhood, kids in cars could roll down their windows and hear Van Halen from blocks away. Soon the house and backyard were overrun with buzzed young people.

For Heublein, the size of the party would turn out to be the least of his problems. After Charles Levor got into a late night argument with another teenager, the teen left the party swearing that he'd be back to settle the score. As the *Star-News* reported, he'd kept his word. He returned with fifteen to twenty of his friends, who came armed with "two knives, a shotgun, possibly another gun, and a blunt instrument, possibly a bottle or pipe." Within moments, shots rang out. Levor was wounded with "50 buckshot wounds on his backside," and two other men were injured, one with a serious stab wound and the other with a contusion from a blunt object.[206]

The chaos of the evening left a lasting impression. Tom Hensley, a friend of Edward's, says, "I was in the driveway and saw the two shots. Levor ran and stumbled and fell right at my feet. I don't care whether you're at war or in Los Angeles, when someone pulls out a gun like that, it is a scary deal. Maybe it was the first drive-by shooting, back forty years ago."

== ==

Some weeks later, Van Halen set their sights on another gig. In an effort to get teenagers to take part in the celebration of Pasadena's centennial, city leaders encouraged a committee of civic-minded teens to organize a free concert by local bands, which would be held on the steps of Pasadena's city hall. While the groups wouldn't be paid, the January 1974 concert would allow them to perform in front of a crowd of thousands.[207]

The quartet soon heard that they were one of four bands to make the cut. Each act would play for one hour. At 8:00 p.m., the show would open with Scottie and the Hankies, a 1950s rock and roll revival act, followed by Kismet, a jazz band. After Van Halen played, Headwinds, a progressive rock group, would close out the night. With the pieces in place, committee chairman Michael Jensen told the *Star-News* that he foresaw few pitfalls, other than rain or too large of a crowd.[208]

That Friday evening, about two thousand young people had gathered in front of the stage as the Hankies got things underway. Steve Bruen, the group's guitarist, remembers that he and his bandmates "were wearing wigs and did kind of a Sha Na Na '50s revival show. It was a blast." After Kismet came and went, the audience had swelled to nearly five thousand, far more than the organizers had expected.

With the smell of pot hanging heavy in the air, Van Halen appeared. As Roth led the band through its set, the crowd got unruly. Spectators loaded on booze and pills started fighting. Teens with hooded eyes and wobbly legs leaned and pushed backwards in all directions to get clear of the scrums. Within these openings, drunks pounded each other into submission. Dana Anderson says, "I remember that gig. It was really violent. A guy named Taylor was there with me. He was the kind of guy who played football and worked out all the time, and he had a horrible temper. We were getting ready to leave and somebody bumped him and spilled his beer. He hit this guy so hard that the first thing to hit the ground was his head. And I think the cops came right after that. I'm sure he was badly hurt."

The Pasadena police had seen enough. Backstage, two agitated officers cornered committee members, telling them that between the brawls and bottles that had smashed into police cars, the show had gotten out of control. If things didn't calm down, they'd pull the plug on Van Halen.[209]

After an intense conversation, a compromise was brokered. Roth made a halfhearted statement asking everyone to "cool [out with] the drinking." In response, the crowd booed and jeered. During the remainder of Van Halen's performance, cops pressed their way through the crowd and began confiscating alcohol, pouring out, according to the *Star-News*, enough "booze to fill a liquor store."[210]

The city hall gig is a lost landmark in Van Halen history. That night, Van Halen played in front of their largest audience to date, one comprised largely of their fans. "The city hall gig was a Van Halen crowd," says Karen Imler, who attended the concert. Scott Finnell of the Hankies adds, "All the people who showed up didn't know us from Adam, but they knew Van Halen. It was all the kids who went to their parties." All of this meant, as guitarist Terry Kilgore observes, that this show was one "that made them more popular" across the city. After years of gigging around Pasadena, Van Halen was now capable of drawing thousands.

= =

A month later, another opportunity materialized. Jack Van Furche', the teenage son of a successful doctor, had just applied to become a member of a custom van club. "I was trying to get into the club at the time," he remembers. "And they always gave everyone an initiation of some sort. And mine was, 'Jack, you've got to throw a party for the club.' They thought, *Heh, his folks ain't never gonna to let him throw a party at their place.* I came to the next meeting a week later with my stepdad, and he said, 'All right, let's go! How many kegs are we ordering?' . . . Two days later I was voted into the club."

It's no surprise that the club wanted Van Furche' to host a party. His parents' residence was an English Tudor mansion nestled in the heart of San Marino, one of the most elite zip codes in the Golden State. "Jack's house was huge. It was like a castle," explains Debbie Hannaford Lorenz, who was dating Jack at the time. The backyard covered two-and-a-half acres, landscaped with terraces that sloped downward from the back of the house and bordered by mature trees. The lowest terrace levels featured tennis courts and a pool. In sum, it was a property tailor-made for a gigantic backyard party.

The next day, the phone rang at 1881 Las Lunas. Van Furche' says, "I called Eddie and said, 'This gig's for my van club. I've got to have a real good band. Can you be there?'" The two teens then met and came to an agreement. "We did everything on the

EDWARD VAN HALEN
Lead Guitarist of Mammoth

1881 Las Lunas   796-76[

Mammoth lead guitarist Edward Van Halen's business card, 1973. CHERI WHITAKER

back of a little business card that he signed and wrote everything down for me, and he goes, 'Here it is. We'll see you there!'" Years later, Edward explained to *Rolling Stone*, "We used to play backyard parties down in San Marino, the real rich part of Pasadena, where Roth lived. The parents were away for the weekend, the kids would have a party and hire us. We'd get a little Abbey Rents stage, cheap lights, and charge a buck."[211]

Meanwhile, Van Furche' and his club printed up hundreds of flyers and spread them everywhere.[212] The handbill promised "Refreshments + Dancing," along with music by Van Halen, all for two dollars.

By the day before the party, it was clear that the promotional campaign had worked well — perhaps too well. Van Furche' explains, "Back then there was KMET-FM radio, and on Fridays and Saturdays if anything was happening in town they'd always announce it over the radio. Somehow, one of my flyers had gotten over there, and over the air they said, 'Hey, Van Halen's playing this weekend on Arden and Oak Grove.'"

On the afternoon of March 9, preparations began at the Van

Flyer for Van Halen's epic March 1974 backyard party, which drew a crowd of thousands. FROM THE COLLECTION OF TOM BONAWITZ

Furche' residence. Down on the tennis courts, Van Halen tested its lighting rig and soundchecked on its rented stage. Back up at the house, a local liquor store delivered a dozen kegs. Van Furche' and his friends also worked up a plan to keep freeloaders from jumping the property's walls. Reinforcements for this effort would come from members of the Vagos, an outlaw motorcycle club, who, after an invite from the van club, had added the party to their social calendar.[213]

By dusk, it was clear that a significant percentage of the San Gabriel Valley's young people had decided to attend. Lorenz recalls that from early in the evening "people were coming into the backyard saying how long it took them just to walk to the house." When they told her which streets they'd parked on, she'd say, "That far away? You couldn't even get any closer than that?" But once she glanced back up at the house, she better understood what was transpiring. Under the archway that led to the backyard, she remembers that people stood shoulder to shoulder as they struggled to enter the yard.

When the big yard had nearly filled up, Van Halen started to play. Lorenz recollects, "They were in the very back of the backyard. You could see them through the tennis court fence, so from everywhere you could see, because the backyard went higher and higher. They actually got to play for quite a long time. It was amazing." Down on the courts, kids boogied. Karen Imler says, "I remember dancing at that party while Van Halen did the blues and some Led Zeppelin."

By 9:30 p.m., the party was raging. Scores of kids milled around inside the home. The backyard was a sea of humanity. "I remember standing facing the house," Lorenz says. "It's packed like sardines in this whole backyard. It was solid people. There were thousands of people there. There were people into the front yard."

Just then, the rhythmic whump of helicopter blades sounded. As everyone looked up, a three-and-half-million candlepower spotlight illuminated the yard.[214] Chris Holmes, who later went on to platinum success with 1980s shock-rockers W.A.S.P., remembers, "This was a huge party. It got outta hand so the cops showed up and of course they brought the helicopter, which was shining a light down that lit up all the kids in the yard." After the spotlight did nothing to scatter the crowd, the pilot began ordering people to disperse over the chopper's loudspeakers.

Van Halen and the partygoers were having none of it. Edward and Mark turned their amps to ten while Roth cracked one-liners. "When the helicopter came over, the band just thought it was funny," Lorenz says. Van Furche' adds, "The helicopter was flying overhead for about forty-five minutes with the spotlight, and Dave was hamming it up. From the start, he saw that light and he just used it by singing in it, because the light was right there on the stage — right there on the guys. There were instant spotlights."

Meanwhile, dozens of San Marino police officers fought their way onto the property. Lorenz remembers that as the copter hovered, she and her friends stood in the middle of the yard with their backs to the house, watching Van Halen. "Then all of a sudden, a policeman taps me on the shoulder and I turn around and everything behind me was completely empty of people. I never even noticed that everyone behind me was gone! I didn't have a clue." Van Furche' observes, "It took the police over an hour to get through the crowd back into the tennis courts where the band was. They finally got stopped when a cop removed Roth's microphone from under the spotlight."

Lorenz, who was living in the house at the time, made her way into the residence and found some friends in Jack's bedroom. With the lights off, Lorenz and the others looked out the window at the chaos in the long circular driveway and up on the street. "Everyone was pissed off at the police for ending such a wonderful night," she remembers. Out in the yard, partygoers hurled rocks and bottles at the police.[215] Janice Pirre Francis, who later helped promoters put on Van Halen shows, saw kids on nearby streets "turning over trash cans, lighting them on fire, and destroying property."

Closer to the house, a mob of kids had set upon a police cruiser. "You know how you can rock a car back and forth to get it to flip over?" Lorenz says. "I watched it happen. We were up in Jack's room looking out the window and sure enough they'd flipped over a police car in front of the house."

In the days that followed, partygoers spun tales about the night in high school hallways. An account of the event even hit the local paper. The *San Marino Tribune* reported this "van gathering" had backed up traffic for miles and "a disturbance," punctuated by thrown projectiles, had broken out around eleven o'clock.[216]

The Van Halen brothers still remembered this party twenty-five years later. In an interview, Alex recalled that "four cop cars got turned over" that night. Edward said, "I'll never forget we played a backyard party once. It was written up in the paper. Nineteen people got busted and stuff. I'll never forget a group of guys took one cop and they took his handcuffs and they handcuffed him around a tree with his own handcuffs!"[217]

By the same token, San Gabriel Valley police forces weren't going to forget either. Along with the tumultuous city hall concert, the Van Furche' party made clear that when it came to dealing with Van Halen and its fans, it was time to take the gloves off. Francis observes that the Van Furche' party was the one most responsible for giving "backyard parties and 'keggers' such a bad name" among authority figures. Still, the members of Van Halen saw it as business as usual, just on a larger scale. "Wild teenagers?" Edward remarked. "Yeah . . . that was our audience."[218]

= =

A few days later, Roth called Miranda. He remembers that Roth said, "What can you do for us?" Miranda likely mentioned that Algorri had a cousin who worked with the Beach Boys and Jan and Dean. A more immediate incentive was a chance to play Gazzarri's. Roth said, "We've already auditioned. Bill Gazzarri doesn't like us." Miranda explained that the self-proclaimed "god-father of rock and roll" had recently hired Algorri and Miranda to audition bands for him, freeing him from a task he despised. They'd make sure that Van Halen got to play a couple of sets one

David Lee Roth and Edward Van Halen rehearse in a
garage in Altadena, California, early 1974. ELIZABETH WILEY

night when the club was open for business, so the owner could
size them up. Thanks to Algorri and Miranda, Van Halen had
another Gazzarri's audition.[219]

The guitarist and lead singer of Van Halen confer
at practice in Altadena, early 1974. ELIZABETH WILEY

The quartet was determined to succeed this time. They
retreated to their new practice location, a battered garage located
at 1940 Maiden Lane in Altadena, on a property owned by a friend

Alex Van Halen pounds out a beat at rehearsal, early 1974. ELIZABETH WILEY

of Roth's, Elizabeth Wiley. Their four-hour rehearsals, which transpired six days a week, took on an extra intensity.[220] Taylor Freeland,
who often watched them practice, remembers the routine: "They'd
go through their sets, and if they had a song they needed to work on,
it would be like this: Alex would count in with his sticks, *One-two-
three-four!* And it would sound *just* like the record. Then somewhere
in the middle, you'd get Edward yelling, 'No no *no!*' Alex would
scream, 'What the *FUCK*?' Then there'd be arguments. Then you'd
have to go out and have a smoke. Then they'd do it again. This went
on for years." Vincent Carberry says that while Red Ball Jet practices
had been all about fun, the one he saw in the Maiden Lane garage
was "very grim and serious. They were just all *business*."

Kilgore, who was close friends with Edward, points out that
there was one band member who made sure everyone stayed on
task — or else. "No one remembers," he observes, "that Al ran
that group and pretty much had last word due to several reasons,

the main [one] being that he could easily beat the shit out" of anyone who didn't agree. When Alex would power through several cans of Schlitz Malt Liquor — the band's favorite — he'd take on all comers. "I recall lots [of] sparring with Stan Swantek, me, Ed, Gregg Emerson, and whoever else happened to be around."[221]

= =

On the day of their audition, Algorri and Miranda, along with Putman, helped the four musicians load in their gear. "If you can envision it," Miranda says, "you'd walk into Gazzarri's and it had this stage in the middle, and then to the right and the left you've got two other smaller stages." In the compact upstairs area, there was another stage. As Van Halen set up on one of the downstairs side stages, the band members looked around. The walls were papered with huge black-and-white photos of some of the former winners of the club's trademark "Miss Gazzarri's" dance contests, including sex kitten Barbi Benton. Fluorescent posters, which would glow under black light when the club was open for business, also hung on the wall. But with the house lights up, the club was a dirty, dingy place.

Indeed, Gazzarri's circa 1974 was a far cry from the club that had showcased the Doors and Buffalo Springfield back in 1967. "Gazzarri's was not doing well at the time," Algorri concedes. "It had a sleazy reputation. I hate to use that word, but it really did. It had fallen from the pinnacle." Dave Connor, a musician who also played the club in 1974, agrees: "Gazzarri's had a sense of already having seen its day. The Whisky was more of a place you would want to play that was higher up. Gazzarri's was seedy. It was not a happening venue. You had the sense that it had been at one time, but it really had that quality that its day had passed it by."

When nine o'clock rolled around, Van Halen started playing in front of a sizable crowd. Roth had dressed for Hollywood success,

Edward Van Halen solos at Lanterman Auditorium in La Cañada, California, November 22, 1975. MARY GARSON/HOT SHOTZ

wearing a skintight little boy's sweater, hip-hugging London Britches jeans, and platforms.[222] Even Alex and Edward, who still thought that a T-shirt and dirty jeans made for a good stage outfit, had dressed up for the occasion. "So around the time we auditioned to play Gazzarri's on the Sunset Strip," Edward told *Rolling Stone*, "I got some platforms and nearly broke my ankles."[223] The shy Stone, meanwhile, had refused to glam it up, leaving the band's vocalist and guitarist, as Edward remembered, looking like two "long-haired, platformed, goofy lookin' fools!"[224]

While Roth had long pushed for this image change, the truth is that ambitious young rock musicians in Hollywood dressed this way, thanks to the influence of glam rock. At Rodney Bingenheimer's English Disco, glam rock stars like David Bowie hung out amidst scores of wildly dressed teens. According to *Newsweek*, "The dance floor is a dizzy kaleidoscope of lamé hotpants, sequined halters, rhinestone-studded cheeks, thrift-store anythings, and see-through everythings. During the breaks, fourteen-year-old girls on six-inch platforms teeter into the back bathrooms to grope with their partners of the moment."[225] This outrageous atmosphere made the English Disco, and Hollywood by extension, what the *New Musical Express* described as the "the mecca for the sub-teen groovers of Southern California and horny British Rock musicians."[226]

That night at Gazzarri's, however, it was clear that Van Halen had changed more than their dress. They also dispensed with the abrasive hard rock that club owner Bill Gazzarri hated, instead offering up a set of radio-friendly material. "We learned 'Mr. Skin' by Spirit," Edward told Steven Rosen, so "we actually attempted to do stuff that wasn't us, just to get a gig."[227] Algorri remembers, "They did a pretty commercial set. They definitely had some good ZZ Top songs that they played. Their set was very punchy and very good."

After the show, Algorri and Miranda tracked the band down. The four musicians sat on a wall behind the club, smoking and drinking as they talked about the gig. When the two promoters walked up, Roth asked what Bill Gazzarri thought about Van Halen.

Algorri said, "He didn't like you guys at first."

Having tried out at the club three times now, Roth saw red.

Miranda quickly said, "Wait a minute. No, that was at first, man. Algorri talked to Bill. He chilled out."

Algorri went on to explain that they'd lined up a regular booking. "We're going to work on getting you guys in here, if you want to play."

Within a few days, the parties had signed a contract. Van Halen would perform from April 4 to 7 and from April 11 to 14, with a cut of their payment going to Algorri and Miranda. As soon as the last pen left the paper, Roth had achieved a goal he'd long pursued. He'd front a band that would do a weekend engagement on the Sunset Strip.[228]

= =

But before Van Halen played their first full weekend at Gazzarri's, they had another show to perform. It was in San Marino on March 29, but this time at the city's high school, where Van Halen would open for Honk, a successful surf rock band.[229]

On the night of the concert, something like a thousand people were in the auditorium, including a freshman named Robyn McDonald.[230] She watched as Van Halen performed some covers and originals. Then Roth, perhaps inspired by Jim Morrison's exploits in Miami back in 1969, tried a wardrobe trick. McDonald remembers, "David started unzipping his pants and started to pull them down mid-song." The school's principal immediately made a beeline for Roth. "Principal Jack Rankin," McDonald explains, "walked onstage and made David pull them up."[231] After the show, Rankin, like so many other residents of San Marino, had seen enough of Van Halen. Mark Stone remembers, "We were told afterwards that we couldn't play there again . . . We were banned from the school because Dave was so lewd."[232]

Before they left the campus, Algorri met two young ladies, one of whom had a particular interest in Van Halen's singer. Algorri recalls, "After the thing, two girls had come to the stage door. One was very beautiful, a very dramatic-looking gal. They had been in a black Cadillac limousine outside. It turned out that the beautiful girl's mother was an actress. I don't remember the name, but she was a well-known actress from years before. She had gotten wind of David Roth and had this unbelievable crush on him."

This beauty, it turned out, had a proposition for Van Halen. "She said, 'I want to help pay for a demo tape.'" Because Algorri and Miranda didn't have the money to bankroll a recording session, this sounded promising. Algorri found Roth and filled him in. Roth replied, "Yeah man, this sounds great." After introductions, the girls drank beer with the band in the parking lot, made plans to book some studio time over the next few weeks, and got more acquainted with Roth.[233]

On the night of April 4, Miranda poked his head out of the Gazzarri's entrance. The line was long and the club was buzzing. Van Halen played three sets that evening, which Miranda says featured a "lot of Top 40" plus the occasional original. "They had originals but not a lot of originals to play every set." Over the course of the weekend and the one that followed, Algorri recalls that they "started bringing in a huge number of people, because the band obviously had this huge following. It was these Pasadena kids who all started going on a regular basis. They became a sensation."

Even though the band felt elated about their Gazzarri's break-through, Alex and Edward felt increasingly dissatisfied with their bass player's performance. Stone could sometimes be "unprofessional," which became a problem as the band played bigger and bigger gigs. "Stone used to piss them off back in the backyard party days," Eric Hensel recalls. "They'd take a break between sets and Alex would have a hell of a time finding him to get the next set going. I remember Ed calling for him on the PA a couple times, and then Ed would grin, but you could tell he wasn't happy about it. Stone was usually the last one back from breaks, because he'd be off smoking dope with somebody."

This interest in partying, of course, was something shared by all the members of Van Halen. Bill Maxwell notes, "Mark liked to drink, but so did they." But for however many intoxicants the rest of the band took, Stone seemed to be taking more. "I guess Edward had a problem with Mark's memory," Burke says. "He couldn't remember songs."

Years later, Edward offered details about Stone's decline. "We started playing clubs like Gazzarri's," he explained, "and the old bass player we had used to smoke too much pot and hash. We had a repertoire . . . that you *had* to remember, and he'd be so high, he'd be playing a different song."[234] In 1995, Edward offered more details to *Rolling Stone*: "We had this bass player who was really creative but smoked too much hash. He was going to school to be a pharmacist — swear to God. He spent more time at home building LSD molecules. We were playing parties with a repertoire of a hundred songs, and he wouldn't remember stuff."[235] These mistakes, which jeopardized the band's progress, particularly irked Alex, says Maxwell. "Stone and Alex did not see eye-to-eye. When the drummer and the bass player don't see eye-to-eye, you've got problems."

= =

While the problems with Stone festered, Van Halen continued to gig. In early 1974, the band hooked up with a Los Angeles entertainment impresario named Ray Engel. Engel, however, was not a rock promoter. Engel hosted sex-themed parties.

Engel hired Van Halen to perform at the Proud Bird nightclub on April 26. In the advertising material, Engel proclaimed, "If you want to go to something really far-out & different, then join us" for "Glamour, Glitter, Insanity . . . Circus Acts, Costumes, Body Painting, Celebrities," and, courtesy of a quartet from Pasadena, "Rock 'n' Roll."[236]

Elizabeth Wiley, who accompanied Van Halen to this "Freak Ball," recalls that she and Dave took in the sights. Walking around together, they marveled at the "strange things" they'd "seen for sale in the booths," including "nail-studded beds, cat-o'-nine-tails, thigh-high boots with pointed metal-tipped toes and . . . auditions for porn films."[237]

After Van Halen finished, Roth "met a gal," as he wrote in *Crazy from the Heat*. He "wound up back at her place, went into her room." When he opened his bloodshot eyes in the morning, he saw that "every square inch of her walls and her ceilings and the facings of the bureau were covered with pictures of rock and roll singers." Roth, future frontman extraordinaire, had bedded his first professional groupie.[238]

= =

The following Friday, Van Halen headlined a concert at PHS Auditorium, with two other bands in support. Brown Eyes, a six-piece funk-jazz band, opened the show, followed by Snake, an Arcadia-based power trio, fronted by Michael Anthony Sobolewski. Anthony, a barrel-chested, easygoing young man, not only played bass in the band, he also served as lead singer, *de facto* manager, and van driver.[239]

Anthony, it turns out, had grown up woodshedding and working on his bass chops just a few miles away from where Roth and the Van Halen brothers had grown up. Like his future bandmates, Anthony, his siblings, and his parents had moved to the San Gabriel Valley during the 1960s. Anthony, who had played trumpet as a child, took up the bass in the late 1960s. His first group, Poverty's Children, was a family affair, with his brother Steven playing drums and a friend, Mike Hershey, playing guitar.[240]

Like the Van Halen brothers, Anthony had parents who supported his musical endeavors. With him and his brothers all bitten by the rock-music bug, their parents allowed them to take over their Arcadia garage. Joe Ramsey, who grew up near Anthony, recalled, "Mike was great when we were younger. He was two years older than me. I met him through his younger brother; we were in a band together. We used to rehearse at his parents' house. They had a rehearsal room, which was a soundproofed garage, that you could practice in . . . You could be loud and no one cared."

Rock group, The Black Opel, warms up for a Battle of the Bands competition among bands at the three junior high schools May 10, from 7:30 to 10 p.m., at the Arcadia High School Little Theater. The Black Opel, from Dana Junior High School, is led by T. J. Noone, drummer. Mike Sobolewski, plays bass guitar, left. Mike Hershey is on rhythm guitar. Not shown is Brad Becnell, lead guitarist. Cash prizes totaling $90 will be awarded the three finalist bands. The deadline for applications has been extended to May 7 at 4:30 p.m. Students attending can vote for their favorite. Applications are available at the schools and at the recreation department.

—News-Pos. Photo

Future Van Halen bassist Michael Anthony Sobolewski with one of his early groups, circa 1969. JEFF HERSHEY

Anthony practiced in the garage with his different bands. One was a short-lived power trio called Balls. Werner Schuchner, the band's guitarist, says, "We did Led Zeppelin and Humble Pie. We had a good drummer, and Mike sang really well."

Another of Anthony's bands was called Black Opel, which once again featured Mike on vocals and bass. Ramsey recalls, "They played a lot of Blue Cheer and, as my then-thirteen-year-old brain allows me to remember, a remarkably faithful version of 'Fire' by Jimi Hendrix with Brad Becnel burning on the lead guitar. Brad was an absolute prodigy. He was probably about sixteen years old and playing wailing fast guitar solos. Great!"[241]

For Anthony, this gig with Van Halen wasn't his first encounter with Edward, Alex, and Mark. As he told an interviewer in 1998, "The first time I ever saw those guys play . . . there was a carnival that [Arcadia] High School would have every year on the football field, and their band happened to be playing, and they were called Mammoth. It was Eddie, Alex, and their bass player then, his name was Mark Stone. Eddie was doing the lead singing."[242]

Two years later, Anthony, like Roth and the Van Halen brothers, was attending PCC. Even though they hadn't actually met, their paths had crossed. Anthony, who majored in music, explained, "I'd be going to a jazz improv class, and I'd pass Alex in the driveway, just leaving his. We'd kind of look at each other but act real cool, because it was the rival band thing. You never really said hi or anything, you just barely waved. But everybody knew who everybody was."[243]

= =

On the afternoon of the gig, Van Halen faced a crisis. Anthony recalled that Snake "had a PA system that I used to borrow from one of the teachers at Arcadia High School . . It just so happened that [Van Halen's] PA blew up during soundcheck. So I remember Eddie coming up to me and asking if they could borrow our PA." The affable Anthony replied, "Yeah, sure. Fine."[244]

A few hours later the show began. After Brown Eyes played, Snake, with Anthony on lead vocals and bass, Tony "Codgen" Caggiano on guitar, and Steve Hapner on drums, took the stage. The trio went for the throat by opening with KISS's "Nothin' to Lose."

From the side of the stage, the Van Halen brothers watched

Anthony. Ironically, in Snake, Anthony found himself in the same position that Edward had been in before Roth joined Van Halen. Anthony explained to *Guitar World* in 1991, "I was the lead singer in my band, and I didn't really feel comfortable in that role. I just wanted to concentrate on my bass playing."[245]

Nonetheless, he did both well, which started the wheels turning in the brothers' heads. As Edward told *Guitar Player* in 1978, "We were all tripped out because he was lead singing for his band and fronting his own band."[246] Undoubtedly, they also took note of the fact that Snake performed songs like the James Gang's "Walk Away," Beck, Bogert & Appice's "Superstition," and Johnny Winter's "Still Alive and Well," which were part of Van Halen's repertoire.

About fifteen minutes later, the headliner came onstage.[247] Roth strolled to the mike as the applause subsided. After taking a breath, he announced, "Welcome everybody. We're Van Halen and our business is *whalin'*!"

With that, Van Halen thundered. After opening with a lumbering, sludgy Stone-penned song called "I'm With the Wind," they played covers like Captain Beyond's "Raging River of Fear," Grand Funk Railroad's "I Come Tumblin'," and ZZ Top's "Waitin' for the Bus."

They also performed more of their own songs. These included "I Can Hardly Wait," which featured a riff that Edward would eventually rework into "D.O.A." on *Van Halen II*; "Glitter," which had appeared on the band's fall 1973 demo; and an embryonic version of "Outta Love Again," a tune with an ascending middle riff that showed the influence that Captain Beyond's "Dancing Madly Backwards" had on Edward's early songwriting. "In a Simple Rhyme," one of the band's most polished original songs, also made the set that night, along with another from 1980's *Women and Children First*, the boogie-blues rocker "Take Your Whiskey Home."

As Van Halen jammed, Anthony watched Edward and Alex. Anthony vividly remembers "standing on the side of the stage, watching them play, and I'm saying to myself, *These two guys are great. They have some incredible chops!*" Roth, with a stage-prop cane in hand, then sauntered over to him. "All of a sudden Roth comes struttin' over to me, he had some little vest on and his hair was skunked: it was dyed black with a white skunk stripe down the center. He says, 'Hey, How do you like my boys?'"[248] After one look at Roth, Anthony said to himself, *Jesus Christ, get this guy away from me!*[249]

In the middle of the set, Alex and Edward both took long solos. Edward's was a crowd-pleaser, even if the brothers had borrowed part of its sequence from Cactus. "If you listen to 'Eruption,'" Cactus's Carmine Appice said in 2006, "it's the same thing as the beginning of our song 'Let Me Swim.' I never realized it, but if you listen to both, there's a chord, then there's a guitar thing, then it goes '*Bim, Bam, Bowmmm,*' it changes the key, then there's more guitar. That's the same intro we had for 'Let Me Swim.' Exactly."[250]

Their second to last song of the night was "Believe Me." This song, which disappeared from the Van Halen canon before they recorded their debut album, highlighted the progressive side of Van Halen, with its odd time signatures, stop-start breaks, and some absolutely killer riffs.

The set closer, "Show Your Love" — later renamed "I'm the One" for Van Halen's 1978 debut — then screamed from the speakers. With its speedy shuffle beat, it sounded like a turbo-charged version of "I'm Going Home." After a final flourish, Van Halen waved goodbye and left the stage.

When Edward and Alex saw Algorri backstage, they pulled him aside and whispered, "We're getting rid of Mark. We want to approach this guy."[251] Soon after, they caught up with Anthony. After shooting the shit about life at PCC, they prepared to go their separate ways.[252] Before they parted, however, Anthony said to Edward, "Maybe we could jam some time."[253]

== ==

In the days that followed, Edward didn't forget about Anthony. The guitarist was taking a scoring and arranging class over at PCC with Jonathan Laidig, Roth, and a friend of Anthony's, Mike Franceschini.[254] Edward let Franceschini know that Stone was on his way out of the band. Franceschini then gave Anthony's number to Edward.[255] Within two weeks, the phone rang at the Sobolewski residence in Arcadia. Anthony remembers, "I got a call from Eddie and Alex one night, and they asked me to come over and jam with them."[256]

Anthony concedes that Edward's and Alex's musical talents intimidated him. "I was playing backyard parties," he told Steven Rosen, "and these guys were playing Gazzarri's in Hollywood."[257] He asked one of his brothers to take the ride over to Altadena with him for "moral support."

When he got to the Maiden Lane garage, he noticed that Roth was nowhere to be found.[258] Regardless, they tuned up and started playing some highly technical material. "Those guys were musically so advanced and far ahead of what we had been doing in Snake," he says. "We'd been doing mostly four on the floor, straight ahead rock and roll. They were doing this 5/4 stuff. I was just trying to keep up with them." Anthony added, "I guess I surprised them, because I hung right in," which Anthony credits to the facts that he was "into playing jazz on the bass" and that he'd taken a jazz improvisation course at PCC.[259]

In the midst of this three-hour jam session, Anthony felt a "magic" vibe in the room. As he told Steven Rosen, "You get together and you jam with people and you can play blues in all twelve keys and it's like, 'Yeah, nice.' Or else you start playing one thing and we'd just go off . . . Al had a case of Schlitz Malt there and we had a few beers and kept playing and playing." Finally, when they'd finished, the brothers conferred and then asked, "Hey, do you want to join the band?" Anthony briefly huddled with his own brother, who "was really blown away," before looking back at Edward and Alex and saying, "Well, yeah!"[260]

= =

But before the band could cut Stone loose, the opportunity to do the demo materialized. The studio time needed to be used immediately, so Stone, without yet knowing his fate, would play on the session. After an early morning beer run, the quartet spent the day at Cherokee studio in the San Fernando Valley. The resulting tape contained recordings of "Take Your Whiskey Home," "In a Simple Rhyme," "Believe Me," and "Angel Eyes." The latter song, a gentle ballad that Roth performed alone on a twelve-string acoustic, showed the impact of soft-rock performers like James Taylor and the Eagles on Roth's early songwriting. The tune, which the band considered for inclusion on *Van Halen II*, remains officially unreleased to this day.

With the session wrapped up, everyone drove to Hollywood to meet with Algorri's cousin. "My cousin is Rick Donovan," Algorri explains. "He set up the Cherokee Studios demo. He was a protégé of Roger Christian, who co-wrote a lot of early Beach Boys songs." Donovan was then a producer and vice-president for a label called Custom Fidelity, which did Top 40 compilation albums. Algorri gave Donovan the tape. In the end, though, Donovan "wasn't very impressed, so that didn't go anywhere. My cousin didn't think it was a commercial product." This episode damaged Algorri and Miranda's credibility with Van Halen, and their business relationship ended a few weeks later.

= =

As rumors spread about Stone's future with Van Halen, musicians expressed surprise that change was looming. Peter Burke says, "Mark Stone was a good player. He had really good meter and his sound was wonderful." Brent Pettit agrees and adds, "I had a lot of respect for Mark Stone. He's an intelligent person. He would listen to us play, and then he would ask you, 'Hey man, how did you do that? Can you show me?'" Bill Maxwell notes that along with being a talented musician, Stone "wrote *a lot* of stuff" that Van Halen played during this period of time.

But even if there weren't other issues with Stone, the fact that he didn't like to sing made him a poor fit for a band that now emphasized harmony vocals. When Paul Fry bumped into Edward, he said that firing Stone wasn't going to be an easy thing to do. "Paul," Edward replied, "I just don't want to sing by myself anymore." Indeed, vocals were the major sticking point. "Stone was an exceptional musician," Algorri says, "but there was a rub there, because he would not sing and they wanted harmonies. That was the problem. That was the reason he got booted out."

From Stone's perspective, his divided loyalties between his schoolwork and the band, more than anything else, had taken a toll on his playing. "I was split between these two things," he explained. Ultimately, "I just couldn't keep up with them," and so "we met one day, and they actually asked me to leave."[261] As Alex diplomatically put it to Steven Rosen, "The reason we had to let Mark go was that it seemed his interests were elsewhere than music."[262]

At the same time, however, Anthony's talent and focus made this move possible. Burke says that many of Edward and Alex's friends who'd seen Snake perform at PHS thought that "Mike sang better than Dave." Moreover, Anthony's commitment to music matched that of the other three members of Van Halen. Werner Schuchner says, "One thing I always thought was that Mike was important to Van Halen being so together, because he was very serious. I remember he got his dad to take us to a place where we

Bassist Mark Stone practices with Van Halen in
Altadena, California, early 1974. ELIZABETH WILEY

got new Acoustic amps. I don't remember who paid for them, but
I remember him being real serious like that." As Leiren explained,
"You really got to have that little extra. It's the only thing you've

The classic Van Halen lineup goofs around at David Lee Roth's father's home in San Marino, California, summer 1974. ELIZABETH WILEY

got to want. Stone didn't quite have that. He enjoyed the music. He enjoyed playing, but he also liked to party. He didn't have that same dedication where you eat, live, breathe, and sleep music."[263]

For Stone, all of this was hard to accept. "For a long time," he conceded, "it really hurt. It was tough. It was tough leaving that band, because I knew they were destined for greatness. It's just like they say, 'Don't leave before the miracle happens,' and I did."[264]

= =

Ultimately, this lineup change highlights that Alex, Edward, and Dave recognized that they'd laid the groundwork for something special. Their time together had produced a mutual understanding that their particular mix of talents and personalities, despite all of their artistic differences, engendered a musical synergy that gave Van Halen its musical power and popular appeal. All through the summer of 1973, the brothers had gritted their teeth as Roth warbled through one pitchy version of "Cold Sweat" after another, grinning and strutting his way around the stage. Roth, in turn, had been frustrated with the brothers' determination to play technically sophisticated heavy metal music rather than more accessible pop material. But in the months that followed, the three core members of Van Halen had found a way to meld their musical visions so that the instrumental brilliance of the Van Halen brothers could flourish alongside Roth's entertainment-first notions. Anthony, with his strong backup vocals and great chops, just seemed like the missing piece of the puzzle.

THE BATTLE
OF PASADENA

The Los Angeles County sheriff's deputies, dozens strong in riot gear, trotted down Pasadena's Madre Street. Ear-splitting music — courtesy of "VANHALEN," according to the flyers strewn on the ground — blared out of the well-lit backyard at the end of the long block. As they moved towards the massive party, deputies pushed past scores of wasted teenagers laughing and stumbling down the suburban road, which was lined with cars. Overhead, a police helicopter circled in the cool November air, its spotlight shining down on the property. The pilot, his voice booming through the chopper's loudspeaker, announced, "Attention! This is an unlawful assembly! Disperse! Failure to do so will result in your immediate arrest!"

When the deputies arrived in front of the ranch home, their commander evaluated the situation from the curb. The house was set back about seventy-five yards from the street. Drunken and stoned kids filled the front and back yards and streamed in and out of the house. He estimated that as many as fifteen hundred people were on the property. *Goddamn kids. Where are their fucking parents?*

He looked at his deputies' faces. They were spoiling for a fight. Like him, they'd grown tired of spending their weekend shifts breaking up big Van Halen backyard parties in unincorporated areas around the San Gabriel Valley. But this was the biggest one he'd ever seen, and it was happening in one of Pasadena's nicest neighborhoods. It was also utterly out of control. Earlier in the evening, deputies who'd responded to noise complaints faced a barrage of rocks and bottles from the property. *Probably thrown by the same fucking kids who flipped over those San Marino police cruisers at that giant Van Halen party back in March.* It was time to send a message.

The commander faced his men and ordered them into assault position. They formed a phalanx, their green and gold helmets gleaming under the streetlamps. They lowered their visors, raised their riot shields, and elevated their batons to the ready position. The Battle of Pasadena was about to begin.

== ==

A few months earlier, Don and Mary Ann Imler had informed their son, Denis, then twenty-two, and their teenage daughters, Debbie and Karen, that they'd be taking a month-long trip in June 1974 to their vacation home in Mexico, without them. "They loved to travel," Karen, the youngest of the three, recalls. "My father was older and had just retired from the L.A. County Sheriff's Department. He was a deputy inspector. He was about as high up in the department as you could get. His area was juveniles and narcotics."

Debbie explains that her mother always believed that her children would act appropriately while their parents traveled. "My parents were gone all the time, so there wasn't a lot of supervision," she says. "My mother would say, 'You behave yourselves! I trust you!'" Debbie nodded earnestly, thinking, *Yeah, right!*

Almost immediately after their parents' car pulled out of the driveway, Denis hatched his plan to host the Imlers' first backyard party. Their house was well suited for such an event. It sat on a full acre, and there was another half-acre of undeveloped land behind the rear property line, making for a deep backyard.[265] Its location, which was literally right across the street from Art Agajanian's house, was ideal too. It sat on the corner of Madre Street and Huntington Drive, a busy six-lane road that was one of Pasadena's main thoroughfares, making the house easy to find. They'd supply cold keg beer and hire a hot live band. When it came to picking the group, the decision was easy. All three of them wanted Van Halen to play.

"I went to school with Alex and Edward," Denis explains. "Alex was in my grade. We all hung out together. I was close with them, and after the band got started, we partied together." Debbie, who'd worked with Roth at London Britches, also knew the Van Halen brothers well, even if some of her friends didn't approve of her friendship with Edward and Alex. "They were from the other side of the tracks. My family, and my friends who lived in our neighborhood, Chapman Woods, had a privileged upbringing. They'd ask, 'Why do you want to hang out with *those* guys?' That came from the fact that they were working-class kids. I'd take them to parties and my friends would say, 'Um, why are you friends with *them*?' But I liked them as people, not just because of their music."

Even though Karen didn't know the band members as well as her siblings, she *loved* Van Halen's music. "Well, when I was about fourteen or fifteen, I went to a backyard party that wasn't very big. We sat down in the grass, and I watched Eddie play. I remember being just awestruck by his talent. I was just totally into rock, and I knew the music. I had gone to a lot of concerts at a very young age. And in hearing him and in comparing him to the actual artists who did those songs, I remember thinking, *This guy is going to be famous*. I went up to him afterwards and said, 'You sound better than the musicians that actually play that music. You play it better than they do.'"

Denis wasted no time. He called Alex and asked if he could hire the band to play on a Saturday night in June. Denis says, "The party was an opportunity to play in front of a huge crowd, and it would be inexpensive for everyone since I only charged a dollar." For their services, Denis would pay them a flat fee of three hundred dollars.

From the band's perspective, taking this gig was a no-brainer. They'd make more money in a few hours than they could make playing a weekend booking on the Strip. They'd also have the chance to further expand their fan base by playing in front of hundreds of kids. As Roth declared in later years, "We figured that at first we should just grab any gig we could, whether it was in some grubby high school gym or at a garage sale, because we knew that would be the quickest way for us to build a following."[266]

= =

In the days before the party, the Imlers told their friends that Van Halen would be playing at their home. Denis, in a rare moment of caution, decided not to distribute flyers, figuring that word of mouth would be enough to guarantee a big turnout. The sprawling Chapman Woods neighborhood was home to dozens of teenagers; some families had seven or eight kids, and everyone knew everyone else.[267] Even if more people than he expected showed up, the large property could handle the crowd. He ordered ten kegs, a small stage, and some lights.

= =

When that Saturday arrived, Michael Anthony felt butterflies in his stomach. As the newest member of Van Halen, this gig was his first backyard party with the band. He'd played many yard parties with Snake, but those were jam-with-your-pals, jeans-and-T-shirt affairs. He knew that Van Halen backyard parties were cut from a different cloth; they were bigger and rowdier.

Bassist Michael Anthony, sporting some gold lamé, holds down the bottom
end at Lanterman Auditorium in La Cañada, California, November 22, 1975.
MARY GARSON / HOT SHOTZ

But there was another reason for Anthony's unease. Even
though the quartet glammed it up in Hollywood, Anthony
expected that he'd dress in his usual backyard party garb. But
before the gig, word came down from Roth: they'd be wearing
their Gazzarri's stage clothes in the Imler backyard. Anthony
explains, "Those guys had been down in Hollywood at Gazzarri's
and they knew what would set them apart, and this definitely
made us different from the other bands in the area. But that was
Dave's influence. If it had been up to Ed, Al, and me, we would
have been wearing jeans and T-shirts."

By early evening, the party was rocking. There were a few
hundred kids in the backyard. Some mingled in front of the stage,
which faced the kidney-shaped pool. Others splashed and swam in
the pool. But the biggest crowd was around the kegs.

Before long, the members of Van Halen emerged from the

house, one by one. Roth, of course, was bare chested and wearing impossibly tight pants, and even Edward donned a black cape and silver lamé pants.[268] The last one out of the house was Michael Anthony, a sheepish look on his face as he stared at an audience that included his close friends and his girlfriend, Sue. He recalled, "The first backyard gig I ever did with them was at a party on Huntington Drive. My [future] wife had made a gold lamé outfit for me. I could barely bring myself to walk though the crowd wearing it."[269]

Near the stage, a thirteen-year-old aspiring guitarist named Dave Shelton looked on in awe. Despite Edward's virtuosity and Roth's charisma, the first thing about the bash that comes to his mind today is Anthony's garb. "I remember Michael Anthony was wearing a little tiny gold sparkly vest," he says with a chuckle. "It made him look like an organ grinder's monkey. All he needed was a little pill hat and he was all set!"

Van Halen got the party off to a rousing start by playing some ZZ Top. As the kids grooved and cheered, Roth strutted like a gamecock with the band thundering behind him. As the crowd's excitement grew, people pressed up against the small stage. Shelton says, "I remember standing next to Eddie. They just had this column PA system and people were leaning on it and they were all yelling, 'Get off the PA! You'll knock it over!'"

With the beer flowing and spirits running high, Michael and Edward stepped off the stage to take a break as Dave and Alex prepared for the band's drum solo. With Alex behind the kit, Roth kneeled in front of the drums

Carl Haasis saw this bit of stagecraft. "Roth would do his pose where he rocks back, like on the back of *Van Halen*. He had a plastic tube in his mouth and the tube is going to the small airhole of the tom drum. So Alex would be beating on it, and Roth would be exhaling so it would go *do do do dooo*. It would be raising the pitch, because he's blowing air into the drum." Shelton's sense is that this part of the act didn't come off quite as well as the rest of the show. "Ah, it was kind of lame," he says with a smile. "He was down on his knees sucking on the thing."

Inside the house, Denis was having a grand time when a buddy clapped him on his back "Cops are here!" his friend yelled in his ear. Denis took a final gulp of beer and headed out the front door.

His eyes set upon a group of Pasadena police officers standing in his yard. Some kids retreated from the officers and from the line of black-and-whites parked along the curb, their colored lights spiraling in the darkness. Others stood their ground, too stoned to care.

After Denis identified himself as the homeowner, the officers explained that they'd received noise complaints. If Denis wanted the party to continue, he'd have to get the kids out of the street and make sure the band turned it down. Denis nodded and apologized, assuring the officers that he'd quiet things down and keep people on the property. With that, the officers turned and headed back to their cars. The party would go on.[270]

While it might seem surprising that police would allow a massive teenage party to continue, Eric Hensel explains that up until the summer of 1974, the Pasadena police were largely "friendly" towards teens and had "kind of a don't see, don't tell thing" when it came to parties. He says, "If your party got too loud, and you did get complaints, they'd send a couple of cars over." Many times, the officers' "kids were at those parties too" so they'd be loath to arrest anyone. He continues, "You'd see the cops pull up in front of the house. We'd be standing there smoking a joint or something. People would be all over the place: on the front lawn, in the backyard. Here would come these few cops and they'd walk up and find the owner and tell him they'd had noise reports. 'We will let the party go on if you turn it down and move everybody into the backyard. You've got to get everybody off the street and into the backyard.' They'd let the thing run to midnight or until one.

Van Halen would play a couple or three sets before somebody shut it down." Roger Renick, a singer who performed at many backyard parties, adds that even when the cops broke things up, there was little drama. He remembers, "For a long time Pasadena parties seemed to have a formula that worked, and for the most part everyone knew the routine. Flyers, admission price, kegs of beer, lots of people, big backyards, band played, police came, party ended, and everyone was pissed but left peacefully."

Ultimately, the first Imler party ended without incident. Debbie says, "At the first party, Van Halen played all night. We didn't really get bothered by the police other than stopping by to say, 'Get the people out of the street.' It was a really fun night." When things wound down, the Imlers and their friends worked into wee hours of the morning to pick up trash and to help the band break down their equipment.

After Denis paid the band, he and his siblings counted the fistfuls of money he'd collected at the door. Even after paying his expenses, he'd ended up a few hundred dollars richer. As Denis smiled, Debbie observed that another positive development had come out of the evening. It turned out that "their neighbors seemed okay" with backyard parties, since the police had never returned. Ultimately, this premise would be tested in just a few short months.

= =

When Don and Mary Ann Imler returned home, they seemed only mildly annoyed after hearing about the party. The house looked in good shape, and surely their neighbors' accounts of huge crowds and lines of cars were exaggerated. Regardless, the children were old enough to take care of themselves, and so they planned to return to Mexico in November, this time with some of Don's friends from the sheriff's department and their wives. Flush with success, the Imler siblings looked forward to doing it all again.

In early November, Denis, Debbie, and Karen set out to make their next bash the best backyard party in Pasadena history. Of course, they hired Van Halen, once again for three hundred dollars. But for this second party, they doubled the keg order and employed better staging and lighting. Denis says, "We set up lights from Hortie Van Lighting in Pasadena so we could illuminate the bigger stage, which was on this concrete slab in the yard by the pool. We had a pool house. We mounted spotlights on the roof of the pool building so we could put lights on the band." According to Roth, all of these components are "what made Van Halen's backyard parties different from anybody else's backyard parties."[271]

These preparations aside, Denis had a couple of other tricks up his sleeve. To stop people from sneaking onto the property without paying and to keep rowdy partygoers out of the house, Denis and his friends erected a hundred yards of temporary chain-link fence, complete with a gate, along the Huntington Drive side of the property. Some of his friends, acting as security, would prevent revelers from coming onto the front side of the property from Madre Street and direct everyone to enter — and pay — at the gate. Guests would then flow straight into the backyard.[272] At the time, Denis says, he believed this would allow him to "control the crowd" of partygoers.

= =

To increase the turnout — and profits — Denis printed flyers for the band, his friends, and his siblings to distribute. The week before the party, "We took thousands of flyers and we just went everywhere, high schools, and all the way out to Van Nuys and gave them to everybody. We were just party animals," Karen says with a laugh. The flyer promised a night of "Beer & Music" featuring "VANHALEN," all for a "$1.00 a head donation."

At high schools all over Los Angeles, kids passed them around.

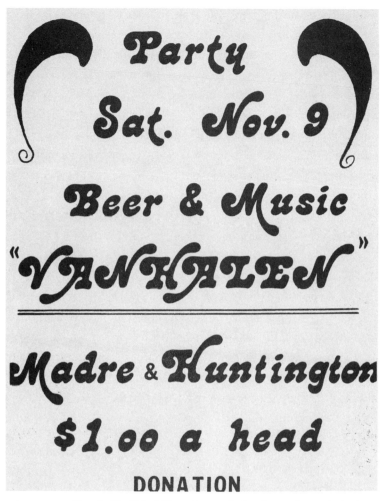

Flyer for Van Halen's November 1974 backyard party that sparked a riot in a sedate Pasadena subdivision. FROM THE COLLECTION OF TOM BONAWITZ

Lori Cifarelli, who attended Mayfield Senior School, an all-girls Catholic school, remembers, "You'd bring flyers to school. They'd be all over: *A buck! Open party!* Everybody and anybody would go; you'd pay a dollar to get in, there were kegs of beer, and of course there was always pot around. Usually it was Van Halen that was playing. Wherever the flyers took us, we went."

The week of the party, Van Halen took the Imlers up on their offer to let the band stay and practice at the house. Debbie says Van Halen "left their equipment in the house. On Thursday and Friday, they practiced in our living room. That was cool." Karen underscores the incongruity between party-hearty Van Halen and the room's morally upright décor. "When the band practiced in our living room," she says, all of her father's sheriff's department "plaques and his commemorative police ashtrays were right there."

Along with a practice space, the Imler home had another added attraction for the band. The house was always filled with girls, including Debbie, Karen, and Edward's girlfriend Kim Miller, who were all gorgeous. Karen remembers, "One time when I ran into Dave, he said, 'You know what I think of when I think of your place?'"

"No. What?" she answered.

"I think of the song 'La Grange,'" Roth replied with a smile, referencing ZZ Top's ode to the Chicken Ranch, later immortalized in *The Best Little Whorehouse in Texas*.

Karen took it all in stride. She laughs, "I'd joke around and answer the phone at the house, 'Mustang Ranch!' There were always girls there, so a lot of guys would come around. What can I say? It was kind of like that. It was a house with a lot of young girls and no parents."

= =

On Saturday, Van Halen moved their equipment outside and ran through their set. Jeff Touchie, who'd spent much of the week at the house, remembers, "We just hung out in the back and they played. Even though I had seen them a million times, it was always good. Back then, you never got tired of Van Halen, because Edward was amazing; he'd just sit down and do some riffs. And Alex could just go on the drums. They'd play a song, take a break, and joke around. They'd get ready to start something and say,

'What do you think about this?' And they'd do a little jam. It was always entertaining. We'd just drink beers and shoot the shit. It was laid back and kicked back."

Meanwhile, all across Los Angeles, hundreds of young people got ready. They checked their stashes and chilled their beer. They called friends, passed the word, and made plans to caravan over to Pasadena. They'd be coming from San Gabriel Valley communities like Duarte, Flintridge, La Cañada, and West Covina. Even San Fernando Valley teens from Glendale and Calabasas would be making the long trip to the corner of Huntington and Madre. Leiren explained that for kids looking to get loose, a Van Halen gig would be *the* place to be that night. "Anytime you wanted to find *anybody*, you'd go to the Van Halen backyard parties."[273]

While it seemed that nearly every young person in Pasadena knew of the party, even those who'd not gotten the word knew how to find out about the evening's action. Marcia Maxwell says, "There was a certain liquor store, Allen Villa Beverage, on Allen Street and Villa. That's not too far away from where the Van Halens lived. People would tell the owner, Larry, 'I'm having a party. Here's my address,' so *everyone* knew to go there to give and get information. We'd go there faithfully every weekend. All the gals would get all dressed up, we'd drive over there, and we'd come in and say, 'Where's the party?' And off we'd go! There was usually a party every weekend. If it wasn't Van Halen it was some other band. There was a *lot* of partying going on."

Around seven, Van Halen hopped onstage and tuned up. Roth joked with his bandmates as he looked out upon the big backyard, which was already swarming with hundreds of kids. From the gate at the back corner of the property, young people stampeded into the yard and jockeyed for position in front of the stage. Despite Denis's efforts to make everyone pay, some Chapman Woods locals, who knew their way through the brushy terrain behind the house, snuck into the backyard. Others attempted to vault Denis's Huntington Drive fence or slip in through the front yard, only to be turned back by the host's friends who guarded the property's perimeter.

Onstage, Roth looked back at Alex one last time before grinning broadly at the crowd. He raised his arm, put the microphone to his lips, and screamed. Just then, Roth fired off the band's pyrotechnic flash pots, sending black clouds ascending skyward. He noted in his autobiography, "Put a little gunpowder in the tins, and then when you hit the foot switch, it sparks it off and you get a great big colorful 'fooomm!' — a smoke bomb."[274] All the while, Edward played a blazing solo as an introduction to the band's high-powered set opener. [275] Van Halen's senses-shattering assault had begun.

Around the stage, kids gathered and jammed to the music, but right up front, clutches of girls had their eyes glued to Roth. Debbie recalls, "Roth would wear low-cut tight bell-bottoms. He had this nice hairy chest. He liked flashy stuff. A lot of times he'd just wear no shirt and some flowing scarf. He had this gorgeous flowing long blond hair." Roth's appearance and persona had a particularly strong effect on her sister, Karen, who had a massive crush on Van Halen's frontman. "He wore these hip hugger pants," she recalls. "He was very sexy."

Out in the streets, cars jockeyed for parking spaces and kids on foot moved with purpose towards the Imlers' house, knowing that once Van Halen began playing, there was no saying how long the party would last. Debbie Hannaford Lorenz says that when she hears a Van Halen song today, she is transported back to those moments right after arriving at a backyard party. "I have that memory of walking down the street with all the cars and the music just echoing everywhere, and you know it's a Van Halen party. It was such an exciting, electrical feeling. You were so excited to get to go. I loved it. I loved that sensation that you'd get through your whole body."

Neighborhood residents felt sensations too — their windows rattled and cars cruised by their houses, honking their horns and burning rubber.[276] Karen Imler says, "It was crazy. Huntington Drive turned into and sounded like a drag strip."

By 7:30, frustrated residents began calling the police. Touchie explains that the Imlers "lived right on the border between Temple City and Pasadena. Chapman Woods was unincorporated, so sometimes the Pasadena police would show up and sometimes the sheriffs would show up." For whatever reason, on this night the law enforcement response would come from the sheriff's department station in Temple City.

In the meantime, the party was raging. Van Halen played everything from funky numbers by James Brown and the Rolling Stones to skull-crushers by Humble Pie and Montrose, with a few originals to boot. Roth and Edward fed off the crowd's energy while standing under the spotlight, which shone down from the pool house roof courtesy of Edward and Alex's old friend Ross Velasco.[277] As Roth wrote in Crazy from the Heat, "We had rented a Trooperette spotlight . . . We'd put it on top of the work shed, which is on the other side of the swimming pool, and shine it down on us. You'd open it up wide enough that you've got the whole band until there was some singing or solo . . . then you would make the spot smaller so you could bring some focus to the proceedings."[278]

Under the beam of light, the packed crowd surged, with the most wasted kids held upright by the press of the crowd. Around the pool, partygoers pushed each other into the water and ran around on the patio, laughing uproariously. Wet T-shirts abounded, according to Touchie: "People were throwing each other in. Girls were running around half naked and drunk and jumping in the pool!"

Suddenly, people standing at stage right scattered as plate glass splintered. Dana Anderson explains, "I vividly remember the party on Madre and Huntington. I dropped PCP that night, so I was bouncing off the walls. I don't remember a whole lot except walking through a plate-glass door that was right [alongside] where the band was playing in the backyard. I walked right through it barefoot. And not a scratch on me! I didn't even remember. People had to tell me, 'You broke the door, man!'"

Things were just as wild inside the house, which, despite Denis's efforts, was full of people. Marcia Maxwell says that at Van Halen backyard parties there'd be "lots of drunkenness, a lot of fun, a lot of drugs in the house. There'd be lots of quaaludes, mescaline, mushrooms, and peyote. Cocaine — people would be wearing their spoons and their razor blades around their necks. It was so tacky. People would wear a coke spoon around their neck as a status symbol."

At the gate, Denis and his friends crammed currency into their pockets as a huge crowd waited to get into the party. Denis would occasionally pause, pointing and gesturing at his friends to grab kids trying to sneak into the backyard. Also hanging around were kids who didn't want to pay but couldn't be bothered to jump the fence. They just stood along the fence line and listened to Van Halen.

Even though Denis was making money hand over fist, a serious problem was developing. Debbie observes, "Huntington Drive is a huge, wide boulevard, and the gate keepers couldn't get the kids in the yard fast enough. The crowd spilled onto Huntington, which has a speed limit of forty-five miles per hour." Before long, three lanes of traffic were blocked, and horns blared as drivers attempted to snake their way through the groups of kids on the blacktop.

With traffic backing up, Denis yelled to his friends to stop collecting money. "We just started shoving people into the yard without taking money just to get them off Huntington," Debbie says. "The kids were coming by the hundreds, and we could not get them in fast enough."

Sometime after 8:00, the Temple City sheriff's deputies paid their first visit. Denis Imler recalls, "The party had only lasted an hour before the L.A. County Sheriff's Department responded." According to the *Pasadena Star-News*, the deputies located Denis at the gate and warned him to "tone things down" or the party would end. Denis promised that he'd do just that as he continued to herd people into the yard. As the crowd thinned on Huntington Drive, the deputies returned to their cars and drove off.[279]

But after their departure, urgent calls kept coming into the department's switchboard. There were so many cars in the neighborhood that for the first time in history, there was L.A.-style bumper-to-bumper traffic right on Madre Street. Kids wandered everywhere in Chapman Woods. They pissed in bushes. They parked on people's lawns. Broken glass and trash littered the street. And the noise! It sounded like an air raid was underway. Unworldly screams and piercing squeals echoed throughout the neighborhood, and the stadium-style cheering hadn't ceased. One resident even swore she'd heard explosions. Deputies' radios crackled to life with orders for all available units to converge on the corner of Huntington and Madre.

Once again, deputies rolled up. One quick look at the scene made it clear to the unit commander that Denis Imler had done little to "tone down" the party; in fact, the number of people on the property had about doubled in the last hour. Denis remembers, "They found me and said, 'The neighbors won't tolerate this. We're shutting this down.' The party was so big it was stopping traffic on Huntington Drive. They told me I was hosting an 'unlawful assembly.'" As the conversation continued between Denis and the ranking officer, other deputies ordered everyone in earshot to go home. *Now.*

Denis, who was the son of a Los Angeles sheriff's department commander, knew that the deputies now meant business and that the party *had* to end. He made his way through the crowd and went to the stage. This was a feat in and of itself. "It was like Woodstock," Touchie says. "You'd look over and just see this mass of people in front of the stage. To maneuver through and get up there to the stage was next to impossible. It was just a wall of people."

After yelling and waving, Denis caught Roth's eye. Van Halen played on as Roth pranced over to the party's host. Roth leaned down as Denis yelled, "They're going to shut it down! You guys need to stop playing!" Denis waited for Roth to stop the song, but the Van Halen frontman just kept singing and dancing. "He ignored me, and they kept playing. Roth had control of the whole thing; he egged the crowd on." A frustrated Denis decided to take matters into his own hands. As he headed through the broken sliding glass door, he glanced up at the sky. A police helicopter was approaching.

Denis found Debbie and told her the party was over. She recalls, "So Denis came running in the house and disconnected the electricity to the stage." Denis then headed into the yard to assure the deputies that the party was ending.

In through the back door bounded a sweaty, wide-eyed Alex Van Halen. He yelled to Debbie and everyone within earshot, "Who keeps pulling the electricity?"

"Denis did," Debbie informed him.

"That's bullshit!"

He plugged the band back in, returned to his kit, and Van Halen resumed playing. Debbie says then "this happened again, back and forth between Denis and Alex."

Around this time, an instigator out on Huntington Drive killed any chance for a peaceful end to the party. Denis says, "Eventually, when the police ordered people to disperse, someone threw a beer bottle that hit a patrol car." Debbie adds, "There were bottles thrown at the police cars parked on Huntington Drive. I can't remember who did it, but I remember he was just a real trouble-maker. He broke windows and a windshield."

The *Star-News* reported that this first flurry of projectiles triggered a number of copycats. Deputies "were met with a barrage of rocks and bottles" as they congregated around the property. Touchie saw kids hurling projectiles from the backyard over the fence and onto Huntington Drive. "There were fifteen to twenty cop cars on the Huntington Drive side of the property," he says.

These rowdies "jacked up about six cop cars." What had begun as a Van Halen backyard party had now become a full-scale riot with a Van Halen soundtrack.[280]

As deputies on the scene retreated, backup units saddled up in Temple City. Tense calls came over the radio about the "unlawful assembly" in Chapman Woods. Deputies gathered up their riot gear, angered that their comrades were under attack. But perhaps all this was inevitable. Van Halen backyard parties had been getting bigger and more disorderly over the past months; it was only a matter of time before one of them turned into a riot. No matter. The officers were well trained, and had a whole range of crowd control methods they could employ. Truth be told, the whole department had run out of patience when it came to Van Halen backyard parties.

= =

Standing on the pool house roof, Ross Velasco could see the flashing lights of at least two dozen patrol cars, all converging and congregating a quarter-mile down on Madre. As the officers stepped onto the street, they grabbed riot shields and donned their helmets.[281] Equally alarming, the department had brought a paddy wagon, suggesting that mass arrests were imminent.[282]

Velasco looked down into the yard and hollered a warning to Peter Wilson and his friends, who soon joined Velasco on top of the structure. Wilson says, "We decided to go up on the roof so we wouldn't be affected when the bust came. We had a bird's-eye view of everything. We could see the sheriff's staging area and the cars amassing down the street, so we knew it was coming down." He figured he'd sit tight and watch the proceedings, since he and his friends had set themselves up nicely by "raiding the liquor cabinet" and "maybe the medicine cabinet," he concedes with a laugh.

As they played, the four members of Van Halen saw Velasco

pointing and knew their performance was about to end. The backyard couldn't get any fuller. The helicopter hovered above, its light shining down and its loudspeaker blaring "Disperse!" This song would be the night's last.

With the band thundering behind him, Roth knew exactly what do for a grand finale. As Edward, Alex, and Michael concluded the song with a crescendo of drums, bass, and guitar, Roth triggered the band's bank of smoke pots once again. As stunned onlookers recoiled, six mushroom clouds of smoke rolled into the night air and sparks rained down from the sky. All the while, Edward's fingers flashed up and down his fretboard as Roth screamed his guts out. Fellow backyard party musician Bill Hermes observes, "The flashpots were a brilliant idea, because they tattooed a Van Halen memory onto your brain from the shock of them going off!"

Word of the impending raid spread quickly. Tom Broderick hustled back to his car with some of his friends. He told *The Inside*, "I remember sitting outside when the cops all pulled up and parked up the street . . . They all came running down the street in formation with their clubs and helmets in military style. We were all just tripping."[283] Hensel had just bugged out as well when lines of deputies trotted past him. He says, "They showed up in Pasadena with fifty or sixty cop cars and four guys in each one with full riot gear. My friend and I just happened to be leaving when they showed up. We watched the cops going in; it was an amazing thing to watch. I'd never seen anything like it in Pasadena." In *Crazy from the Heat*, David Lee Roth recounted what this very moment felt like: "Cop cars show up parked in a line, all with the flashing lights and lots of flares. It was all very exciting and kind of scary, and you might go to jail, and your parents might have to come get you out, and even maybe pay for a friend or two. It was great."[284]

= =

Sensible partygoers knew it was time to split. "The helicopter was always the first warning," Terry Vilsack says. "When it comes, everybody just flies — just scatters. It's like when you turn the light on and you watch the cockroaches go!"

But for those kids who were too stoned to run or too drunk to know what was happening, the police assault came with little warning. After they'd gotten into formation, deputies surged into the yard, batons swinging and Mace in hand, with tear gas in the air. Wilson looked down from the roof in amazement as "they formed a line right underneath us. They proceeded to push everyone out of the yard with their batons. People were running and panicking. They were dropping their stashes on the ground." Roth termed this the "surround and pound" strategy: "The cops would come bursting in, in a great big line, kind of like football style."[285]

With their backs to the pool house, the police charged, violently herding the crowd out of the yard. Peter Burke remembers, "The sheriff's department showed up and started shoving people around really brutally. I mean girls. It was pretty hairy." Art Agajanian recalls, "The Temple City Sheriff's Department was very hard on kids. They used Mace and tear gas. They billy-clubbed kids."

Law enforcement next sought to clear the roof. "I remember them grabbing people," Karen says, "like my sister's boyfriend at the time, they pulled him off the roof." Ross Velasco, who'd been operating the lights all night long "tasted Mace for the first time" that night.

Caught in the middle of the melee, Denis could only stand and watch as panicked partygoers and enraged deputies trampled the landscaping and knocked over all of the patio planters. Kids caught inside the pool fencing vaulted over it in an effort to escape, with the deputies lunging for them, handcuffs in hand.

Then one hapless kid who tried to leap the fence caught his foot and fell right on the pool's water supply line, severing it. A geyser of water sprayed onto the patio, forming a quickly growing pool. An alarmed Debbie Imler watched as the water flowed closer to the stage. She remembers, "All this water started gushing out and cascading down towards the stage and all of the band's electrical equipment." In a fit of anger, she grabbed the young man who'd severed the pipe and punched him square in the face.

Standing nearby was Peter Burke. He says, "I remember there was some sort of flood that started flowing right into the equipment. I'm the one who stepped up with a push broom and said, 'Hey man, *look out!*' Then Edward grabbed the broom from me and shoved the water back while everybody else fixed it. That was my contribution to the show!" With water pouring into the yard, Denis sprinted to the water main and shut off the water to the house.[286] Later that night, a shaken Edward would tell Debbie he "was very afraid he was going to get electrocuted."

Meanwhile, the police confronted the band. Roth explained that the group's strategy for busts was to shrug their shoulders and say to the police, "Man, we're with the band. This is our equipment. We don't know nothing about this, man. We were just hired to play what we thought was going to be a normal party. There's nothing fucking normal about this party at all. All we want is out. We're with you, man."[287]

But Michael Anthony recalls that this line failed to work its magic at this particular party: "The cops said they were going to arrest us. I thought we were going to jail. That really scared us. Yeah, those backyard parties were something incredible. There were like two thousand people in this backyard."

Although the band members didn't go to jail, twenty-one kids did get hauled away in handcuffs for charges ranging from narcotics possession to "suspicion of failure to disperse," in the words of the *Star-News*.[288] Once in the hands of the Temple City deputies, a young person's troubles were just beginning. Steve Bruen explains that the sheriff's deputies "were much worse than the

Pasadena cops. Pasadena cops would smell pot in your car and say, 'Just put it out and go home.' Temple City cops would drag you out, beat you, and harass you all the way to a cell. They'd say, 'Are you crying for your mommy yet?' That kind of crap."

After clearing the yard, the commander and his deputies barged into the house and confronted the Imlers. Karen remembers, "The cops were just storming through the house. They were yelling at us, and they had their riot gear on with their helmets and their batons out, and they were telling us all to leave. I remember they hit my brother in the head." Karen Imler adds that seeing her brother struck and one of her girlfriends in cuffs enraged Debbie. "My sister was yelling, 'You Nazis!'" Karen recalls. "It was kind of funny. But then they made us all leave, even me! From my own house!"

With everyone in the front yard, negotiations began. The ranking officer eventually agreed that a handful of people, including the Imlers, could remain in the house. Karen's close friend Patti Smith Sutlick explains, "I just remember standing out in front with [Karen]." She selected "the people that are going to stay at her house. Edward was one of them; I don't know if Alex was." With that, the deputies left and the remaining guests headed inside.

After Denis iced his head and counted his money, he and Debbie headed down to the jail to bail out their friends. They returned after a couple of hours, realizing that even with all of the cash he'd made, he still didn't have enough money to bail anyone out. Sitting with his friends and family, he observed that even though it had been a great party, he knew he'd "overdone it when people were still driving up to the party after the police had broken it up."

= =

The following Monday in Rosarito Beach, a fat orange sun hung in the late afternoon sky. As Don and Mary Ann Imler watched the spectacular sunset and sipped margaritas, their friends arrived at the vacation home after driving down from Pasadena. In their luggage was a copy of Monday's *Star-News*.

Here accounts vary about how the Imlers received the news that a backyard party riot, featuring Van Halen, had erupted at their home. Gary Baca, an Imler cousin, *swears* Don and Mary Ann knew about the party while it was happening. He says, "Denis's parents were sitting at their vacation cottage at Rosarito Beach in the Baja. Like everyone back then, they got TV from the States with an antenna. Whatever they were watching got interrupted as the TV switched to a live feed from a helicopter, showing their home surrounded by police. So they saw it live, on TV. That's how they found out about the party."

But the Imler children tell a different tale. Debbie says that Don's friend pulled him aside and whispered that he had something to tell him. Out of their wives' earshot, he handed Don the *Star-News*. "My father opened the paper and saw this article describing the party." The piece, which appeared on the second page of the first section, featured the headline "21 Arrested in Pasadena Party Melee" and reported that "a rollicking crowd of 1,000" had laid siege to the Imler property.[289]

After Don read the piece, the pair talked. He asked his friend, "Should I tell Mary Ann and go home to L.A.?" His friend counseled him not to tell her and to stay, because the party was long over.[290] However, leaving his wife in the dark didn't stop Don from wondering about the current condition of his home and yard. "He wasn't pleased," Denis remembers.

= =

Among San Gabriel Valley natives of a certain age, Van Halen's performance at the Imler residence is the stuff of legend. Karen Imler summarizes, "It was just wild. Through the years, anyone that I run into has always brought it up, and even the band." Terry

Kilgore asserts, "At the Agajanians' and the Imlers', they were packing twelve to eighteen hundred people into those backyards." The fun and excitement that these celebrations generated only fueled the demand for more. Dana Anderson says that the same question always popped up among his friends: "We were always like, 'Where's the next Van Halen party?'"

David Lee Roth, perhaps better than anyone else, grasped the effect that the Van Halens' backyard party "campaign" had on building Van Halen's "following."[291] In 1987, he asked a *Penthouse* interviewer, "Do you remember those early Mickey Rooney–Judy Garland movies? In those films it was always 'Hey, Mr. Ziegfeld is coming to town! I have a backyard. We can turn it into a stage!' I've spent the last ten years of my career taking a million-dollar stage and attempting to turn it into a backyard."[292] Roth knows. Backyard parties like the Imlers' made Los Angeles Van Halen Country.

THE CONTEST

David Lee Roth swigged a beer and soaked up the surroundings as he listened to the roar of the crowd on this June 1976 night. Young men with flushed faces stood with their chests pressed up against the stage of the Rock Corporation nightclub in Van Nuys. Hot, sweaty bodies packed every square inch of the dance floor, forming a throng consisting of everyone from motorcycle gang members and underage teenage boys to hard-drinking women and young Valley girls. Outside the entrance, muscle cars rumbled down the street as the club's burly bouncers held back groups of denim and leather-clad men who just didn't want to hear that there literally was no more room inside "the Rock." They, like everyone else on the crowded street, didn't want to miss the action that was just about to take place.

Onstage, Roth reached for the microphone, and said in a deep, affected baritone, "Ladies, it's last call for contestants for the wet T-shirt contest! *Last call!*" Soon after, club owner Jeff Simons, accompanied by a dozen or so young, drunk women wearing sheer white tank tops made their way under the hot lights. As the girls lined up next to a small wading pool, Roth introduced the first girl as she stepped into it. Once Roth finished his sexually suggestive banter, she shot a hand in the air and waved to the crowd as Simons poured a pitcher of ice water down her chest, turning her tank translucent. On cue, Van Halen kicked into Aerosmith's "Walk This Way," giving the drenched girl the chance to shake and shimmy for the crowd. As this process was repeated, drunken men leaned forward, screaming and slapping each other on the back in euphoria. Onstage, Van Halen grooved their way through every riff. Roth and the rest of Van Halen, Simons later said, were very much in their "element during the wet T-shirt contests."

As the last of the girls took her turn, she impulsively decided to try to improve her odds of winning the contest's significant cash prize. She brazenly raised her soaked top, exposing her ample chest. A deafening roar came from the crowd, which grew louder as some of the other girls quickly followed suit. With the hot, wet, topless young ladies wiggling onstage and pandemonium sweeping through the crowd, a knowing smile formed on Roth's face. At this moment, his band was right in the midst of the most brilliant promotion he'd ever seen staged in a Los Angeles bar.

A couple of men lingering at the very back of the club, however, disagreed. Standing on an elevated platform near the Rock's jukebox, two undercover members of the Los Angeles Police Department's Vice Squad had now seen all they needed to see. They hopped down from their perch and prepared to end this now-illegal event.

= =

The beginning of 1975 saw Van Halen seek broader horizons. While backyard parties in Pasadena and gigs at Gazzarri's remained the group's stock-in-trade, Van Halen began to look beyond both its San

Gabriel Valley home and Hollywood for new venues to play. "We had a big bulletin board with a map and little stickpins," Michael Anthony remembered in 1978. "There are hundreds of clubs and other places to play in California — we played them all, five forty-five minute sets a night, averaging about six nights a week."[293]

Yet when Van Halen pored over this map and called these clubs, they discovered that the places that seemed most interested in hiring them were dive bars, such as Pomona's Walter Mitty's, that attracted a blue-collar, rough-and-tumble clientele. "We went through a lot of rough times," Alex said. "Years of playing some of the shittiest biker bars that you'll ever know. In the middle of the second set, someone's getting knifed outside, and half of the audience goes out to watch it while we're still playing. That discourages a lot of people."[294] Terry Kilgore, who played this same circuit, remembers that they were "shitholes. Edward used to call all those places 'the pits.' They were all horrible. They were all dirty dumpy hamburger bars with fat waitresses that served beer."

The band logged long miles on L.A.'s freeways, driving west from Pasadena to the San Fernando Valley, down south to the seaside at Redondo Beach, and due east to Pomona. Reflecting back on this moment in the band's history, Roth explained in 1978 why, even as Van Halen remained a Tinseltown also-ran, the four musicians didn't get discouraged about their prospects outside of the San Gabriel Valley: "Southern California is a huge, huge place. There's [sic] a lot of outlying areas. You have Orange County, which is a hundred miles away from San Bernardino, which is 190 miles away from the beach. And as we played all of those towns, we got away from Hollywood. Van Halen was never big in Hollywood, but we were big in San Bernardino."[295]

Ambition aside, this suburban strategy was hardly a recipe for financial success. While sometimes the band might make over a hundred dollars for their five or six hours of onstage work, Leiren remembered a few nights, after the band chose to take a cut of the door rather than a flat fee for performing, "when the band didn't get a penny" after playing.[296] Still, even when the band earned a tolerable wage it barely covered expenses. "We were making seventy-five bucks a night," Edward told the *Record* in 1982, "not even enough to pay for gas and strings and drum heads." (Because of this low pay, the Van Halen brothers supplemented their income in other ways — mainly by posing as Pasadena and San Marino city employees and charging homeowners to stencil street numbers on their curbs.)[297]

Even though they left the four musicians poor, these gigs furthered the band's development in three important ways. First, these dive bars helped transform Van Halen into a band that, by 1978, would be powerful, seasoned, and skilled enough to thrill stadium crowds. Most immediately, this involved playing, as Roth put it, "five [sets] a night of hard rock, no slow stuff," to audiences largely comprised of alcoholics, speed freaks, cycle enthusiasts, and incipient felons from L.A.'s industrial hinterlands, all of whom wanted their rock hard and their beer cold and, initially at least, had never heard of Van Halen.[298] By winning over these rowdy audiences, Van Halen developed what Roth would later term the "habits" and "attitudes" that separated the great bands from all the rest.[299]

Second, these long nights of gigging also allowed the quartet to test drive and tweak their original songs. Although bar owners like Simons expected an up-and-coming unsigned band like Van Halen to play popular songs that their customers would know, Van Halen took liberties with this policy as they worked to craft a body of their own material. "We probably had the largest repertoire of anyone around," recalled Anthony. "It included everything from James Brown to the Kinks. And we'd always try to stick in one of our own songs, but about one per set was all we could get away with."[300] According to Alex, the best way for a band to "get away" with slipping in its originals was to get patrons "dancing to a song they know" and then "just segue into one of your own songs and they'll keep going."[301]

Most importantly, though, Van Halen committed to playing at bars like Mitty's because they believed that these places would help the band make a monster truck–sized name for itself throughout Southern California. As Roth told Steven Rosen, this component of the band's vision was that "we'd play the clubs and the bars and our following [would keep] growing, which was the whole idea, to make the following grow. And if you heat people up enough, if you excited people enough, they would talk and then eventually the record companies would hear about it . . . [and] you'd get discovered and signed."[302]

Even though getting signed seemed like a pipe dream in early 1975, the band stood ready to do the work necessary to raise its profile, regardless of whether or not it provided a quick payoff. "Even when we were working and we made no money at all when we played," Alex said to an interviewer in 1978, "we felt in our heart that this was the music the people liked and what we liked. So it didn't matter moneywise, because if we had not made an album we'd still be playing the same music . . . We loved playing and the people had a good time."[303] Thus the band resolved to grind it out on the dive bar circuit until enough of the city's rock fans had become Van Halen fans.

= =

In the late spring of 1975, Van Halen got the word that they needed to add a new pin to their nightclub map. A small club called the Rock Corporation had opened its doors in Van Nuys. While the venue would feature nationally known acts like Captain Beyond, Iron Butterfly, and Canned Heat, the Rock would also give unsigned bands a chance to ply their trade. Most likely, the band had also heard a piece of information about the club that they had deemed useful: its owner, Jeff Simons, was a former roadie for Bachman–Turner Overdrive (BTO). After Roth or Alex called the Rock and secured an audition slot, they all drove to the Valley.[304]

When they arrived, the foursome met the Rock's manager and pulled on their grimy coveralls. As they unloaded, each of them took in their surroundings. The club itself was located on a gritty commercial stretch of Oxnard Street, with little to recommend it to those looking for the beautiful side of the City of Angels. Indeed, the *Los Angeles Free Press* described the Rock's location as an "unpicturesque" example of the Valley's "industrial underside" standing "all too near the center" of life in Van Nuys.[305] Situated across the street from a power station, it was an ideal spot for a business that featured loud live music.

The inside of the Rock likewise offered little in terms of ambiance. As they stepped into the dimly lit club, the smell of stale beer and dirty ashtrays assaulted their nostrils. A shallow puddle of spilled beer, stained brown by dirty boots and discarded cigarettes, covered part of the dance floor. The club's rough-hewn wooden walls were haphazardly plastered with gig posters, photographs of celebrity visitors, and a growing collection of autographed cymbals. Along with pinball machines, pool tables, a jukebox, and an imposing wooden bar, the club also featured a small stage situated in one corner of the room.

While the band set up onstage, owner Jeff Simons worked in the Rock's small, cluttered office. He typically left the amateur band auditions to the club's manager, so he didn't bother to watch when this Pasadena quartet began to play. He didn't hear Alex count in by clicking his sticks, and the significance of Van Halen's audition song didn't immediately register in his mind. But after a couple of bars, Simons looked up from his desk. Van Halen had launched into BTO's massive 1974 hit, "Takin' Care of Business." To his ears, Van Halen's version sounded nothing like the original. It sounded thin, tinny, in fact.

Suddenly, a flash of anger surged through him. *These fucking guys know I worked for BTO.* Unwilling to be manipulated, Simons strode out of his office and climbed onto the club's stage. He yanked Edward's cord out of his amp, bringing the song to a grinding halt. Turning to Edward, he yelled, "Hey, your fucking band sucks! Pack your shit and get the fuck out! Try practicing too before you audition again!" Upon hearing this, Roth went ballistic. Edward, meanwhile, looked stunned as Simons said a few choice words to Roth before walking off and slamming the door to his office.

= =

Even in the face of another failed audition, Edward's dedication to his craft never wavered. Kim Miller, who probably spent more time with Edward than anyone outside of the band, recalls that nothing interfered with her boyfriend's love affair with his instrument. "Edward sat on his bed to play his guitar. He played for hours, which was not unusual at all for him. He only stopped for food and sometimes just fell asleep. It's what he loved to do most. By the time I came into his life he really didn't play along to records or even play songs [*per se*] — I guess he did this at practice. He just played riffs and jammed freestyle. Edward also did play guitar at my house a lot; he would bring it with him unless we had plans to go out. I was so [accustomed] to him . . . playing his guitar. I rarely paid a lot of attention; it wasn't amped and sounded like 'Eruption' all the time, but with less structure."[306]

Edward also spent time with his friend Terry Kilgore, a burly, intense guitarist whom he'd known since he was a little kid. As Edward told *Guitar World*, "A really good friend of mine named Terry Kilgore and I were the so-called gunslingers in Pasadena back in the mid-'70s."

Their friendship grew out of mutual admiration. "We jammed together and would trade licks and have a lot of fun," Edward explained.[307] Jonathan Laidig, Terry's bass player at the time, recalls, "The two of them, they'd get together, and if you can imagine it, the two of them played face to face. It was kind of like they pushed to make each one get better. The guitar was Terry's life, and it showed. At that point you could put him and Eddie together in a blind test and you couldn't tell them apart." Carl Haasis adds, "Terry Kilgore's a great guitar player. He and Ed were like neck and neck back then. At one point they sounded kind of like each other."

Their shared sense of respect led both young men to watch while the other practiced with his band. Terry took in Van Halen practices. Edward, in turn, watched Terry's band rehearse, talking to his friend on breaks about guitar gear and tone. In fact, Edward recounted to *Guitar World* that he first discovered MXR, a guitar effects company he now endorses, at Kilgore's place. "I went to one of his band rehearsals once, and that was when I first saw a [MXR] Phase 90."[308]

Around 1974, Kilgore started giving guitar lessons. One of his early pupils was a fourteen-year-old Chris Holmes. Holmes, later of W.A.S.P., explains, "When I was a young kid I took guitar lessons from Terry Kilgore. I could get high school credit for taking these guitar lessons."

To pay for his sessions, Holmes got a summer job. He says, "I was painting houses in La Cañada and Flintridge. One day I looked in the window of this house we were painting, and I noticed all these gold records lining the walls. I knocked on the door. I asked the lady that answered about them and she told me they were Harvey Mandel's awards. I was like, *Huh, I don't know who that is.*"

When Holmes showed up for his next lesson, he mentioned that he'd been inside the home of a musician named Harvey Mandel. Holmes asked Kilgore, "Who's Harvey Mandel?"

"He's a great guitarist, that's who he is. Next time you're there working get his phone number for me."

Holmes says, "I did, and Terry went up there and met Mandel."

At that time, the twenty-nine-year-old Mandel had already had a career that would be the envy of guitarists everywhere. He'd grown up a blues prodigy in Chicago. Mandel then joined the ranks of boogie-rockers Canned Heat and would perform with them at the Woodstock Festival. Not one to stand still, Mandel then became a member of John Mayall & the Bluesbreakers, a band that had incubated Edward's guitar idol, Eric Clapton. He also recorded two solo albums, *Baby Batter* (1971) and *Snake* (1972).

When Kilgore showed up at Mandel's home, he asked the famous guitarist for lessons. Kilgore says, "I just wanted to take lessons from him, because I loved the way he played." He didn't hide his enthusiasm after his first session and arrived at practice raving about Mandel's talents. "I was playing with Terry in 1974 and 1975 when he was taking those lessons," Laidig says, "I know he was really jazzed about taking them from him."

Kilgore, who always kept tabs on the latest guitar techniques, was particularly interested in learning Mandel's unique two-handed tapping technique. While playing lead runs, Mandel would use his pick-hand fingers to sound, or "tap," notes on the guitar neck in a stuttering and meandering fashion.

Mandel, it turns out, had learned the unorthodox method from a former bandmate. In 1972, Mandel had joined a Los Angeles–based blues-rock band, the Pure Food and Drug Act. Mandel shared guitar duties in that group with a wildly creative player named Randy Resnick. During the band's long live jams, Resnick would often tap notes with his picking hand. Mandel took notice.[309]

In the months that followed, Mandel woodshedded the technique. Mandel told writer Abel Sharp: "Randy was the first guitarist I ever saw tap, and he had his own little way of doing it . . . After I saw Randy Resnick doing it, I got on it. I started doing it all over."[310] On his 1973 solo album, *Shangrenade*, Mandel showcased a style that featured the two-handed technique as the centerpiece of his lead playing.

After learning it from Mandel, Kilgore started to experiment with the method. Chris Holmes recollects, "The next time I took a lesson with Terry, he was doing finger tapping." Kilgore also showed his bandmates and his soundman, Kevin Gallagher, the technique. Gallagher explains, "So Terry started showing up with this [tapping] stuff that Mandel was teaching him. I never really met Mandel. But they were pretty tight, and he shared a lot of this stuff with Terry. My understanding is that Harvey started that style of playing and showed it to Terry."

It didn't take long for Kilgore to share this novel method with Edward. Gallagher says, "I can recall at least one time when I was doing sound in Jon Laidig's basement that Eddie was sitting on the basement stairs learning that stuff from Terry."

Before Kilgore gave Edward a tutorial on finger tapping, it's quite likely that Edward knew that a few forward-thinking guitarists occasionally used their pick hands in this fashion. Edward, a player who could hear a song once and then play right along, surely *heard*, for example, when Billy Gibbons offered up a quick tap during his solo on ZZ Top's 1973 barnburner "Beer Drinkers & Hell Raisers" (a song Van Halen covered frequently in the early days).

But while Gibbons's technique involved adding nothing more than a single-pinged note to his solo, Mandel's approach saw him construct entire lead lines around the use of tapping. It was embedded deeply in his compositions, rather than a bit of guitar flash used to spice up a solo, and it opened up Edward's eyes. Kilgore says, "That's where, believe it or not, Edward picked up on the second hand style. I said check this out [and tapped], and he went, *Wow*. He started doing it. I had a lot of ideas that ended up in Edward's hands. He had a few that ended up in mine for sure."

Even though Kilgore's demonstration made an impression, there are only a few observers who can recall Edward using his right hand on the neck onstage before 1977. Guitarist Dennis Catron, who regularly caught Van Halen live during these years, says he never saw Edward use his full-blown two-handed technique "until about the time they got signed [in 1977]" but is adamant that onstage he "did little ones, like one note," à la Gibbons in "Beer Drinkers," as far back as 1975. Guitarist Donny Simmons recalls he heard Edward "experiment" with tapping during a soundcheck at the Golden West Ballroom in the summer of 1975: "I'll never forget. We'd done our set and we were headed back to the bar to get a beer. I turned around, and I was all like, 'What in the fuck is he doing?' Think about hearing that for the first time after you're used to hearing Bad Company. What's all this [*imitates tapping noise*]? I was all, 'What was *that?*'"

Edward's occasional single finger taps aside, there's no evidence that between 1975 and 1976, Edward employed the flowing two-handed hammer-on and pull-off style that would become his musical signature after the release of *Van Halen*. During those years, Edward apparently toyed with what he'd learned from Kilgore, hitting a few pick-hand notes here and there while onstage or in practice, but wouldn't unleash his game-changing take on the technique until the early summer of 1977, just months before Van Halen would enter the studio to record their debut.

= =

While Edward expanded his guitar horizons, Van Halen regrouped and re-auditioned, and within two weeks, Simons had hired them. He observes that he booked Van Halen because they drew people to the club. The Rock Corporation's operation was ultimately "driven by the crowds. If you got the crowd in you got booked." As the weeks passed, Van Halen began to build its Valley fan base.

One of those early fans was a wild eighteen-year-old brunette named Valerie Evans Noel. During the summer of 1975, Evans remembers seeing Van Halen on many a Saturday night at the Rock. She was immediately taken by Edward's playing. "Look, anyone can do the 'Canned Heat Boogie,'" she points out, "but there was no intensity like it when Eddie played. It was surreal, and he was so young." At the same time, she emphasizes that Roth played a big part in Van Halen's appeal. "Back in the day," she says, "there was no one really like David. His voice was amazing and he had a great body. He would wear a bandanna, no shirt, hip huggers, and had a Black Oak Arkansas vibe." His stage presence and look, accordingly, drew many a female closer to the stage. "His following with women was amazing," Noel recalls.

In between sets, Noel would walk backstage to shoot the shit. She remembers, "The dressing room was this little alcove with a curtain. It had a bench with a cushion. Van Halen would be drinking and smoking." Because the club didn't pay very well, Noel says the foursome took advantage of the club's free drink policy for working musicians: "I remember that Van Halen would always be drinking to make their money" as they "got their buzz on before the next set."

At the Rock, getting your buzz on typically involved pills, which were popular in the 1970s. Unlike trendy Sunset Strip nightclubs, where cocaine was king, the Rock was ruled by pharmaceuticals. "Coke was too expensive" for the Rock's patrons, Evans observes. "You'd split an eight-ball and it cost a fortune and you'd have a buzz for an hour." Pills, in contrast, "were *huge*. We would look on the floor and just pick up pills that people had dropped. The Rock had a big downer crowd. 'Ludes, Tuinals, and Seconals were all the rage." In fact, she remembers one night when she played rock-paper-scissors with Edward for a Tuinal.

Also in the club on Saturday nights was a beautiful teenager named Iris Berry. Before she became a fixture on the Los Angeles punk scene, Berry was a self-described "Valley girl with a good fake ID." She remembers going to see Van Halen at the Rock, where she took in the group's sets of hard rock covers. She says the band "drew well," attracting a rough crowd composed of young rockers and bikers. Berry declares that Van Halen packed the club largely because of their "great frontman," who knew exactly how to grab the attention of onlookers. In Berry's case, this would involve a seductive Roth whispering in her ear between sets.

As the weeks went by, the four musicians began performing some of their own songs at the Rock. In the middle of the evening, they'd follow up Stray Dog's rumbling "Chevrolet" with their bluesy "Take Your Whiskey Home." During the last set of the night, Trower's propulsive "The Fool and Me" would lead into the catchy original "She's the Woman." "Once we knew the people" were "becoming big fans of the band," Anthony explained, "we [would] start popping off some of our own stuff."[311] Oftentimes, patrons had no idea that these tunes were Van Halen compositions. Tom Broderick observes that they "slipped originals in and it was like nobody in the audience knew."

= =

While Van Halen had found its niche at the Rock, Edward continued to struggle with a persistent problem: his amplifier volume level. Ever since Mammoth's ill-fated 1973 performance at the Posh nightclub, which had ended with the owner cutting the band's power, he had tried to find ways to get his distinctive guitar sound (the tonal character produced by a guitar player's hands, instrument, effects, and amplifiers) from his favorite Marshall Super Lead amp without deafening club patrons.

The most obvious solution — to use a less powerful amp — wasn't something that Edward liked to do. Haasis found this out in the summer of 1975. He arrived at the Rock for the first set of the night and was surprised to see that while Edward had his typical setup of two Marshall speaker cabinets, his amplifier was turned around on top of his cabinets, so the guts of the amp were visible rather than its nameplate and knobs. Regardless, Haasis says,

"I knew it was a Sound City Fifty Plus, a little head." After Van Halen moved through a brisk opening set, Haasis approached him.

"Hey Eddie, what are you playing through tonight?"

Edward shook his head and frowned. "Eh, it's a Sound City."

Haasis paused as Edward took a drag off his cigarette. "Why do you have it turned around?'

"I don't want anyone to see it. I'm embarrassed."

"Where's your Marshall?"

"It's in the shop," he said with a disgusted look on his face.

"Well the Sound City sounds great."

Edward shook his head again and muttered, "Whatever."

Haasis says that Edward just "didn't want to hear" that this lesser amp sounded good. Haasis remembers that in fact, "It sounded great, because if he played through a home stereo he'd sound the same. It's in his hands, like any guitar player."

Edward disagreed. He believed that his sound largely depended on that one amplifier, and there was no good substitute for it. So he tried different ways to cut the amp's volume while still keeping it on ten. "I did everything," Edward told Steven Rosen, "from keeping the plastic cover on it to facing it against the walls to putting Styrofoam padding in front of the speakers."[312] None of these solutions worked. "I need[ed] an amp I could play in clubs," Edward explained to *Esquire*. "We wouldn't get hired, I would play so loud, you know, I'm going, what can I do? What can I do?"

By the summer of 1975, Edward had found a solution. Looking to supplement his primary Marshall, he bought a second Marshall amp. But when he got it home, plugged in his guitar, and turned it on, he heard nothing. "I'm going," he recounted to *Esquire*, "fucking thing doesn't work. I got ripped off." With the amp still on, he walked away in a huff. When he returned after about an hour and played through it again, he found that "there's sound coming out, but it's really quiet." Edward then realized that the amp wasn't a standard 110-volt Marshall; instead it was a 220-volt model designed for use in Europe and not the United States. He thought, *Hey, wait a minute. It sounds exactly like it's supposed to all the way up, but it's really quiet.*

Ever the tinkerer, Edward had an idea. He grabbed a screwdriver and removed a light dimmer from the wall. He wired his main amp into the house's electrical system, in the hopes that he could drop the amp's voltage with the dimmer. Instead, the house went dark as he blew a fuse.

Still thinking his idea could work, he headed over to Dow Radio, a Pasadena electronics supply store. He walked in and asked, "Do you guys have any kind of super duper light dimmer?" The clerk replied, "Yeah, it's [a] Variac variable transformer." When the man brought one to him, Edward looked at the cube-like metal box. He recalled, "[on the] dial you could crank it up to 140 volts or down to zero. So I figured, if it's on 220 and it's that quiet, if I take the voltage and lower it, I wonder how low I can go and it still work?"

Edward's idea worked like a charm. He remembered, "It enabled me to turn my amp all the way up, save the tubes, save the wear and tear on the tubes, and play at clubs at half the volume. So, my Variac, my variable transformer, was my volume knob. Too loud [makes knob turning sound], I'd lower it down to 50." While today attenuating a tube amp by starving it for voltage is a well-known way to deal with intolerable volume levels, at that time Edward had hit upon something both unique and useful. He resolved to keep this discovery to himself. [313]

= =

One late summer afternoon, Edward's old friend and fellow guitarist Jim Steinwedell drove to the Rock to say goodbye to Edward before going off to college. Steinwedell had first met him back in 1972, when he had loaned him his Marshall head after Edward's had blown right in the middle of a Mammoth backyard party in La Cañada.

Walking into the darkened club with one of his band's roadies, Steinwedell was struck by the number of huge, menacing bikers sitting at the bar double-fisting drinks. "My roadie and I were by far the smallest guys in the place," he says. "I'm six-foot-two and was 235, and John's six-foot-four and was 270." Told that Van Halen was in the "dressing room," the two hulking men found them at the rear of the club, sitting behind "an accordion plastic room divider that you would pull away from the wall to create a space to dress in semi-privacy."

After saying hello, the pair hung around during soundcheck. As Van Halen played, Steinwedell was taken aback by both the "killer" sound flowing from Edward's setup and the fact that his Marshall amplifier sounded thick and full even though its volume was relatively low. This reduced volume particularly perplexed him, because decibel levels were a "perennial problem" for the era's working guitarists who used powerful tube amplifiers.[314]

Once the band took a break, he asked his friend what he had done to get such an amazing tone at a reduced volume.

"Oh it's this new DiMarzio pickup," Edward said evasively.

"Bullshit," Jim retorted. "What is it?"

"Ah, um, it's these old tubes in my amplifier."

Growing tired of his friend's dissembling, Steinwedell gently but firmly pressed his smaller friend against the wall and asked again, "No, really. How'd you get that sound at that volume?" Finally, Edward admitted — after swearing his friend to secrecy — that he'd started using the Variac. As he showed it to him, they both agreed that along with volume reduction came another unexpected benefit: it made his tone richer and warmer. In later years, Edward credited this breakthrough for helping him attain the signature tone — his self-described "brown sound" — that would achieve legendary status among guitar players after the 1978 release of *Van Halen*.[315]

= =

A few months earlier and fifty miles away from Van Nuys, guitarist Donny Simmons and his band Stormer had ended their second set of the night at Walter Mitty's. As Simmons set down his Les Paul, he saw the club's owner, Larry Ward, headed to the stage with two familiar faces in tow: David Roth and Edward Van Halen. Ward strolled to the microphone and announced, "Hey everyone! I want to introduce you all to a dynamite new band called Van Halen! These guys will be playing here very soon, so watch for them."

Simmons, who liked Edward and Dave but also knew that Van Halen was a great live act, felt deflated as he considered this new competition for bookings at the club. A smiling Edward, oblivious to his friend's mixed feelings, turned to Simmons and earnestly said, "That was a nice blues, dude! I guess we'll be playing together off and on." Simmons thought, *Oh, just fuckin' great.*

When the members of Van Halen first showed up at Walter Mitty's, they barely blinked an eye at their surroundings, considering some of the other less-than-savory places they had already played. Mitty's stood in a tough industrial neighborhood on the east side of Pomona. In his autobiography, Roth writes that the small club "was out in the middle of nowhere."[316] Across the street, military contractor General Dynamics operated a huge manufacturing plant, its property line surrounded by a formidable chain-link and barbed-wire fence.[317] The rest of the street included frontage for two trailer parks, a liquor store, a couple of bars and, incongruously, an adult bookstore and an evangelical church, the Pomona Revival Center.[318] This was hardly a slice of California suburban paradise.

When the club was open for business, Mitty's customers ran

Walter Mitty's Rock'n Grill Emporium, Pomona, California, as it looked in 1976. LESLIE WARD-SPEERS

roughshod over the seedy neighborhood. Leslie Ward-Speers, Larry's daughter, remembers that most patrons parked in "a big dirt field at the end of the building. When it rained it was just nasty and muddy." They also parked on both sides of the street and when bands played, "people would be waiting for spaces and fighting, and cars would be moving in and out. It would just be total chaos." Bikers, who were the club's best customers, lined their choppers up along the sidewalk. "The bikers parked rows and rows of motorcycles," Ward-Speers says. "You wouldn't believe how many — all the way down the front of the building."

The interior of the club also lacked amenities. Speers says succinctly, "It was a well-used place." After passing through the entrance, customers came to the bar area. "The bar was really long and people had carved things in it," she recalls. Pool tables filled part of that space, and tables were arranged around the walls. A partition bisected the club and large cutouts in it allowed those sitting at the bar to see the dance floor and the bands. Leiren described the stage, which was against the back wall of the club, as "a postage stamp . . . with like two feet in front of the drum kit, which was pushed up against the wall. Then there was probably four feet or six feet on each side of the drum kit."[319] Rounding all of this out, Ward-Speers recalls, was a perpetually sticky floor along with "that stale beer and cigarette smell. It was just nasty."

After Van Halen got the gig, their San Gabriel Valley fans came to see them in Pomona. Few of them, however, had ever been to this kind of neighborhood. Charlie Gwyn, a then-twenty-one-year-old from Duarte, recollects that an older friend took him to Mitty's to see Van Halen. "I was scared at the time," to enter the club's dark interior, "because the crowd looked older and tougher than I had seen at local parties."[320] Cary Irwin, a La Puente product, confirms that Gwyn's fears were not unfounded. "Walter Mitty's became this real hip place for all these bands to play at," he explains. But "there were quite frequently severe fights. I remember one night I went there some guy got thrown through a plate-glass window and cut his neck really bad. It turned into a big deal."

Van Halen would gain firsthand knowledge of Mitty's violent clientele. In the midst of their fifth set one night, they witnessed a murder on the club's dance floor after members of two rival motorcycle gangs got into a deadly fight. "One time late in the evening," Edward remembered, "we just saw a guy's intestines hanging out of his gut." As the band watched in horror, the stricken man reeled away from his knife-wielding attacker and then "fell to the ground; there was blood everywhere."[321] As Roth recounted in his autobiography, the club's lights suddenly came on and Van Halen quickly left the stage. "But the next night," he explains, rumors raged that certain aggrieved bikers were "coming back to exact revenge." Van Halen still performed, but just to be safe, they "pulled the amplifiers a few more feet away from the walls than usual, in case we had to jump behind the amps if there was a shoot-out."[322]

Despite these dangers, people turned out in large numbers to catch the band's shows. Joe Carducci, a La Puente guitar player whose band played Mitty's, witnessed this in the early summer of 1975. "I remember standing way in the back and the place was packed," he says. Taking one look at Roth, a friend of Carducci's yelled in his ear, "Who's this guy trying to be, Jim Dandy?" Carducci replied, "Man, if they just had a guy who could sing!" He explains, "I meant that in the sense of somebody who had a really, really good rock and roll voice. That was what was in my head. Man, then these guys would be unbelievable!"

Here Carducci hits upon two themes that would resurface once the band hit Hollywood's Starwood nightclub in May 1976. First, Roth, who'd abandoned his glitter rock image, now offered up skintight leather pants and a bare torso while performing. When paired with his swaggering stage presence and raspy voice, he reminded observers of Jim "Dandy" Mangrum of Black Oak Arkansas, a southern rock group that had fallen out of fashion over the last couple of years. Second, Roth's voice was, at best, a work in progress and was, in the opinion of many observers, the only thing that detracted from Van Halen's greatness.

Regardless of Roth's shortcomings, Van Halen had found their Pomona outpost from which to build an east L.A. fan base. This, of course, fit perfectly with the band's overarching objectives. Roth told *BAM* in 1977, "Like most new bands that just start out, our short-range goal was to get exposure and soak up experience by playing in front of anyone who would listen." [323] Over time, the band would "build our audience and people will talk and go, 'Oh hey, you've really got to see this band tomorrow night.'"[324]

And as much of a grind as performing at a dive bar like Mitty's could be, the four men found ways to embrace the experience as the crowds grew. "We went out and played and played and played," Alex told *Modern Drummer*. "Sure we didn't have any money and sure this broke down and sure there were lousy people we had to work with, such as pseudo managers and club owners. But the audiences were always there and it was a great time. Some people call it paying your dues, but we just called it having fun. We had a good time. I wouldn't have wanted it any different."[325] Roth likewise explained to the *Los Angeles Times*, "We were happy playing all the clubs. We were working towards something. We were hungry, we were accomplishing things."[326]

In later years, this positive mindset translated into nostalgia. Alex remarked, "To me [Mitty's] was the epitome of a rock and roll club. And every night we played there I had this vision that we were playing some sort of large arena."[327] The club, Anthony added, "held three hundred people, and we'd have seven hundred, a thousand people inside. It was your ultimate sweaty small stage." Van Halen's lineup "used to get a great sound in that place. When we were grooving, the whole club would be happening."[328] On those nights, Van Halen mixed their originals and covers together with abandon, as patrons danced and cheered.

This infectious energy, when coupled with the band's singular appeal, led to jam-packed houses. In fact, the Van Halen phenomenon at Mitty's was so remarkable that owner Larry Ward awoke one Saturday morning and said to his sixteen-year-old daughter, Leslie, "You've got to come down and listen to this group. You'll really like them." When she showed up in the early evening, she saw that "people were lining up down the street and down around the building to get inside." After her father snuck his underage daughter inside, he told her, "Keep your head down and don't let anyone see you too much." She followed his instructions by lingering in a corner, where she watched the club come to life. Van Halen, she says, "would just pack my dad's bar. It was all you could do just to get in the door. It would be standing-room only. Once you got inside all you could do was stand up and just look. There was no sitting down in that place that night." After Van Halen began blasting through some Bad Company and Led Zeppelin, she "was just mesmerized.

To hear this sound that was so different from everybody else and to hear it live like that — they were so good."

In between sets, Ward-Speers stepped outside to smoke a cigarette. Staying close to her father's towering bouncer "Bear," she drank in her surroundings, taking note of "all these bikes parked up and down the sidewalk. These guys would come out and they'd have chains coming out of their pockets. Big wide leather straps around their wrists, wearing vests and jeans and big thick leather boots, long hair, and long beards. They were pretty rough. They were intimidating."

Meanwhile, Ward and Bear worried that the local authorities would be paying the club a visit that night. "The police and fire department used to come a lot for being overcapacity and the noise," she explains. "When David and Eddie's band was there, it was a given. You almost expected them to show up."

Inside the club, Roth earned his money. He'd call for the crowd's attention, then step off the stage, microphone in hand, and barge into the tiny ladies room. He'd speak to the outraged women crowded inside, asking them, tongue-in-cheek, to show him their IDs in order to confirm that they were of age, as bikers leered through the doorway and cheered. As the laughs reverberated, Roth would return to the stage and continue the set, playing, as he wrote in his autobiography, "everything from old Rod Stewart to [the] Ohio Players."[329] To paraphrase Roth, Van Halen might not have been big in Hollywood, but by 1975, his band was getting big in Pomona.

= =

Several months later in Van Nuys, Jeff Simons felt sick as he looked over the Rock's books for the spring of 1976. His club's finances were dire. Between bartenders who robbed him blind and the Department of Alcoholic Beverage Control's fines for underage drinking, the Rock wasn't making much money. To make matters worse, he was *losing* money on Thursday nights, regardless of which band was onstage.

A few days later, Simons and a couple of friends sat down and brainstormed ways to bring more cash into the Rock's till. After tossing ideas around, they resolved to introduce a promotion for Thursdays since the bar had done better after Simons had put promotions in place for Tuesday ("Girls' Night") and Wednesday ("Suds Night"). Eventually one of them suggested a "beauty pageant" of sorts — albeit updated for the sexually frank 1970s — that he'd seen successfully staged elsewhere: a wet T-shirt contest.

Simons now faced a decision. This type of event would likely pack his club, but it would also test the tolerance of the Van Nuys city officials who already kept a close eye on his establishment. Would they put up with girls getting nearly topless onstage? The impulsive Simons thought, *Fuck it. The bikers will dig it. Let's do it.*

That first Thursday night, Simons's lack of planning was evident. The club owner just stepped onstage between sets, threw down a piece of Astroturf to catch some of the water, and ran the contest. Renee Cummings, a Rock regular, remembers, "Jeff winged it from day one. He just said, 'Let's get these girls up onstage and let's do it. We'll make up the rules as we go.' It wasn't organized; nothing was ever organized at the Rock. It was Jeff's fly-by-night idea, and it worked." Despite its haphazard nature, the contest had attracted the attention of law enforcement, as undercover officers were in house that night.

The next day, Simons considered ways to improve to the contest. For the following week, he'd make it the evening's centerpiece, complete with signup sheets and a wading pool. He'd spread word of the event with flyers and, in an age when truckers and many other drivers communicated via Citizens' Band radios (CBs), with announcements over the airwaves. He'd offer a more substantial cash prize to encourage more girls to participate. He'd also have one of his best bands, Van Halen, onstage. Simons felt energized as he set these plans in motion.

= =

The next Thursday afternoon, a buzz was in the air about the contest. More cars and motorcycles cruised past the Rock than usual. The club was more crowded than normal, and the office phone was ringing incessantly. High school kids even hung around outside, hoping to see the big show. Fred Whittlesey and his friends in Reseda had "learned there was this thing called 'wet T-shirt night' at the Rock Corporation. For boys in their late teens, this sounded like a really good idea. I'm sure we heard, 'Hey guys, there's wet T-shirt night and they don't check IDs!' That's all we needed to know."

By the time darkness fell on this June night, the neighborhood around the Rock was swarming with people. Evans says, "The line was literally all the way from the club up to Van Nuys Boulevard, which was a quarter of a mile away."

Inside the club, Noel's friend Renee Cummings could barely believe the size of the crowd. She explains, "There were so many people that at times you could not walk from the front door to the bathroom. The regulars were there, but then you had people who came in from all over." This included Edward's old friend, Dana Anderson, and teenagers like Whittlesey.

Finally, around midnight, it was time for the main event. The Rock was jammed and people stood three-deep around the bar trying to order drinks before the contest began. Three hours earlier, Roth had announced, "Remember, it's two-for-one night next Thursday."[330] He then said, his arm outstretched, "Ladies, you can sign up at this side of the bar for the *wet T-shirt contest!*" Noel recollects, "Sometimes twenty-five girls would sign up, sometimes less." Girls wrote their names on the list, including some who Simons describes as "ringers" — particularly well-endowed ladies from places like Tujunga or Chatsworth whom bikers had recruited for the contest.

After Roth announced that the contest was underway, a buzzed Simons bounded onto the stage with the contestants, including Cummings and Noel, and a deafening cheer arose from the crowd. In 1981, Roth told *Oui* what happened next: "It was a great scene. I'd be the MC, with the band behind me. I'd interview the contestants.

"'And what do you do for a living?'

"'Oh, I'm a donut waitress from Canoga Park.'

"I'd make a dumb joke, the place would crack up, and she'd jump into a kiddie pool and get wet.

"'And honey, what song would you like to hear?'

"'Oh, I'd just loooooove [Edgar Winter's] "Free Ride."'

"'Al, it seems this lady would like to take a free ride.'

"The audience," Roth recounted, "went into hysterics."

With that, "Jeff took pitchers of ice water and poured it down what we were wearing, which was a string tank, like a belly shirt. Then you would dance," Noel says.

As each girl stood in the pool, Van Halen, Roth recollected, would "play." Then "she does her twitch and bump, and the rest of the girls bounce in."[331] Cummings explains, "We were wasted! There was nothing better to do in those days than get wasted. You had to let your hair down! So we're getting our tits wet? Big fucking deal!" She adds that, yes, the competition got so heated that some of the girls started "stripping down to nothing." The only one not smiling in the midst of all of this was Alex. Noel recollects that he became incensed because his drums, along with the girls, had been drenched.

Somewhere across the bar was Anderson. "At the Rock Corporation," he says with a laugh, "we were in Dave's world. It was crazy! It was like Dave was an MC for a game show. He was totally in his element with the wet T-shirt contest. The guy who ran the club would pour a pitcher over the chicks and they were just loving it! It was free love back then. It was packed. You couldn't get in the place."

Onstage, the show continued. Roth remembered that on some nights, "at the end, the judges [were] too fucked up to make any decision so we [had to] run all the contestants through again, five, six hundred people standing on top of each other, drunk, and screaming."[332] On other nights, however, Simons decided the contest through applause.

On this particular night, just as Simons began calling for an audience vote, a commotion broke out at the back of the club. Cops from the Van Nuys Division of the Los Angeles Police Department had arrived. Noel says they "were in the back. There was a scuffle, and then they worked their way through the packed crowd to the stage." At the same time, Simons recalls, a backup call had also gone out to units from the North Hollywood Division, which came in full force to help end the contest, arrest the participants, and clear out the club. It would take, in fact, both divisions to shut down the Rock that night.[333]

But with nearly a thousand people in the Rock, all of this happened in slow motion. Simons observes, "It actually took time for the police to work their way through the crowd to stop it." After the officers fought their way through the throngs of belligerent, drunken patrons, they got onto the stage and handcuffed Simons and the girls who they believed had bared their breasts. Noel says, "Girls were pulled offstage at one point, which really put a damper on the evening. The police were sending a message: *We're a force to be reckoned with.*"

Even as the police dragged away Simons and the others, the members of Van Halen were all smiles. The police ignored the band, especially after Roth told the cops that Van Halen had nothing to do with the contest. Even so, the notoriety that came from the contests and the police raid was invaluable. Like the big backyard busts of prior years, the events at the Rock helped to cement Van Halen's reputation as Los Angeles's best party band.

= =

In 1982, Roth shared an anecdote with the *Los Angeles Times* that highlights the band members' belief, even when they were playing "the pits," that they would one day reach the height of rock and roll success: "I remember back to the days standing in the parking lot with Alex, drinking beers behind the building after a gig, and saying, 'Al, someday, man, we're gonna make it. Someday, you and me, we're gonna be drinking beer in the *Forum* parking lot.'"[334]

That same year, David Lee Roth sat for an interview with MTV's Martha Quinn. She asked Roth, "How do you map out a show that you're going to do?" His answer reflects the lessons he learned at the Rock and elsewhere and underscores the importance of these years for Van Halen's later success. Roth replied, "It's a constant movement. Who needs dead space? A lot of people have nothing to say in between songs . . . I love talking. I love telling jokes. For me this is just one big wet T-shirt contest."[335] Roth's analysis here is absolutely correct. Starting in 1978, Van Halen took the swagger they'd learned playing dive bars and hosting wet T-shirt contests in Los Angeles and unleashed it on an unsuspecting American public. Rock and roll — and America — would never be the same.

THE GOLDEN WEST

His hair damp with sweat and a post-show cigarette between his fingers, Edward made his way through the throngs of fans at the Golden West Ballroom on May 9, 1976. The numerous friends, acquaintances, and strangers he passed reached out to congratulate him for his band's gutsy and powerful performance. Van Halen, despite the immense pressure of opening for the well-respected English rock band UFO, had gambled by choosing this night to play its first-ever set of all original material. They had done so knowing that many of Hollywood's tastemakers and stars would be there, all eager to see UFO and its young guitar superstar Michael Schenker. While omitting their usual crowd-pleasing cover songs had been a high-risk, high-reward move, the electric atmosphere inside this Norwalk concert venue told the tale. Van Halen had delivered.

After saying thanks to one last well-wisher, Edward entered the men's room. He set down his beer to take a piss when a familiar figure approached. Edward didn't know his name, but he knew he was a dealer who had supplied him with some cocaine the previous weekend at the Golden West. Moving close to Edward, he bellowed, "Yeah! You guys were *bad!*" Edward, ever modest, said, "Thanks, man," and took a drag off his cigarette. Leaning in, the dealer then motioned to a stall and whispered, "Do you want a toot?" Edward, ready to start his post-show celebration, nodded.

Edward closed the stall door as the dealer produced his vial. He asked, "How much can I take?" The dealer, his face flushed and his pupils as big as saucers, said, "Hey, take as much as you want." Edward didn't hesitate. He shoveled two big bumps into each nostril, said thanks, and headed out of the bathroom.

Within minutes something was terribly wrong with him. Rudy Leiren explained to Steven Rosen: "By the time he got back up to the stage to start loading the equipment he just started coming onto it. He started going into convulsions — kind of his body started freaking out and he started doing this thing like he was playing air guitar, like freaking out." As his bandmates and crew huddled around him, Edward's face was drawn taut, like a mask. His jaw was locked and his eyes fixed. Panicking, Alex yelled in his ear and shook him, and yet his younger brother remained rigid and unresponsive. Edward Van Halen was dying.[336]

= =

As 1975 came to an end, the four members of Van Halen would have been hard pressed to conclude that they'd made any real progress towards getting a recording contract. Musical talent aside, Van Halen's brand of heavy metal was woefully out of step with the "L.A. Sound," the country-tinged soft rock that dominated the city's — and the nation's — pop music culture. Los Angeles–based recording artists like Neil Young, Joni Mitchell, Graham Nash, and Jackson Browne made the major labels millions of dollars as their records flew off the shelves and their songs jammed the nation's airwaves. As a result, the industry's A&R reps scrambled to sign the next Little Feat, not the next Led Zep. Whether young rock musicians like the members of Van Halen knew it or not, the major labels had concluded that heavy metal was a relic.[337]

This grim assessment of metal's future meant that Van Halen would be frozen out of high-profile rock venues like Hollywood's legendary Starwood Club. Looking back at this period in the band's history, Roth remembered that Van Halen found it "impossible to get bookings in Hollywood. The Whisky was closed and you needed connections to play [the] Starwood."[338]

Instead, the group, like the city's other innumerable unsigned heavy rock acts, slogged it out week after week by playing every place from low-rent bars to improvised concert halls. While the band regularly packed the sizable Pasadena Civic Exhibition Hall, the quartet still played backyard parties, and even performed at aging western swing-dance ballrooms, like the Golden West, which, in order to keep the lights on, now hosted rock concerts.

Then there was the band's longstanding gig at Gazzarri's. Despite the steady work, the fact that Van Halen was now the *de facto* house band at this venerable Hollywood venue actually hurt the band's chances for advancement. Because the club's management demanded that its acts perform almost all cover songs, Van Halen couldn't showcase the original compositions that might interest record executives. As Runaways bass player Jackie Fox explains, because of this policy "serious bands did not play Gazzarri's. If Van Halen was doing a lot of shows at Gazzarri's, it would have tainted industry opinion about them." In other words, none of the record industry's major players ever considered signing a "Gazzarri's band." Music critic Ken Tucker, who covered the scene for the *Los Angeles Herald Examiner*, dismissed the venue as "a real dump, where bad heavy metal and hard rock bands tried to make a start. It wasn't seen as a particularly desirable showcase, within the music industry at least."[339]

Herein lay the root of Van Halen's dilemma. Gazzarri's paid the bills — albeit barely — but just paying the bills meant going nowhere fast. "It's easy to get in a rut," bassist Michael Anthony explained to the *Los Angeles Times* in late 1977, because "you can go to a place like [legendary L.A. Top 40 club] Big Daddy's and make $1500 a week playing other people's hits." Yet as Anthony pointed out, "You can do that the rest of your life" and never get a record contract.[340] In December 1975, Van Halen seemed destined to be an also-ran on the L.A. rock scene, thanks to the quartet's identity as a copy band. But by May 1976, Van Halen stood poised to reinvent themselves as an original act that would stand or fall based on the strength of their own songs.

= =

"Before I saw him play, I'd heard of him, like everybody did. You'd hear about a guy locally," says Tracy "G." Grijalva. In 1975, Tracy G. was an introverted sixteen-year-old from the L.A. suburb of La Puente. He remembers that Van Halen was playing backyards, little halls, and parties around the San Gabriel Valley, and "so you were hearing about him. *Oh you've got to check out this band Van Halen. You've got to check out this guitar player.*"

Tracy, who'd one day serve as metal legend Ronnie James Dio's guitarist, was skeptical. He already had his local idol, Donny Simmons, a Jimmy Page lookalike who strapped on a low-slung Les Paul and played searing, bluesy solos for the hard rock cover band Stormer. For Tracy and his guitar-playing friends, the talented Simmons was the guitar god of La Puente, Pomona, and West Covina. There was nobody better in that part of L.A. Tracy explains, "When you're sixteen, you kind of think you've seen everything, almost, and you haven't seen shit, but you don't know that yet. So how fucking good can Van Halen be, man?"

On the last Sunday of the year, Tracy got a chance to find out. Van Halen was headlining the Golden West, with Stormer as one of its two opening acts. On the afternoon of the show, Tracy and his friends caught a ride to Norwalk with the venue's lighting operator.

After they arrived, Tracy and his friends entered the club. "I walked into this place," Tracy says, and "it seemed like the Forum to me, because I hadn't been anywhere. It was a little hall and bands were soundchecking." Tracy recalls his excitement as a young musician staring at a real stage: "You're like *whoa*! There's nothing but Marshall heads, equipment, and that's it. I was just hypnotized."

While Tracy and his friends watched, the groups prepared for the show. After a few minutes one of the musicians, wearing a grey mechanic's coverall, walked towards them from the stage. "My friend says, 'This is Van Halen's guitar player. This is Ed Van Halen.' I'm like, 'Hey.' I was really fucking shy so I was afraid to say hi or anything," Tracy remembers. "He was all like, 'Hey nice to meet you, man.' So he sat down, right next to me." Tracy mustered up his courage and peppered him with questions about his gear and his band's stage setup. After a few more minutes of shooting the shit, Edward hopped up and said, "Okay dude, nice meeting you. I've gotta soundcheck."

He walked back to the stage and strapped on his wood-grained Ibanez Destroyer. He looked at Alex as he counted in before Van Halen launched into the galloping "Sweet F.A." by British glam rockers the Sweet. Although the four musicians were just warming up, Tracy thought, *Wow. They sound pretty good.* Even more striking was Edward's stage presence. "His whole look, and his whole way he stood and the way he played? Fucking forget it. I'd never seen nothing that came off like *This guy's God on guitar.*"

As showtime approached, the hall filled. Tracy and his friends stood in front of the stage and before long, the house lights dimmed. Tracy says, "The first band, Maelstrom, plays, and

Van Halen gets down to business at Lanterman Auditorium in
La Cañada, California, November 22, 1975. MARY GARSON/HOT SHOTZ

they're great." As a young guitarist experiencing his first concert,
he kept thinking, *How's Van Halen gonna be better than that? I've
never even seen a band that good.*

"Stormer comes on next, and those are my guys," Tracy
remembers. "There's my guy, Donny Simmons, up there. He's the
rock star, ripping with the Les Paul." Tracy watched as Stormer
ran through a set punctuated with Foghat and Bad Company
covers. "They played and they're better than Maelstrom. I'm
thinking, *How can Van Halen be better than this?*"

Tracy, like the rest of the crowd, waited for Van Halen. Then
suddenly the lights dimmed and from behind the purple velvet curtain, Roth, like a sideshow barker, yelled, "Ladies and gentlemen!
Van Halen!" The curtain parted and the Pasadena quartet appeared.

Tracy recalls, "I see these four guys, but they don't look like the
guys I saw setting up the equipment because they're all done up
and they have their rock shit on. They open up with a song called

Van Halen, standing tall in their platform shoes, rock out in La Cañada, California, November 22, 1975. MARY GARSON / HOT SHOTZ

'Man on the Silver Mountain' by Rainbow. I almost passed out, dude. It was like being with the perfect woman. I don't know how else to put it. Because they didn't just have a guitar player like you'd never seen. It's the whole fucking band. You've got God on the lead vocals. He looked perfect, and all the women wanted him. It didn't really matter how he was singing. Who cares? He looked great. He was great with the people, and they've got the drummer from hell and a bass player who's right there." Tracy stood motionless as Van Halen finished its opener with a flourish.

He then turned his full attention to Edward. "The guitar player was playing an Ibanez Destroyer," he recollects. "It hung on him perfectly. He held it perfectly. He played it perfectly. He had his own sound and fire. I went, *Holy fuck*." As a budding player, Tracy struggled to comprehend what he was seeing and hearing. He explains, "He did stretches with his really long piano fingers," unleashing "pure shredding picking and bluesy, soulful harmonics." Tracy, who today is a world-class rock guitarist, explains, "Everything that I didn't know about yet, it was all being crammed in my face when I was sixteen. I was like, *What?*"

Van Halen moved through its set, doing the future-classic "Runnin' with the Devil" and a few other originals, which Tracy remembers as "fucking better than the covers." He says, "I'd never seen a unit work like that and sound like that."

As the show built to a climax, Edward played his unaccompanied solo, which would be entitled "Eruption" on *Van Halen*. Simmons watched from the side of the stage and recalls, "'Eruption' was in the middle of 'House of Pain.' I said to myself, *Whoa! How the fuck did you come up with this shit?* He didn't brag to anyone. He didn't go, 'Hey man, check it out! I learned all these licks.' He just pulled them out. He didn't talk about it." After an encore, the band took a bow, waved, and exited.

Tracy, with audience members around him buzzing as they headed for home, stood in stunned silence. Then Tracy's buddy roused him out of his stupor, reminding him that they needed to find the lighting man so they wouldn't miss their ride. Tracy followed his friends up to the stage and walked, tentatively, behind the curtain.

"So the concert's over and I'm standing there behind the curtain like a little scared kid waiting for the lighting man," Tracy explains. "I'm looking at Eddie. He's sitting on the side of the stage dangling his legs, and he's shaking his head, smoking a cigarette, almost like, *Eh, that was a fucked night. That sucked. I didn't do good.* He wasn't happy, and I could hear him talking to a couple of people, saying, 'Eh, the sound was shitty.'" Tracy, awestruck, couldn't even bring himself to approach Edward. "I was too young and too shy. He blew me away so bad. I just stood there."

Walking past Tracy came his guitar idol, Donny Simmons. Without warning, Simmons kneeled down on the stage near Edward and lowered his torso and arms, as if to say, you're the king now. "He started bowing down to this guy Eddie. I'm just standing in the corner, just looking at my hero just completely give it up to some other dude. Then his words were, 'You're the fucking greatest thing on two legs.' I'll never forget it."

= =

In March, Golden West Ballroom promoter Dan Teckenoff called Roth. He offered the quartet, who now regularly played the venue, an April date for a show he'd bill as "The Spring Jam," which would also feature Maelstrom and Eulogy, a hot, young band from Orange County.[341] Roth conferred with Alex, and the band signed the contract.

On the afternoon of April 11, Eulogy's seventeen-year-old guitarist, Rusty Anderson, showed up at the Golden West for his band's first performance at the nightspot. Anderson realized that he was the first of his bandmates to arrive, so the La Habra native settled in to watch Van Halen, a band he had never seen before, soundcheck. Anderson, who plays guitar for Sir Paul McCartney, remembers, "Just watching them I was going, *Wow*. They were very understated in a certain way because their whole presence is pretty intense."

After Van Halen finished, Eulogy played a couple of songs and then left the stage. The group's bass player, Dirk Van Tatenhove, then headed to the men's room. Soon after he got into the bathroom, the door flew open. "Their singer comes in, who I find out later is named Dave Roth. I was at the stall and he's at the stall next to me. He goes, 'Sorry, Eulogy, for taking so *long* with the *soundcheck!*' He said it in his kind-of iconic way, which by the way, he talked that way onstage too. He looks at me and goes, 'Do you want some coke?' I looked at him with a straight face — and I'm serious — and said, 'Thank you, but I'm not thirsty.' At eighteen years old, I had honestly no idea what cocaine was. I thought he was offering me a drink. So that's my first recollection of meeting Van Halen."

Backstage, Eulogy's drummer, John Nyman, overcame his initial intimidation and drank beers with Alex, his counterpart on the skins. "The Van Halen guys scared the shit out of me," Nyman confesses with a chuckle. "They were much more adult and very sure of themselves. They were aggressive. They were adults, and they were *working*. When you're sixteen and someone's twenty-one, they're much older. They were scary in an awesome sort of way."

As Alex cracked open another Schlitz Malt Liquor, he gestured for Nyman to follow him across the room. "Alex showed me a hole in the wall in the little dressing room," Nyman remembers. "He had punched the wall. I think he was mad at Eddie. They had gotten into a fight. I remember thinking, *Oh yeah, they're brothers.*"

They talked tools of the trade, drumsticks and drumheads, and about what it meant to be a working musician. "They were gigging, from what he told me, like six nights a week at that point, just bar after bar and gig after gig." Nyman says that Alex then sat him down and gave him "the long *'here's how you've gotta do it, buddy'* talk."

After Maelstrom and Eulogy performed, Van Halen took the stage in front of a sparse crowd. While the other members of Eulogy had departed, Nyman and a friend had stayed to watch Van Halen. He insists, "Van Halen was just completely on fire. It was a

Edward Van Halen in La Cañada, California, November 22, 1975. MARY GARSON/HOT SHOTZ

great show that they played to about, oh, twenty or forty people. There was nobody there, and they were just *smoking*. They kicked ass to *no one*." The professionalism inherent in giving your all when almost no one's watching made an enormous impact on the young drummer: "Wow, that was a big lesson to me. They're doing it for themselves. They're going to kick ass and if you want to ride along and enjoy it, great, but if you're not here, well that's your tough luck." This stood in sharp contrast to Nyman's "teenage musician point of view, which was *I'm here to get some pumping up from the audience because I wish I were a rock star*. No, no, no. They *were* rock stars."

"That band was tight," Nyman declares, and "everything was just on the edge of energy. When I say on the edge, they weren't speeding up, but [it was] as if they were on a surfboard on a wave, [as if] they would all be on the nose of the board dangling their toes off the edge." Van Halen, he says, "had achieved this intensity. Alex would end one song with a really big flourish and then they'd go right into the next song. That one night they kept this going — for no one! There was no one there and they just kept up this incredible intensity. My friend Michael and I were like, 'Oh *fuck*! These guys are going to be big. This is crazy.'"

= =

Despite gigs at good-sized venues like the Golden West, Dave, Alex, Edward, and Mike knew that for all their sweat and dedication, Van Halen was still just headlining beer bars and converted dance halls. And even though their band name was up in lights on the Sunset Strip, they had made no progress on the Hollywood front. In fact, Van Halen had just celebrated its second anniversary at Gazzarri's, a hollow milestone for a band pursuing a record deal.

One weeknight in early April, Rodney Bingenheimer, "the Mayor of the Sunset Strip," stood inside the legendary Rainbow Bar and Grill on the Strip with his close friend Hernando Courtright. Bingenheimer, a fast-talking, diminutive man with a shag haircut, knew seemingly everyone he encountered on the Strip, but tonight, things at the Rainbow were dreadfully boring. On typical evenings, Bingenheimer might hold court at the bar, chatting with admirers. This evening, though, cocktail waitresses sat around talking, filing their nails, and smoking, their tables empty. The club's booths, often occupied by rock luminaries like Led Zeppelin and Deep Purple, and the royalty of the Hollywood groupie scene, stood empty.[342] Courtright, the handsome, dark-haired son of a successful Los Angeles hotelier and a Runaways insider, finished his drink and suggested he and Bingenheimer depart.

For no particular reason, the pair headed west on Sunset. They crossed North Weatherly Drive before they realized they were standing in front of the least hip club in Hollywood. They glanced up the Gazzarri's marquee, which was emblazoned with VAN HALEN. This name meant nothing to them.

They paused and looked at each other. They knew, like every other member of the Tinseltown in-crowd, that Gazzarri's offered up weak talent and weaker drinks to clueless tourists, fading celebrities, and suburban kids who didn't know the difference between Linda Lovelace and Linda Ronstadt. Thus, the two men entered the club on a lark — what Courtright terms "an accident" — just "to see what was happening."

As they entered, their expectations of a brief visit punctuated by snickers dissipated as they listened to the group onstage. Instead of an amateurish band playing limp Top 40 covers, this accomplished and powerful quartet interspersed R&B songs by Wilson Pickett and the Isley Brothers with hard rock tunes by Queen and Trapeze.[343] Between songs, the charismatic lead singer flirted with the clutches of sexy teenage girls who stood near the high stage as he bumped-and-grinded his way through the set.

Another round of tunes, this time by ZZ Top and Aerosmith, came next, only to be followed by a stand up routine directed at Russell, the club's oft-intoxicated Asian doorman. Russell, whom one Gazzarri's regular describes as looking "like a Kamikaze pilot who survived" a plane crash, jokingly gestured at Van Halen's singer.[344] After setting up his punch line, the frontman bellowed into the microphone and stabbed a finger towards him, exclaiming, "That's because Russell looks like something out of a *National Geographic* magazine!"[345]

Other song choices came out of left field. "Maid in Heaven," by highbrow prog-rockers Be-Bop Deluxe was followed by "Fopp," by one of the singer's favorite funk acts, the Ohio Players.[346] With the musicians churning through the verses, he belted out the words of this freaky call for carnal pleasure only to be joined on the chorus by the bass player, who nailed the song's impossibly high notes.

Even when the music stopped, the performance continued. For those in the know, Van Halen's singer hammed it up with an absurd but amusing prop: a big glass beaker, situated on a speaker,

Edward Van Halen harmonizes at Gazzarri's
on the Sunset Strip, 1976. MARY GARSON / HOT SHOTZ

filled with white powder and outfitted with a dinner spoon. With a shit-eating grin, he would shuffle over, scoop out a big spoonful of "blow," and pretend to snort it while the guitarist tuned his axe.[347]

Bingenheimer said about the experience, "I was there with a friend, Hernando Courtright, and we just knew that they were gonna to be the next big thing."[348] His friend agrees, noting, "They were just so amazing doing these covers." Yet Bingenheimer, who had a gift for spotting trends, is quick to point out that for all of Van Halen's greatness, the female response was what convinced him that they were going places: "Girls are constantly setting the trend. We could just tell by the vibe of the club," which was "packed and filled with hot females."[349]

After the last set, Bingenheimer and Courtright introduced themselves to Van Halen. "We went up to them afterwards," Courtright explains, "and said to them, 'Do you guys do originals? Because your covers sound like originals.' They said, 'Yes, but we can't get into Hollywood. We play in Pasadena and Arcadia and other places out that direction. But for some reason we haven't been able to crack the code and get into the Hollywood clubs and play originals.' We said, 'Well, we can help you with that.'"

The next afternoon, Bingenheimer and Courtright went to the Starwood. They ascended the stairs and headed to the office of Ray Stayer, who booked the nightclub. Courtright says, "We just about ran there the next day and said, 'You've *got* to book this band. We've seen God! They're the Godhead!'"

Despite Bingenheimer's clout, Stayer balked. "Well, I don't know," he replied, "[I've] never heard of Van Halen." When they told him that the band played Gazzarri's, he shook his head, a reflection of the club's poor reputation. Desperate to make his case, Bingenheimer then exclaimed, "Yeah, but these guys attract a lot of beer drinkers!" He knew, he admitted later, that "bar owners always like" a band that will drive alcohol sales. Finally, Stayer relented and agreed to give the band "a shot." He promised to book Van Halen on an open Monday night in mid-May.[350]

After leaving the Starwood, Bingenheimer went to Gazzarri's to find the Van Halen guys. He spotted Edward on the sidewalk in front of the club, talking to a friend. With excitement coloring his voice, Bingenheimer told him the good news. He then suggested it was time for Van Halen to bid farewell to Gazzarri's: "You guys should be playing the Starwood — it's more happening." To Bingenheimer's amazement, the young guitarist seemed less than enthused with this idea. "No, we like it here," Edward replied. "Bill [Gazzarri] treats us so well." After some more lobbying by Bingenheimer, the guitarist said he would pitch the idea to the others and get back to him.[351]

= =

Back in Pasadena, the band held a meeting at Roth's place. By this time Dr. Roth had purchased a new home at 455 Bradford St. In a reflection of his success as a surgeon, he and Dave had moved into a twenty-four-room, 14,000-square-foot Italianate mansion set on two-and-a-half acres of beautifully groomed grounds, with a tennis court and swimming pool. Kim Miller, who spent many days wandering through the house while her boyfriend and the rest of the band practiced in the basement, recalls, "My favorite room was the library. It was airy and bright with arched windows, floor-to-ceiling bookshelves, and a fireplace. You looked out over three manicured terraced yards surrounded by mature trees licking the sky. I could live in that room. It was my idea of heaven."[352]

Down in their basement practice space, Van Halen hashed out the pros and cons of a Starwood booking. First, they knew that playing a competing club would anger Bill Gazzarri, who was notoriously territorial about his talent. As Roth explained in *Crazy from the Heat*, telling Gazzarri that the Starwood had hired Van Halen was certain to result in being "threatened and banished to the seventh level of hell."[353] Second, the club did provide a steady income to Van Halen, sometimes supplemented with an extra twenty dollars shoved in Roth's palm by Gazzarri after a particularly successful night. If its owner, in a fit of anger, fired them and then they flopped at the Starwood, they would be out of Hollywood and out of pocket altogether.

Yet the most salient issue was that the Starwood was, in early 1976, L.A.'s premier rock nightclub. Practically every up-and-coming professional group in the mid-'70s played there, from power-trios like Stray Dog and ZZ Top — two of Edward's favorite groups — to blues icons like Albert Collins and Albert King. Young glitter rockers like Mott the Hoople and Slade, rock legends like Buddy Miles and the Spencer Davis Group, all of them had headlined the Starwood. Unsigned bands like Van Halen rarely played there.

Therefore, at the Starwood, Van Halen would have to perform a set of all originals, something the band had never done before.

They'd have to dig deep to put together a forty-five-minute song list, which would necessarily include not just their best tunes, such as the relentless "House of Pain" and throbbing "Runnin' with the Devil," but deeper cuts like the funky "She's the Woman" and the prog-rocker "Believe Me."

When some in the room expressed doubts, a confident Roth dismissed their concerns. He knew that this was the best opportunity that had come Van Halen's way in years. He reminded the others that they'd spent the better part of the past two years trying to build a following by playing everywhere from Redondo Beach to Rancho Cucamonga and from Pomona to Pasadena. They'd played in parks. They'd played in hotels. They'd gigged in Masonic temples, backyards, Top 40 clubs, and Catholic girls' schools. They'd provided musical entertainment for sweet-sixteen parties and wedding receptions. Hell, they'd even shared a bill with a screening of the 1969 Peter Sellers and Ringo Starr comedy *Magic Christian!*[354] They'd performed, at one point, twenty-three nights *in a row*.[355] Roth pointed out that he'd even walked into the Starwood earlier in the year, only to be told that Van Halen couldn't even audition, much less perform there. Bingenheimer and Courtright had given them an opportunity that they couldn't afford to pass up. As Roth explained to the *Los Angeles Times* in 1978, "We knew we had to do something to get us out of the bars where all we could do was play other people's hits. We had to develop a following; people who'd realize that we could do more than play Aerosmith songs well."[356]

When Roth finished, the others spoke. Alex and Anthony agreed that they needed to take this risk. Edward, however, remained unconvinced. What if Gazzarri fired them? What if the band bombed at the Starwood? He was against it. While he thought that the others could rise to the occasion, he wasn't sure that he could do the same. Edward Van Halen, who in less than three years would be acclaimed as the best new rock guitarist since

Jimi Hendrix, was gripped by a sense of insecurity so strong that he was hesitant to play the Starwood.

Roth, attuned to his guitarist's fragile psyche, countered with a suggestion designed to bolster his confidence. The band had just been booked to play a gig with UFO at the Golden West on May 9. That night, he explained, Van Halen could play their first set of all original songs in front of what promised to be a packed house. That way they could work out any kinks in their new song list at least a week before playing the Starwood.

Everyone turned towards Edward. The guitarist pursed his lips, took a deep drag on his Camel, and exhaled. "Okay," he said.

= =

On a Monday night in late April 1976, Edward, perhaps to pre-pare himself for the impending Starwood booking, drove to the Starwood to check out a funk rock group called Straight Jacket. Arriving before the show started, he walked into the dressing room and said hello to an acquaintance, drummer Skip Gillette, who later played with Ronnie Montrose's Gamma. Also in the room were Gillette's bandmates, the singer of the funk outfit Rufus, Chaka Khan (who was engaged to Straight Jacket's manager), and Michael Kelley, a friend of Gillette's and a young drummer who had manned the skins for a number of Los Angeles hard rock cover bands.

While Kelley chatted with Gillette, Edward picked up Straight Jacket guitarist Tim McGovern's Fender Mustang and plugged into a little practice amp. He began playing an obscure tune by Trapeze, "You Are the Music, We're Just the Band." Kelley's ears perked up. Not only was this guy a great player, his offbeat song choice told Kelley that he was a serious student of hard rock. Kelley asked Gillette, "Who's the guitarist?" Gillette replied, "That's Ed Van Halen. I'll introduce you."

Kelley and Edward shook hands. He told Edward that he loved

Trapeze and that his playing sounded great. Edward said thanks, then mentioned that his band, Van Halen, would be playing the Starwood with two other local bands on May 17. Kelley recognized the Van Halen name from the Gazzarri's marquee and from flyers he had seen around the city, saying, "Oh I know you guys. My band plays a lot of the same clubs."

Edward's expression suddenly turned grim. He confessed to Kelley that despite playing Gazzarri's innumerable times, he was "scared" to play the Starwood. "I'm not sure I can do it," he told Kelley. The drummer smiled and told him that playing the Starwood wouldn't be different from playing any other nightclub. Edward shook his head, finding Kelley's words to be cold comfort and said, "We've never played a place like this before." Kelley says, "I knew he had been playing around town doing covers with Van Halen for years, so in light of this, his fear and nervousness over Van Halen's upcoming all-originals Starwood debut struck me as being funny and humble."

Kelley then told Edward he was heading out. Before he walked away, Edward asked him, "Will you come back and see us?" Kelley said, "Yeah man, sure. I promise. I'll be there." Edward, imagining the humiliation inherent in playing a deserted Starwood, said earnestly, "Thanks. When you come, though, can you bring some friends?"[357]

= =

But before Van Halen played the Starwood, they needed to take on UFO. After poaching nineteen-year-old German *wunderkind* guitarist Michael Schenker from the Scorpions, the band, rounded out by vocalist Phil Mogg, bassist Pete Way, and drummer Andy Parker, released their classic 1974 album *Phenomenon*. The next year, the quartet hit pay dirt with *Force It*, a powerful statement of UFO's musical growth.

In early 1976, UFO retreated to the studio again and emerged with its latest album, *No Heavy Petting*, and a new band member, keyboardist Danny Peyronel. To support their new LP, which would be released on May 7, the five musicians flew to Los Angeles at the very beginning of that month They would spend the next few days in residence at the Starwood, where they would be introduced each night by the perpetually enthusiastic Bingenheimer.

When not onstage, they laid siege to Hollywood's Sunset Marquis Hotel. They sat wasted by the pool in their mirrored sunglasses, soaking up the Southern California sun, and enjoyed all of the decadent activities that the City of Angels had to offer. And to end their L.A. campaign was one last windfall: they signed a five-thousand-dollar contract with some small-time promoter to play in someplace called Norwalk, with some local band they had never heard of before and presumably would never hear from again.[358]

= =

Across the city in Pasadena, Roth kept his eyes on the prize. Ever since their band meeting, he'd heard all about the London-based group's prowess. He knew of Schenker's reputation as hard rock's newest and youngest guitar god. He'd laid eyes on the magazine photos of him in full guitar-hero mode, his straight blond hair draped in front of his face and his fingers bending the strings on his trademark Gibson Flying V. Despite all of this, Roth knew his band and his guitarist were better.

Anthony and the Van Halen brothers, initially at least, were not as sure. UFO was a great group and Schenker was an *amazing* player. They were road tested after years of touring and were about to release the album that everyone expected would make them superstars. To counter this thinking, Roth began pumping up his band for their looming encounter with UFO. Much like Muhammad Ali before a prizefight, Roth motor-mouthed to Alex, Edward, and

Michael — and anyone who would listen — that on Sunday, May 9, the mighty Van Halen was going to shock the world.

On a Thursday in late April, Tracy was back at the Golden West. Ever since he'd first seen Van Halen, he'd kept his eyes peeled for their flyers. "I went to every Van Halen gig I could possibly get a ride to, because I didn't even drive yet," he recollects. On this day, Tracy had arrived at the club after Van Halen's soundcheck but well before the show's starting time.

Wandering around the near-empty ballroom, Tracy spotted Roth. "Dave was walking around with his coveralls on, his roadie clothes. I knew who he was now, because I'd seen them a few times." Although he found Roth intimidating, Tracy greeted the Van Halen singer.

"Hey Dave! What's going on, man?"

"Hey. What's goin' on?"

"Your band's far out!"

"Yeah, we're pretty hot."

"Oh man, your guitar player's amazing."

"Yeah, the kid's pretty good."

The teenage guitarist then asked the all-important question regarding the source of Edward's formidable talents. "So, um, how much does he practice?"

"Well, lemme put it to you like this, kid," Roth said in a matter-of-fact tone. "When he's eating breakfast, he's got the guitar with him and he's practicing. He's always playing."

"Oh fuck. He's amazing, man."

"Yep," Roth said, without a trace of humility, and began to walk away.

"Wait," Tracy blurted out. "One more thing. I've seen a flyer. In a couple of weeks you guys are playing here with UFO. That's fucking *Michael Schenker*! You guys are gonna open up for 'em, huh?"

"Yeah we're gonna open up for them, but I feel sorry for him."

A perplexed Tracy cocked his head. "Who? Whattya mean?"

"Edward's gonna blow him off the face of the fucking earth."

"*What?*"

"I feel sorry for Michael Schenker. Edward's gonna wipe the floor with him."

Tracy just stared, not believing what he was hearing.

"Okay, kid, I gotta go. Enjoy the show." With that, Roth strutted towards the stage.

Tracy recollects that Roth talked up his guitar player "with all the arrogance that any man could have. I saw so much confidence coming out of him, it was frightening." More importantly, Tracy notes, Roth's cocksure attitude about Edward had to have given his guitar player an enormous boost. "Sometimes when you ask a singer about his guitar player," Tracy observes, "he's going to be all arrogant and make it all about himself, like, 'Yeah, he's pretty good, but it's all about me.'" Not Roth in the weeks leading up to this gig. He clearly believed that "Eddie was the up-and-coming motherfucker." Guitar god Michael Schenker? Tracy reiterates that Roth's attitude was "Sorry! Goodbye! Who's next?" Tracy says, "Dave knew it. *I'm going to predict the future, watch.* And he did. Because he knew."

= =

On the day of the show, the phone rang in Donny Simmons's apartment.

"*Yehhloow.*"

"Donny?"

"Yeah. Who's this?"

"It's Ed."

"Hey. Whassup, bro?"

"Hey. We're playing with UFO tonight."

Simmons knew about the show at the Golden West. "We were all UFO fans. I'd already seen them a couple of times that week at the Starwood," he remembers, and he was eager to see them for a third time. Van Halen? He'd seen them dozens of times, so they were just an afterthought. Maybe he'd even skip their set and just show up for the headliner.

"Yeah, Ed, me and my girl, we're gonna go."

"Well, I'm gonna pull out all the stops tonight."

"What does that mean?"

"I'm gonna kick his ass."

The line went quiet as Simmons tried to process what he'd just heard. "Whose ass?"

"Schenker's," Edward declared.

"What? What are you talking about? No one's gonna kick Michael Schenker's ass. What are you — fucking nuts? *Are you crazy?*"

Simmons says today, "Eddie already knew. In retrospect, it was *My plan is to take over the world.*" He told him he'd be there to see Van Halen. Edward said thanks and the line went dead.

That same afternoon, Dennis Catron, a sixteen-year-old budding guitarist from Whittier, and a friend drove to the Golden West. Once inside, Catron and his companion saw Van Halen getting ready to test their levels. Catron had seen them a number of times, including a memorable Thursday night billing in 1975 with guitarist George Lynch's band, the Boyz.

Catron, like every savvy fan on the local scene, thought Edward was one of the best young guitar players around and was excited to see him play. As Catron stared at the stage, Van Halen roared into one of their own songs. "We went inside early and watched Van Halen soundcheck." Catron recalls, "They were *on.*"[359]

Nearby, Mogg and a couple of his bandmates stood bleary-eyed after days of hard partying. UFO's singer felt like a zombie, but he gathered that Van Halen was no run-of-the-mill cover band. Like an out-of-shape champion boxer who climbs into the ring with an upstart fighter he'd underestimated, Mogg knew UFO was in trouble.

As the members of UFO stood with surprised looks on their faces, Catron watched as Mogg called over one of UFO's roadies. He yelled something in his ear, and the man left in a hurry. When he returned a few minutes later, he came bearing a couple of gifts for Van Halen, which he placed on the stage. Taking this in from a few yards away, Catron surmised that Mogg had "coyly sent Van Halen two wine jugs" to try to get the openers off their game.[360]

As night fell, the club came alive. Simmons, who was there as promised, remarks, "The place was gigantic. Because it was out towards the beach it was packed with surfers and surfer girls. The girls! The surfer girls had blonde hair and peeling noses from the beach. Oh my goodness. It was like, *whoa!*" Catron adds that those nights "there in 1975–1977 [were] Valhalla. Girls still dressed on the glam side with the glitter heels and pixie cuts, every band had a good guitar player with a Marshall, and there were so many bands then."[361]

On an evening like this, with rising stars UFO on the marquee, even well-connected Hollywood denizens made the long trip to Norwalk. Jackie Fox points out that the distance between the Golden West and Tinseltown was "quite a schlep." She says, "I was only there twice in my life. I really never went to shows there, because it was just too far away. It sounds snobby but it's true." In fact, "We'd never go to Norwalk or Covina or any of those places unless there was a band playing there that for some reason wasn't playing in L.A. proper, and that didn't happen very often."

But it was happening tonight. Fox, along with her fellow Runaway Lita Ford and Bingenheimer, now sat in a dressing room and partied with UFO. "Lita and I had gone to see UFO because we were fans," Fox remembers. "I think we must have met them [already], or they had put us on the [guest] list anyway, because we were backstage." As show time approached, she "asked somebody, 'Who's the opening act?'" Someone mistakenly told her,

"Oh, some band from Orange County." She thought, *Eh, I don't need to see some band from Orange County.*

Minutes later, Bingenheimer went onstage to introduce the opener in question. Michael Anthony and the rest of Van Halen stood behind the curtain, eyes fixed and jaws set, as Bingenheimer grabbed a microphone and began talking up Van Halen to the nearly two thousand fans in the hall. Van Halen's bassist remembers, "We were ready to play with UFO. That was our first all-originals gig. We wanted to make a good impression in front of Rodney and everyone else who would be there. It was a big gig for us."

"So let's welcome, from Pasadena, Van Halen!" With that, the curtain parted, and Van Halen lit into the fast-paced "On Fire." Roth slithered across the stage as he sang. Edward's fingers gripped his guitar neck with a fury, harmonics and power chords blasting out of his stack of Marshalls. As the song reached its first chorus, Michael, Edward, and Dave all screamed in unison into their microphones — *I'm on fire!* - - as Edward's thick chords rebounded off the rear of the hall.

Backstage, Fox and Ford cocked their ears as the powerful tune pierced the walls. As Edward lit into an incendiary solo, Fox turned to Ford and said, "These guys sound pretty good. Maybe we should go check 'em out?" She recalls, "So we went out and watched them, and we were both completely blown away. We *had* to find out about this band from Orange County."

Van Halen's assault on the Golden West continued apace. A one-two punch of the crushing "Somebody Get Me a Doctor" and a boogying "Show Your Love" concluded with Roth, his bare chest glistening with sweat, declaring "We're gonna do all *Van Halen* music tonight!" A fist-pumping "Runnin' with the Devil" followed, with Anthony's throbbing bass thumping the chests of onlookers.

About halfway through the set, Alex soloed. Patti Smith Sutlick recalls, "It was like you could see crystals floating in the air

[Alex] was so fast. Everyone always talks about Edward, but back in those days I thought Alex was the talented one."

For this important night, Alex, like the rest of his band, strove to make a professional presentation. To hide the milk crates that served as the foundation for his drum riser, Alex had roadie Jeff Burkhardt drape and staple a continuous length of black fabric to his plywood drum platform.

But Alex had even bigger plans. Before the show he placed an array of smoke pots in an unorthodox location — right under his riser. As he explained to Burkhardt, when he set them off during his solo it would appear as if his drum set "was blasting off."

With his hands flying around the kit, Alex trigged the fiery effect with a footswitch. Burkhardt recalls, "Boom! They go off and, just as he wanted, it looked somewhat like an Apollo rocket launch." But the impetuous drummer hadn't carefully measured the amount of black powder he'd used, thinking that if a little bit would be good, a whole lot would be great. Not surprisingly, Burkhardt recollects, "The fabric surrounding the drum riser" was suddenly "burning pretty good."

Burkhardt sprang into action: "I ran across the stage, bending down to grab the fabric on the way. I yanked all the staples out but here's this flaming black riser curtain following me the rest of the way across the stage on Mike's side. But I just kept running and a guy off to the side of the stage saw me coming and opened the back door for me. I ran outside, dropped the fabric, and stomped it out." In all, the episode took less than ten seconds.

Meanwhile, Edward faced his own equipment problems. He and Leiren, in crisis mode, hovered over his guitar backstage. Joining them were Jimmy Bates and Steve Hall, guitarist and drummer, respectively, of Stormer. Hall explains, "Me and Jimmy Bates went backstage when Alex was doing a drum solo. Eddie came off, and Eddie and Jimmy were talking for a minute. They were looking at his guitar, and Jimmy was doing something to it. I went to say something to Eddie, and he had this look on his face. Eddie was in this bad state of mind. Bates said, 'Don't talk to him right now. His sound's all fucked up.'"

After some repairs, Edward regained his composure and went back onstage. After a few more songs, Roth, breathing heavily, asked the roaring crowd, "Do ya wanna hear some electrical guitar?" Alex pounded his toms as Edward stepped into the spotlight and banged out the first few chords of "Eruption." In the five-plus minutes that followed, Edward put on a tour de force performance that distilled the tens of thousands of hours of performing and practicing he'd done since the late 1960s. His blitzkrieg began with some hummingbird-quick tremolo picking, partnered with a rollercoaster of double-stop bends. He wrung meaty artificial harmonics out of the lower strings and set them off with a fluid finger vibrato. A torrent of blazing legato hammer-ons and pull-offs poured from the speakers before he halted his assault.

He then walked over to his effects rack, which sat inside a tall, black, hollowed-out World War II–era practice bomb. Standing upright, it looked every bit like the Little Boy atomic weapon that had leveled Hiroshima back in '45. Twisting knobs on his Univox echo unit and hitting chords, he conjured up a reverb-drenched interlude reminiscent of Jimmy Page's work on Led Zeppelin's "Dazed and Confused."

Guitarist Dave Macias was out in the crowd and recalls, "It was standing-room only. Eddie started doing 'Eruption' but I couldn't see the stage well. I was thinking, *What the hell is he doing to get that sound? Is it a machine?* I stood on my chair, but a bouncer ran over and told me to get down. Everyone was jumping up and down and screaming their heads off."

With smoke from theatrical pyro apocalyptically billowing from the nose of the bomb, the guitarist concluded with a burst of speed picking. His echo unit modulated the piercing notes, making them sound like a science fiction ray gun amplified through a stack of cranked Marshalls. For those onlookers who may have gotten too stoned, the effect sounded *exactly* like a real UFO was landing in Norwalk. Simmons, after witnessing this amazing performance, could only think, *Maybe Eddie was serious.*

After the band members powered through the end of the set, they came offstage for a moment, wiping sweat, chugging Schlitz Malt, and lighting smokes as the crowd roared. They then ran back onstage, and, perhaps still a bit unwilling to fully embrace their new identity as an all original act, tore into their only cover of the night, KISS's "Rock and Roll All Nite."

Out in the audience, Tom Broderick, who knew of the band's plan to play only their own material, turned to his friend and yelled, "Aw, they shouldn't have done that!" To this day, Broderick thinks, "They should have went all the way with all originals, but that was one of their big party tunes at the time."[362] Mark Kendall says, "It was a pretty good little crowd. If I had to guess, maybe fifteen hundred people, maybe two thousand? But, man, they *ripped it up,* and you knew right then that this band, there is no denying they're going to go. It's going to happen." Chris Koenig, who later managed Mötley Crüe singer Vince Neil's first band, Rockandi, sums things up by declaring, "They just destroyed the place."

With the curtain closed and the crowd still buzzing, Mike, Alex, Dave, and the band's roadies began striking the stage. Just then, an overdosed Edward staggered up to them, his body quivering and his arms making uncontrolled motions. After a few panicked moments, Alex and the others grabbed the unresponsive guitarist and dragged him backstage, where they encountered Teckenoff and his assistant, Francis. The cool-headed promoter insisted that they take the stricken Edward to the hospital. Leiren watched as Alex and other Good Samaritans "got him out to the car [but] they couldn't get him into the car. They couldn't get him bent over, 'cause he was so rigid. Finally Alex had to punch him in the stomach to get him to double over so they could push him into the car."[363] Francis explains that this terrifying scene is "one of my most vivid memories of Van Halen at the Golden West Ballroom. I was fearful. I didn't know this drug. The reaction that he had was frightening. It was a serious thing." As she and the others looked on, Alex sped away and raced to Norwalk Hospital.

＝ ＝

Meanwhile, Bingenheimer, unaware of the ongoing drama, introduced UFO. The English band then kicked into the up-tempo "Can You Roll Her" from their just-released album. At the outset, at least some onlookers thought that the band was playing well. "UFO came out and did their thing," Koenig remembers, "and they were great."

But as the quintet's set progressed, it was obvious that they were drunk, high, or hungover, or maybe all three, and thus were not ready to follow Van Halen. Catron, who was a massive UFO fan, explains that the five musicians "were drunk and played horribly."[364] He surmises that Van Halen's aggressive performance took "something out of UFO as they looked self-conscious and not at all like they were enjoying themselves."[365] Their set included all of their biggest songs, but they never got into sync, and before the show was halfway over much of the crowd had lost interest. At the end of their set, UFO walked offstage while the audience applauded halfheartedly.

When they returned to play an encore, UFO delivered what Catron terms an "awful" rendition of one of their early hits. At its conclusion, he watched as Mogg, "with his three inch platforms . . . walked over and kicked bassist Pete Way's Marshall stacks to the ground. I fully expected Pete to kill him after that, but instead he took off his gorgeous black Thunderbird bass and heaved it into the pile. That pretty much summed up their evening."[366] Simmons witnessed the same thing and remembers that the band's German guitar player also got into the act: "After UFO got done with their set, Michael Schenker kicked over two stacks of Marshalls, because he was pissed off." Macias adds, "At the end of the show I remember him smashing his Flying V across his amps." UFO wandered offstage, smashed amps and shattered guitars feeding back in their wake.

After the show, Simmons and his girlfriend went backstage. "I was in line to meet UFO and the guy [Teckenoff] who ran the Golden West Ballroom, who knew us really well, said, 'Ah, Donny it's really not a good idea. They are not in a very good mood.' I'm like, *Oh my God. These guys are gonna go somewhere. Eddie's pissed off Michael Schenker!*"

Meanwhile, Roth had gone back onto the floor to bask in the glory of Van Halen's triumph. Koenig recollects, "When you left the auditorium you had to go through this hallway, and at the end of the night when everyone was leaving, Roth was just standing back there leaning against the wall with his shoulders up, [and] his hair all messed up . . . He's just leaning there so that everybody who walks out has to see him. It's funny because I used to hate guys like that, but that impressed me. It was his shtick. It was his thing. He was a rock star and he wanted everybody to know it. I thought that was pretty cool. I was like, *Wow, look at Roth*." When the crowd thinned, Roth returned backstage.

In Van Halen's dressing room, the mood was subdued as everyone anxiously awaited word from the hospital. Roth idly talked with Bingenheimer, Ford, and Fox, while some of Van Halen's inner circle and crew lingered nearby.

Suddenly a scowling Mogg appeared. Leiren listened as UFO's singer, oblivious to Edward's condition, gave Roth an earful about the effect that Edward's onslaught had on the fragile psyche of *his* guitar player.

"Hey! *Your* guitarist really fucked up. He fucked with the mind of Michael Schenker!" Mogg stood close to Roth, his eyes narrow.

"Hey now, come on, man. You know! Edward's doing his thing, Michael's doing his thing," Roth said in a singsong voice, trying to smooth-talk his way through the tense exchange.

Mogg's face flashed with anger. "No *you* don't know, *man*. *You* don't understand. You really fucked with Michael!"

The throng in the room parted as Mogg stalked off.[367]

Putting things in perspective, Kendall believes that despite all of Roth's and Edward's talk and Mogg's anger, "Eddie didn't try to do anything to UFO. Every show I'd seen him play was like that. With those guys it was like every show was their last. They were so confident, and they played that way. If you're going to play guitar on the same stage with that guy, be prepared to bring out everything you own. And I was a huge Schenker fan and I saw that show and I stayed for UFO. I'm sorry, but Eddie got him that night. It was blistering. It was an offensive."

= =

At the hospital, Edward was quickly wheeled into the emergency room. The attending physician immediately placed a tube down his throat, while nurses checked his vital signs and started him on oxygen. By this time, Edward's parents had gotten the awful news and had made their way to Norwalk. Later, the doctor would walk out of the ER and remark to Jan, Eugenia, and Alex, "If you got him here a few minutes later, you probably would have lost him."

Leiren explained that this was Edward's parents' "first shock of drug abuse." It was the "first they'd ever heard, or ever thought, or ever conceived of their kids being involved with drugs."[368] Edward, too, had to come to grips with what had happened to him, explaining to a radio host in the mid-'90s: "I OD'd on PCP, thinking it was cocaine. That's when I first got exposed to that stuff, and I didn't know what it was."[369] Despite his brush with death, in later years he would look back on it with black humor, telling Leiren, "I'm crazy now. I go nuts trying to get all this music out of my head. I'm afraid of what I would have been like if I hadn't burned up all those brain cells!"[370]

NO COMMERCIAL
POTENTIAL

After a seemingly interminable wait, the Aucoin Management secretary escorted Van Halen into the well-appointed Manhattan office. KISS's manager, sporting a thick mustache and a wide-lapelled sport shirt, had his feet up on his imposing mahogany desk. "Sit down boys," he said, gesturing to four leather chairs. "I'll be with you in a minute." With Roth and Alex in the lead, they walked across the garish shag carpet and sat down. Gold and platinum records lined the high walls. Documents, promotional photographs, and albums covered the desk, all illuminated by sunlight streaming through the fourteenth floor windows.[371] In the street below, midtown traffic on Madison Avenue moved in fits and starts on this cold November morning. Right in front of the four musicians, KISS's manager, Bill Aucoin, smoked a fat cigar while a diminutive man worked with polish and brush on his Italian loafers.[372]

Aucoin leafed through a folder without speaking. A minute passed, then another. Finally, Alex broke the silence, saying, "Where's the paperwork? So where do we sign?" Michael Anthony recalls, "We really thought this was it: he sat us down because he wanted us to sign a contract." The man behind America's biggest rock band put down the folder and set his eyes on Van Halen.

= =

In October 1976, KISS bassist Gene Simmons wanted more. To be sure, he had already enjoyed more power, fame, money, and women than whole cities of normal men enjoyed in a lifetime. KISS was now America's biggest rock band. Over the summer, they'd performed in front of sellout crowds across the country, capped off by an explosive performance in front of forty-three thousand fans at Anaheim Stadium. Their new single, "Beth," had just cracked the *Billboard* Top 20, and their latest album, *Destroyer*, was nearing platinum certification. But sitting in his Hollywood hotel room, he gave KISS's achievements little thought. Instead, he focused on his newest ambition: to manage and produce a young rock band.

After Simmons had voiced this idea a couple of weeks earlier, everyone from Hollywood hangers-on to young musicians had begun feeding him band names. But there were individuals whose opinions he trusted more than others. These included Runaways bassist Jackie Fox, guitarist Lita Ford, and their good friend Rodney Bingenheimer. Their consensus was that the best two unsigned bands in Los Angeles were Van Halen and the Boyz, a quartet that featured hotshot guitarist George Lynch and powerhouse drummer Mick Brown, both later of the 1980s glam metal act Dokken.

By October, Bingenheimer was long sold on Van Halen's greatness. After catching them at Gazzarri's back in April, he'd seen them at the Pasadena Civic and introduced them at some of their June Starwood shows.[373] So as soon as Simmons asked him which unsigned local rock band he liked best, Rodney blurted out, "Van Halen!" Simmons looked down at the pint-sized DJ, furrowed his brow, and asked earnestly, "What the hell kind of name is that?"[374]

Van Halen performs a lunch-hour set at Glendale College
in Glendale, California, fall 1975. MARY GARSON / HOT SHOTZ

Michael Anthony, Edward, and Alex Van Halen in
Glendale, California, fall 1975. MARY GARSON / HOT SHOTZ

Edward Van Halen bends a note on his Ibanez
Destroyer, fall 1975. MARY GARSON/HOT SHOTZ

Fox and Ford also had Simmons's ear. The two sexy musicians
would chat him up at the funky Sunset Marquis, a Hollywood
hotel that regularly hosted the members of Cheap Trick, UFO,

David Lee Roth, wearing an Acme Siren Whistle around his neck, belts it out, fall 1975. MARY GARSON / HOT SHOTZ

and KISS. "If we knew somebody who was staying there, it would be a fun place to go and hang out," Fox says. "You have to remember we were all teenagers and we were still living with our parents. You'd take any excuse to get out of the house and if that meant hanging out by the pool drinking a vodka gimlet with rock musicians, well that was cool."

By the middle of October, Fox had already talked up her favorite bands to Simmons. So when the topic came up again while poolside, she and Ford told him — and KISS frontman Paul Stanley, when he made an appearance — that Van Halen and the Boyz had a Starwood gig on November 2. Fox recalls, "I'd keep bugging them that they had to go see this band the Boyz. Lita and I found out Van Halen was going to be [playing with] them and I said, 'Gene, you've gotta trust me — you guys have got to trust me. You *have* to go see these bands.'"

Fox and Ford's enthusiasm for Van Halen was genuine. Neither of them had forgotten the experience of seeing them wipe the floor with UFO at the Golden West Ballroom that past May. But the cerebral Fox, thinking about which act would be the easiest sell to the record-buying public, figured that Simmons and Stanley "would like the Boyz." She says, "They were a little more mainstream sounding. Van Halen was doing music that no one had ever done before. They had a really unique sound. At the time, they didn't seem as commercial" as the Boyz.

Mass appeal aside, Simmons just couldn't get past the Pasadena act's moniker. He told the girls that he thought Van Halen was "a silly name for a group. It sounds like Van Heusen, the shirt company."[375] They laughed, reiterating their admiration for the two bands. Simmons listened but was noncommittal about whether he'd go to the Starwood.

It turns out that KISS's bassist was keeping his cards close to his chest. He soon decided not to wait until next month to start evaluating these acts. While Van Halen wouldn't be playing in Hollywood until the Starwood show, he learned that the Boyz, along with a few other local bands, would be gigging at what was billed as a "Halloween Party" at Gazzarri's on Wednesday, October 27.[376]

Simmons and Stanley went to Gazzarri's that night. In 1976, the public had no idea what the members of KISS looked like, so when the two dark-haired men and their entourage walked into the club, they attracted no attention. Singer Myles Crawley, whose band Eulogy was on the bill, says, "On any given night, there were like four bands playing. We'd each play a couple of sets throughout the night, so it was this constant barrage of music."

As all bands did at Gazzarri's, Eulogy played covers, including the KISS anthem, "Rock and Roll All Nite." After they came off-stage, a man with dark curly hair approached them. "A guy walked up to us and introduced himself as Paul Stanley from KISS," Crawley says. "We were like, 'Yeah, come on. No way.' But it turned out it was Paul and Gene Simmons. They just happened to be there that night checking out all the bands."

After wishing Eulogy well, Gene headed upstairs to catch the Boyz's performance. The band's singer, Michael White, remembers, "KISS was absolutely at the peak of their popularity in the fall of '76. Everyone came down dressed as KISS. I'm not exaggerating; probably ninety percent of the kids came dressed in KISS makeup and costumes. When we saw all those kids dressed like that, as a joke we said, 'Let's add a couple of KISS songs to our set.' We used to do 'Firehouse' when we soundchecked. We also threw 'Detroit Rock City' into the set. We did those two songs to end the set."

Between sets, a stranger approached White. "I'm standing around after the set and this fucking huge guy walks up to me and says, 'Hi, I'm Gene Simmons. I really liked the way you did our songs.' I knew it was Gene once I looked at him. Paul was there too. Some guy they were with handed me a business card from Casablanca Records. I still have that card."

Simmons then asked, "Where are you playing next? I liked your set. I'd like to bring some record company people down to see you."

A wide-eyed White replied, "This Tuesday we're playing at the Starwood."

"Okay, I'll be there with the record company. You guys be ready."
With that, Simmons, Stanley, and the others departed.

A stunned White tracked down his bandmates: Lynch, Brown, and bassist Monte Zufelt. He told them what had just happened, but, assuming he was pulling a practical joke, they told White to stop fucking around. When White showed them the card, the quartet got gleeful. "Everyone was all excited," White says. They exchanged high-fives and yelled.

= =

A couple of days later, Fox and Ford visited with Simmons again at the Sunset Marquis. Sitting by the pool, they reminded him about Tuesday's show. This time, Simmons agreed to go. They'd be joined by Stanley, the stunning model Bebe Buell (Simmons's then-current companion), Bingenheimer, and Hernando Courtright.[377]

By the weekend, Hollywood buzzed with the news that KISS had been on the prowl at Gazzarri's. Sunset Strip denizens shared stories of seeing the two dark-haired men at the club or in a booth at the Rainbow later that night. The Boyz, eager to hype KISS's interest in them, told members of their circle that Simmons and Stanley planned to attend their Starwood show.

But among Van Halen and Boyz fans, there was another reason for excitement about the gig. On that night, two of the best guitarists on the scene would face off. Michael Kelley, a Starwood regular, explains, "Everyone was talking about Eddie and George playing back to back. We thought it was going to be like Tombstone, Arizona, in 1881. Two gunslingers would fight it out, but only one would come out on top."[378] Lynch, in particular, had something to prove after a personally disastrous 1975 double billing of the Boyz and Van Halen. "The first time I saw Eddie play was in the Golden West Ballroom," Lynch stated later. "He was amazing . . . He had a lot of fire and a great tone. I was embarrassed for myself. I thought, *This is ridiculous*. I immediately went back [home] and started practicing. I stayed up all night saying, 'I sound awful. I play awful.'"[379]

As was the norm at the Starwood, the two bands on the bill would alternate sets. The Boyz would play first, followed by Van Halen. Then after an intermission, the two groups would play again in the same order. Kelley, who was at the Starwood on that fateful Tuesday, explains that while "it sounds logistically insane in this day, that's how it was done: two bands, two sets per night, alternating."[380]

That night, Simmons and company showed up at intermission. They were seated at tables in the VIP balcony. From their perch they could look down at the audience, which numbered about three hundred, and the stage. Whispering and finger-pointing began soon after they arrived. "It was a big deal," Kelley says, "because at that time no one had seen the members of KISS without their makeup." Earlier in the evening, Kelley felt certain that KISS would appear, because unlike most nights, "The upstairs VIP area, which was normally very easy to get into, was suddenly off-limits and no-go."[381]

Around eleven, the Boyz returned to the stage. White remembers that as a unit, his band didn't perform well. Over the past few days, they'd "rehearsed and rehearsed" in order to be at the top of their game for KISS. But White says what happened instead was "we burned ourselves out." That night, "my voice was shot and we were tired."

Kelley has a different take, at least in regards to the Boyz's guitarist. "George was really killing it!" While he can't be fully certain, he believes that "this may have been the gig when George actually passed out briefly during the second set because of a combination of heat and his personal intensity; he was delivering the goods like he was possessed!"[382]

After the set ended, Simmons headed backstage. White remembers, "They came and hung out with us upstairs; they schmoozed us. Bebe Buell was with Gene. He announced, 'We're taking a band back to New York to record for a new label we're starting.'"

Then through the walls rumbled Roth's introduction of his band. Simmons recalled that he heard, "All right, ladies and gentlemen, here they are! From Pasadena . . . " Simmons, still hung up on the band's name, shook his head as Roth shouted, "Van Halen!"[383] Out on stage, the foursome ripped into their opener.

Van Halen's stage volume soon made communication impossible. "Van Halen started playing," White says, "and then it was too loud backstage at the Starwood to keep talking. Simmons yelled, 'We're going to go out and see them.'"

Simmons returned to the VIP area. "The first thing I thought," he told Steven Rosen, "was Dave looked like Jim Dandy, and they had kind of an old-fashioned look. But within two numbers I thought, *My fucking God, listen to these guys.*"[384] By the third song, Simmons was "floored" by Van Halen.[385]

What hit home for Simmons was the band's enthusiasm and power. "The sound, the approach, and the look all fit," he said later. "There was a lot more choreography — y'know, the old KISS choreography, where everybody would shake their heads back and forth together. They looked like they were having a good time."[386] But more importantly, the band was generating atomic-level energy in front of a somewhat listless crowd. "They did well, but there was no tip-off that this was gonna be the next sensation, at least as far as the audience was concerned. But the whole group, especially David, was playing the stage as if it was Madison Square Garden. And that's the sign of greatness. You've got to be good in the first place, but when you treat a small, intimate gathering as if it's a spectacle, you have the makings of a star."[387]

Of course, a seasoned musician like Simmons couldn't help but notice Edward's talent. "As soon as Eddie started playing, the thing that struck me right away was that the guy was amazingly fast and light on touch . . . Eddie was just swimming over that fretboard, and I couldn't believe the control he had. I don't remember him using the tremolo bar that much, but he was bending the neck a lot." His influences, too, seemed unusual to Simmons. Instead of the conventional Beck-Page-Clapton blues trinity, what Simmons "heard was a much more classical influence."[388]

Courtright stood nearby, watching Simmons. He recalls, "We were in the VIP section at the Starwood when Gene saw the band. I sat near him and kind of just observed." Simmons, Courtright says, sported a poker face. "He wasn't standing on the table and going *Yeah!*" The Runaways insider, who harbored his own aspirations to manage Van Halen, explains with a laugh, "He didn't want people to know his enthusiasm, because that would raise the dollar value. So you play it cool. He was just watching. He was looking at the band the way I did — he saw dollars. When I saw Van Halen play I always thought, *This band will change your life if you manage them, because they're going to go someplace.*"

As the set climaxed, Simmons, without a word to Stanley, tapped Bingenheimer on the shoulder and pointed backstage. With "the Mayor of the Sunset Strip" in tow, KISS's bassist set out to stake his claim.[389]

Down below, audience members took in the show as well. Photographer Mary Garson, who shot many of Van Halen's early promotional photos, remembers, "I was there the night at the Starwood that the Boyz played with Van Halen. Gene Simmons was there. The Boyz *sucked*. Van Halen had a great night; I thought Dave was amazing." Nearby was Steve Tortomasi, Roth's old high school acquaintance, who now promoted Van Halen's Pasadena Civic shows. He says, "I remember telling the guys, 'The night that KISS came down, you guys did one of the best sets of your life.' And I'd seen them play many, many, many shows from high school days on up." By the time their encore was wrapping up, their power and charisma had stirred the Starwood. "That set they laid down that night, along with the crowd reaction, was just unbelievable. It blew everybody away." Right before the band left the stage, Tortomasi wended his way through the crowd to congratulate the guys on their knockout performance.

In the small dressing room, Van Halen let loose. They stood with their roadies, girlfriends, and a few friends, chugged some beers, and bullshitted about the set. When the door swung open after a knock, Tortomasi recognized Bingenheimer but not the other man with him. "I'd never seen those guys without their makeup," he says.

"Hey everyone!" the uber-enthusiastic DJ said, "This is Gene Simmons of KISS!"

After some introductions, Simmons said, "Well, we just wanted to come and see you."

Alex powered through his beer and guffawed before saying to Simmons, "Well that's fair, because we went to see *you* at the Forum."

Simmons's face creased with a small smirk.

Tortomasi thought, *Wow, that's a ballsy thing to say.*

"It was lighthearted," Tortomasi explains, "but it was cocky of Alex."

The unflappable Simmons then made his pitch. "Look, I'd like to help because I think you guys can make it. I'm not stroking you, I'm not interested in doing anything for myself, but I love your band and I'd like to help you."[390]

Continuing, he asked, "Are you guys on a label or anything? Do you have a manager?"[391] They shook their heads but mentioned that a certain "yogurt manufacturer" had recently offered to support the band. "Please do me a favor," Simmons implored, "don't do that."[392]

Simmons then lectured the band, telling them, "You guys are going to make it. Just be careful that you don't get screwed business-wise." Edward recalled that Simmons "wised us up a lot" by warning them to "watch out because people will take advantage of you. They end up rich, and you'll be sitting there ten years later saying, 'Look at all of the stuff I've done and I ain't got a penny.'"[393]

As Simmons talked contracts and bottom lines, Anthony felt his head spin, and this time, it wasn't from Jack Daniel's, his favorite beverage. "My first impression of him was that he was a great businessman. He had a real, no-nonsense, business-oriented look about him," Anthony recalled. "We actually learned a lot from him. After talking to him for an hour, he made me really wonder whether I really wanted to be a musician. He started talking to us about accountants and lawyers, and it all sounded pretty heavy and a little scary."[394]

Eventually, Simmons pulled all four aside. He told them that he'd like to sign them to a management contract and try to get them a record deal. The band quickly agreed to accept his help. Edward remembered that before he left the Starwood for Pasadena, Simmons handed him his hotel phone number "and asked me to call him as soon as I got home that night." By the time the band got back to Pasadena, "it was three or four in the morning. By six that morning we were in Village [Recorders] sitting with Gene. I was blown away."[395]

After convening at the Santa Monica studio, the first order of business was to evaluate Van Halen's originals. "I wasn't just going in and saying, 'Okay, let's record,'" Simmons explained later. "They gave me a cassette of the tunes — there must have been over twenty on there — and I picked thirteen to record. Didn't like 'Ice Cream Man' . . . The last one, 'House of Pain' is on 1984, though it sounded much tougher then, much closer to 'Runnin' with the Devil.'"[396]

Along with their instruments, effects, and amplifiers, the band had another unique prop to offer to Simmons: a car horn noise-maker that would later be immortalized on the opening track of their debut. Pete Dougherty, who lived in the Roth guesthouse in 1976, explains, "I took some horns out of an Old Ford station wagon. It was a '52 or something like that. And Dave gave me some old horns." Roth knew that Dougherty was an electronics genius who'd know how to turn the horns into a stage prop. After successfully wiring them together, Dougherty and Gary Nissley, who'd known the band since their high school days, made a tape of the horns. "Gary and I recorded them and gave Dave the recording," along with the horns, which they'd mounted on a board. "Al thought it was pretty clever what I did with the horns. It ran on a footswitch." While it's unclear if the quartet hauled the horns down to Village Recorders or just brought the tape to Simmons, the blaring horns would become a permanent part of Van Halen's sonic history.

During the November 3 session, Simmons's admiration for the band's guitar player grew as each track was recorded. "What amazed me was when we got into the studio, Eddie got a lot of his effects direct. Where you usually get the effects after, from the board, he had the effects down pat, so all you had to do, basically, was mike it. He really knew what he was doing."[397]

Simmons also found a use for the horns, adding them between verses and tagging them to the end of the blistering "House of Pain." As the song faded out, Simmons gradually dropped the pitch of the horns as they segued into "Runnin' with the Devil." He explained, "I wanted to connect [the] two tunes together, so I just slowed down the tape so it wound up in the same key."[398]

= =

Soon after the session wrapped, Simmons called Aucoin. He told him he'd found this hot new group in Hollywood and that he'd just laid down thirteen tracks with them in the studio. This demo, he explained, now just needed some overdubs. Simmons hoped that if Aucoin liked them as much as he did, KISS's manager might take them on as clients and then put them on KISS's label, Casablanca Records. Then down the road, KISS might even take Van Halen on tour with them as an opening act.[399]

Aucoin asked him the band's name. "Van Halen" was the answer, and Simmons continued his sales job. An impatient

Aucoin cut him off, saying, "Yeah, I've heard of them. I've heard their name when I was in L.A."[400] Simmons continued, telling his manager that Van Halen was *great*. After a bit more back and forth, Aucoin sighed and said, "Okay, we'll fly them to New York."[401]

While Aucoin would later concede that he'd badly bungled Simmons's proffer of Van Halen, he had a larger agenda when it came to Simmons and his new hobby.[402] KISS's new single, "Hard Luck Woman," had just hit radio, and their new album, *Rock and Roll Over*, would arrive in stores on November 11.[403] Perhaps more importantly, tour rehearsals were scheduled to begin at New York's SIR Studios on November 7.[404] He needed him back in New York immediately.

After he hung up with Aucoin, Simmons called Edward. He told him that he and his bandmates should pack, because they were flying to New York City to finish the demo.[405] Van Halen's guitarist remembered, "Gene had this master plan that he'd produce us, but the rest of the guys in KISS were getting a little uptight, because he was spending time with us instead of with them."[406] Because Michael and Alex had completed all of their bass and drum tracks, Anthony says that it really wasn't necessary for the band's rhythm section to go to New York. Regardless, Simmons told Anthony they were all going because "he wanted us together as a band."

= =

After they arrived in New York, Simmons got them rooms at the venerable Gotham Hotel, so they were smack dab in the middle of the city. Simmons recalled that for Van Halen, "It was 'Oh my God, we're in *New York*.' That first-time feeling . . . I'm sure it was a little bit too much. They wandered around, went to record stores, and I was rehearsing to go on the road with KISS."[407]

Despite his responsibilities to KISS, Simmons was determined to finish the demo. He booked time at Electric Lady Studios, a legendary facility that his band frequented. With the drums, bass, and most of the background vocals completed, Simmons planned to spend most of his studio time with Edward and Roth. He wanted Roth to lay down more lead vocals and Edward to overdub guitars, a task the guitarist had never undertaken before.

On the day the session began, all four members of Van Halen walked into Electric Lady with Simmons. Anthony, in particular, was struck by the experience of standing in Jimi Hendrix's own studio. "The best thing about going to New York," he says, "was that we got to go into Electric Lady. They took us into the vault and showed us all of these tape boxes of Hendrix recordings. All I could think about was all the amazing music on those reels."

After Anthony "sang a couple of backgrounds," he and Alex departed. Van Halen's rhythm section then explored the city. Anthony remembers, "Alex and I didn't have much to do in New York except goof off. Alex and I stepped out of the hotel and into the street every day and had hot dogs from the vendors. We thought it was so fucking cool that you could get a hot dog right on the street," he laughs.

While Alex and Anthony had fun in the Big Apple, Simmons, Edward, and Roth worked on the demo. After knocking out Roth's vocals, Simmons focused on thickening up Edward's contributions to songs like "House of Pain," "Big Trouble," "Somebody Get Me a Doctor," and "On Fire" by having him double solos and add harmony lines. The guitarist recollected, "It was my first attempt at overdubbing, which was very bizarre. I remember asking Gene before we started, 'Can't I just play the way we do [live]?'"[408] Edward said his first tries went poorly, because he "just didn't know how" to overdub since he "hadn't even played with another guitarist."[409]

Simmons patiently coached the guitarist as they worked. He pushed the talkback button and said, "Here's what you do in the studio — you play your rhythm parts on one track and your solo parts on another."[410] When that didn't seem to help, Simmons added that all overdubbing meant was that "you have to play to yourself."[411] Edward explained later that his biggest stumbling block was that he was "used to playing the main guitar all the way through so it sounds like one guitar."[412]

Despite Simmons's mentoring, the man who'd become the most influential guitarist since Jimi Hendrix was stumped. From the other side of the studio glass, he told the KISS bassist to give him a few minutes. "I said, 'Hold on, guys, now I have to think of another part to play first.' There'd never been another guitar playing there. Now I have to think what I could play there."[413]

Eventually, Edward started getting the job done. But after years of playing in a power trio format, the sound of multiple guitars threaded through Van Halen's tunes seemed wrong. While reviewing one track's overdubs, he said to Simmons, "Whoa, that sounds odd to me."[414] Ultimately, the studio experience in New York taught Edward a valuable lesson: "I quickly learned that I didn't like overdubbing."[415]

In later years, Edward claimed that the demo was never completed.[416] What exactly he meant is somewhat unclear. Here Edward could have been referring to the fact that Simmons has often maintained that the demo contained thirteen songs, even though only ten have ever leaked into the public realm, so perhaps three of the songs remained unfinished. And while the ten songs from the demo that have surfaced sound polished, it's possible that Simmons's intention was to add extra guitar to all the tunes, rather than just the few that ended up with overdubs. But regardless, what likely happened is that between Edward's slow pace and Simmons's tight schedule with KISS, the clock had run out. The recording sessions would have to end.[417]

Simmons now turned his attention to mixing the tape. For this task, Simmons selected Dave Wittman, one of Electric Lady's house engineers. Wittman, who'd trained under the legendary Eddie Kramer and would later work the board on smash albums like Foreigner's *4*, already had an impressive resume of recordings to his name, including KISS's *Dressed to Kill*. Wittman says, "I was constantly working with Gene and/or Paul doing various demos. We were seeing a lot of each other back in that period."

The pair would work in Electric Lady's Studio B. Wittman explains, "I seem to remember that there were four or five songs I ended up mixing." Wittman's recollection of four or five songs fits with the number of tracks that Edward, Roth, and Gene had worked on in New York, so it's likely that the rest of the demo had been mixed in Los Angeles. "The one thing that sticks out in my mind is the song 'Runnin' with the Devil.' I loved that song. I'm going, '*Wow!* This is cool! This song is really great.'" Gene sat back and let the engineer work, occasionally telling him "maybe more of this" or "less of that" as Wittman adjusted the levels. In under a week of work, and for an expense of $6,500, the Van Halen demo was in quasi-finished form.[418]

Before he presented the tape to Aucoin and took his protégés to meet him, Simmons wanted to make sure they looked the part. He recalled that because the band hadn't brought their stage outfits from home, they were hanging around New York City in street clothes. That wouldn't impress his manager, so he took them shopping for some stylish rock garb. He remembered "telling them they couldn't walk around in sneakers if they want to try out for the labels. So I got them leather pants and boots."[419]

While Van Halen waited to meet Aucoin, Simmons focused on his own band. Starting on November 7, KISS rehearsed at SIR Studios for their upcoming tour, which was scheduled to last several months. All the while, though, Simmons assured Van Halen that he remained committed to guiding their career and finding them a record deal.

They knew, of course, that when push came to shove, KISS would always trump Van Halen in Simmons's world. "We were somewhat concerned," Anthony explains, "because Gene said he wanted to manage us and yet he was about to take off on some massive Japanese tour or something like that with KISS."

In addition, they all remained somewhat unsatisfied with the recordings they'd made. As Rudy Leiren explained to Steven Rosen, when it came to the demo "they really weren't happy — particularly Ed — with the way that Simmons was producing the tunes."[420]

When compared to the band's albums, it's clear why Van Halen didn't love the Simmons demo. Roth's singing sounds strained in spots, particularly on the opening track, "On Fire." Simmons's vocal coaching is clear on "House of Pain," as Roth adds some awkward "God of Thunder"–style growls to the chorus. Alex's drumming is stiff, and the tempos of songs like "Runnin' with the Devil" sound off-kilter, either too fast or too slow. And while Edward's playing is certainly respectable, the recording does little to capture the world-changing brilliance that dominated every track on Van Halen's debut. In fact, Michael Anthony put in the best performance on the demo. His solid bass lines and his fantastic background vocals shine on every song.

A few days after KISS's rehearsals began, Simmons invited Van Halen to SIR to watch the proceedings. On a break, the band stepped away from their instruments. Simmons then strolled over to Van Halen. After some small talk, he said, "Bill [Aucoin] is coming by, why don't you guys play on our equipment and do a little showcase for him?" Not wanting to pass up a chance to play in front of one of the most powerful men in the record industry, the quartet said yes.[421]

The four musicians walked onstage, sizing up KISS's equipment. Alex sat down behind Peter Criss's kit and tried to get comfortable as Anthony adjusted the strap on Simmons's bass. Edward studied Ace Frehley's amps and picked up his Les Paul. As soon it was around his neck, he felt uneasy. "I didn't even have my own guitar. It was really funky," he said later.[422] Even after tinkering with Ace's axe, "The guitar was totally alien to me."[423]

Soon enough, Aucoin entered. He said some quick hellos and encouraged the guys to start playing, which they did. Although afterwards he'd assure Van Halen that he liked their performance, his true opinion was quite different.[424] He told interviewers in later years that it was clear "they were nervous." The band's vocalist "didn't really sing that well." Even though he liked Edward's guitar playing, Simmons had built him up "to be a phenomenal guitarist," and when he saw him perform at the showcase, he thought he just played "okay."[425]

But ultimately Aucoin's assessment came down to the group as a unit and the quality of their tunes. By the time they'd finished, he just wasn't sold on the "band in total." And perhaps more importantly, he "wasn't sure that there was a song that we could really get behind."[426] Regardless, Aucoin thanked the guys and said he'd meet with them the next morning.

Meanwhile, there was another member of KISS who was taking an interest in the goings on with Van Halen: Paul Stanley. While Gene had mentioned to Edward that the other members of KISS were feeling "uptight" about their bassist's focus on Van Halen, Stanley, in particular, felt compelled to actively intervene. As he disclosed in *Face the Music*, Simmons hadn't told him in Los Angeles that he planned to take Van Halen into the studio. Stanley would only find out about their work at Village Recorders after the fact. He termed this "secretive" behavior at best "sneaky," and at worst "dishonest."[427]

At some point during Van Halen's visit to New York, Simmons brought the demo to Stanley and Aucoin. Stanley recalled that Simmons, still uneasy about the band's moniker, said that he'd tell Van Halen that they'd be shopped to labels under the name Daddy Long Legs. Simmons then played the tape.

Later that day, Stanley and Aucoin "spoke — without Gene — and agreed to pass on Van Halen." Stanley claims that this had nothing to do with the band's talent, but rather with the damage that Gene's new hobby could do to KISS's upcoming campaigns. "We passed to protect KISS, which needed our daily focus to continue building on all fronts. Gene's wandering eye was clearly a potential risk to all we had accomplished and all we were working toward."[428]

= =

The morning after the impromptu showcase, Van Halen sat in Aucoin's office. Aucoin, not wasting a word, quickly shot down Alex's notion that he had a contract for Van Halen in his hands. He said, "I don't see any commercial potential" in Van Halen. "Besides that, I've got my hands full because I just signed a band called Piper," a Boston-based act that featured a then-unknown singer named Billy Squier.[429]

Continuing, Aucoin centered on what he saw as the band's biggest liabilities. The first problem was that the group's songs weren't catchy enough. "I just don't hear the melodies," Roth recalled that Aucoin told them. "Hits are required in this day and age." If Aucoin's benchmark for songcraft at that time was the power pop of Piper, it's clear why he passed on Van Halen. Piper's ultimate commercial failure aside, the material on their first album *sounded* radio-ready. The songs on Van Halen's demo simply weren't as polished.

The second problem was that he didn't like the band's vocalist. "Dave," he said to Roth, "maybe there are a couple other acts that I handle that we could get you to work with." To the rest of Van Halen, he said, "maybe another vocalist would work." But the bottom line was "Gene has his own career, he's in KISS, and barring any other permutations, I don't think I can work with you."[430] With that, Aucoin dismissed them.

When Simmons heard that Aucoin had passed on Van Halen, he was shocked. He sat down with him to try to change his mind. He played the demo again. "I said, 'This group is *the next big thing*.'"

"It's too derivative," Aucoin countered.

Simmons retorted, "Listen to how *unique* the guitarist is!"[431]

Aucoin conceded that the guitarist was talented, but what about the fact that Roth looked just like Jim "Dandy" Mangrum of the now out-of-fashion southern boogie-rockers Black Oak Arkansas?[432] Simmons told him he was crazy, "because nobody knew who that band was" anymore.[433]

In the end, Simmons knew that all of this had less to do with Van Halen and more to do with KISS. Simmons later said that the bigger issue was that "the rest of the guys in the band were angry that I was turning my attention" to Van Halen.[434] Ultimately "nobody wanted to listen" to him about Van Halen any longer.[435] On his way out of Aucoin's office, Simmons's glared at his manager and said, "You're gonna eat those words."[436]

= =

Back at the hotel, Roth felt demoralized as he packed. He knew that the rest of the band was stunned by this turn of events. As Edward said later, "Here we are, totally bummed out because we thought this was our one shot to make it, and it didn't pan out; it didn't work."[437] Roth, like the others, understood that at that moment KISS was America's most popular group. If *Gene fucking Simmons* couldn't get them a record deal, how would they ever get one? Roth wrote in his autobiography, "I felt terrible. Wow — had I had let the band down?" He was particularly worried because he "didn't know what the Van Halens were thinking at the time." Roth knew that some observers back home whispered that his vocal ability paled in comparison to Edward's masterful playing. Would the brothers, after hearing Aucoin's opinion, now want to get rid of their lead singer?[438]

Before Van Halen left town, Simmons met with them. He tore up the contract they'd signed with his Man of a Thousand Faces production company and told them they were free to use the demo to try to get a deal elsewhere. He'd be back from tour in the spring, and if they still didn't have a recording contract, they could still expect help from him.[439] Just "give me a call," he said, "and we'll do it again."[440] Simmons shook their hands and gave them money for plane tickets back to Los Angeles.[441]

= =

After landing back in Los Angeles, the band members prepared to head home. While Michael caught a ride back to Arcadia, Alex, Edward, and Dave stood outside the terminal and waited for Roth's old friend Stanley Swantek and his brother David to pick them up and take them back to Pasadena. Edward, looking back on the whole whirlwind experience, said it left the band feeling "totally bummed" and ended up being "really depressing."[442]

The Swanteks soon rolled up, setting the stage for what David Swantek terms the "most dramatic" Van Halen moment he'd ever witnessed. With Stanley behind the wheel, Roth grabbed shotgun as the other three piled into the back seat. David remembers, "They were all bummed" about what had just gone down with Simmons, "Eddie and Alex in particular." As they got on the freeway, the car was silent and the mood morose.

After another minute, Roth swung around in his seat. With his voice raised, he said, "Look, don't think for a second that this is over! This is how it's gonna be. We are really going to go into recording studios. We really are going to be a big name. You'll see. Just keep at it!"

The Van Halen brothers shook their heads. "We had our big break and we lost it!" one of them said to Roth.

"No, no, no! That's not what this is. This is just a flicker of what's eventually going to be a *lot* more."

David Swantek says that this episode just fortified his belief that Roth "was really the driving force that kept them going, even though they had all the talent, to be honest about it. I remember that scene in the car like it was yesterday. That's the thing about David Roth and Van Halen. They knew where they were going, even back then. They really had a fix on it."

= =

Back in Pasadena, the band regrouped. They went back to gigging at places like the Pasadena Civic, Walter Mitty's, and the Starwood. They also thought about what to do with their demo tape. At least from Edward's perspective, the band initially "didn't know where in the hell to take it; we didn't know anyone" in the recording industry who'd be interested in hearing it.[443]

Roth, however, had ideas. By December, he'd gotten the tape into the hands of Bingenheimer, who had a popular radio show on KROQ. On December 14, Roth joined him on the air to debut "Runnin' with the Devil." Roth, ever the shrewd promoter, lavished praise on the DJ, giving him *all* the credit for bringing "some of the fellas from KISS" to the Starwood. Roth then recounted their New York trip and recording session — without mentioning Aucoin's verdict — saying, "What we have here is one hell of a demo tape." And just like that, Van Halen got its first real airplay.[444]

= =

In April 1977, KISS came off the road and Simmons returned to Los Angeles. As he recounted in KISS's official biography, "I wrote 'Got Love for Sale' at the Sunset Marquis, when we got back from Japan, along with 'Christine Sixteen.'" He also had another song that he'd worked up called "Tunnel of Love." With his rough work tapes lying nearby, he picked up the phone and called the Van Halen home. He asked Alex and Edward if they'd like to work with him at Village Recorders again, this time to demo these three songs. If the brothers would lay down drum and guitars, Simmons could add bass and lead vocals to the tracks.[445]

None of this sat well with Roth. In *Crazy from the Heat*, Roth charged that "Gene Simmons's true interest" in Van Halen "was in conscripting Ed Van Halen into their show in some form or another, get him to play on a record, get him to help write guitar solos, get him into the band."[446] Leiren shared Roth's suspicions. "As a matter of fact," he told Steven Rosen, "I know he wanted to get the band away from Dave. He didn't like Dave at all."[447]

Further support for the idea that Simmons's intentions weren't pure comes from Pasadena native Wally "Cartoon" Olney, who hung around the brothers quite a bit in 1977. He told *The Inside*, "I was at [the Van Halen home] several times, and Gene had called there and Ed was going, 'No, man, I don't want to play.'" After he hung up the phone, Edward vented to Olney: "God, he calls me constantly and won't leave me the fuck alone. It was cool that he made the tape for us, but I don't want to be in a band with him. I've got my own band."[448]

Ultimately, the brothers decided to do the session. But when Edward, Alex, and their techs showed up at the studio, an unexpected guest accompanied them. "Simmons would look at me with horror," Roth recalled. "*Horror*, 'cause I was on to his game way early."[449] Leiren adds, "Dave wanted to be there whenever they did anything, because he suspected what Gene was up to. He felt that, *Hey, this guy is trying to undermine my interest here and I want to keep an eye on it*. There was always a little static there between them."[450]

With Roth and Leiren looking on from the control room, Gene, Edward, and Alex set up. They recorded the basic tracks for the three songs live. Simmons then listened to the playback and gave the performances a thumbs up.

To finish the tracks off, Simmons asked Edward to lay down some solos. Within a few moments it was clear to Simmons that

Edward's skill level had grown "leaps and bounds" since November. "The control he'd developed on the instrument since I'd seen him last was just incredible," Simmons remembers. "He was *flying* on that thing. He was using the wang bar by now, and because the [sound] level was so loud, he could continue to hit the fretboard without picking the string. It sounded like a roller coaster ride — almost as if he was playing and someone was messing with the speed of the tape."[451] While things went smoothly on "Love for Sale" and "Tunnel of Love," they hit a stumbling block when it came to "Christine Sixteen."

Just as he had done in New York, Simmons coached Edward, trying to convey his vision for the song's lead guitar parts. Leiren recalled, "It's funny, because at first Edward wanted to play it the way he thought it should be played. Gene would go, 'No no no! Too intricate! Simpler, simpler!' So he tried it another way."[452]

This new solo still didn't match what Simmons was hearing in his head. He reiterated that he wanted a less technically complex lead break. "Simpler! Simpler!" he told him after each attempt. Six takes later, Simmons felt unsatisfied and Edward felt frustrated.

Finally, Roth could take no more of Simmons's inability to coax the proper performance out of Edward. Roth said to Simmons, "Can I talk to him?" Simmons nodded, "Sure, go ahead."

Roth marched into the studio and spoke to Edward. Using what Leiren termed "baby talk," he attempted to put what Simmons wanted into words that Edward would understand. Leiren said, "I don't remember how he said it, but he got the message across to Edward and then the very next take Edward played it just the way Gene wanted it. [Simmons was] like, 'Yeah! Yeah! That's it — *That's it!*'"[453] After Roth's assistance, Simmons was so satisfied with the result that "when the band recorded it for *Love Gun*, Ace pretty much copied Eddie's solo note for note."[454]

But did Ace actually *play* that solo on *Love Gun*? Leiren, who watched the whole session, doesn't think so. "To this day," he told Steven Rosen in 1985, "I will *swear* that that guitar solo on 'Christine Sixteen' is the same one that Edward laid down. Just listen to the sound quality. It sounds just like Ed [playing] on the *Love Gun* album. To me it sounds exactly like when I was standing in the control room watching and listening. *Exactly!*"[455]

= =

As the summer of 1977 began, Simmons stayed in Los Angeles and remained in touch with the Van Halen brothers. Kim Miller recalls that Gene took her and Edward to see Cheap Trick.[456] At other times the God of Thunder would show up at Van Halen's shows at the Whisky a Go-Go. Brian Box says, "Gene Simmons used to come to a lot" of their Whisky gigs. Patti Fujii Carberry, whose boyfriend was Roth's old friend from high school, was in Van Halen's dressing room one night when Simmons made an appearance. "We were upstairs at the Whisky when Gene Simmons came in, and we talked to him. He sat backstage with us." Patti, who is of Japanese descent, recalls the incident vividly because Simmons spoke to her in Japanese.

By July, Simmons was on the road again with KISS, only to return in late August for three shows at the cavernous Los Angeles Forum. Before the stand began, the Van Halen brothers got a call from the KISS camp, telling them that tickets for the band would be waiting for them at the will-call window. Roth unloaded about this episode in his autobiography: "There were scenes like, 'Oh, all you guys are invited to the big KISS show down at the Forum,' and I would show up and there would be no tickets for me. The Van Halens would be inside, comfortably ensconced in the back room with Gene and his pals. Of course I knew what was up, and I was super protective of the band at the time, or people like that would have picked us apart right away."[457] Once again, Leiren offers confirmation: "Gene came back to town with KISS, he called up the guys, 'Hey come down to the show.' When they got down there, there were tickets for everybody except for Dave. No tickets for Dave. Dave said, 'Fuck it' [and] split."[458]

= =

Despite the passage of years, Roth never forgot this snub. According to Leiren, Roth bumped into Simmons in Los Angeles in the spring of 1984, sometime before Van Halen played the Forum in May. Roth greeted Simmons warmly and, in his inimitable Diamond Dave style, said, "Hey Gene! How you *doing*? Good to see you!" The two stars spoke for a few minutes before Roth said, "Hey we're going to be playing the Forum. You want to come down to the show?"

Simmons smiled and said, "Sure. Great. I'd love to."

"Okay, I'll take care of you."

The night of the sold-out show, Simmons went to the will-call window. "Tickets for Gene Simmons," he said. After a couple of minutes, the clerk returned and informed Simmons that there were no tickets for that name. Leiren told Steven Rosen, "Dave swore someday he'd get his revenge, and he got it. He left no tickets for Gene Simmons. Payback is a motherfucker."[459]

RIGHT OUT
OF THE MOVIES

Van Halen's 1977 signing to Warner Bros. Records by producer Ted Templeman and label executive Mo Ostin is the stuff of rock legend. "They came in [to the Starwood] one night when we were playing for free," Roth mythologized to *Record Mirror* in July 1978. "Having watched the set, they came backstage and offered to sign us up with Warner Brothers."[460]

After years of striving for this moment, the band members found the experience surreal. Edward said the two powerful men appearing in their dressing room was a "heavy thing, man."[461] Roth told the *Los Angeles Times* that the night felt like "a scene right out of the movies."[462] The motion picture analogy used by the band's singer was no accidental turn-of-phrase. The band's late 1977 Warner Bros. Records band biography quotes him saying "We always knew we'd be discovered, but when it happened it was right out of the movies."[463]

While the movie metaphor captures the storybook nature of that fateful night, it does little to tell the full story of how

Templeman and Ostin ended up at the Starwood. Van Halen's Warner Bros. "discovery," it turns out, depended on many behind-the-scenes maneuverings that put the four performers in the perfect position to get their long-awaited record deal.

= =

In the summer of 1976, Kim Fowley heard a lot of street talk about a promising local group. "It came to my attention that there was this band at Gazzarri's at the other end of the Sunset Strip," the fast-talking promoter and producer said. Even though Fowley was always in search of pop music's "next big thing," the idea of visiting that nightclub turned his stomach.[464] He remembered, "It was two blocks away from the heart of the Strip but it might as well have been two thousand miles away. Gazzarri's was for all the troglodytes from the hillbilly sections of L.A.; all the redneck enclaves like the horrible Inland Empire. I'd see these loser kids hanging out in the parking lots near the Rainbow and London Fog. It was awful. The word polyester was invented with Gazzarri's in mind."

Still, the Runaways manager couldn't dismiss all of these impassioned testimonials he'd heard from "blondes with big tits" and "redneck kids" hanging out on the Strip. "All they'd talk about," he explained with a grunt, was this Pasadena band called Van Halen![465]

Fowley, who'd grown disgusted with the recent trend of "all these people trying to create New York or London bands in L.A.," went to the club. "And there they were." That night, Roth laid his best used-car salesman pitch on the influential Fowley, telling him that Van Halen was the "ultimate band" in town.[466]

Soon after, the pair lunched in Hollywood. "We ate at Denny's one afternoon," Fowley recalls, "and he told me that David Lee Roth and Van Halen were going to rule the world." As Fowley listened, he considered the band's strengths and weaknesses. He says, "I thought Eddie and Dave were good; I thought Dave was a combination of Black Oak Arkansas's Jim Dandy, and Al Jolson. I thought the drummer was okay. The bass player didn't really fit, but that didn't really matter. To me, they were just another version of Led Zeppelin." Once he finished his monologue, Roth asked, "Will you help us?" Fowley agreed to do so, undoubtedly thinking about the innumerable times he'd profited from helping bands get record deals.

Fowley then made a few calls. One of them was to Denny Rosencrantz, the Mercury Records A&R representative who'd signed the Runaways. Fowley encouraged him to come see the quartet at the Starwood. Rosencrantz, hoping that Fowley had just handed him another marketable act to sign, said he'd come to the show.

As promised, Rosencrantz appeared. He found Fowley in the VIP balcony and grabbed a seat. In truth, they could have sat or stood anywhere in the club, because it was deserted. Fowley estimates there were about eight people in the audience when Van Halen started playing.

It didn't take long for Rosencrantz to make his views known. He looked over at Fowley, shaking his head and laughing. "He *hated* them," Fowley recalls. With a smile on his face, Rosencrantz yelled, "It's an awful band, but keep trying, Kim!" Before leaving, he informed Fowley for future reference: "I'm not interested in signing Jim Dandy fronting Led Zeppelin."

Between sets, Fowley went backstage and told the band that Rosencrantz had passed. A crestfallen Edward asked, "Will you still help us even though Mercury said no?" Once again, he said he would help.

= =

It's important to note that even more music industry figures had received a heads-up about Van Halen in the second half of 1976.

Joe Berman, who was a fixture on the Hollywood scene, says, "I saw record company people at their shows before Gene Simmons ever came into the picture. I didn't know these people, because I wasn't in that part of the business at that time. I can't remember names, but A&R guys were aware of what was going on with this band in town. I'm sure they were coming to check them out."

In one instance, musician and record executive Herb Alpert took a look at Van Halen. Edward told *Rolling Stone*, "I remember a long time ago, we were playing and someone told us, 'A&M Records is here to see you guys.'" Alpert, like Rosencrantz, saw no potential in the band. After finding himself put off by Edward's wild playing, he told the band that their "guitarist is too psychedelic and [has] too much uncontrolled energy." Years later, he conceded to Edward, "One of the biggest mistakes I ever made was passing on you guys. I didn't understand what the hell you were doing 'cause it was so unorthodox."[467]

Yet even industry figures who embraced the unorthodox, like legendary producer Bob Ezrin, didn't think Van Halen was worth their time. Hernando Courtright explains, "I tried through my friend Scott Anderson, who was working with Bob Ezrin at the time, to bring Ezrin to see the band. Bob just couldn't be bothered. He was too busy. He had worked with Alice Cooper and he had just done Peter Gabriel's album. Scott just couldn't get him focused to come out and see the band. I don't know if Scott was not selling it right, but I know he said, 'You've got to see this band. You've got to lock in on this band. This band's going to be huge.' We told the band, 'I don't know what the story is, but he's just not motivated.'"

Anthony explains that this type of thing happened frequently. They'd hear that record executives would be coming to see them, only to find that no one had shown up. This even occurred when Dr. Roth made calls to record labels. Anthony recalls, "On occasion, he'd say that he was going to send someone out to see us, but what we'd do is have the reserved card out on a table, and nine times out of ten it would still be there at the end of the night."

= =

Meanwhile, Fowley hadn't forgotten about Van Halen. By early November 1976, he was helping to line up acts for the re-opening of a Sunset Strip landmark, the Whisky A Go-Go. The club, which had spent the last three years operating under different guises, including as a disco, would start featuring local rock acts at the end of the month.[468] Elmer Valentine, the club's owner, told *Billboard* that he believed the timing was right to start booking unsigned bands, because "punk rock, which is so hot in New York now, may well be due to hit Los Angeles."[469] The man that Valentine entrusted with the task of capitalizing on this abrasive new musical trend was Marshall Berle.

Even though he's well known for being the nephew of comedian Milton Berle, Marshall Berle became the Whisky's booking agent after building an impressive music industry resume. Back in 1960, he went to work as an agent for the famed William Morris Agency. He started up their West Coast music department and within eighteen months had signed the Beach Boys. Later, he worked with rock legends Creedence Clearwater Revival and Spirit.

In early November, Berle left a message for Fowley, asking if he knew of any hot local bands he might consider for the Whisky. When the Runaways manager returned the call, he reminded Berle about his newest act, the pop-punkers Venus and the Razorblades, before dropping another name on Berle. He said, "There's this band Van Halen. Even though Danny didn't get it, I think there's something there." Fowley, always thinking about his own publishing revenues, then made a request of Berle. "If you end up managing them, just make sure I have a song on their album."[470] He then passed Roth's phone number on to Berle.[471]

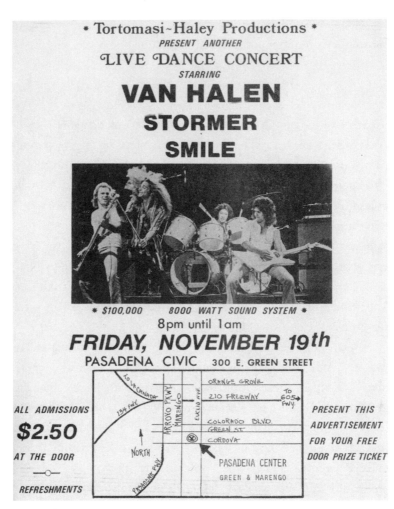

* Tortomasi~Haley Productions *

PRESENT ANOTHER

LIVE DANCE CONCERT

STARRING

VAN HALEN
STORMER
SMILE

* $100,000   8000 WATT SOUND SYSTEM *

8pm until 1am

FRIDAY, NOVEMBER 19th

PASADENA CIVIC   300 E. GREEN STREET

ALL ADMISSIONS

$2.50

AT THE DOOR

REFRESHMENTS

PRESENT THIS
ADVERTISEMENT
FOR YOUR FREE
DOOR PRIZE TICKET

Flyer for Van Halen's November 1976 concert at the Pasadena Civic, where
Marshall Berle, who later managed the band, first saw Van Halen perform.
MARY GARSON/HOT SHOTZ AND STEVE TORTOMASI

When Berle called Roth, he let him know that he was considering booking Van Halen at the Whisky. Roth reacted with
enthusiasm, and suggested that Berle come check out his band at
their upcoming show at the Pasadena Civic. Berle agreed to do so,
telling Roth that he'd come bearing the Whisky contracts.

On November 19, Berle drove to the gig, which he expected would be a small affair. He soon realized his mistake. "When I got there on the night of the show, to see what I thought was just another punk rock band," he saw the parking lot filled with a fleet of Camaros, Mustangs, and custom vans while herds of teenagers made their way into the Civic.[472] When he arrived at the building's entrance, he was told the show was sold out. He recalls, "There were 3,500 people at the Civic in Pasadena. I couldn't even get in! I had to go backstage and do the whole 'I'm an agent' number just to get in."

Standing in the packed hall, Berle felt the electric vibe as an army of screaming teenagers greeted Van Halen and cheered their every move. He remembers, "It was great! I just couldn't believe what I was seeing. It was one of those things that you see once in a lifetime, and I saw it twice: one time at the Palladium when the Beach Boys opened for Dick and Dee Dee, and then with Van Halen. Only twice in my life have I seen a band that no one's ever heard of in terms of commerciality that just blew me away. It just happened to be two of the greatest bands in the history of music."

After the show, Berle went backstage and found Roth surrounded by a harem of young beauties. Roth excused himself, shook Berle's hand, and introduced him to the others. Berle, still buzzing from Van Halen's blistering performance, complimented them and said, "You guys should have a record deal."

To Berle's surprise, the four musicians suddenly turned cold. He says, "Eddie Van Halen turned around and looked at me. Then the brothers looked at each other, and then at Dave and Michael. Then the brothers looked at me and went 'Yeah. *Right.*'" Shrugging off their comments, Berle reiterated, "I'll get you a record deal. Let's play some shows at the Whisky." The band signed the contracts.

For some time, Berle had no inkling why they'd responded in that fashion, until someone told him about Van Halen's recent trip to New York. Tired of hearing people promise everything and deliver nothing, Van Halen thought Berle would do little more for them than get them into the Whisky.

Berle, who says that he harbored no aspirations to be Van Halen's manager at that time, held up his end of the Whisky bargain. Van Halen was among the first acts booked by Berle. The club, which had built its storied reputation by showcasing some of the greatest talent in rock history, sought to become ground zero for the city's burgeoning punk rock scene. Thus, Berle hired acts like glam-punk oddballs Zolar X and Fowley's Venus and the Razorblades and proceeded to put them on bills with a decidedly un-punk rock quartet from Pasadena.

= =

Soon after their Whisky debut, Van Halen met a young man who eventually became one of their most valued employees. In 1976, a teenage Pete Angelus had driven from the East Coast to Hollywood. He'd then landed a job at the Whisky, which involved getting bands off- and onstage in a timely fashion and, eventually, working the stage lights.

After a slow night at the club, Angelus struck up a conversation with Roth. Angelus said he'd made short films back on the East Coast and had an interest in lighting and staging. Roth then asked Angelus about Van Halen's show. Angelus shot straight, telling the singer that while he thought his band was great, their show featured some "very repetitive" aspects that could be improved. Roth, intrigued by Angelus's suggestions, invited him to an upcoming rehearsal.

Angelus arrived at the Roth mansion the next day. After Diamond Dave buzzed him through the gate, Angelus drove down the long driveway. He met Van Halen's frontman outside a back door that led right into the kitchen. When they stepped

VAN HALEN RISING | 246 | GREG RENOFF

inside, Angelus did a double take. "I was really caught off guard," he recalls, "because somebody had spray-painted on the kitchen cabinets NO MILK!

"I said to Dave, 'Um, are you guys remodeling? What's going on here?'

"'Nah, man, there's no fucking milk in the refrigerator and it really annoys me.'

"'So you've gotta spray paint that? You can't just jot that down as a note and leave it for somebody?'

"That was my first impression of entering their world."

Angelus apparently fit right in, because he soon went to work as a lighting and production consultant. He remembers, "So I said, 'Okay, I will design a lighting show that will step things up a little bit,' to make them look like rock gods, so to speak."

═ ═

With Angelus in their corner, the band continued to perform all over Los Angeles. Bookings at the Whisky continued in December, but the band also played at the Golden West, the Starwood, and the KROQ Cabaret, a short-lived West Hollywood nightclub that was housed in a former disco.

At the Cabaret, they'd shoot the shit with Bingenheimer and gig with bands like Venus and the Razorblades, punk-rockers the Quick, and Randy Rhoads's neo-glitter quartet, Quiet Riot. At soundchecks, Edward and Alex put their fellow musicians on notice about their exceptional musical skill. They played scorching renditions of fusion songs from Jeff Beck's *Wired*. They also slammed out "Quadrant 4," from Billy Cobham's *Spectrum*, a jazz-rock tune they'd nick for "Hot for Teacher."[473]

A few weeks later, Van Halen gigged with a young hard rock band from San Francisco, Yesterday & Today. Drummer Leonard Haze remembers, "The first time I met them I was down in

Hollywood. We went and saw them at Gazzarri's. The next time we were playing at the Starwood, Roth came down. We talked, drank, smoked a couple of joints, and just got to be friends."

They played three gigs together in January. They lined up two shows at the Starwood, but the night before those shows started, they played at the Golden Bear nightclub in nearby Huntington Beach. Hoping for a little beach time, both bands got to the club early on January 17. Haze says, "Dave and I were sitting out on this brick wall that was by a cement walkway. There was sand on one side and you've got street on the other. We were smoking a joint, like Dave and I usually did. Eddie comes walking out. He's sitting there, smoking with us."

After the three got high, Edward pulled out a harmonica. Haze says, "He goes, 'Man, I just bought this thing.' And he's blowing it like he's played that thing *forever*. Dave goes, 'Doesn't that just piss you off, man?'"

While Edward blew his harmonica, a musician who'd just come from a nearby jazz club approached carrying a saxophone case. Once he was in earshot, Edward asked, "Hey dude, is that a tenor or an alto?"

"A tenor," he replied.

"Dude, I've always wanted to play a tenor!"

"Um, yeah, okay, cool."

"Hey I've got a reed in my guitar case! Can I blow on your sax if I get my own reed?"

The saxophonist paused.

Roth chimed in, "Come on, man. Do it. Let him do it. He's never played one before. Go ahead and give him a shot. Here, smoke this joint with us. This could be fun."

Putting his case up on the wall, the man sat down and said, "Yeah, you've got your own reed? Go ahead and get it."

Edward left and then returned with a reed. Edward then started to play. His raw musical talent stunned Haze. "And so in five minutes, Eddie was blowing the shit out of that saxophone. I mean like a serious sax player. He was playing it like he had been playing it all his life. It was amazing. It blew me away."

The next afternoon, the two bands reconvened at the Starwood. Once again, Edward showed off his unmatched musical abilities. When Yesterday & Today soundchecked, Dave, Edward, and Alex watched.

On a break, Edward jumped behind Haze's kit. Haze chuckles at the memory. "I told him, 'Get off my fucking drums, man! You can't even play.' He goes, 'What do you mean, I can't play?'"

Roth, as he was wont to do, interjected. "No, it's not that he can't play. You give it to him, and he'll play it." Haze then watched as Edward played his drums "like he had been practicing. It wasn't like a guy getting sloppy and blowing it here and there. He was just *on it!* I was like, 'Goddam, dude, stop that!' I said [*laughs*], 'You let him do that on your kit, Al?' Al goes, 'I'm not around when he does it!'" Haze observes, "The guy could play anything. That's what amazed me about him. Playing guitar, he was great. Watching him do stuff on harmonica and play my drums; the guy is the most talented human being I've ever laid my eyes on."

Edward then picked up a guitar as the San Francisco rockers resumed their soundcheck. Haze says, "[Guitarist] Joey Alves and Eddie hit it off. Joey loved playing rhythm for a guy who could solo. So the two of them would jam, and they were having a great old time. Matter of fact, you know that [technique] where you hit a chord and then you turn up the volume knob? Joey showed that to Eddie, because we had a song that had that in it. Eddie goes, 'What are you doing on that song 'I'm Lost'?' Joey goes, 'I hit the chord with the volume off and then I bring it up slowly.' Eddie's like, 'That's cool!'"

Later, someone whispered to Van Halen in the dressing room that record company executives would be coming to the shows. Although Berle has no recollection of inviting anyone down for these gigs, it's possible that his promise to get the band a deal got Van Halen thinking that he'd already worked his magic.

But no executives ever made themselves known to Van Halen on those nights. The band again felt deflated. Edward tied one on to drown his sorrows.

Out in the parking lot, Yesterday & Today packed their van as a loaded Edward stood nearby. When the band's vocalist and lead guitarist, Dave Meniketti, started to drive off, Edward staggered over and stuck his head in the driver's side window. Meniketti recalls, "He was crying to me, 'When are we ever gonna get a record deal?'"[474]

The members of Yesterday & Today, who had a record contract, offered Edward some words of encouragement before pulling away. Haze says, "They were one of my favorite bands during that era. I was amazed they hadn't gotten a deal. I was amazed that Warners hadn't come and seen them, especially because of the stuff Eddie was doing. You know, they were right down the street. That's a fucking no-brainer if you ask me!"

= =

While Tom Broderick remembers that in early 1977 the band "fully expected" to be signed soon, the disappointments did weigh on them even as they continued to work harder than ever. Maria Parkinson, who later appeared in David Lee Roth's "Yankee Rose" video, says, "I remember one time I saw David on a break from rehearsing. They were playing at the Whisky and they didn't get signed. I remember David being very frustrated and upset. In the meantime they still practiced like crazy."

Dana Anderson saw a similar determination in the Van Halen brothers. One day in January 1977, he heard Alex's drum tech Gregg Emerson ask Alex and Edward, "What are you going to do if you guys don't get signed? What are you going to do for a living? You don't have any experience at anything." Anderson recalls, "They looked at him like he was crazy. 'What do you mean, *if*? We're going to make it.'" He emphasizes the fact that "they were determined from a very young age. They had the drive and the determination. I think they got it from their dad and the Dutch upbringing."

= =

The band regrouped and reflected on how far they'd come. They'd put Gazzarri's in the rear-view mirror, and now with steady bookings at the Whisky on their calendar, they prepared to say goodbye to Walter Mitty's. Chris Koenig saw the band's final show at Mitty's. He recalls that the quartet let loose onstage. "The last Walter Mitty's gig was fun. They announced 'This is it!' They were *on*. They did Johnny Winter, Edgar Winter, and KISS. They were just having a blast. They all changed instruments. I think at one point Eddie was playing drums."

Koenig, who stood by the stage, adds, "I was so close, and the show was so crazy." He laughs, "I remember at one point I was standing in the front, and I had a pitcher of beer, and Roth asked me for it. I handed it to him, and he poured it over his head, which at the time pissed me off because, hey, I spent two bucks for that! It's funny, years later I ran into him at the Country Club [an L.A. nightclub]. I said, 'Hey, you owe me a pitcher of beer!' I told him the story and he started laughing."

= =

Back in Hollywood, their Whisky bookings had earned them praise from the *Los Angeles Times*. Critic Richard Cromelin, whose review also highlights the embryonic nature of Los Angeles "punk rock" in late 1976, had this to say about Van Halen and "Edwin," the band's guitar player: "Even though the group is associated with the local punk-rock scene, its highly developed musical attack and conventional image give it a good chance of moving from the L.A. circuit into national popularity. Edwin Van Halen is the heart of the group . . . The material itself is pretty fundamental, but [Edward] Van Halen's resourcefulness keeps things interesting and steers the music clear of formulized heavy metal monotony."[475]

The good reviews continued into January 1977. Cromelin labeled the group "the slickest and most commercially promising of the local outfits" and praised "the dazzling guitar work of Ed Van Halen" which "more than compensates for some material that, while perhaps thin on paper, comes to vibrant life onstage."[476]

More importantly, the dean of the city's critics chimed in about Van Halen. Robert Hilburn, who'd been one of the first American journalists to recognize Elton John's star power, wrote, "The fastest moving of the unsigned bands appears to be Van Halen, a heavy metal quartet from Pasadena." In the same piece, Bingenheimer gave the band his stamp of approval, saying, "I wouldn't be surprised to see them signed and on a big tour soon. They should be playing the Forum as a support act by the end of the year."[477]

This buzz helped Berle get the band on a high-profile bill with Santana at the Long Beach Arena on January 30. Years later, Michael Anthony called the experience of opening this arena show as an unsigned band "amazing," but that night the heavily Hispanic audience had little love for Van Halen.[478] The *Long Beach Press Telegram* reported that the "hard-core rock band from Los Angeles whipped the crowd into an avid boredom."[479] In fact, even before they'd played a note, the crowd broke into a chant of SAN-TAN-A! SAN-TAN-A! The MC, preparing to introduce the band, walked over to Roth and asked, "By the way, what label are you guys on?" Roth shot back, "Shut up and just introduce us!"[480]

= =

At this juncture, Berle moved to set up a label showcase. He called the Starwood, which often hosted such gigs, and blocked off a couple of nights. He then rang up the band and, without telling them about his plans for a showcase, let them know that he'd booked Van Halen into the Starwood on February 2 and 3. Next, he called the Warner Bros. Records switchboard.[481]

When Berle got Templeman on the phone, he said, "Ted, I've got a band for you." He told him that their name was Van Halen and that he should come see them at the Starwood. Berle says, "I pitched them to Ted because he had an expertise in three-part harmony, and they were doing that in some of their songs. Plus Ted had a *huge* resume of hits." Indeed, Templeman, then an executive vice-president and house producer for the label, had overseen successful LPs by Van Morrison, Little Feat, Captain Beefheart, the Doobie Brothers, and another West Coast heavy rock quartet, Montrose.

Templeman recalls that he was happy to hear from Berle, whom he'd "known for ages." But he was at a loss when his old friend said the name "Van Halen." He asserts, "That was the first I'd heard of them, when Marshall Berle told me. I was busy. I wasn't on the street at that time. That's why he called me." Despite the recent run of positive press and big gigs, Templeman had no inkling that Van Halen was practically right on his doorstep. He told Berle he'd come check them out, since he knew the former agent had good instincts. "He always had his finger on the pulse," Templeman says.

On Wednesday night, a reserved sign sat on an empty table in the VIP section. But the blond Templeman, who looked more like a surfer than an industry executive, was in the house. "So I went down there one night," he remembers. "I kind of went in the back. I went in, but I didn't let them know I was there. I saw Ed, and I was just fucking knocked out. He was the best musician I'd ever seen in person."

Of course, Templeman couldn't help but notice Roth as well. "Dave was playing to an audience of ten thousand, when there

A PLACE OF MUSIC

STARWOOD

8151 Santa Monica Blvd. ● 656-2200

JAN. 31-FEB. 1	**THE DOGS**
FEB. 2-3	**VAN HALEN**
FEB. 4-5	**PAPA JOHN CREACH**

FORMERLY OF JEFFERSON STARSHIP

DANCING—NO AGE LIMIT

Ad for Van Halen's performances at Hollywood's Starwood Club, February 1977. On these two nights, Ted Templeman and Mo Ostin of Warner Bros. Records first saw Van Halen live. AUTHOR'S COLLECTION

were about eleven people in there," Templeman told *Newsday*. "He was performing and sweating and jumping whether anybody was out there or not. He was wearing outrageous clothes."[482]

As the set moved along, Templeman focused almost exclusively on the band's guitarist. "Ed was still playing those hammer-ons while he was jumping in the air . . . Ed had Jimmy Page's moves down, he could play with a cigarette in his mouth. I signed them because of Ed, because he was such a great player. I figured there's Art Tatum, Ornette Coleman, and this kid."[483]

Looking back, Templeman emphasizes that his background as a working musician led him to lock in on Edward's virtuosity when other A&R men had found the same frenzied playing too avant-garde. "I don't think most A&R guys really knew their stuff when it came to guitar players, or musicians. I was kind of a snob, because I played jazz trumpet. I played bebop and everything else, so I was looking at Ed as a musician, rather than the group," Templeman says. "I think if you're an A&R guy just looking for a pop group you might get a little scared by Van Halen. But you've got to remember, there's a plethora of bands out there, and a lot of people — listeners at the time — weren't sophisticated enough to know how great Ed was. They wouldn't know." But he knew.

Having seen enough, Templeman exited. He says, "I don't think the guys knew the first night I was there. I had heard about them, and I wanted to see what was going on. Once I saw Ed I thought, *I don't want to talk to them until I have the guy with me who can sign them.* So that's why I made sure I had Mo with me the next night."

== ==

The next day, Templeman shared his experience with label president and chairman Mo Ostin and the company's other top executives. After he mentioned the name Van Halen around the office, someone handed Templeman a cassette copy of the Gene Simmons demo, which he'd never heard. He then tracked down his partner-in-crime, engineer Donn Landee. Landee recalls, "Ted came back after the first night at the Starwood and said, 'We're going to sign them. You've gotta hear this guitar player.'" Templeman then pushed play on the Simmons demo. "We listened," Landee says,

"and Ted said, 'We gotta go get these guys.' Ted loved Eddie."
Templeman also called Berle and told him he'd be coming down
to the Starwood with Ostin in tow.

Templeman explains that he was thinking strategically by
inviting only Ostin. Typically, he would have asked his best friend
and the label's top A&R man, Lenny Waronker, to come along.
But he knew that Waronker, who produced "L.A. Sound" singer-
songwriters and country-rock acts for the label, would find a hard
and heavy act like Van Halen distasteful. "Lenny was not into
heavy metal, ever, ever, ever," Templeman says.

Ostin, in contrast, liked heavy music. The bearded and bespec-
tacled label executive, Templeman says, "was more open to [hard
rock and heavy metal] than Lenny, I knew he knew this stuff — I
knew he appreciated it — and so that's why I took Mo instead
of Lenny." Templeman also knew that Ostin had signed rock
superstars the Kinks and another revolutionary guitar player to
Warner's sister label, Reprise, back in the 1960s. "Mo signed Jimi
Hendrix," Templeman explains. In fact, Mo had been watching at
the Monterey Pop Festival when Hendrix set the music world on
its ear. Templeman told Ostin, "You've got to check these guys
out," in the hopes he'd have a similar reaction that evening to the
virtuoso guitarist that Templeman had just seen.

As Michael Anthony remembered, the Thursday evening was
unremarkable: "The night we got discovered by Ted Templeman
and Mo Ostin was just another night." Berle said to the group, "'Hey
there are some important people here to see you.' People say that
all the time, so we just said, 'So what, we'll play our normal set.'"[484]

Perhaps because of the mid-week booking and a passing
shower, once again the club wasn't crowded. Still, the band set out
to level the place. Alex recalled, "We were playing to about twenty
people at the Starwood Club in Hollywood — but that didn't stop
us from doing our usual big show."[485]

As he'd promised, Templeman appeared with Ostin and another label executive, whose name has been lost to time. Berle recalls that he was happy to see Ostin, who, like Templeman, was an old friend who he'd known since the early 1960s.

The four men then headed upstairs to the VIP area and sat down. Edward's playing once again grabbed Templeman: "Let's put it this way — without Ed, there wouldn't have been a Van Halen. That's for sure. I saw them and I thought, here's this genius. I'm thinking, *There's Art Tatum, there's Charlie Parker, and there's this fucker.* I went, 'Goddamn, he's the real deal.'"

In fact, Templeman says, he put the flaws he saw in the band out of his mind because of Edward's greatness. "I signed them based just on Ed. *Boom!* That was it. I was signing Ed as a guitar player and the band I was going to make work around that, because I thought he was the greatest musician I'd ever seen in my life! I'd never seen anyone play live like that, except when I used to go to jazz concerts. I saw Dizzy Gillespie, I saw Miles, and all these people, but Ed played better than almost anyone else I'd ever seen live. I saw it *instantly.* I wanted to sign them on the spot."

Ostin, too, was impressed. Between the band's Hendrix-like guitar player and their knockout version of "You Really Got Me," Ostin saw the makings of a commercially successful act. Years later, he recounted, "I heard them onstage and turned to my colleagues and said something crass: 'They sound like money.'"[486]

Berle, who knew the band's talents well, says that his pre-gig call for the band to "play good" had been far exceeded by the four musicians, who were "fucking great" that night. When the house lights came on, Ostin turned to Berle and asked, "Are you the manager?"

Berle said no.

"You are now," Ostin replied.

In their small dressing room, the band members congratulated each other on the excellent performance. "We got done with the set," Edward told Jas Obrecht, "and we're all going, 'Hey, it was a good set. All right, guys!'"[487] With no label executives in sight, the band cracked a few cold ones and flirted with their girlfriends.

Just then, there was a knock on the door. Anthony remembered, "It was kind of rainy that night and we thought, *Nobody's coming,* and after we finished upstairs it was like, 'How do you do? I'm Mo Ostin and this is Ted Templeman.'" The stunned quartet stammered hellos and sent the girls packing as Berle and the executives entered.[488]

As the girls filed into the hallway, Leiren made his way down the corridor from the stage to the dressing room. He told Steven Rosen, "I remember the girls standing in the hallway going, 'Oh man, why do *we* have to get out? Those guys are *fucked!*' They were pissed! I knocked on the door and they said, 'You can't go in there!' Then they opened the door — I had the guitars in my hand and they let me right in! I knew who these big shots were so I go, *Man, there's* no way *I'm going to miss this.*"[489]

Inside the room, Ostin and Templeman told the band that they'd enjoyed the show. Anthony said, "Our mouths dropped to the floor, and I remember Mo saying he really loved the way we played 'You Really Got Me,'" a song he'd helped bring to the American market.[490] Templeman, too, "got off" on the song that night and made a mental note that the Kinks classic might be an excellent candidate to include on a Van Halen album.[491]

The pair then got down to business. Edward remembered that Ostin "asked us if we were signed. We said no. He then asked if we had a manager. We said no. Finally he asked if we had an agent, and we said no again!"[492] At that point the executives encouraged them to cement a formal relationship with Berle, the man who'd told them about Van Halen.[493]

Eavesdropping as he cleaned Edward's guitars, Leiren heard Ostin and Templeman say that they'd like to book some studio time with the band.[494] Anthony remembered, "Ted said, 'I'd like to do a demo with you sometime; get together in the studio and do a few songs and see what develops.'"[495] When Ostin proffered a letter of intent for them to sign, the band demurred, telling him that they'd "have to think about it" before signing anything.[496]

With that, the Warner Bros. team took down the Van Halen brothers' phone number and said, "Don't sign with anybody else," before heading out the door.[497] Roth observed that there was no chance of that happening: "We all stood around with our tongues hanging out, going 'Yessir, yessir.'"[498] Leiren remembered that once the executives departed, "Everyone was like, 'Alright! This is the big time!'"[499]

The next day, the phone rang at 1881 Las Lunas Street. It was Warner Bros. Records asking again if Van Halen would sign with the label.[500] Alex didn't wait long to say yes, since the band had already decided that they would take the deal.

Within hours, the four musicians, along with Berle, reconvened at the label's Burbank headquarters. After scheduling a demo session at the legendary Sunset Sound Studios with Templeman and engineer Donn Landee, they signed the letter of intent with the label.[501]

═ ═

From the standpoint of their career hopes, the band couldn't have been happier. Templeman and Landee had been the brains behind the Montrose debut album, which was one of Van Halen's favorite rock records.[502] But more importantly, Warner Bros. Records had long embraced hard rock and heavy metal. As writer Warren Zanes observes, "[As early as 1972] Warners was laying the groundwork for an era of heavy metal that would surprise many in its staying power."[503]

From the band's perspective, this made Warner Bros. their ideal label. Haze says, "They wanted a Warner Bros. deal. That's what

Dave told me, anyway. He said, 'Everyone's got good deals, but we want to be on Warner Bros.' It was all of the bands that were there like Sabbath, Deep Purple, and Montrose. They had a stable of *the* heavy rock bands. Then they had commercial access. They had a lot of radio promotion guys [on board], because they had the Doobie Brothers and stuff like that too. So Warner Bros. was really diverse." Edward felt the same way, telling Steven Rosen, "Warner Bros., man, that was always the company I wanted to be with."[504]

Knowing that nothing would be set in stone until the final rounds of negotiations drew to a close, the band celebrated in a low-key fashion. Larry Abajian, who owned the Van Halen family's favorite liquor store, Allen Villa Beverage, remembers, "The day they signed, Alex and Ed came in and bought a bottle of champagne and a package of paper cups."

But if they'd hoped to keep things quiet at first, they soon found out that wasn't going to be possible after the *Los Angeles Free Press* reported on February 11: "Local favorites Van Halen have signed with Warner Bros., marking them as the first band of the new wave of young groups to work their way through the local clubs onto a major label."[505] With the news out, Roth headed over to KROQ on Sunday to tell Bingenheimer. Koenig recalls, "I was actually at KROQ hanging out on Rodney's show when Roth showed up with a case of champagne, saying, 'Rodney, we got signed!'"

= =

Within a couple of weeks, Van Halen entered the studio with Ted Templeman, Donn Landee, and second engineer Richard McKernan. Edward remembered that the band didn't decide which facility to use: "Donn and Ted had basically done all the Doobie Brothers stuff there; it was one of their favorite places. I didn't know anything about studios, so wherever they wanted to go was okay."[506]

The band might not have known it, but by working at Sunset Sound, they were walking in the footsteps of rock's giants. Led Zeppelin, Alice Cooper, the Rolling Stones, and the Doors had recorded there. Along with the Doobie Brothers, Templeman and Landee had recorded Little Feat and Montrose at the fabled studio.[507] In preparation for the sessions, Landee reserved a generous amount of studio time.[508]

In the meantime, Templeman and the band held a pre-production meeting. They worked up a list of twenty-five tunes to record based on Van Halen's lengthy song list, which the band members had written out on a wall in Roth's basement.[509] At that meeting, Edward told Templeman that based on his experiences with Simmons, he preferred not to add extra guitar tracks to their songs. Templeman agreed to that plan, since he'd already learned at the Starwood about Van Halen's wall of sound.

On the first day at Sunset Sound, Templeman watched Van Halen tune up. Edward's ragtag effects setup caught his eye, and he looked on in amazement as the guitarist tested his rig. Templeman recalls, "He had this little board with all these things jury-rigged, like string and gum putting shit together. He'd put it all together and step on these little things. He was a fucking little genius. He sounded great. That board was just something he brought when we did the demo."

Once Landee rolled tape, Templeman watched in wonder as Edward worked. Unlike most guitarists, who needed multiple takes or multiple tracks to get their parts right, Edward just blazed through the songs, solos and all, in one take. Templeman says, "With Ed, I couldn't believe it. When we did the demo, he would sit there and just play. When he came to the solo, he would play the solo. I'd say, 'Do you want to put the chords underneath it?' He'd say no. But that's what sounded so great about it. They were playing as a power trio, because there was no rhythm guitar underneath the solo." McKernan says that Edward's vision for the demo sessions came to life because other than "a couple of over-dubs" the tracks were in fact done live.

Things moved at a dizzying pace. Alex, Michael, and Edward stood together in the room, with only baffles separating them, and recorded the instrumental tracks for each song live. Roth ensconced himself in the vocal booth and sang along. Templeman, who was unprepared for how quickly the band could work, says, "We just knocked 'em all down in one afternoon — boom, boom, boom!" Landee, who'd recorded bands since the late 1960s, says without qualification, "They were the most prepared band I had ever heard or recorded," so in the end, "we didn't need the extra studio time."[510]

= =

Templeman and his engineers had reason to be impressed. The band's song list was long and deep. It included six of the eleven songs that would end up on Van Halen's debut and eight other songs that would end up on Van Halen's first six albums in one form or another. To settle their debt with Kim Fowley, the band also recorded a hot version of a KISS-like song called "Young and Wild," which had been written by Fowley and Venus and the Razorblades' Steven Tetsch.

Even though the demo sizzles with energy, there are a few clunkers. Edward later explained to Steven Rosen that the demo included a few songs that "Van Halen–wise" were "kind of dated. They're a little dumber rock."[511]

The next day, the quartet knocked out their backing vocals. To conclude, the band recorded the Roy Rogers classic, "Happy Trails." Before they sang, Roth asked, "What else is left?" Anthony, surely thinking of the whirlwind nature of the experience, yelled, "Insanity!" Apart from a few vocal fixes by Roth — which he completed about a week later on the same day that Landee mixed the tape — the demo was completed.[512]

= =

While the band had a blast recording the demo, there was a less pleasant task ahead: getting legal representation and signing the final contracts. Anthony remembered, "Next thing I know, it was contract time. We scrambled out and [hired] a lawyer that Roth's old man got us."[513] The man that Dr. Roth suggested was an entertainment attorney named Denny Bond. He'd worked for singer Paul Williams in the 1970s, and in later years would be Lee Majors's publicist.[514] In the liner notes on *Van Halen*, the band gave "Special Thanks" to Dennis Bond, Esq.

Gary Ostby, the live-in groundskeeper at the Roth estate who'd become tight with Dave, points out that Dr. Roth had become a big Van Halen supporter by 1977. He says, "Dr. Roth didn't like [Dave's musical pursuits] at first, but as Van Halen started growing, he became more tolerant. He became a fan. He'd try to help them out every chance he could with the attorneys he knew; he would turn Dave on to them. And Dave had a business sense anyway, so he'd know if the guy was good or not. Even though the guy was *always* onstage, he made a lot of good moves."

Ostby adds that Roth understood that record companies almost always ended up in the catbird seat when the ink was dry on contracts. "He knew all the horror stories that you'd hear, even back then, about how the record companies are ripping people off and taking more than they were due." After they initially committed to Warner Bros. in February, Roth told Ostby, "We ain't giving away *anything*." Ostby says Roth's confidence came from the fact that "he had good attorneys from his dad to advise them."

Before any agreement was final, the band needed to tell Bond how they intended to handle their songwriting credits. Apparently, that decision had been made years earlier. Edward, who later lamented the arrangement, said: "We sat down at Dave's father's house and said, 'Well, what are we going to do if we make it?' I said, 'Split it four ways. There are four people, right?' That was before I found out that I was the only one who writes.'"[515] Soon after, the negotiations ended.

═ ═

On March 3, 1977, guitarists Carl Haasis and Gary Putman showed up early for Queen's *Day at the Races* concert at the Forum, making their way into the arena more than an hour before showtime.

While the pair checked out the stage, Edward walked up to them. They asked, "Hey man, what's up?" Edward laid some big news on them. "We fucking got signed today!"

Haasis said, "Whattya mean?"

"We're going to put a record out! A real record! We got signed!"

Haasis recalls that Edward went on to say, "'We got $150,000, and eighty thousand of it is going to go to this . . . ' He kind of broke it down." Haasis says that he and Putman, who were still playing in bands that specialized in copy material, stood dumbfounded as their friend shared the great news.

═ ═

Finally, it was time to celebrate. Roth visited George Courville and asked if they could throw a party at his house, since Roth's father had just laid down the law about late night gatherings at his home. Courville chuckles, "Dave came over and said, 'Can we use your house?' Stupid me, I said yes." [516]

Courville says that in true Van Halen style, the band threw a legendary bash. "There were about three hundred people at that party, with about twenty-one people standing in my tub/shower smoking and tooting at any given time. I passed out around 2:00 a.m. on the couch, with four holes in my walls: two in the bathroom, one in the kitchen, and one in the living room. I woke up at 3:00 a.m. to a food fight going on in the kitchen. Eddie, Alex, Dave, and a few friends had opened a case of beer on the kitchen floor and were doing a slip and slide thing. Meanwhile, they had taken all the food out of the refrigerator, piled it up on the kitchen table, and made a three-foot-wide by two-foot-high salad. The empty jars were included and mixed into the salad. By 6:00 a.m., I could have opened up a recycling center for all the empty bottles, cans, cups, and food plates everywhere."[517]

= =

These were indeed days of celebration for Van Halen. After years of hard work, Van Halen had finally secured the major label deal they'd long dreamed about. Now it was time to get ready to record their debut.

VAN HALEN

In March 1977, Ted Templeman was riding one hell of a hot streak. He'd produced numerous hit albums, and his upcoming schedule included sessions with proven acts the Doobie Brothers and Little Feat and promising newcomers Nicolette Larson and Van Halen.

In the case of Van Halen, he couldn't help but liken them to Montrose, the muscular quartet he'd produced back in 1973. And that's what worried him. Montrose had had *all* the pieces in place for a breakout debut: solid songs, an earthshaking bassist, a monster drummer, a masterful guitarist, and a powerful vocalist by the name of Sammy Hagar. Despite those advantages, *Montrose* staggered to a disappointing No. 133 on the *Billboard* album chart before disappearing from it forever.

When he did a similar accounting of Van Halen's assets, he felt confident about the band's deep song list, virtuoso guitarist, and rock-solid rhythm section. But when he compared the two singers, he thought Roth came up short. Templeman says, "I didn't think I was going to keep him" in the band after seeing Van

Halen at the Starwood. Wanting to hear how Roth performed in the studio, the producer withheld further judgment until after the mid-February demo session. Templeman recalls that what he heard on tape didn't assuage his fears. In fact, he says that at that time "Dave really made me nervous, because he couldn't sing."

Templeman thus considered replacing Roth with Hagar, who was then a solo artist. He says, "I actually wanted Sammy in the band at the time, because I had done Montrose. I know that was on my mind in the beginning." He explains that this plan made sense, because Edward loved Montrose's debut. Still, at that time Templeman never brought this idea to anyone in the band, even though he recalls mentioning it to Lenny Waronker and perhaps Donn Landee.

While Templeman ruminated, Roth refused to rest on his laurels. While many aspiring rock stars under contract with Warner Bros. might have gotten lazy, Roth worked hard. Within weeks, Roth's creative mind, clever lyrics, and improved vocals had convinced Templeman that he had all the requisite tools to front Van Halen.

Roth's labors, and those of his bandmates, would eventually bear fruit inside of Sunset Sound. In just fifteen days, Van Halen recorded one of rock's greatest debut albums, one that would make them America's hottest young rock band just months after its release. For Van Halen, this kind of success is a story of talent and hard work winning out in the end. For David Lee Roth — who could have been bounced out of Van Halen in early 1977 — it's a Rocky-like story of winning when the odds are stacked against you.

＝ ＝

Despite Van Halen's eagerness to start recording, the band entered hurry-up-and-wait mode after finishing the demo in February. Anthony remembered, "We didn't go into the studio for a long time, because Ted was doing a Doobie Brothers project."[518] As it turned out, he wouldn't be done cutting tracks with the Doobies anytime soon. Templeman explained in 1981 that unlike Van Halen, a band that can "go into the studio and blow it right out," a Doobie Brothers' album "takes a lot longer" to record.[519] With Templeman and Landee indisposed, Van Halen kept working.

Roth led the way. Although there's no evidence that he knew of Templeman's misgivings, Roth did hire a vocal coach in the spring of 1977. As he self-deprecatingly told *Winner* in 1986, "I took some vocal lessons for a while and obviously they didn't make my voice much better."[520]

Nonetheless, Roth did set out to become a better singer. Jim Burger remembers waiting in Roth's driveway for his friend Pete Dougherty (who lived in the property's garage apartment) when he heard singing coming from the main house. He looked and saw that "Dave was practicing his voice lessons up on the second story of the mansion. He'd tell us he wasn't taking 'singing lessons' — they were voice lessons."

Roth practiced religiously. Gary Ostby says Van Halen's main man "went through his exercises every morning" — which for a rock-star-in-training like Roth, began no earlier than 11:00 a.m. — and then every hour on the hour. Ostby says, "He was always doing his scales, *A-E-I-O-U*, and all that. He was with a voice coach way before their album ever came out."

With studio sessions looming, Roth knew the stakes were high. But he also knew that his own flaws as a singer would be magnified on an album featuring a guitarist as talented as Edward. Lisa Christine Glave, who was Dave's friend in those days, thinks that Roth worked so hard "in 1977 because he knew that Eddie was a virtuoso. If he was going to stay in this band, he realized he was going to have to take his performances up a notch. Eddie could take a tin can with three strings and make it sound like a

Stradivarius. To keep up, Dave had to really work at it. Eddie's talent was more inborn."

Significantly, Roth had made previous efforts to tune up his pipes. During his early '70s stint at PCC, Roth took a summer class, Music 172: Advanced Vocals, with an instructor named Gloria Prosper. For the final exam, students needed to sing five different songs in five different vocal styles, including pop, rock and roll, rhythm and blues, and Broadway. Roth, who likely failed the class after not turning in any written work, did give the final assignment a go. In front of his classmates and Prosper, Roth sang four of five required songs, all covers: Chicago's "Wishing You Were Here," John Brim's "Ice Cream Man," Donny Osmond's "Go Away, Little Girl," and Peter, Paul and Mary's "If I Had My Way."[521]

While it's unclear how Prosper and Roth's fellow students responded to this particular performance, at some point Prosper gave Roth some general feedback. Debbie Imler McDermott says, "I'd see him sitting outside the music room all the time. I'd walk up, say hi, and sit down and talk with him. I remember one day he was sitting there looking forlorn. I walked up and asked him, 'What's wrong?' He said, 'I'm taking this voice class, and my teacher said I've got a terrible voice and I'll never amount to anything.'"

= =

While Roth worked, Templeman pored over the demo. After a few weeks, he had a change of heart when it came to Roth. Whatever vocal shortcomings Roth possessed, Templeman knew that inside of Sunset Sound he "could go to work on whatever it was and try to fix it."

He also came to love Roth's songwriting. He says, "Once I got through that demo, I knew that Dave had something to say. He had a lot of depth and comedic skills. He was pretty amazing."

Templeman's newfound appreciation grew after he heard some songs that Van Halen had written since the demo session, like "Atomic Punk" and "Ain't Talkin' 'Bout Love." "I really did my homework," he remarks, "and what I learned was that those were Dave's lyrics, and he was a great lyricist. And I knew he was smart. And that's hard to come by, somebody who's really, really bright like that." Templeman says that in the end, "Sammy was a great singer, but Dave was a great writer."

Resolved to move forward with the current lineup, Templeman scheduled pre-production meetings. Here the band's inexperience encouraged them to defer to their producer. "We had Ted Templeman," Anthony recalled, "who was kind of like being the band leader at that point, telling us, 'Yeah, you should do this.'" With "us being new in the studio and the whole [recording] thing," Anthony said, "we were just like, 'Yeah, yeah,'" to whatever he suggested.[522] The producer says that while he did call the shots, the band ceded that authority to him. "Let's put it this way," he says, "all they did was say, 'Yeah. Whatever you want.'"

The first order of business was to pick tunes for the LP. Templeman says, "I pretty much wanted their album to be up and playful." In other words, he wanted nothing to do with gloomier songs like the *Island of Lost Souls*–inspired "House of Pain" or the Nightmare on the Bayou–themed "Voodoo Queen." He explains, "I just looked away from those songs" lest the album come off as "morose." Thus, any chance that Van Halen's debut would become a dark, doomy affair was scotched well before the band recorded their debut.

Instead, the vibe would be Southern California sunshine with a sugar rush. Songs like "Feel Your Love Tonight," "Show Your Love," "On Fire," and "Ice Cream Man" fit with this upbeat feeling. According to Templeman, everyone saw eye to eye on this point. "They were kind of gravitating towards happier stuff," a philosophy they'd largely remain committed to throughout their career. "If you go through the years, and if you listen to 'Jump' or 'Hot for Teacher' or 'Panama' they have an 'up-thing' to them."

Still, there was space for shadow on the LP. Remembers Templeman, "'Runnin' with the Devil' was dark and great the way it should be," and would make the final cut, as would "Atomic Punk" and "Ain't Talkin' 'Bout Love." These last two songs, interestingly enough, had been inspired by the city's punk scene, with the former allowing Roth to declare to the legions of punkers that he was the Strip's true alpha male.[523]

After watching them work on the demo, Templeman resolved once again to track the sessions as live as possible, an approach backed by Edward. This stemmed in no small part from the well-rehearsed group's talents. "They were so good live in the studio," Landee comments. "Not many bands could pull that off. We knew they could do it. We wanted it as raw as we could make it." Landee recalls that even before they recorded demos, Templeman and Landee intended to minimize overdubbing. "They don't know this," Landee remarks, "but we spoke between ourselves and decided we were going to discourage them from doing anything other than a 'live' recording."

To hear Templeman tell it, recording Van Halen depended on little more than rolling tape: "My job with Van Halen is to put a microphone in front of them and get the take."[524] Templeman recognized that Van Halen's ability to deliver live was what made them magical; he knew better than to conceal that talent under layers of studio effects.

Still, one band member harbored reservations about this approach. "Ted at that time was one of the most purist kind of [producers] around," Alex said later. "He wasn't interested in special effects. He wasn't interested in overdubbing. As a matter a fact . . . at the time I would have liked the record to be more like a Zeppelin record, which had layers of sound. But Ted [would have] nothing to do with it. He wanted to record the purity of it."[525]

Of course, nothing on *Van Halen* would sound more pure than Edward's monstrous guitar sound and dynamic playing. "When I recorded Van Halen's debut," the producer told *Guitar World*, "my strategy was just to take the guitar and blow it up all over the face of the damn map, because I thought it was the most amazing thing I'd ever heard."[526]

This approach all flowed from Templeman's awareness that Edward's instantly recognizable style made him a rarity among players. "Certain guitar players, no matter how well they play, just don't have a sense of how to make their instrument sound distinct."[527] Edward did, and thus his guitar would be front and center in the mix. As Michael Anthony would explain, "When we recorded our first album, Ted Templeman, our producer, was so into Eddie's playing. Everything was really oriented around the guitar."[528]

≡ ≡

What further encouraged Templeman to focus on Van Halen's guitarist was the great leap forward he'd recently made as a player. Carl Haasis, who'd seen Edward perform dozens of times since 1973, observes, "When I talk to people about Van Halen, I say, 'The two things he's known for, the whammy bar and tapping, happened at the very last moment.' He's playing for years and years and years, and that happened in the span of six months. All of a sudden he's doing this tapping. Isn't that crazy? You'd think, *Oh, this guy's been doing this for twenty years.* No." During the months leading up to recording the band's debut, Edward would radically alter his style.

The first step in this sequence began around December 1976 when Edward started playing a guitar he'd modified himself: a Stratocaster, loaded with a humbucking pickup and equipped with a whammy bar. When paired with his favorite Marshall head, his Variac, his effects pedals, and his own gifted hands, Edward's guitar sound was now astonishingly powerful.

At the same time, the introduction of the tremolo bar made Edward's style more wild and unpredictable than ever. Tracy G. recalls that he first saw Edward play this type of instrument at an early 1977 show at Walter Mitty's. "So he has this bar thing going, and he was using it like I never heard anybody use it, with the giant dive bombs, with that *wrooom* and all that."

And Edward still wasn't done changing his style. Tracy, who had rarely missed a Van Halen show, went to see them at the Whisky in the early summer of 1977. Again, Edward offered up something unexpected. He came out "with the Strat and he'd painted it white and he'd put electrician's tape crisscrossed all over it." Because Edward's unconventional-looking "Frankenstrat" — which he later painted in a unique black-and-white-striped pattern — would transform the way 1980s heavy metal guitarists decorated their instruments, it's easy to overlook how striking it was to those who first laid eyes on it.[529] Tracy explains, "I was standing there with a bunch of other guitar players. You could tell, because they were the ones with their fucking mouths open."

Edward had yet another surprise for everyone at the Whisky that night. After an introduction by Roth, Edward stepped into the spotlight. Tracy says, "He starts to do 'Eruption,' and he breaks out the finger tapping for the first time I'd ever seen it. I remember I turned to my friend and said, 'Oh no. That can't be.' I had never seen it. I had never heard it. I literally just bowed my head. I said to myself, *Fuck! What the fuck is that? Are you kidding me?*"

What astounded Tracy, and everyone else who saw Edward debut this technique in the summer of 1977, was its unorthodox nature. Edward used his right hand index finger to strike notes on his fretboard while simultaneously hammering on and pulling off notes on his guitar neck with his left hand. In doing so, he created music that sounded wholly different from the fretwork of more conventional rock guitar players. At this moment — months before the release of Van Halen's first album — Edward's tapping was setting the agenda for heavy metal's guitar heroes of the 1980s.

Here it's important to underscore the significant differences between the two-handed finger-tapping technique that Edward debuted that summer and what he'd learned from Mandel via Kilgore and from Gibbons's work on "Beer Drinkers." *Guitar Player*'s Jas Obrecht observes that the approach involved the creation of "spiraling, keyboard-like arpeggios."[530] Edward's 1977 technique unleashed torrents of flowing notes, rather than single pings or stuttering runs of tapped notes. In short, it was revolutionary.

Still, Edward did have sources of inspiration in late 1976 that might have encouraged him to revisit what he'd learned back in 1974. On September 14, 1976, Jeff Burkhardt took Edward to see Derringer, guitarist Rick Derringer's new quartet, open for the Runaways at the Starwood. That night, guitarists Derringer and Danny Johnson tapped a few notes early in their set before showcasing their take on the technique during the galloping "Beyond the Universe." Burkhardt explains, "It has that guitar solo at the end. Danny and Derringer bent their strings up and touched [*makes tapping sound*] strings in harmony at the end of the solo. Ed was standing right next to me; he was like eight inches away from me. And when they did that I kind of looked over at him and he had his head kind of cocked to the side. You could tell that all of a sudden the mechanics were working."

Edward got another dose of the technique right before Christmas. On the evening of December 20, Edward was walking on Santa Monica Boulevard when he bumped into his longtime rival, guitarist George Lynch, who'd just left a band practice.[531] Lynch and Edward exchanged pleasantries and found out they were both headed to the same place. Lynch says, "After a rehearsal, me and Eddie walked to the Starwood together" to see Canned

Heat. When they arrived, the marquee said a special guest would be joining them: Harvey Mandel.[532]

Lynch later explained what they saw. "We both witnessed Harvey Mandel from Canned Heat do a neo-classic tapping thing" during his guitar solo. He added later with a chuckle, "It was rudimentary, but it was tapping, which woke everybody up. Everybody went home and ripped it off."[533]

However these two experiences affected Edward's playing, it's a fact that he started woodshedding the tapping technique in the next few months. During that span, he created a paradigm-shattering approach to the instrument. And by the time he unveiled his two-handed method, it was a fundamental part of his style. Kilgore observes, "Like Jimmy Page, he could take something and own it like it was welded into his playing."

While Edward has always been publicly cagey about what inspired his two-handed tapping, he would privately credit Mandel. Journey guitarist Neal Schon told journalist Dan Hedges that Edward had confided in him when their two bands toured together in early 1978: "I was listening to 'Eruption' and all these other tunes, going 'What the hell is this kid *doing*?' I couldn't figure it out. I'd never seen that one-finger thing before. Later, I talked to Eddie and he told me how Harvey Mandel had done some stuff like that in the early days. I recalled seeing Mandel, but Edward took it to the limit."[534]

Perhaps the last word here should go to Kilgore; he's the first to concede that Edward was the difference-maker. Kilgore explained that when he tapped in the mid-'70s, all he did was "tag a note here and there." Edward, he maintained, is the player who "perfected it." If Mandel was "the guy who pioneered this tapping thing," Edward "took it three levels beyond that."[535]

= =

Apart from Edward's playing, Templeman also took inspiration from Montrose's first album. With its short, powerful songs, killer guitar tones, and brash production, it seemed like the perfect blueprint for *Van Halen*. Templeman remembers, "They pretty much liked Montrose so much that Ed wanted to borrow Ronnie's Marshall head for this recording. They'd named their band name just like Ronnie's last name. Van Halen really wanted to be exactly like Montrose." Michael Anthony agrees, saying, "Ted Templeman produced [Montrose], and I remember all of us in Van Halen telling Ted that we wanted to sound big and bad, just like them."[536]

Significantly, Templeman's Montrose experience had taught him a lesson: Van Halen needed a hit. He says, "Montrose never had a hit record, because they didn't have a hit single." At this juncture, Templeman thought that none of the band's originals sounded like pop singles. Thus, the Kinks' "You Really Got Me" would make the cut. As Edward Van Halen remembers it, "Ted felt that if you redo a proven hit, you're already halfway there."[537]

= =

Finally, in late August 1977, Van Halen entered Sunset Sound's Studio Two. Anthony concedes that they were all nervous: "As confident and full of ourselves as we came across on that record, the truth is, we were all pretty scared. I remember we put our headphones on and kind of looked at each other like, 'Wow, we're really doing this. Hope we don't mess up!'"[538]

To get loose, they treated Sunset Sound like Roth's basement. Edward told *Guitar Player* that once things got underway in the studio, they started "jumping around, drinking beer, and getting crazy."[539] Peggy McCreary, who served as one of the second engineers on the album sessions, remembers the band's exuberance. "The best thing I remember," she says, "was how enthusiastic and excited the band was just to be there."[540] "We had a lot of laughs, a lot of fun," Templeman told writer Warren Zanes. But it turned out "they were having a little more fun" than their producer, thanks to a certain white powder. "They would go into the other room, and I wasn't quite sure what they were up to. They had their own word for it: Krell. Ed would say to the roadie, 'Call Krellman.' I didn't figure it out for a while."[541]

To capture a live feel, Van Halen would record the basic tracks as a quartet, and thus try to perform in the studio as they did onstage. The best way to achieve this goal was to have the band track inside of Studio Two's spacious thirty-one-by-twenty-four-foot performance area. Templeman and Landee got the ball rolling by situating the drums in a location that would allow them to make eye contact with Alex from the control room. Templeman recalls, "In Sunset Two, I always put the drummers in the same place. With Little Feat I put Richie in the same corner I put Al in. With the Doobies I'd put the drummer over in that corner too. If they were just to the right-hand side, Donn could see them. I put Al in the same place. That way I could talk to Al. I could do a hand sign to him and he would look over and go, 'Yeah.'"

With Alex ensconced, the production team placed the others nearby. While Roth would sing in an adjacent booth, Michael and Edward would cluster around the drummer with only baffles separating the three instrumentalists. In fact, Edward so desired an intimacy with Alex and Michael that he would dispense with wearing cans. "I can't stand to wear headphones," he declared. "I feel like I'm in a glass bottle, separated from the rest of the guys. I never wear headphones in the studio, I just stand right next to Al and play."[542] The guitarist, like the rest of the band, would also play *loud*. "I use two [Marshall amps and cabinets]," he told Steven Rosen in 1978, "because I like to feel it too while I'm playing."[543] Even though Templeman and Landee sometimes spent days getting a good guitar sound, Edward quickly nailed things down.[544]

Still, the guitarist and his tech were unwilling to stand pat. McKernan explains, "Rudy always said, 'Eddie does everything himself,' but Eddie and Rudy masterminded his sound. They took pickups and rewound them with different gauge wire to see if that made a difference. They were always experimenting. But the real key was the Variac. They hooked it up between the amp and the wall. They'd use a lower voltage for the rhythm stuff when they wanted to sag out the amp for that thump. Or they would put a lot of voltage through it and push it almost to the limit and the amp's tubes would sizzle. That's what they would use for leads; they'd turn it up and get that sizzle. They were trying to do the same thing with pickups that they had done with the Variac." Templeman observes, "Ed was never locked into anything. He was all about exploring whatever he wanted to do. He was a very inventive, creative guy."

Landee, too, remembers Edward as a player who'd try almost anything to get the right sound. "Ed was totally committed to his sound and his craft," the engineer says. "I knew this after I was miking his cabinets for the album. I said, 'I want to get this microphone as close as possible to the speaker here.' He just took a knife and cut the grill cloth completely away, right in front of me. I didn't ask him to do it. He just did it. His sound came from being totally prepared."

With all of this attention focused on Edward, Michael Anthony felt like the odd man out. The very experience of entering Sunset Sound left him overwhelmed and frightened, and no one educated him on how to sound good on tape.[545] "The first album was weird," he later told Steven Rosen. "I discovered I didn't really know how to get a good sound in the studio with my fingers. Not to really slam Ted, but I wish he would have worked more with me too on that first album because . . . you can hear a lot of clicking and slapping on the bass." The producer, in Anthony's estimation, didn't pay much attention to the album's bottom end, because he "was infatuated with Edward's guitar playing and made that known." During the first album sessions, Anthony would ultimately discover that he "had a lot to learn [about] playing in the studio."[546]

= =

On Tuesday, August 30, tape rolled. The first track they recorded was "Atomic Punk." To create an appropriately primitive opening for the fast-paced song, Edward clicked on his phase shifter pedal and scraped the heavily callused heel of his right hand across his strings to create a riff that any beginner punk guitarist could mimic with ease.[547]

The next day, August 31, the band laid down the basic tracks for four more songs. The first was "Feel Your Love Tonight," a song propelled by an infectious riff that sounds like something the Beach Boys would have written if they'd been a hard rock band. As Roth explained in 1978, "'Feel Your Love Tonight' is the way you feel when you go out on a weekend night."[548] Alex agreed and added, "It's about what everybody feels on a Friday or Saturday night . . . you jump in your car, you pick up your girlfriend, and you're gonna have a good time. Well, with Van Halen, every night's a Saturday night."[549]

Next up was what would become the album's opener, "Runnin' with the Devil." Here Templeman acknowledges his debt to Simmons's work. The way he recollects it, "They brought me a demo I think they had done with KISS of 'Runnin' with the Devil.' We pretty much used the same horn intro for that thing." As the song fades into full volume, those salvaged horns roar like a 747 landing at LAX before giving way to Anthony's bass thumps. During Edward's solo spot, Landee and Templeman gave headphone listeners some ear-candy by panning Edward's rhythm guitar between channels, another flourish they'd borrowed from the Simmons demo.

But Templeman *had* reinvented the song. He primarily did so by recalibrating the song's cadence. A tune that had bounced along at a spirited pace now took on a menacing lumber. As Roth put it, "'Runnin' with the Devil' is how you feel when you feel like going out and strutting your stuff."[550] It's new tempo matched Roth's Chippendales dancer–meets–Jim Dandy vibe perfectly; what had been a stiff march now swaggered with attitude.

Templeman and Landee also remade "Devil" by making Edward's guitar sound like the roar of the gods. Ted Templeman, who always liked "a real good live echo chamber," placed one of Edward's cabinets inside one of Sunset Sound's reverb rooms and then had Landee treat the sound with the studio's EMT Plate Reverb unit.[551]

Set within the song's expansive sonic landscape were Roth's vocals. As the album's opener, it would be critical for establishing Roth as a bona fide vocalist. After Roth sang with the band, Templeman had him run through the song two more times. The Sunset Sound track sheet for "Devil" reveals that Roth's vocals on the first verse are a Templeman/Landee compilation of two takes, while the second and third verses appear to be drawn from individual Roth vocal attempts.

McKernan and Templeman explain how this played out in practice. McKernan says, "For *Van Halen*, Roth sang with the band as they played out in the big room. Then we went back and fixed the vocals by doing the traditional cut vocals." The band's producer adds, "We had him in the same booth every time, and we'd record that. We'd save a lot of the vocals. Sometimes we'd have him go back in there, and we'd punch him in and put him on another track, and we'd combine them later."

Here Templeman's skill paid dividends; he coached Roth so he'd shine. Anthony said, "Ted was Roth's mentor when it came to lyrics and melodies for the vocals. For the most part, Dave had a few licks down that he did over and over, so Templeman was in there and tried to suggest different lines."[552] In the end, what Roth set as a goal was "getting a feeling, or feelings, across" on tape, which "doesn't take the voice of a Caruso, a flawless technique, or purity of tone."[553]

In the end, "Devil" would capture the definitive David Lee Roth vocal. His singing, complete with screams, yelps, and whoops, wouldn't win him a Grammy for best vocal performance, but those affectations made him instantly recognizable. On the same album side that allowed the rock world to discover that no one played guitar quite like Edward Van Halen, listeners learned that no one sang quite like David Lee Roth.

As the band worked, tempers flared in the pressure-cooker atmosphere of the studio. Alex remembered, "If I was in the middle of a take and Ed told me I was rushing or slowing, I'd tell him he was out of tune. He'd throw the guitar down but . . . neither of us drew blood."[554]

During cool-down periods, Templeman would track the drummer down. "Alex Van Halen," Templeman observed, "never says much, but he has great ideas. So I'd maybe be at the Coke machine and he'd say, 'Hey Ted, did you ever think of trying this?'" Templeman would respond, "Wow, God, I wish I'd thought of that, Al. That's great! Why don't you say more?"[555]

Alex did start saying more, especially to his brother. Templeman explains, "Al was really good at helping Ed dial stuff in. He'd say, 'Ed, remember this? Ed, remember that?' Al was almost like an associate producer. He was always in there helping Ed remember things and do things that Ed did and stuff like that. He was this integral part of the band in this odd way that people don't know about."

The next song on the list was Van Halen's two-chord masterpiece, "Ain't Talkin' 'Bout Love." On this track, the production team came up with the idea of giving a song that started off as a punk parody a psychedelic flavor. Edward told *Guitar Aficionado*,

"The first time I used a Coral Sitar was when Donn Landee rented one from S.I.R. (Studio Instrument Rentals) for me to record overdubs for 'Ain't Talkin' 'Bout Love.' Either Donn or Ted suggested I overdub a sitar underneath that melodic part I played for the solos."[556] Even though Edward thought the unfamiliar instrument played like "a buzzy-fretted guitar," the track turned out spectacularly.[557] In 1983, Templeman revealed, "One of my favorite tracks I've ever done is 'Ain't Talkin' 'Bout Love.' As a production, I really loved that one."[558]

The last song cut on the second day of tracking was the Kinks' "You Really Got Me," a riff-based rocker that would become the perfect vehicle for Van Halen to prove that they'd reinvented heavy metal. Edward Van Halen explained, "We turned that song into a jet plane compared to the first version. We brought it up to date. It's just an old tune we always used to play in the bars when we did a lot of oldies. It went over very well live and fit well into our style of music."[559] Donn Landee recalls that the band cut the song quickly, and after playback they responded to their engineer's work with a burst of enthusiasm: "They did it in two takes, and I remember they gave me my first standing ovation at the board."

On Thursday, the first day of September, work continued with "On Fire." By this time, the song's arrangement had changed from the demo version. Perhaps after some input from his brother and Templeman, Edward cut out a tremolo bar–saturated tease between the first pre-chorus and the second verse; on the album track, the band gets right to the chorus. And in a gesture that might be taken as a final warning regarding Van Halen's coming assault on middle America, Roth added a siren-like scream for the song's close, another feature that hadn't appeared on the demo.

For "Ice Cream Man," Roth performed a song that he'd been singing well before he ever joined Van Halen. But even if he could sing it in his sleep, he still needed to croon out the song's opening with only a soft acoustic guitar as backing. There would be no end-of-the-world playing from the rest of the band to hide behind. This song was a Roth vehicle; it was up to him to sell it.

In one sense, the very fact that the song made the LP with this arrangement makes clear that Templeman now had confidence in Van Halen's vocalist. But the song's mix, with the acoustic set back, is the real tell. Roth is more naked here than on any other song on the album, and his strong blues voice fills the speakers. As much as any track on the LP, the opening of "Ice Cream Man" proves that Roth's hard work on his vocals had paid off.

In light of his later status as a rock sex god, Roth's performance on the opening verses is quite tame. The song's lyrics, which suggest that this vendor of sweet treats has more than lemonade to offer the ladies on his route, presented Roth with a golden opportunity to leer like Jim Dandy and lemon-squeeze like Robert Plant. But Roth sang it in a manner that wouldn't even make a sixteen-year-old virgin blush.

After the third verse — and a swaggering "Alright, boys!" — Roth's bandmates transform the song from an acoustic blues-shuffle into a searing electrified boogie. Edward's solo is another jaw-dropper, one that had given him fits as he sat at home, wondering, "Fuck, man, what kind of a solo am I gonna do [on] this?" But with its combination of swing and virtuosity, he hit all the right notes.[360] The song concludes with just a hint of Roth-as-Lothario. He croons his guts out, promising that his flavors are guaranteed to satisfy.

"Show Your Love" was Thursday's last song. It's a manic blues shuffle fueled by Krell and malt liquor, one that paid tribute to two Van Halen backyard party favorites, "I'm Going Home" and "Parchman Farm." While those tracks cooked, Van Halen's boogie here is hot enough to melt rock. The rhythm section locks in and sets toes tapping. Roth's sass and leer come with the perfect touch of Landee echo, making him sound like he's singing from the top of Mount Olympus. Edward serves up one dive bomb and whammy slur after another before unleashing not one but two burning solos with so many artificial harmonics that ZZ Top's Billy Gibbons must have stood and applauded the first time he heard it.

Just when it seemed like they'd keep the pedal to the metal, the quartet slammed on the brakes and served up an incongruous barbershop quartet vocal breakdown. On paper, the idea of R&B-styled doo-wop joining forces with adrenalized metal sounds like a career-ender, but as with so much in the early Van Halen catalog, there's no sense that this detour takes the band into unfamiliar territory. In fact, it sounds like they'd been woodshedding the Five Satins' 1956 hit "In the Still of the Night" on off-nights when they weren't flattening Gazzarri's. But this unexpected wrinkle in the Van Halen sound — just like the band's later efforts with offbeat tunes like *Diver Down*'s "Big Bad Bill (Is Sweet William Now)" — ends up smooth as glass; there are no lines that reveal where Van Halen ends and the Five Satins begin. It's all Van Halen.

The finishing touch on this track came later. The song was re-titled at some point between the day the song was recorded and the time Landee finished working with the master reels. Perhaps to prevent two songs on the album from having a title that included the phrase "Your Love," the band decided to rename the song "I'm the One." Hence, while the track sheet says "Show Your Love," the front of the tape box reads "I'm the One," a title written on top of a thin layer of Wite-Out.

= =

Starting on Friday, September 2, Van Halen worked on over-dubs and background vocals, a process that would take them the good part of a week to complete. These overdubs added splashes of color in surprising ways. For instance, on "Feel Your Love Tonight," Templeman added two tracks of handclaps and a tambourine (!) track. Likewise, "You Really Got Me" took on two tracks of "moans" for the song's breakdown.

Guitars, too, needed to be added. Edward overdubbed a rhythm guitar to provide backing for his "Feel" solo. For "Ice Cream Man," he laid down some blistering call-and-response fills for the song's climax. On "Devil," he played a solo on top of the rhythm guitar he'd laid down on the live tracks. "Ain't" saw Edward add the sitar. "On Fire," too, has a guitar overdub track listed on the track sheet, but it seems likely that whatever was recorded didn't make the LP.[561]

Also on the agenda was a distinctive part of Van Halen's sonic palette: background vocals. Roth explained later that the three-part harmony, an aspect of the band's sound that he'd always championed, originated from his "old Motown learning . . . Everything I was listening to at the youth club dance was, [sings] "Standing in the Shadows of Love," but that's where the harmonies come from. And that dates back to early Van Halen stuff . . . we had no keyboard, we had no pumping brass section. What are we going to do to add a little color to the chorus? We'll sing. Let's get some harmonies going here . . . This is the Temptations played to the background of 'Heartbreaker' by Led Zeppelin."[562]

To fully realize this part of Van Halen's sound, all four band members, and even Templeman at times, sang backgrounds.[563] The way Templeman remembers it, "A lot of times the background vocals were Michael Anthony and Ed. I would sing with them and then later Michael would double Ed's part too."

But Van Halen's unsung hero in this department was Michael Anthony. The bassist, whose strong vocals had helped get him in the band, was as important to the Van Halen sound as Roth's screams and Edward's solos. In fact, his singing was so powerful that the others started calling him "Cannonmouth." He remembered, "A lot of our harmonies we sang live out of one mike, and

Edward and Dave would be right on the mike and here I'd be all the way in the back of the room against the wall. They had to keep me farther away, because I was so loud."[564]

These harmonies, as much as any other aspect of Van Halen's musical presentation, helped assure that Van Halen would never be mistaken for a traditional heavy metal band. While the average metal band's gang choruses sounded like they'd been tracked in a dungeon, Van Halen's sounded like they'd been cut on a sun-drenched beach. Anthony observed, "Being able to sing three-part harmony was a big thing that set us apart from other heavy metal bands. It added a more sophisticated pop element that most metal bands weren't able to replicate."[565] This, more than any other factor, made Van Halen's heavy metal sound as sweet as cotton candy.

For all of the attention heaped on the band's singer and guitarist, Roth is the first to concede that Anthony's vocals were a signature aspect of the band's sound. In 2012, Roth told *Rolling Stone* that Anthony possessed "arguably one of the greatest high tenor voices ever." He continued: "In our tiny little corner of the universe, that voice is as identifiable as the high voice in Earth, Wind & Fire, as identifiable as the high voice in the Beach Boys. Van Halen is an indelicate house blend of both."[566]

== ==

On Wednesday, September 7, Van Halen returned to cutting basic tracks for the remaining songs. Perhaps because another act had laid claim to Sunset Sound's Studio Two, the band relocated to Studio One. Templeman can't remember why this move was made, but says, "With Van Halen we only used [Studio One] because we couldn't get into Studio Two."

In their new environs, the band set out to finish their album. "Little Dreamer," a mournful ballad, opens with another razor-sharp riff by Edward. In between verses, he smoothly slips out of the song's primary guitar line to add some snarling fills, another distinctive aspect of his style. For the solo, he plays with as much restraint as an amped-up Edward Van Halen was capable of in 1977. While he put his whammy bar to good use with some Hendrixian bends, he matched that with some Claptonesque lyricism that paid homage to the song's melody.

With nine songs in the can, Templeman still needed a second single. Edward then offered up the riff for what became "Jamie's Cryin'." Templeman and Roth immediately heard its potential. Roth recalled, "We heard Edward fooling around with his guitar between takes, and we yelled, 'Hey man, that's just what we need on the album.'"[567]

During a late night session, "Jamie's" came to life. Roth, in a *Los Angeles Times* interview, explained the band's writing method: "We just stand in a circle and hum at each other. Ted gets in there and says, 'Let's try that.' Doing the lyrics is a spontaneous thing too. I get a brown paper bag or the back of a magazine or something like that and scratch out the lyrics. Usually within an hour or so I have something together and read it to the guys. If they like it we go ahead and do it."[568]

Intriguingly, the song's hook, based on a heartbeat of an open-string riff, resembles KISS's "Christine Sixteen," perhaps an unsurprising development considering Edward and Alex's work on that KISS track. But while the "Christine" riff opens a tune that sounds like an *American Graffiti*–inspired throwback to the 1950s, "Jamie's Cryin'" turned into what Roth would describe as a "Cosmic Cha-Cha."[569] Putting a fine point on it, he told the *Guardian*, "We're the band that sold a Ricky Ricardo rumba in 'Jamie's Cryin'.'"[570]

According to Roth, his first vocal attempts on the song were a disaster. In *Crazy from the Heat*, Roth explained what happened next: "I went out and sat in the little basketball court area outside of [the] studio . . . I ate half a cheeseburger and drained a soda pop and smoked half a joint. Walked in, knocked out 'Jamie's Cryin'' in forty minutes."[571] On "Jamie's," Roth rose to the occasion, as he did on every track on the LP.

The resulting track is indubitably a pop song. Ted Templeman observes that even though *Van Halen* is a heavy album, "those guys had pop sensibilities. For example, 'Jamie's Cryin'' or 'Dance the Night Away.' They'd write these pop tunes." Roth, too, considered it a radio-friendly track, but he went to pains to explain that "Jamie's" wasn't just fluff. As he told the *Cleveland Plain Dealer*, "I don't consider it bubblegum. It ain't. It's a pop tune. I grew up with that stuff, with the Dave Clark Five and the Beatles."[572]

≡ ≡

The next day, September 8, Templeman and Landee sat in the control room while Edward worked through his solo for an upcoming Whisky show.[573] "When we were recording our first album," Edward remembered, "our producer, Ted Templeman, heard me practicing it for an upcoming gig and asked, 'What the hell is that?' I said, 'It's a thing I do live — it's my guitar solo.' His immediate reaction was, 'Shit, roll tape.'"[574]

Templeman's interest surprised Edward. As Edward explained to Steven Rosen, "I just didn't think it was something we'd put on a record. He liked it, Donn liked it, and everyone else agreed that we should throw it on."[575]

The band's three instrumentalists quickly cut the track. In Edward's words, "I played it two or three times for the record, and we kept the one, which seemed to flow."[576]

What was captured on tape sounded apocalyptic. "Eruption" (first titled "Guitar Solo," according to the song's track sheet), takes flight after a quick drum fill and a power chord. Edward sends notes and harmonics soaring before diving down with some gravity-defying tremolo bar bends. Alex and Michael then fire off a flak burst of three chords. Edward maneuvers again, twisting and turning, strafing and bombing before turning on the jets and heading skyward with a flurry of notes. He recedes again, leaving only a descending low note in his wake. After another pause, he attacks again, faster than ever. He weaves and twists and then unleashes his secret weapon: his two-handed tapping technique that would astound and confound guitarists across the world. Finally, an atomic blast, courtesy of Edward's Univox echo chamber, concludes this minute and forty-three seconds of open warfare on the guitar world.

Amazingly, Edward felt disappointed with the way the track turned out. He explained, "I didn't even play it right. There's a mistake at the top end of it. Whenever I hear it, I always think, *Man, I could have played it better.*"[577] Still, after years of dissecting guitar solos by every band from Aerosmith to ZZ Top, he knew what ended up on tape was unique. "I like the way it sounds; I've never heard a guitar sound like it. It's not that my playing was so great, it just sounds like some classical instrument. Donn really made it sound like more than it is, in a way."[578]

After a few more days of guitar overdubs (on "Jamie's"), background vocals, and Roth vocal patches, Van Halen rested. According to Landee's tape box notations, he printed alignment tones on the third master reel on September 13, bringing the studio work on *Van Halen* to a close about two weeks after the band had entered Sunset Sound.[579]

The next step was to mix the album. Despite some objections from the band, Templeman and Landee worked alone. "Up until 1984, Donn and I always mixed by ourselves. No one was ever allowed in our mixes — *ever*. If the band's there, you can really get tripped up; it's better to give it your shot. They didn't like it at first, but I would mix it with Donn."

Still, Templeman says that he and Landee had such a simpatico relationship that it just made sense for them to work alone: "So when Donn and I started doing *Van Halen*, I would look over at Donn and he knew what I wanted, usually +2 at 10, or something like that. So we both *heard* the same. So people would come in and see us, I'd look over at Donn and he'd look over at me, and he knew *exactly* what to do. It was *amazing*."

During the mixing process, Landee had a vision for how to arrange the album's sonic landscape. "On the mix," Templeman explains, "we'd put the guitar on the left and always put the echo return on the right. That got a neat sound. That was Donn's idea, I think. It was really good." Landee later explained that the idea grew out of the band's live tracking. "It made sense, because we didn't want to overdub guitars," Landee told Dave Simons. "If you put the guitar right down the middle with everything else, you'd wind up with the whole band in mono! So it seemed like a reasonable idea."[580]

= =

Once the mix was completed, Templeman invited the foursome into his office to hear the results. While Alex wished the album had turned out heavier, and Michael wished his bass sounded crisper, in general the band seemed satisfied. "They sat in my office to hear the first mix of the thing," Templeman recollects. "They didn't complain much but — they went with it. After I mixed the stuff without them, they were good for four or five albums. They never questioned it."

Edward, for his part, remembered that while he'd harbored doubts about Landee and Templeman's approach, what he heard on tape made him a believer. "By the time Donn got through with it, I really liked it."[581] He also had praise for his producer: "What he managed to do was put our live sound on a record. I mean, a lot of people have to do a bunch of overdubs to make it sound full. It's a lot easier to make a lot of instruments sound full than a guitar, bass, and drums. That's where Ted comes in — he knows his shit. He's the man."[582]

Landee then finished off the project by himself. "Here's another thing about Donn," Templeman says. "Donn would master the fucking records. You could never find an engineer who could do the mastering. He was damn good." After Landee made the album's sound consistent across its eleven tracks, *Van Halen* was complete.

Some days later, Warner Bros. Records' bean counters tallied the bill for the Van Halen project. Remarkably, the album cost about a third of what the typical late-'70s major-label recording project ran, an outcome that didn't get overlooked by the industry. "When an act is well-rehearsed, recording can be relatively inexpensive," veteran rock scribe Harold Bronson wrote in late 1978. "For instance, Van Halen's debut album, which is approaching platinum (sales of 1 million units), was recorded for $54,000."

In contrast, Fleetwood Mac overran their Warner Bros. budget by more than $400,000 when recording *Rumours*. As Con Merten, the manager of Cherokee Studios, explained to Bronson in 1978, "I doubt whether any albums in the Top 20 cost less than $100,000, and I would guess that the average cost would probably approach $150,000," or approximately $544,000 in 2014 dollars.[583] Edward, in later years, recalled that between the speed of the recording process and the low cost, "people couldn't believe it" when they found out about Van Halen's sessions. "Back then, bands like Fleetwood Mac and Boston were spending something like three years on [an] album, so you can just imagine the cost."[584]

= =

To be sure, Van Halen's debut is a landmark in rock history. And while many of the plaudits for the LP have been showered on guitarist Edward Van Halen, the guy who really came through in the clutch was David Lee Roth. While few listeners would contend that Roth's vocal prowess matched that of 1970s superstars Ian Gillan, Robert Plant, and Paul Rodgers, Roth had created a distinctive vocal persona. Roth sang with brio and sass, power and energy, personality and charm. He was having a great time fronting Van Halen, and it sounded like it on tape.

And that really was the whole vision behind Van Halen's first album. Templeman wanted fun, humor, and sunshine, and he got it. As Roth explained to *Rolling Stone* soon after the album's release, such Van Halen songs offer "an attitude, a feeling — like driving down the Strip with a load of girls, the radio on, and a couple of cases of beer . . . The lyrics just come from our experiences: the cars, the girls, the beer, the parties, the sweat, and the fun."[585]

Of course, *Van Halen* sounded like that because it was a snapshot in time, not an elaborate production that pasted together disjointed performances logged over months of work. As Roth explained, "The album was done on the first or second take exclusively. You can get lost in the studio if you're not careful. With overdubbing, you can get everything musically perfect. But that human vibe, that intangible thing . . . that's the thing for Van Halen."[586]

CALM BEFORE
THE STORM

With their album finished, Van Halen felt confident about their chances for commercial success. Roth, naturally, didn't hold back when asked in late 1977 about the band's future. He boasted to *Raw Power*, "We started in the little bathroom places and now we're at the Whisky, and we're probably gonna take over the world as soon as our record comes out on Warner Bros.," which Roth predicted would be in January.[587]

But one glance at the 1977 *Billboard* charts should have given Roth and the others pause about their prospects. While established metal bands like KISS and Ted Nugent had hit records, young heavy metal and hard rock acts like Judas Priest and the Bill Aucoin–backed Starz had limited sales success despite releasing solid albums. And even if the Sex Pistols hadn't sold millions of units, the massive buzz surrounding their riotous Warner Bros. Records debut seemed to signal that punk would come to define the future of heavy, aggressive music.

But what dominated the charts — apart from disco, which showed no signs of abating as a trend — was soft rock. In fact, the latest LPs from two L.A.-based acts, Fleetwood Mac and the Eagles, had each achieved blockbuster success. Meanwhile, Peter Frampton's breakthrough 1976 live album, *Frampton Comes Alive*, remained near the top of *Billboard* charts for all of 1977. All of this added up to one inescapable fact: very few people in the music industry saw a bright future for hard rock and heavy metal.

Accordingly, musicians and industry executives shared that same sentiment when it came to Van Halen. Terry Kilgore's take was that in 1977, "Warner Bros. didn't give a shit about Van Halen; their money was on the Sex Pistols, even though the Sex Pistols were incredible fuckups who couldn't do anything right." Keyboardist Drake Shining says the belief among many Pasadena musicians — driven in no small part by jealousy — was "Oh yeah, *right*. Warner Bros. Records! This is just a tax write off for the label. Their album will get buried over at Warner headquarters in Burbank." Incredibly, there's evidence that some inside of Warner Bros. Records thought this way. Roth remembered, "The first thing the director of promotions told me before our first album was about ready to come out was 'Hey, don't get your hopes up. Your kind of music is pretty passé. It's all about the Sex Pistols and the Clash now. I want to warn you [up] front.'"[588]

By the end of the year, all of this would come to a head between Van Halen and Warner Bros. In the meantime, they gigged just frequently enough to leave no doubt that they were Los Angeles's best young rock band. Behind closed doors, however, the band would confront an internal matter that threatened to undermine their future prospects, even as they all looked ahead to the day their debut would finally drop.

= =

Almost immediately after Van Halen completed work at Sunset Sound, people began asking about the LP. Gary Putman recalls, "I remember seeing them at the Whisky when they were finished recording the album. They were around. Eddie and I had a brief conversation. I remember him telling me he was pretty happy with how it turned out. We'd run into them and they'd talk to you for a minute."

Putman, who was a big fan, was smart to see them at the Whisky in September. Their management and record label, wanting to keep the focus on the band's forthcoming release, told the quartet to limit their live appearances. Joe Ramsey, who'd gigged with Van Halen in the past and then ran an Arcadia nightclub, remembered, "I tried my damndest to get Van Halen to play the Marquee West. Mike Anthony was an old friend, and they really wanted to do it, but it was during a weird time when their album was ninety-nine percent finished and their management didn't want them to play anywhere, let alone a hometown gig."

As a result, a band that had played most nights of the week now found itself sidelined. "There was like this six-month drought in 1977," Rob Broderick remembers. "It was like they weren't allowed to play." The band members passed the time, incongruously enough, by hitting the links. "A bunch of us would go out, play golf, and drink Schlitz Malt Liquor on these three-pars. Sometimes they would come and hang out. They weren't playing live," Broderick says. Dana Anderson turned up for these outings as well. He recalls, "We'd play a little three-par in the Arroyo Seco. It was all about getting drunk in the California sun."

One of the few shows Van Halen did play in the fall of 1977 was at the Movieland Cars of the Stars Exhibition Center in Buena Park, Orange County. The promoter hauled in a couple of flatbed trucks to serve as an outdoor stage and hired Van Halen, Orange County favorites Eulogy, and a last-minute addition to the bill, a punk-flavored group called the Strand. Significantly, Tom

Broderick recalls the October 8 gig only happened because it was a makeup for a previously scheduled Cars of Stars show, suggesting that if Van Halen's management had had its way, the band might not have appeared at all.

Van Halen's low profile clearly had not reduced interest in the band: by the day of the show, more than four thousand tickets had been sold. The Strand, who were amped about the gig, arrived early. When they popped their head inside of the dressing room (an unglamorous mobile home trailer) they encountered Edward, who'd already started warming up. Strand guitarist Fred Taccone remembers the scene: "He put the guitar on and didn't take it off until he got offstage. He played every single second. Practicing, practicing, practicing."

A couple of hours later, the Strand played a barnburner of a set that got the crowd roaring. As Taccone recalls, "People really liked us, and we did good at the Cars of Stars gig, because there was a whole movement of people who were like: *Out with the old, in with the new*! We did some of our own material, some Roxy Music, some *Raw Power*–era Stooges, and a Sex Pistols song. When we played 'God Save the Queen' in front of four thousand people, the crowd *erupted*. People hadn't heard something like that. You can be Van Halen all you want, but people were like, wow, what the fuck is that? It worked."

After the Strand bid the crowd farewell and Eulogy took the stage, Taccone asked Edward what he'd thought of his band's set. Taccone's take is that Edward had taken note of the passionate response that the Strand had received from the crowd. "Eddie knew that something was happening on the scene," Taccone remarks. "When we got done opening for them, he looked at me and said, 'You guys dress a lot more rad than you play.' I didn't take offense to it, because Eddie's a nice guy. But he had no problem with speaking what he thought. I wouldn't say it was arrogance, because he earned everything. But his fear was that pretty soon, Van Halen might be obsolete. Eddie was suggesting that you guys are good, but you're not *that* good. You guys are doing the new wave thing, and that's why everyone likes you."

After Eulogy finished, Roth and the others got their game faces on and hit the stage around 10:00 p.m. Right out of the gate, Van Halen was on fire. Dirk Van Tatenhove, Eulogy's bassist, observes, "You know the old Maxell tape advertisement, with the photo of the guy sitting in the chair with his hair blowing back? Now, it wasn't like I wasn't confident in Eulogy, our singer, our songs, and of course Rusty Anderson on guitar. But Van Halen was an extremely powerful, invading force. They were very special, because when they played it was like being on the deck of an aircraft carrier: *Whoooom!* It was like a jet taking off."

Taccone watched as well and was particularly struck by the persona that the leather-clad Roth now projected onstage. He points out that in the early to mid-'70s, glam rock had topped the charts. In fact, even as late as 1977, it continued to serve as the model for many local L.A. bands like Eulogy and Quiet Riot: "All of the guys in bands like Quiet Riot were really into the makeup and the feminine, Bowie, androgynous thing. In fact, Randy Rhoads got really popular in L.A. because he was like a miniature Mick Ronson [a guitarist for David Bowie]. That feminine thing — even Rod Stewart and the Stones at that time were doing that."

But at some point, Taccone observes, Roth had taken a detour from the glitter-rock mold that had captured his imagination back in 1973 and 1974. He laughs, "Everyone at that time was like, 'I like Bowie.' But for some reason, maybe the guys in Van Halen saw Jim Dandy and Black Oak Arkansas at the [1974] Cal Jam, and it just clicked with David Lee Roth. He said, *I want to be Jim Dandy,* as opposed to, *I want to be Bowie.* If you've ever seen Jim Dandy back in the day, he's exactly David Lee Roth. It's all about the cock rock."

At this gig, girls went wild for the shirtless Roth. Taccone recalls, "They were like, 'Wow, look at this guy! Wow, look at that!' David Lee Roth was the first local guy to open the shirt, show the hairy chest, and say, 'We're here to par-*tay*. I'm here for sex. I'm here to *have* sex.' He looked like a complete Neanderthal, and he moved onstage like a fucking Chippendales dancer, like a stripper. David had a new way of doing things. It was unique. Look at Randy Rhoads during that exact period of time. He was very effeminate. Van Halen wasn't doing that. They'd play some dance and get fucked up on coke and fuck chicks."

= =

The band's next gig, which took place on October 15, would be their last show at the Pasadena Civic. Steve Tortomasi, who promoted a total of four Van Halen shows at the Civic, recalls that he hated saying goodbye to Van Halen, because their partnership had been so fruitful. As Tortomasi tells it, "We kicked ass at that first [October 1976] Van Halen show. It was an all-cash show. Eventually, the kids just overran the gate. I couldn't even stop them. After that I wasn't sure we'd cover our expenses, but by the end of the night, I had so much money, I couldn't carry it. Now, remember, we are all kids and it's the '70s. If you made ten thousand bucks back then, you thought you'd hit the lottery, but we made a *ton* of money." Anthony agreed that this run of Civic gigs showed the band they were on the right track: "When we played the Pasadena Civic . . . those shows were when I was starting to realize that, wow this could happen. This is like big time . . . I'd try to get my parents to come down and watch. I'd say, 'Hey, check it out, we're playing a [real] concert. We're doing it.'"[589]

For this final show, Tortomasi and Van Halen wanted to break their own attendance record. The promoter hired two local bands, Terry Kilgore's new group, Reddi Kilowatt, and a blues-boogie trio called Smokehouse, to warm up the crowd.

Tortomasi also printed a mind-boggling 100,000 flyers for the

Tortomasi~Haley Productions
PROUDLY PRESENT
A FAREWELL CONCERT
∗ $100,000   8000 WATT SOUND SYSTEM ∗

VAN HALEN
LAST PASADENA PERFORMANCE BEFORE U.S. AND EUROPEAN TOUR
WITH
SMOKE HOUSE
INTRODUCING

REDDI KILOWATT

SATURDAY, OCTOBER 15th

Doors open
8pm

ALL ADMISSIONS
AT THE DOOR
$3.75

3.25 *WITH FLYER*

PLENTY OF
CHAIRS AVAILABLE

PRESENT THIS
ADVERTISEMENT
FOR YOUR

50¢
DISCOUNT

PASADENA CIVIC   300 E. GREEN STREET

Flyer for Van Halen's final performance at the Pasadena Civic, October 1977.
David and Edward's flashy stage garb underscores how sharply the band's
image had evolved since their jeans-and-T-shirt days. STEVE TORTOMASI

bands and the small army of kids the promoter hired to distribute.
He says, "What we'd do is flyer every single high school from La
Crescenta all the way to San Marino and Arcadia, twice a week.
Then every weekend we'd hit all the clubs in Hollywood. We'd go
up and down Mulholland Drive where everybody parked and put

them on cars. We'd put them on every influential telephone pole; we'd put them everywhere. My plan back then was to put out so many flyers that people couldn't stand looking at them anymore."

Roth and the rest of Van Halen joined in this project. Roth explained to *Tiger Beat*, "We used to drive all over town putting flyers up on every lamp post, bathroom wall, gym locker, just so that people would get to know our name and come and see us play."[590] As Anthony told *Guitar for the Practicing Musician*, it all paid off: "I'd look out and see five thousand kids that we'd drawn because we put fliers on everyone's car at Anaheim Stadium, where Aerosmith was playing an outdoor show."[591]

Despite this massive marketing effort, Tortomasi and the band weren't done. Tortomasi had rented huge spotlights, which he set up in the Civic parking lot. On the night of the show, they'd send beams of light into the sky to make it easy for kids to find the venue. He had also paid for radio advertisements, which he and Roth worked up with their resident electronics wizard, Pete Dougherty. Tortomasi remembers, "Roth's house was an old mansion, and there was a [garage apartment] in the back that Dr. Roth had rented out to Dougherty. He had some audio equipment in there. I said, 'Okay, David, we're going to use your voice on them.' We put some music to them and brought them to KROQ."

= =

On the evening of October 15, friends and fans mingled with the band before the show. Jan Van Halen was there in his lederhosen, having arrived at the Civic straight from a gig of his own. A few Warner Bros. executives, including a vice-president and Ted Templeman, made an appearance as well.[592]

Tortomasi then huddled with Van Halen. At a prior Civic show, he explains, Van Halen had blown off their flash pots and filled the hall with smoke. "We had a problem with pyrotechnics back then.

There was an angry, drunken asshole named Jack, who was a Civic stage manager. He hated rock music. He told me before this show, 'If they use fireworks, I'm calling the fire department and shutting your show down.'" Accordingly, Tortomasi said to the band, "No pyrotechnics tonight, right?" He made clear that the future of rock shows at the Civic would be threatened if they didn't listen to him. In fact, the fire marshal might even fine him and the band. The four-some nodded, promising they'd eliminate that part of their show.

After the opening acts finished, Van Halen kicked things off with a supercharged "On Fire." Edward's old friend Tom Hensley, who hadn't seen Van Halen perform live in months, was surprised by the band's updated look. They'd donned all new Hollywood-purchased stage clothes, and Edward's guitar had received a make-over. He remembers, "At the Pasadena Civic, Edward came out with the Stratocaster and the stripes and the dog leash chain for a guitar strap with the whole new heavy metal image." As Hensley's observation reveals, Edward's image now bore no resemblance to the days when he performed in jeans and a flannel shirt while playing his Les Paul Goldtop.

Dressed to the nines with the volume on ten, Van Halen roused the crowd with their incendiary set, which featured all the songs from their forthcoming debut, save "Jamie's Cryin'" and "I'm the One." Edward's colossal guitar sound resounded, and Roth's vocals sounded full and rich, leaving no doubt that Van Halen had no peer on the local scene.

Janice Pirre Francis, who'd first seen Van Halen in the Van Furche' backyard back in 1974, makes this exact case. "The Civic would just be packed full of people; it was overwhelming. Nobody drew a crowd like Van Halen. They just didn't. I remember the completely over-the-top loud music, the crowds of people, and that ultimate stardom that the band possessed."

About halfway through the show, the band spotlighted Alex at the tail end of "Atomic Punk." Chris Koenig remembers the ever-growing size of Alex's kit and the powerhouse drummer's solo flair: "Alex had these double deep bass drums. It was literally two bass drums joined together with chains and locks. He'd go through his drum solo, and the band's crew would use fire extinguishers on him. He'd just be enveloped in smoke. Then he'd be done with the solo, and he'd stand up, wearing a gas mask. Everybody would go crazy."

Tracy G. was also in the house. To hear him tell it, Roth held the audience in the palm of his hand. "He'd stand out front with no shirt on going: *Hey motherfuckers! What do ya think of my fuckin' band?* You wanted to hate him, because he was such an arrogant fuck. But you couldn't, because there were all these hot girls there to see him. They all wanted him."

At the end of their taut forty-five minute show, Van Halen blazed into "You Really Got Me." Anthony raced to his microphone and bellowed, "Ted Templeman where are you? This one's for you, baby!" Forty years later, Templeman still remembers what a blast he had at this concert: "I saw them in Pasadena, and it was amazing!"

Van Halen had one more surprise for the crowd. The band's soundman, Tom Broderick, explains, "My brother, Rob, had just finished making these smoke pots for them. We had a whole sequence of them. We set some on top of the amps, some by the drums, and you could hit different buttons to fire them off, and go *this one, this one, these two, these two.*"

Roth recounted in *Crazy from the Heat* what happened next: "We saved all of the smoke pots for the grand finale, hit the last song and fired off all twenty-five at once — in a 4,500-person exhibition hall with the windows closed — and it smoked the place out." They'd laid out so many pots that Roth apparently lost track of one of them. Broderick says, chuckling quietly, "I remember Roth was standing too close to the one right by the drum riser. One went off right by his head!" Backstage, Tortomasi went apeshit as Jack called police. In a matter of minutes, the wail of sirens sounded in the hall.

Onstage, the band coughed and laughed. Roth explained, "[Then] it was like right out of the movies. All the doorways flew open at once, and all you can see [were] those rolling red lights on top of the fire trucks and all of these guys with gas masks and hoses and full-blast fire boots and gear . . . bursting through the door to throw 4,500 of our closest friends out of the building."[593]

Tortomasi, hacking his guts out, stumbled onstage. "I said to Dave, 'What the fuck is wrong with you? I told you they were going to shut the show down and shut down our business for the night! Why'd you do that?'" Roth didn't answer, but Tortomasi knew why they'd done it: "Those guys were on a mission. I'm not angry about it, but to them, it was more important that that show was good than any ramifications of getting shut down by the fire department and losing money."

= =

In the late fall, Warner Bros. Records invited the band and their manager to Burbank to see the cover for their forthcoming album. The unveiling did not go well. Eager to capitalize on the punk trend, Warner Bros. designers had produced a graphic-arts disaster. They'd created an angular, garish logo that rendered Van Halen as "Vanhalen," an unintentional throwback to the group's way of presenting its name circa 1974. They'd used a photo from a nighttime shoot on the grounds of the Roth mansion. Alex, who looks ten-feet tall in the picture, stands close to the lens while the photogenic Roth poses in the background with his eyes closed. While it's unclear if Roth had blinked or if the photographer had asked him to close his eyes, it makes Roth look bizarre.

The response from team Van Halen was resoundingly neg- ative. Berle remembers that he told the Warner executives that the cover sucked. The band could hardly contain their fury. As Edward explained to *Guitar World*, "You should see the first album

cover Warner Bros. designed for us — they tried to make us look like the Clash. We said, 'Fuck this shit!'"[594]

Looking to mend fences, a few days later Warner Bros. executives asked the band and Berle to join them for a lunch meeting. The way then–Warner executive Ted Cohen remembers it, "Warner Music invited the band to [Le] Petit Chateau on [Lankershim] in North Hollywood to discuss their debut album. David Lee Roth

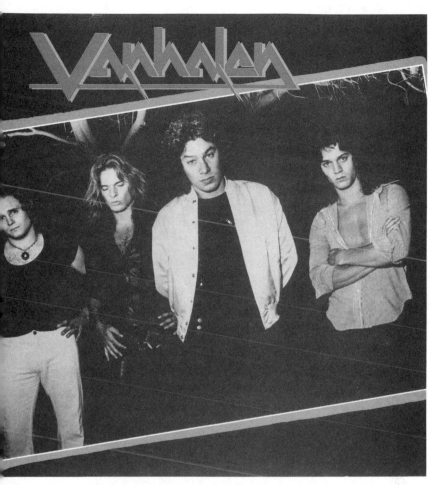

The proposed album cover for Van Halen's debut, as drawn up by Warner Bros. Records, fall 1977. The band, believing the artwork was designed to market them as a punk band, rejected the cover. FROM THE COLLECTION OF MIKE KASSIS

showed up half an hour late, explaining his old Plymouth Valiant had broken down a couple of miles from the restaurant. Out of that lunch, we announced to the guys that they'd be going on a major tour to support their first record."[595]

Berle adds that a few other details had been worked out by the time of this meeting. After the cover debacle, the album release date was pushed back from January to February 1978. For the band's promotional tour, Van Halen's manager and the label had signed a contract with one of the industry's leading booking agencies, Premier Talent. Berle argues that locking up that deal was crucial to an unknown band's chances of success. Berle explains, "You don't just go out and get a tour. You have to understand, industry people at that time wanted to know: *Who the fuck is Van Halen? What's their story?* It was very difficult getting them on a good tour. But by putting them with Premier Talent, which was the most powerful rock agency in the world, I was almost assured of getting them out there on a tour." It turned out that Van Halen would be going on the road with Journey and Ronnie Montrose, a jaunt that was scheduled to last six weeks.[596]

Berle then worked to assemble the team that would tour with the band. Apart from the band's techs, Van Halen would be accompanied by Cohen, who'd work as the band's A&R representative, and tour manager Noel E. Monk, a tough-minded former New York City cop who would join the Van Halen team in early 1978 right after finishing with another hot Warner Bros. Records property, the Sex Pistols.

Soon after, Berle and the band focused on the new album cover. Designer Dave Bhang worked up a new design and photographer Elliot Gilbert took action photos of the four band members during a Whisky photo shoot. In consultation with the band, Bhang created a new gleaming, winged logo fronted by a banner inscribed "Van Halen." Edward recalled that after Bhang "came up with the Van Halen logo," the band "made [Warner Bros.] put it on the album so that it would be clear that we had nothing to do with the punk movement. It was our way of saying 'Hey we're just a fucking rock and roll band, don't try and slot us with the Sex Pistols thing just because it's becoming popular.'"[597]

The label's promotion plan also included videos, which the band shot at the Whisky for the three presumed singles: "Runnin' with the Devil," "Jamie's Cryin'," and "You Really Got Me." Apart from the band's mediocre miming skills, the videos capture the band's image and performance style circa late 1977. Alex's brutalizes his kit while wearing what appears to be a bondage harness. Roth's sporting low-rise leather pants, a wide metal-studded belt, and a smaller waist chain. He's got a gold chain glistening on his hairy chest, he's donning a satin blouse that's open to the waist, and he prowls the stage in his platform shoes with swiveling hips and bulging eyes. The others' clothing choices are only slightly more tasteful. Edward's wearing a striped disco shirt, open to the waist, and maroon polyester pants. Anthony, always the most sensible of the bunch, dons a white scoop neck T-shirt and jeans. Together they project a band image that simultaneously pays homage to heavy metal, disco, and early '70s cock rock.

Around this time, Warner Bros. Records executives had their own reasons for frustration after a Van Halen blunder threatened to hurt the album's rollout. Ted Templeman rang up Edward and told him that he'd just gotten a call from Aerosmith's tour manager, who'd informed the producer that a glam-rock band named Angel had entered the studio to crank out their own version of "You Really Got Me." Edward explained what happened: "I played [Barry Brandt, Angel's drummer] our tape about a month before it was going to be released, and a week later Ted Templeman calls me and goes, 'Did you play that tape for anybody?'

"'Yeah, wasn't I supposed to?'

"'I *told* you. Fuck! I should have never given you a copy!'"[508]

As a result, the label rushed the song to market. This perhaps explains the band's rare red vinyl "Looney Tunes" EP. It features the rejected "punk" Van Halen logo rather than the familiar winged logo, suggesting that the label wasn't going to wait for the band's new iconography to put "You Really Got Me" on vinyl.[599]

= =

To bring the year to an end, Van Halen played two farewell shows at the Whisky on December 30 and 31. With *Van Halen* nearing release, the *Los Angeles Times* paid more attention to the band, even if its critics seemed somewhat underwhelmed by Van Halen. Robert Hilburn, in discussing the band's Whisky engagement, suggested that Van Halen hardly represented the future of rock music: "This isn't new wave. More a Led Zeppelin Meets Black Oak, they've got a Warner Bros. album due next month and are apparently in line for a big push. If you're still into the heavy metal sound, this is your chance to see what it looks like up close."[600] A few weeks later, Terry Atkinson offered measured praise by writing: "Van Halen's music is hard-driving rock with rough edges. There's nothing revolutionary about it, but it's executed in an engaging, sometimes exciting way."[601]

Regardless of the *Times'* opinions, the group sold out both nights. Fans lined up outside the club, and, once inside, had the chance to purchase Van Halen T-shirts, a sign of the band's expanding sense of entrepreneurship.[602]

In contrast to the *Van Halen*–heavy set performed at the Civic, on New Year's Eve the foursome let loose by performing some of the band's more obscure original material. Tom Broderick says, "We talked them into doing a lot of the cool tunes that night, like 'Down in Flames,' 'Show No Mercy,' and 'Here's Just What You Wanted.' They only played that last one a couple of times." Whether the songs were familiar or unfamiliar, the crowd roared. Guitarist Greg Leon says, "Me and some friends ended up seeing them at the Whisky when they were playing a New Year's Eve show. That was a pretty fantastic night." Broderick agrees and adds, "It was a rocking! That was one of my favorite nights."

= =

While it's long been believed that the band played a final pair of dates at the Whisky in February (they didn't), it turns out that the band's last gig before their album's release didn't even take place in Los Angeles. Rather, on January 27, the quartet played at the Snow Crest Lodge in the ski town of Mount Baldy, located northeast of Pasadena in the San Gabriel Mountains. As Tracy G. remembers it, "They had one more local gig at this very small place. Mount Baldy and the mountains are about an hour away from where I live, so I'm begging my friend to take me up there. So we go, and since it's winter, it's snowing. It was right before they took off for the big time."

Janice Pirre Francis made it a point to see this gig too, even though getting to the lodge from the parking lot was no easy feat: "What a scene that was. To get to the lodge you had to ride a ski lift. Imagine now, all of us girls in tight little mini-dresses and high heels having to get off the ski lift without breaking our necks or without having our skirts around our waists!"

Tracy says that he soon spotted Van Halen and their entourage. "When I was walking up to the gig to go in the place," he says, "you walk by the restaurant windows. The Van Halen guys were sitting at the table with their roadies, eating and drinking. I was thinking, *Those guys are like a fucking gang!* I was so envious and jealous. I wanted a band like that, just like a gang, where it would be us against the fucking world. But to get all the right members in a band, that's tough. And there they were, just drinking and getting ready to go on a world tour. The truth is, I was looking at rock royalty, but I was too young to realize it. I just couldn't imagine that they were going to take over the world."

That night, after the openers' gear was struck from the stage, fans started chanting and screaming for the headliner. Tracy looked around, wondering how Van Halen planned to make their entrance. He says, "There's no backstage. There's nothing behind the stage but the wall of the club. So I'm like, *Where are they?*"

Just then an exit door on an adjoining wall flew open. As snow billowed into the room, Van Halen appeared. "They come in from like two degrees outside, and they're wearing their guitars. Everybody's screaming. It was a great show. I could have reached out and touched Eddie's guitar. I was right there."

After this triumphant performance, Van Halen set out to have a night of bacchanalian insanity that would serve as a dress rehearsal for the excesses of their world tour. Tom Broderick remembers that after the band repaired to a handful of ski cabins where they had planned to spend the night, they raged: "There was a really crazy all-night party after that gig with all the skiers and everything; that was an epic party. That night they destroyed the place where they stayed . . . Dave flooded the bathroom and the room he was staying in. I don't know if he was sticking towels in the toilet or what, but there was just mischief everywhere. It was Keith Moon–worthy stuff."

= =

As the band prepared to hit the road, they wrestled with an issue that seemed to threaten Van Halen's chances of success. By this time, Alex's drinking had became a cause for concern in a group whose modus operandi centered on partying. Gary Ostby says, "At that time, Alex was the drunk of the group. He used to drink Schlitz Malt Liquor in the tall cans all the time. A lot of the contention between Eddie and Alex was because Alex would drink too many beers and start screwing up on the drums."

To be sure, Alex's excessive drinking was not a new development. Kilgore explains that when he went over to the Van Halen home in the early 1970s, "by 10 o'clock in the morning their mom would come in with two of those big Schlitz sixteens. That's half a quart of malt liquor. They'd guzzle a couple of them down before noon. I'd have been just lying on the bed after that."

As the years progressed, Alex apparently took to this kind of drinking in a way his brother hadn't — yet. According to Broderick,

"He would go through cases of Schlitz Malt at a party or rehearsal."[603] This seems plausible when Alex's gig preparations are considered. John Nyman, Eulogy's drummer, remembers what he saw before a 1976 Civic gig: "I remember Alex came in there, and he had a floor tom case he was carrying around. I remember thinking, *That's weird. Why doesn't he leave it down with all the gear?* He probably had a sixteen-by-sixteen or -eighteen floor tom case. So he plops it down and opens it and pulls out a cooler full of Schlitz."

His drinking continued when the band performed. Nyman adds that at the Golden West, "I remember Alex talking to me about drum soloing. He said he gets so into it that he doesn't even remember what he played. He did a drum solo [and] he was all sweaty and he poured beer over his own head, which is kind of show biz and very rock and roll, but then he said he didn't remember doing it. He was ascribing it to his intensity in the moment, but as I got a little older I thought, *Well maybe he was just really drunk so he doesn't remember.* He sure played well for someone really drunk. He played *really well.*"

Ostby remembers that this blackout drinking led to a band meeting. "In late 1977, early 1978, they had a band intervention with him, because he was drinking too much. It got to be bad, because he was just fucking up so much. They were really getting pissed. They finally just sat him down, and said, 'Hey Alex, you better cool it, or you're out of the band.' He agreed to cool it and so he kind of calmed down for a little while."

But neither Broderick nor Anthony, who didn't deeply involve himself in this matter, thought that it was anything more than a bluff. Broderick, who saw this whole episode transpire, explained, "They'd never boot Al."[604] Anthony adds, "I don't remember us ever threatening to kick Alex out of the band. We may have sat him down once or twice, but it was never a serious thing. That was probably Eddie more than anyone else who dealt with Alex like that."

These distractions put aside, Van Halen practiced night and day. Broderick recalls, "They rehearsed in Dave's basement for the tour." Right before the band left town, Edward focused on getting the "space echo effect for his solo" just right while the band as a whole "worked on the set they were going to play." Songs were added and crossed off the list, and the band worked to craft a set that would last little more than thirty minutes.

As March loomed, pressure built. The way Broderick remembers it, "I think on one of the last rehearsal days, I had a friend who I had to get out of jail. I thought it wouldn't take that long, but it took forever and I ended up being a half an hour late for this rehearsal. Dave got in my face and read me the riot act about how serious this is and how this is top priority. I said, 'Okay, *okay!*' He yelled, 'Next time, leave your friend in jail!'"

At the tail end of February, trucks arrived at the Roth home to haul the band's equipment to Chicago. The band spent the last night in the basement, thinking about the road ahead. The next day the band, their management team, and their small crew would fly from Los Angeles to Chicago. Gary Nissley, who popped into the basement with Pete Dougherty, remembers, "We were all hanging out in the basement at the Roth mansion the night before they all left. They were all getting ready to go, and they were all kind of looking at each other like, *Is this going to work or not?*" They'd soon find out.

UNLEASHED

In the spring of 1978, heavy metal superstars Black Sabbath planned their tenth anniversary world tour, which would support their upcoming LP, *Never Say Die*. Sabbath singer Ozzy Osbourne, who'd spent his days in a drink-and-drug-induced stupor, suddenly became focused when it came time to choose an opening act. He reminded Sabbath's management and his bandmates about how an upstart KISS had stolen the show when they'd opened for Sabbath back in 1975. He insisted that this time Sabbath book an act weak enough that most audience members would spend their time buying beer and Sabbath T-shirts while the opener performed. As per Ozzy's advice, Sabbath handed down a directive to the band's booking agency: hire "a bar band from Los Angeles" as support.

Sabbath's management dutifully followed those instructions. On May 16, Osbourne, bassist Geezer Butler, drummer Bill Ward, and guitarist Tony Iommi stood backstage at Sheffield City Hall, preparing for the first show of their month-long UK tour. Out of curiosity, Ozzy and the others made their way to the side of the stage to take in the end of their opener's set. They arrived just in time to catch the guitarist's solo spot, a withering sonic assault that dropped jaws all over the venue. The Sabs then watched in stunned silence as Van Halen, as powerful as a Sherman tank, rumbled through "You Really Got Me."

Back in the dressing room, the four Birmingham natives sat together, exchanging concerned looks. As Ozzy later explained to keyboardist Don Airey, "We were just too stunned to speak. We sat there, going, 'That was incredible.'" Soon after, "there was a knock on the door and the best-looking man in the world walked in and said hello." He introduced himself as Dave Roth. At that moment, Sabbath knew they were in deep trouble.[605]

= =

On February 28, Van Halen, the band's management, and crew flew east from sun-drenched Los Angeles and landed in the Windy City. When they stepped outside the airport, icy winds buffeted them. They all pulled up the hoods of their military surplus band-issued parkas and shivered. They'd arrived in the Midwest in the midst of the coldest winter on record.

The tour itself, which would begin on March 3, was a classic '70s billing of diverse acts. After Van Halen performed, Ronnie Montrose would take the stage. Montrose was promoting his first solo album, *Open Fire*. It marked an evolution in sound, as Montrose abandoned mainstream hard rock for Jeff Beck–style fusion. Headlining would be Journey, whose *Infinity* album had come out in January. Like Ronnie Montrose, Journey was also in a transition period that saw the group evolve from a fusion act to a mainstream rock band, thanks in no small part to the recent addition of singer Steve Perry.

Van Halen's status as national newcomers meant that they'd be afforded few privileges. They'd start their set at 7:30, a time when many audience members would not have entered the hall. They'd get minimal stage lighting and almost no opportunities to sound-check. And in light of the band's elaborate contract rider demands on future tours (No brown M&Ms!), the lack of backstage amenities seems ludicrous in retrospect. As Edward explained to Steven Rosen, "Our backstage rider [in March 1978] consisted of four towels."[606]

That night, Van Halen stepped onto the stage, waiting to be introduced. "It was scary walking up there for the first time," Edward remembered, especially since Van Halen only had a half hour to win over the audience. But after the opening number in Chicago, the butterflies subsided and the cheers began. Edward said, "After the first song people liked us," and, in fact, by the end of the night, "everybody loved us." With that, the *Van Halen* tour was underway.[607]

Less than a week into the tour, the band got thrown a curveball. On March 6, they learned they'd have an off night the following day in Madison, Wisconsin, because the Orpheum Theater's stage couldn't accommodate three bands. After a few phone calls, Berle and Monk found a local nightclub, the Shuffle Inn, which was happy to book a band whose debut single, "You Really Got Me," was making its way into the Top 40 on *Billboard*'s Hot 100 singles chart.[608] By showtime, the gig was sold out.

While some managers might have shied away from allowing an ascendant act like Van Halen to perform in a dive like the Shuffle, Berle says that he thought such opportunities played to Van Halen's strengths. He explains, "Wherever we could get a job, I took it, no matter how much money it cost for us to go there. My formula for success was that this was not a recording artist; this was a live rock and roll band. The more people you put Van Halen in front of, the better. They then became your PR. They'd say to other people, 'Oh man, I just saw the greatest band!' So I took everything I could get."

Things followed that script at the Shuffle. Van Halen, who were no strangers to club gigs, laid waste to the venue and left the local rock critic duly impressed. The *Emerald City Chronicle* reported, "The band mounted the stage and launched a full-tilt assault . . . A rough-edged, rowdy, and raw set, Van Halen made no pretense of being the 'hot new national act' that doesn't play clubs anymore. Quite to the contrary, this group grew up in bars and feeds off the energy exchange best found in a close-up crowd." After the band's two encores, Roth baptized the crowd with geysers of champagne as Van Halen left the stage.[609]

Even though the show was over, Van Halen's fun was just beginning. Over the next two nights, the band and its crew set out to destroy the seventh floor of the Madison Sheraton. Tom Broderick told the *The Inside* that the mayhem began with the band members "chasing each other around with fire extinguishers. It was pure madness."[610]

Things got more fun when Van Halen started testing gravity. Berle, relaxing in his room, happened to be looking out the window as a television set flashed by on its way to the ground.[611] "In Madison," he laughs, "I was three or four floors down. They threw shit out the window, like TV sets. But hey, they were kids having a good time." Alex then attempted to toss a table out the window, but before he succeeded, Journey's Steve Perry cautioned him that he'd end up paying for everything he destroyed. Even though the drummer heeded Perry's warning, Van Halen still got to know Madison's finest, who paid them a number of visits during their stay in Mad City.[612]

= =

With the tour's first week behind them, Van Halen focused on converting fans and becoming the bill's main attraction. Roth

CLEVELAND, OHIO
This dramatic aerial view shows the imposing
Terminal Tower and its complex of inter-con-
necting buildings in the foreground. TV
The tall tower to the left is the Federal Build-
ing and on the right is the Erieview Plaza
Tower.
Lake Erie, with its fine shipping and recrea-
tional facilities is in the background.
Photo by Bebman

BRIAN, SUE, JOSH & JAMAICA
SO FAR WE'VE PLAYED
ABOUT 6 or 7 DATES. THE
MORE WE PLAY, THE BETTER
WE GET! WE'VE GOTTEN A
COUPLE ENCORES — NOT BAD
FOR OPENING BAND! JOURNEY
& MONTROSE ARE O.K. GREGG
& EVERYONE DOING REAL GOOD.
KINDA MISS THE BEACH.
LATER! AL & ED.

119 Dominguez A
San Clemente,
Calif.
92672

POST·CARD

Postcard sent by the Van Halen brothers to their old friend Brian Box at the very
beginning of the band's tour in support of Van Halen, March 1978. BRIAN BOX

recalled, "When Van Halen first started out, we opened for
Journey. In fact, they were the first act that we ever opened for
on any kind of national tour with our first record. And when you
first start out on the road like that, then you're very competitive.
You're trying to make your mark, you know."[613] Making a mark
entailed performing the perfect set list, one that would grab the
audience by the throat and not let go. "As a third-billed band,"
Roth explained in the spring of 1978, "every song has got to be an
opener. As long as we're doing a short set we're going to have to
keep going slam-bam-damn!"[614]

Journey, which at first had shown little interest in Van Halen's
performances, paid more attention as the tour progressed. Berle
recalled, "I remember three of the guys from Journey would stand
on Edward's side of the stage. They would only come out of their
dressing rooms when Edward would do his guitar solos, and every

night he would do something different. And they would sit there and crack up in the wings, just being blown away by this young upstart."[615]

By the time the tour arrived in Louisville on March 17, Van Halen had started to gain traction with audiences as well. Berle recalls that as word started to spread about Van Halen, fans started showing up early enough to see the opener. Broderick remembers noticing that some of the guys in Journey seemed put off by Van Halen's meteoric performance and the enthusiastic response they'd generated. "Journey," Broderick says, "became officially frightened of Van Halen at [the Louisville] show."

Journey, hoping to send the ascendant Van Halen tumbling back to earth, started to undermine the Pasadena quartet. Broderick remarks, "Journey started to turn against Van Halen after they saw they were getting blown away. They started sabotaging the PA, and there was nothing I could do. I didn't have a headset, so I couldn't say to someone backstage, 'Look in the backline, something's unplugged.' We were really just screwed and that was it."

But like Roth's idol Muhammad Ali, Van Halen knew how to take a body blow before counterpunching. "They fucked with us," Edward declared. "They gave us a hard time, so we gave them a hard time back." Alex added, "When Journey would be onstage playing, we used to go into their dressing room, eat all their food, mess around with their old ladies."[616] Edward's girlfriend Kim Miller offers confirmation: "They would try to get Steve Perry to come into their dressing room, just to mess with him. It was Alex and the others' goal to try and make him cry! But Edward seemed to like Neal Schon. We would hang out with him and his wife at the hotel."[617]

By the time the three bands arrived at Philadelphia's Tower Theater on March 24, Van Halen had regained its footing. They played a tight, dynamic thirty-five minute set to an audience of hard-to-please rock fans who'd think nothing of booing Santa Claus on Christmas morning. To top things off, they performed a toe-tapping "Ice Cream Man" before leaving to sustained applause. Rock critic Fred Trietsch of *Drummer* came away astonished, telling his readers: "Judging from the audience reaction, it won't be long before Van Halen tops the charts."[618]

Despite the bravura performance in Philadelphia, the next night in New York proved to be a humbling experience. An audience recording documents that most of the crowd was underwhelmed by the band's efforts. As Edward told Steven Rosen about the Journey tour, "Either the people liked us or hated us."[619] On this night, the response at the Palladium ranged much closer to the latter, with some vocal fans heckling and booing Journey's support act.

After the show, things didn't improve. Roth sat for an interview with a snarky Rob Patterson of *Creem*, who later mocked Van Halen as the offspring of heavy metal dinosaurs like Deep Purple and Sabbath. "Face the facts, kiddos," Patterson wrote in the July issue, "when it comes to heavy rock and roll — y'know, the kind of stuff that sounds like a herd of dinosaurs engaging in some prehistoric S&M — a little bit of calculated outrageousness goes a *long* way. So along come Van Halen, led by two Dutch siblings on guitar and drums who grew up in Pasadena and fronted by one David Roth, whose struts and screeches emit a crotch-splitting intensity the likes of which haven't been seen since Jim Dandy Mangrum invented his now passé cock-walk." His message couldn't have been clearer: Van Halen played a contrived form of rock — heavy metal — making the quartet a member of an endangered species, which would soon die off in the face of a new generation of punk and new wave groups.[620]

═ ═

Despite the tough night in the Big Apple, the album was moving units. Anthony remembered that in the spring of 1978, "the album started taking off. It didn't skyrocket, but it was steady."[621] Their single, too, was getting many spins. A West Coast radio executive told *Circus* that within a week of its release, *Van Halen* had become rock radio's most added album: "The single hit thirty-five radio stations the first week, reached another twenty-six the second. After a month, Van Halen was getting airplay on 145 stations across the country." This airplay would prompt *Radio and Records* to label "You Really Got Me" as a No. 1 progressive single for several weeks in the spring.[622]

This radio and chart action led newspaper and magazine reviewers to weigh in about *Van Halen*. To be sure, some did recommend the LP for its power and volume. In the UK, *Melody Maker* sang the band's praises, saying, "It's all there in abundance: screaming guitar solos, thundering riffs, a pounding rhythm section, and tough vocals . . . outstanding and thoroughly recommended." *Sounds* concurred by calling Van Halen "brand new heavy metal heroes" who'd produced "a magnificent debut. If Van Halen can keep the adrenaline flowing for a second album, then Warners have a winner on their hands."[623] Back in Los Angeles, the *Orange County Register* called the album "a hard rock jewel," which was "overflowing with ambitious energy."[624]

Still, the majority of critics came away less than impressed, with most labeling Van Halen recyclers of obsolete heavy metal–*cum*–cock rock. The punk-loving, UK-based *NME* took a flamethrower to *Van Halen*, calling it only "vaguely bearable in places" and excoriating it for its "same old HM excess."[625] On the other side of the Atlantic, *Hit Parader* mocked Van Halen by writing, "With a little practice they just might become the next Uriah Heep. And with another day's practice they could become Arthur Brown or Black Oak Arkansas. But listen to their version of 'You Really Got Me' and you can bet they'll never become the Kinks."[626]

The *Los Angeles Times* and *Rolling Stone* offered more of a mixed message. In the former, Terry Atkinson praised their debut as an "impressive start," before singling out Roth as the band's key defect: "The album's weakness is singer David Roth. His vocals are serviceable but humdrum, resembling too much the screamy kind of singing that has bogged down groups like Uriah Heep. His lyrics, too, are mundane."[627] In the latter, Charles M. Young damned the quartet with faint praise: "Van Halen's secret is not doing anything that's original while having the hormones to do it better than all those bands that have become fat and self-indulgent and disgusting . . . These guys also have the good sense not to cut their hair or sing about destroying a hopelessly corrupt society on their first album. That way, hopelessly corrupt radio programmers will play their music." Towards that end, Warner Bros. released "Runnin' with the Devil" in April as the band's second single.[628]

= =

By that month, the tour had wended its way into the Southwest. In Austin, two reviewers who caught the show on April 12 applauded Van Halen's songs and stagecraft. While she'd call Journey "superb," Margaret Moser of the *Austin Sun* was effusive in her praise of the warm-up act. "Van Halen opened the show with a blast of adrenaline. Brothers Alex and Edward Van Halen, drums and lead guitar respectively, laid out the backbone of their hard, and I mean *hard*, rock. Though their set was too short to get any true feel of their style, they displayed a massive amount of power and drive, not the least of which was shown by lead singer Dave Roth. Roth, in low black leather pants and open shirt, played most prominently to the female portion of the audience, getting down on his knees and kissing hands, accepting a flower and placing it strategically above his zipper."[629]

John Bryant of the *Austin American-Statesman* went further by asserting that Van Halen were the night's real stars. He wrote, "The group had just crammed all the quality and tricks of a headliner show into their thirty-five minutes. Alex did a magnificent drum solo, his brother Edward Van Halen had a lead guitar solo, and Michael Anthony matched anybody's bass solo. Lead singer Dave Lee Roth was all over the stage, leading the league in sweaty, exposed hairy chests and finishing close second in low-riding britches only to a cast member from *Oh Calcutta* . . . The only thing that kept them from stealing Wednesday night's Municipal Auditorium show entirely was the rock concert phenomena that calls for young fans to wander around the lobby during the opening act."[630]

With the album selling and audiences enthusiastic, Van Halen's handlers began angling to move the band onto a bigger tour. For the time being, however, Van Halen said no. Anthony explains, "Our first tour after the *Van Halen* album was only supposed to be six weeks, opening for Journey and [Ronnie] Montrose. But the album was selling better and better. Warner Bros. and Premier Talent wanted to put us right in the big halls when the album started catching." But in order to make sure they had their feet under them, the band chose, in Anthony's words, to "play the smaller places first."[631]

This decision did nothing to reduce the tension between Journey and Van Halen. When Van Halen upturned catering tables after setting a crowd afire, Journey's management gave representatives of Premier Talent and Warner Bros. an earful, saying that Van Halen was one more mistake away from oblivion. But the axe never fell. The way Leiren remembered it, "Journey management would scold us and threaten us weekly that we're off the tour — 'This is it!' Well this went on for a while and we finally asked, 'Are we on double secret probation now? Why aren't we getting kicked off this tour?' And we finally realized: Journey's album is up on the charts a little bit, and ticket sales are going pretty good too. Since we're selling albums, the shows are selling better. The local radio stations were getting lots of requests for Van Halen. People were coming down and they're screaming, 'Van Halen!' So it became very apparent that the majority of the people were coming to see Van Halen."

Still, Van Halen's time with Journey and Ronnie Montrose did wrap up by the end of April. For Neal Schon, who got on well with Edward but found it difficult to perform in the wake of the young virtuoso, this parting came none to soon. "It was like getting your ass kicked every night by the best sword-swinging sushi chef in the land," he'd tell *Guitar Player*. "Ronnie Montrose was supporting, and he hated being in the middle slot. I would tell him, 'Man, I'm glad you have to follow that and not me!'"[632] Montrose, too, would later praise Edward's playing by observing, "The only guy who's really doing something new and different is Eddie Van Halen. He's taken a very basic Stratocaster sound and added a lot of coloration and harmonics to his style. He's one of the only new guitarists who's managed to get past the tremolo bar and feedback tricks that a lot of post-Hendrix guitarists have got caught up in."[633]

= =

After a short transatlantic headlining run, Van Halen hooked up with Black Sabbath on May 16 in Sheffield. Edward and Alex, who'd cut their teeth on Sabbath, surely felt the weight of history on that first night of the Sabbath tour. But all of those thoughts faded after the quartet opened their set with a one-two punch of "On Fire" and "I'm the One." Right in the middle of their second song, however, disaster struck. Edward's guitar went dead for some minutes, bringing the set to a halt. The band would recover and finish on a strong note, but they undoubtedly remained frustrated and embarrassed that technical difficulties had disrupted their Sabbath debut.[634]

Despite this golden opportunity, Sabbath failed to capitalize on Van Halen's misfortunes. Author Paul Wilkinson recalled that Sabbath's set "ended disastrously: the PA broke down after an hour, following periodic blips throughout the earlier part of the set. Bill Ward manfully treated us to an un-amplified and spontaneous drum solo, while the other members sheepishly trudged offstage. I was right at the front, and I could hear Bill shout 'Fuck it!' as he dumped his sticks and trounced off to join them. There was a long pause, and then the house lights came up; someone made an apologetic announcement, and two thousand Sabbath fans were left to make their way dejectedly home." Wilkinson, who loved Sabbath, remembered departing audience members speculating that Van Halen "had sabotaged the PA." But, he writes, "Most of us realized that such a step was hardly necessary. Van Halen were incandescent; Sabbath were merely in decline."[635]

Sheffield set the tone for the rest of this leg of the tour. While Sabbath logged good performances over the twenty-plus UK dates, fans and journalists soon recognized that Van Halen were stars on the rise. While the NME's Tom Noble grumbled that Van Halen was "nothing special," he reported that Newcastle fans went mad for the band: "Before Van Halen had even groped the torchlit way onto the stage, the audience were, to a man, on their feet."[636] Steve Gett, writing in Record Mirror about the Bristol show, observed, "Van Halen's success supporting Black Sabbath has been phenomenal, with at least one encore every night . . . Midway through their UK tour Van Halen is doing very well, increasing in confidence and gaining a lot of fans on the way."[637]

And in Aberdeen, the band received some fantastic news from Warner Bros. Van Halen had gone gold. After years of hard work, and in the midst of a musical environment that was anything but hospitable to their kind of music, Van Halen had achieved a pinnacle of success that only a handful of acts ever attain. Of course, this called for revelry worthy of the occasion. Roth recalled,

A Dickinson Robinson Group Product

DEAR
BRIAN, SUE, JOSH & JAMAICA
WELL WE'RE ON THE END
AGAIN ON OUR WAY HOME
SOUTH LONDON
EVER. IT'S GREAT TO PLAY
WITH SABBATH — BUT WE'VE
ALMOST GOTTEN KICKED OFF THE
TOUR TWICE — ONCE FOR TRASHING
A DRESSING ROOM — AND LAST NIGHT
DAVE THREW A MAGNUM CHAMPAGNE
BOTTLE INTO THE AUDIENCE —
IT CRACKED OPEN SOMEBODY'S
HEAD! SKYROCKETTING INSURANCE
PREMIUMS. WERE YOU IN
NOW.

BRIAN BOX & FAMILY
119 Dominguez Av.
San Clemente, Calif
U.S.A. 92672

Stonehenge, Salisbury Plain, Wiltshire
This famous prehistoric megalithic monument is
situated about 10 miles north of Salisbury. Its origin
and purpose are still unknown, though it is thought
to have been used for sun-worship
PWI/81079

LOVE AL & ED

A second postcard sent by the Van Halen brothers to Brian Box at the
outset of Van Halen's May 1978 UK jaunt with Black Sabbath. In it, they
note that Van Halen was nearly "kicked off the tour" twice. BRIAN BOX

"We celebrated our first gold record in Aberdeen, Scotland, in the
lobby of the hotel." Edward, in a drunken effort to commemorate
the band's achievement, tracked down some gold paint and set
out to redecorate the hallway walls. The rest of the band then
added flourishes to some portraits with shoe polish pulled from
a vending machine. Needless to say, as Roth recounted, police
"escorted" the band out of the country, saying, "Don't ever
come back!"[638]

= =

In mid-June, Van Halen temporarily parted ways with the masters
of metal and headed for Japan. Van Halen played eight dates in the

Land of the Rising Sun, including four in Tokyo, performing in front of subdued but large crowds in theater-sized venues.

Around this time, the Van Halen camp could see momentum building on a global scale. By late June, the album had cracked the Top 30 in Australia, France, and Japan, and "You Really Got Me" had hit the Top 20 in France, Holland, and New Zealand. Back in the States, *Van Halen* had taken its place alongside debut LPs by stars like Foreigner and Boston to become one of the fastest-selling first albums in history.[639] Warner Bros., to keep the album flying off the racks, released "Jamie's Cryin'" in July as the band's third single.

Berle and Premier Talent moved to capitalize on Van Halen's growing success by booking a stretch of summertime American dates. Coupled with a tour with Sabbath starting on August 22 in Milwaukee, in July and August Van Halen would perform everywhere from the cavernous Superdome, as an opening act for the Rolling Stones, to the intimate Armadillo World Headquarters in Austin, Texas. An American tour that was expected to last six weeks had turned into a world vacation.

On June 28, Van Halen prepared to depart Japan. The band's next destination was Dallas, where the quartet would perform on July 1 at the massive Texxas Music Festival alongside platinum-selling acts like Heart, Ted Nugent, and Aerosmith. With the promoters expecting upwards of eighty thousand fans in the Cotton Bowl, this show would take place in front of the largest audience to this point in Van Halen history. Van Halen's crew packed up the band's equipment, cleared customs, and then jumped on a 747 with the rest of the band.

After Van Halen and its entourage arrived in the Lone Star state, they got some very bad news. "When we were in Japan," Berle says, "we shipped the equipment to Dallas and there was a problem. The equipment never showed up." After some frantic phone calls, the band discovered on June 30 that its gear had ended up in Chicago.

Berle remembers that while Edward "had [some of] his guitars, because we could carry those on the plane," almost every other piece of gear the band used was stuck in the Windy City.

With the show happening the following day, Van Halen couldn't count on the airline to miraculously deliver their gear in time for the gig. The band had no other choice than to quickly get substitute equipment. "Eddie was really pissed," Berle says, "because he'd have to rent effects and amps! He had nothing."

On July 1, a blood-red sun rose and began roasting Dallas. Temperatures that day would top out at over 100 degrees, and Van Halen, who'd appear near the bottom of the bill, would hit the stage in the mid-afternoon, the hottest part of the day. By the early afternoon, the gates opened and tens of thousands of fans began filling the stadium, all looking like, according to Mike Simmons of the *Deer Park Progress*, "a herd of Thanksgiving turkeys being paraded into a giant oven." On the Astroturf field, ambient temperatures hit 120–130 degrees, which led scores to faint from the blistering heat.[640]

Backstage, Van Halen stood ready, resigned to the fact that the show must go on, even though, as Leiren recalled, "everybody was totally burned out" from the whirlwind of the past few days.[641] As Alex explained on the radio show *Profiles in Rock*, "It's 1:00, it's 120 degrees. We're getting down to do some business, and I've got a [rental] drum set that comes to my knees."[642]

Still, Van Halen turned up the heat on the Texas crowd. Mike Simmons reported, "Van Halen won over the vast majority of the fans with an exciting forty-five-minute set featuring songs off their great debut album. Lead vocalist David Roth did little prodding to get the fans to respond to such hits as 'Runnin' with the Devil' and 'You Really Got Me.'"[643] The band agreed with this assessment. Edward recalled, "We played in front of eighty-two thousand people on rented equipment and we still blazed!" Roth added, "That was what really made us down in Texas. It was one of our very best shows, and the crowd went *nuts*."[644]

Offstage, Berle watched in amazement. He calls it "one of the greatest shows I ever saw." In his view, the band's guitarist particularly rose to the occasion: "Eddie was understandably upset at the prospect of playing in front of his contemporary musicians for the first time without the amps and the effects that he felt contributed to his signature sound. But in spite of that . . . Eddie still pulled it off to a standing ovation."[645]

Van Halen's incendiary set so burned out the crowd that the rest of the undercard had no chance to make any headway among the thousands on hand. "Other bands that played during the first nine hours simply did not move the audience," Simmons wrote, "partly due to the heat and, in some cases, due to lackluster performances . . . Head East, the band who had to follow Van Halen's dynamite set, was the low point of the concert. They tried endlessly to get fans on their feet but were virtually ignored. Not until their unwarranted encore, 'Never Been Any Reason,' did the fans seem to care. Without a question, Van Halen owned the first nine hours of the show."[646] Only when Heart came onstage hours later did the audience come back to life. On this day, Van Halen went from being a breakthrough act to rock superstars.

Before Van Halen left Dallas, Leiren headed to the airport in the early morning of July 2 to retrieve the band's equipment, which had finally arrived from Chicago. He recounted to Steven Rosen that the band had lustily celebrated their Texas triumph, and so when he met with the customs agents, he took their word for it that all of the band's gear was on hand. A foggy-headed Leiren then signed the paperwork and took possession of the equipment.

Out in the parking lot, he and the band's driver started putting everything into the truck. Only then did Leiren make a terrible discovery. "We started loading," he remembered, "and I realized, 'Hey wait a minute. Where's the bomb?' We had [Edward's] big World War II bomb we used to carry. It turned out there were like four pieces missing." One of the missing items was a three-head

Edward Van Halen solos in front of an arena crowd in southern California, July 1978.

NEIL ZLOZOWER

road case that contained Edward's prized Marshall amplifier, the one he'd bought in the early 1970s and used on *Van Halen*.

Over the following weeks, Edward's bomb and two other items did make their way back to the band. But Edward's "baby," the Marshall, was gone. "Well they found everything but the three-amp head case," Leiren remembered. When Edward heard the news, he was "very, very, upset" about the disappearance of perhaps the single most irreplaceable weapon in his arsenal. "Boy I tell you what," Leiren said, "it was like the loss of a good friend, every minute he was devastated."[647]

= =

After cobbling together an array of substitute amps, Edward and the rest of the band headed to the West Coast. They'd first play a headlining show at San Diego's Sports Arena before returning to the City of Angels to play at the Long Beach Arena on July 8. Berle, wanting to guarantee a sellout, first considered booking the band at the three-thousand-seat Santa Monica Civic, or perhaps playing a "scaled-down, 5,500–seat" setup of the Long Beach Arena. But with album sales going strong and an army of hometown fans itching to see Van Halen, Berle and Premier Talent decided to roll the dice and book the full nine-thousand-seat arena.

Almost as soon as tickets went on sale, it was clear that their gamble had paid off. A nervous Berle called the promoter and learned that within an hour, six thousand tickets had been sold. By the second hour, the concert was sold out. An exuberant Roth told the *Los Angeles Times*, "This is really special. We haven't played L.A. since New Year's Eve at the Whisky. It's like our homecoming. We've been on the road since February and now we've got our first gold record. What better place to celebrate?"[648]

Onstage that night at the Long Beach Arena, Van Halen greeted their raucous fans in explosive fashion. Treating the show like a giant backyard party, they stunned the crowd with an opening barrage of smoke pots, which were just one part of the twenty thousand dollars in "special effects and equipment ordered by the band to give the evening an added spark."[649] Dave Shelton remembers, "To see them at that big of a venue and that big of a sound system was great. They always played great. They were a tight band. It was like, *wow*, Van Halen were our local boys who made it."

The quartet finished their show up with three encores while the audience "roared its approval," according to Robert Hilburn of the *Los Angeles Times*. This frenzied response prompted him to mention Van Halen alongside some rock legends from the City of Angels: "While many bands do well after moving to L.A., it has been years since a homegrown rock group moved on to national attention. Some feel Van Halen could be the biggest L.A.-spun outfit since the Doors a decade ago."[650]

David Lee Roth and Edward Van Halen perform "Ice Cream Man"
in southern California, July 1978. NEIL ZLOZOWER

After the show, pandemonium reigned by the arena's backstage door. Hundreds of friends and fans, including Steve Tortomasi, congregated in hopes of partying with Van Halen. He recalls, "There were a bunch of groupie chicks and probably three hundred other people trying to get backstage. And they had two security guards there with a rope. I feel this tap on my shoulder. I turn around, and it's Mike [Anthony] Sobolewski's dad. He smiles and goes, 'Steve, I can't get backstage, and if you can't get backstage, I know I'm not getting backstage!'"

While the pair spoke, Edward appeared at the door. Tortomasi says, "Everyone's saying, 'Hey Ed! Let us back!' So he grabs me by the shirt and he grabs Mike's dad by the shirt and pulls us to go backstage. But the security guards didn't know who he was. This punk ass security guy grabbed him by the neck threw him on the ground. Hard. The guy choked him. It was brutal. He grabbed him and threw him on the ground because he was trying to pull us backstage. People were screaming, 'Hey man! You don't know what you're doing!' It startled Ed. It really hurt him. Ed got up and said, '*You haven't heard the end of this!*' He was pissed!"

Dave Shelton saw what happened next. "So we were backstage hanging out," he says. "We had lost Eddie for a little bit. He comes back and he's all pissed off. He comes walking past us and he must have management with him and security. Apparently what had happened is that he had gone out to the bus or his car or something to get a camera, and coming back in one of the security guys grabbed him by the throat and put him on the ground, not knowing who he was. Eddie comes back with these guys and he's livid. '*That's the motherfucker RIGHT THERE!*' and pointed at this security guard who had put him on the ground. Eddie was *not* happy about that."

= =

As Edward nursed his sore neck, Van Halen traveled to the Big Easy to open for their labelmates the Doobie Brothers and "The World's Greatest Rock and Roll Band," the Rolling Stones. Naturally, putting a gang of professional drinkers like Van Halen and its road crew in New Orleans, the drunkest city in America, made for an orgy of intoxication. Alex rented a Cadillac, which he drove with abandon. Back at the hotel, he and his drum tech Gregg Emerson ran wild. Michael Anthony explains with a laugh, "Alex and Gregg *loved* to drink back then. Gregg was one of those guys who was always up for doing something crazy. He and Alex would say, 'Let's do [something nuts]!' I'd say, 'Ah, no, I'm not doing that.'"

The bassist adds, "When we were in New Orleans on the first tour, I remember the crew kept bringing back all of these girls, who were actually guys, to the hotel. When we got up that morning, Gregg had two black eyes and was looking *rough*. He said he got in a fight, but it was just as likely that he walked into his hotel door while he was drunk." Unfortunately for Emerson, this transpired right before he made the acquaintance of rock royalty. Ross Velasco adds, "Gregg was so excited about meeting Mick Jagger, but he ended up with two black eyes right before he met him!"

On the afternoon of July 13, Van Halen got a surprise onstage visitor. Anthony says, "I couldn't believe it when Mick Jagger walked onstage when we were soundchecking at the Superdome. My jaw hit the floor." Jagger looked warily at Van Halen's equipment. As Edward later told Rafael Marti, Jagger pointed at his rig and said to him, "Ah wut's this bomb thing?" A starstruck Edward explained that he kept some of his guitar effects inside the bombshell. Jagger, refusing to give Van Halen a chance to upstage the Stones, sniffed and said, "Well, we won't be needing it onstage."

Backstage, the band got ready. Roth later explained that after performing so many gigs in front of so many big crowds, the band felt "more anticipation than nervousness" for a gig like the Superdome show. "I mean, we know the tunes, we know we can do them well. Hey, we've been doing all those songs since way back. We can read comic books onstage while we play, because we know them that well."[651]

Outside the venue, tens of thousands of fans holding general admission tickets lined up near the entrances despite the oppressive heat. Naturally, those hoping to secure prime locations to see the show, and to escape the stifling New Orleans climate, flooded into the air-conditioned arena as soon as the gates opened at 5:30. For Van Halen, this meant they'd perform in front of a packed house of eighty thousand fans.[652]

Even though a *Times-Picayune* critic thought little of Van Halen, the crowd embraced the band.[653] Roth remembered, "That was incredible. Standing up in front of eighty-three thousand people and asking them a yes question, and hearing eighty-three thousand go *Yessss*! The sound almost blew us over backwards.

It sounded like a jet plane taking off!"[654] In September, Roth and Anthony would point to this show as the tour's high point, especially since Van Halen got to return to the stage for an encore at the behest of a screaming crowd.[655]

The next day, Roth asked Alex when he'd be returning his rented Cadillac. Roth explained to DJ Jim Ladd what happened next: "The next morning around breakfast time, I said to him, 'You best call the rental place.'

"He said, 'Yeah, I better.'

"So he called up the rental place. He said, 'Hey man, you've got to come down and pick this car up yourself. I ain't even driving it back into the shop.'

"Guy goes, 'What's the matter?'

"'The right mirror's out of adjustment, the right turn indicator don't work, and the right door don't even open!'

"Guy said, 'Right door doesn't open? I checked that car out myself right before you took it out. Why won't the right door open?'

"Al goes, 'Car's lying on it.'"[656]

= =

Despite Van Halen's growing success, the band still operated within a difficult musical environment. In a reflection of disco's popularity, the *Saturday Night Fever* soundtrack stood like an immovable object at the top reaches of the *Billboard* album chart. And when it came to rock, Van Halen's approach seemed out of step with the industry's dominant trends. Soft rock aside, the Pasadena quartet sounded little like the smooth AOR of Boston, Foreigner, Heart, and Styx, and even less like new wave/punk acts like Blondie and the Ramones.

Many critics concluded that a loud, hard, and heavy band like Van Halen was an outlier, one that offered nothing more than a repackaging of the obsolete heavy metal sounds of the dusty past.

High Fidelity dismissed *Van Halen* in just this manner by declaring: "Van Halen's heavy metal is smooth and ordinary — sort of a Black Sabbath with middle-class Californian professionalism."[657] Anthony remembered that journalists thought nothing of asking the band in 1978, "What do you think now that heavy metal is dead?"[658] Naturally, that question came easy after Van Halen toured with Black Sabbath, a seminal heavy metal act that appeared to be on the decline.

By mid-July, Van Halen — particularly Roth — parried these attacks by offering up a new term to describe their music. In this formulation, Van Halen played neither hard rock nor heavy metal. Instead, Van Halen played "big rock."[659] As Roth told a Houston scribe, "In fact, Van Halen is big rock. We're not a heavy metal band, even though we've been called that."[660] In many an interview, Van Halen's singer went to pains to explain the difference between heavy metal and big rock. "This is the new generation, man," he told the *Dallas Morning News*. "The '80s are here and Van Halen is young and writing that way . . . we call it big rock and it's different from hard rock or heavy metal. We play songs, man. I think in terms of three minutes whether I want to or not."[661]

Of course Van Halen's emphasis on short, punchy songs — tunes that featured the aesthetics of heavy metal played with a pop sensibility — had its roots in Roth's efforts to streamline Van Halen's songs when he'd first joined the band. While it took some time, by 1976 or so, he'd cultivated a culture of radio-friendly songcraft within the band, one that bore little resemblance to the expansive, jam-heavy sound of acts like Grand Funk and Black Sabbath.

While almost all critics — eager to dismiss anything resembling heavy metal — missed this aspect of Van Halen's sound, one observant and influential journalist highlighted this key distinction between the past and the present. Robert Hilburn of the *Los Angeles Times* noted that while Van Halen and Led Zeppelin's music might seem similar, in fact "Van Halen's sound is much more compact than Zeppelin's."[662]

During the month of July, Van Halen offered up their big rock sound to hundreds of thousands of fans at a number of huge rock festivals. They logged one memorable performance on a sultry afternoon at the Mississippi River Jam on Credit Island, near Davenport, Iowa, alongside Journey, the Atlanta Rhythm Section, and the Doobie Brothers.

After the start of their warm-up set was pushed back, Van Halen set out to make the most of their time, as they'd have less than thirty minutes to make their case to the audience. According to the *Quad City Times*, Roth immediately focused on firing up the crowd of twenty-thousand-plus fans by saying, "Get your mind off of the heat and put it on the beat!"[663] Douglas Guenther, who was attending his first concert, recalls, "Van Halen hit the stage and blew me away! Roth was front and center, commanding everyone's attention with his vocals, moves, and rock-god presence. That day was the first time thousands of people there experienced the Van Halen mojo. Eddie was incredible. I couldn't believe what I was seeing and hearing. It gave me goosebumps. I was underwhelmed with Atlanta Rhythm Section, Journey, and the Doobie Brothers when they followed with their full sets. Van Halen stole the show."[664] Asked later that afternoon about what had delayed their set, the ever-quotable Roth shrugged off the question, telling the reporter with a laugh: "My department is sex, drugs, and rock and roll."[665]

The next big show on the itinerary was a rock institution. The Day on the Green Festival, which would be held at the Oakland Coliseum on July 23, would see Van Halen support Aerosmith, Foreigner, and Pat Travers. Despite this roster of heavyweights, the biggest test Van Halen faced was taking the stage after Australian upstarts AC/DC. The way Edward remembered it, "AC/DC was probably one of the most powerful live bands I've ever seen in my life. The energy . . . they were unstoppable . . . I was standing on the side of the stage thinking, 'We have to follow these mother-fuckers?'"

But in another demonstration of Van Halen's mettle and talent, Van Halen stood toe-to-toe with the quintet from Down Under. Edward added, "They were so fuckin' powerful, but I remember feeling that we held our own. I was really happy. It blew my mind. I didn't think anybody could follow them."[666] Photographer Neil Zlozower, who'd just started shooting the band, thought that Van Halen more than held their own: "The band took the stage and devastated every other band that played on the bill that day."[667] Still, dissent came from a *San Francisco Chronicle* reporter, who, in spite of his disdain for Van Halen, made one dead-on-accurate prediction: "Van Halen purveys rock at its lowest common denominator — and probably will be very big before long."[668]

= =

Although the Sabbath tour was about to resume, Van Halen kept working. On August 12, they traveled to Maryland to do a one-off arena performance opening for Ted Nugent at the Capital Centre. That night, they put on their show in front of 20,476 rock fans.[669] Henry Rollins, who later achieved fame as Black Flag's singer, was in the audience. He recalled that he rarely paid attention to opening acts "but this time it was a band called Van Halen. I remember they hit the stage and went into 'Runnin' with the Devil' after Diamond Dave made his drum riser leap."[670]

A few songs into the set, Roth paused to say hello to the packed house. Rollins recounted, "This singer starts talking. He seems to be like a peroxided Mark Twain. He can really turn a phrase. And it becomes evident that the singer in this band doesn't seem to understand that we're not all there to see him. He doesn't seem to know that he's in the opening band; it seems as he's in the head-lining band. *'It's nice to be back in Largo, Maryland!'* Nice to be back?

He's never been here before! What the fuck is he talking about? But it was awesome."[671]

According to Rollins, the crowd so got behind Van Halen that they continued to chant the opener's name even after the headliner's set was underway, leading the Motor City Madman to say "Fuck Van Halen!" to the audience.[672] In later years, Nugent conceded that Van Halen had outshone him that night, declaring, "I don't ever want Van Halen on the same bill as me!"[673]

= =

On August 22, Sabbath began its tour of America with Van Halen in support. After wending their way through the upper Midwest, the two acts were set to appear at New York's legendary Madison Square Garden on August 27. Although this would be Van Halen's third New York appearance (after opening for Journey at the Palladium on March 25, Van Halen had headlined the Palladium on April 28), Roth, perhaps recalling his struggles at SIR Studios back in November 1976, conceded that playing New York made him uneasy, telling the *Aquarian*, "New York gives me the jitters."[674]

In point of fact, Roth probably didn't have to worry. Interviews conducted by *Circus* on the day of the Garden show provided more evidence that the careers of Sabbath and Van Halen were headed in different directions. Ozzy sounded exhausted and paranoid, complaining about a virulent virus that was "wiping [him] out" and about audience members who gave him the "evil eye," an experience he found "frightening." After informing the reporter that he felt "bored to shit" on the road, he conceded that Van Halen "are so good they ought to be headlining the tour."[675]

Roth, in contrast, struck a confident pose. He declared his admiration for fellow motormouth Muhammad Ali and fast food magnate Ray Kroc. He also told the reporter that Van Halen and its crew resembled Attila the Hun's hordes, because both comprised "a group of barbarians who are sweeping around the world non-stop and have a few basic goals in mind and when it's done have a good old barbarian party — after each city is conquered."

Along those very lines, Roth provided *Circus*'s readers with irrefutable evidence that Van Halen's campaign for world domination was succeeding: "They told us New York City, the Big Apple, was the hardest one to crack and in a short space of time we've gone from the three-thousand-seater to the twenty-thousand-seater."[676] The fact that many of those who'd fill the Garden that evening would be there to check out the opening act wasn't lost on the Sabbath camp. Two Sabbath crew members would later write: "Van Halen's presence had a major influence on ticket sales since they were a much bigger draw at home than they were in the UK."[677]

After wowing fans at the Garden, Van Halen got more good news when the band arrived in Philadelphia on August 29. Leiren was backstage at the Spectrum when he was told he had a phone call. As he explained to Steven Rosen, "I go running back and this house guy points to this phone on the wall there at the gig. 'Hello? Yeah.' Well it was Karen calling from the [Van Halen] office. *They found the amps.* I was jumping up and down! I couldn't believe it! I had to call the hotel immediately to tell Ed. Well they had already left to come over for soundcheck. When he got there I had this big shit-eating grin on my face. Whenever something's up, he always goes, 'What?' I told him they found the amp! That was it. *Hip hip hooray!*" After the miraculous return of his priceless Marshall, Edward would retire it from the road because, as his then-tech explained in 1985, "If it's lost we will never be able to replace it."[678]

= =

By late September, the wheels had started to come off the bus for Sabbath. *Sounds* writer Sylvie Simmons, who caught up with the tour in Fresno on September 22, recalled that Ozzy looked "gray and bloated, eyes dead" when she saw him offstage, even though he hadn't hit thirty yet. Perhaps if Simmons had spent a few more days with him, she'd have been surprised that the Prince of Darkness even ambulated at all. The band's tour manager, Albert Chapman, recalled that his workdays often included attempts to rouse a comatose Ozzy: "I'd be kicking doors off hotel rooms to get him out of bed. I mean physically kicking the door down and paying the damages, because it was cheaper than missing a flight and canceling a gig."[679]

Roth, in contrast, seemed fit as an Olympic athlete to Simmons despite his steady diet of drink, drugs, and fast food. The reporter, who watched Roth entertaining a crowd of admirers in a hotel room, remembered the remarkable "contrast between the vitality, energy, and single-mindedness of the support act and the shambolic disunity of the headliners . . . Van Halen looked young, Sabbath looked past it; Van Halen were clearly on the way up, Sabbath were going down."[680]

Things wouldn't get any better for Sabbath when both bands performed at Anaheim Stadium in Los Angeles on September 23 with headliner Boston and an opening act of future Van Halen lead singer Sammy Hagar. Weeks earlier, Berle and Roth had started cooking up a scheme to steal the show from the other bands on the bill. In the middle of the afternoon, while the other bands partied backstage, Van Halen put their plan into motion. They slipped away and hid inside a cargo van. There they sat for hours, drinking, smoking, and pissing in a coffee can, waiting for their big moment.[681]

These cloak-and-dagger tactics were all part of the larger plan. Berle explains that he'd hired four skydivers and bought four wigs, two sets of identical jumpsuits, and two sets of matching helmets. "I had a van there," he recalls, "and the band was inside the van wearing the same jumpsuits. We didn't tell anyone what we were doing. Backstage nobody knew what the fuck was going on."

Soon after Hagar departed from the stage, a plane began circling high above the stadium, an occurrence initially noticed by almost nobody except Van Halen's management and crew. Then out of the airplane tumbled the four parachutists. They deployed their chutes and drifted downward. As they approached the ground, some people began to point and cheer, as they saw that the parachutes were emblazoned with Van Halen logos. Right on cue, a voice blared out of the PA system: "From out of the sky, Van Halen is coming into the stadium!"

Somewhere in the sea of people, all with eyes turned skyward, sat Tracy G. "As they got closer," he says with a smile, "you can see they've got the big *VH* on their fucking parachutes. They got closer and closer and the whole fucking place was roaring. I'm like, *There's no fucking way*. Talk about getting the crowd before they even walk on! Now I don't think it was them, but it didn't fucking matter, because everybody thought it was. They landed in the backstage area, and then they came running out in parachute outfits. I'm like *fuck me*! They rip off the jumpsuits and they've got their fucking rock star clothes on. They throw Eddie his guitar and that's it. I'm like *fuck it*; they had everything, and they thought of everything!"

Berle explains how they pulled off this sleight of hand. "They landed right behind the stage. We did the switch in the van because the real jumpers got in the van. The van pulled up to the stage and they got out with their jumpsuits on. So it was *kind* of believable," he chuckles.

Of course, reporters began asking Van Halen's manager if it was *really* Van Halen who had dropped out of the California sky. Like a magician who won't reveal his secrets, he played along by insisting to the *Los Angeles Times*: "The group had practiced for months for the spectacular entrance." To the band's credit, the caper worked so smoothly that Robert Hilburn refused to make a definitive statement about who actually parachuted, writing that whomever "it was who landed, it was Van Halen that raced arm-in-arm onto the stage in parachute outfits and drew the day's biggest applause." Van Halen, he asserted, was "hard to resist" and was an act that "could well be the heir apparent to Aerosmith's hard-rock American crown."[682]

= =

More tangible evidence of Van Halen's rise to the heights of the rock world came almost immediately after the Anaheim Stadium show. In early September, the band had gotten word that they'd sold more than nine hundred thousand copies of *Van Halen* in the United States.[683] Then, at the end of the month, it was official. Van Halen, a band that couldn't get a record deal back in 1976, had gone platinum. In the September 30 issue of *Billboard*, Warner Bros. Records announced that the quartet had sold one million copies of their LP via a full-page ad.[684] Berle, to commemorate the occasion, surprised all four musicians with Van Halen logo necklaces made of platinum. Warner Bros., to keep the momentum going, released a fourth single from *Van Halen*, "Ain't Talkin' 'Bout Love," in October.

This success came at almost the exact moment that Sabbath's long-delayed Warner Bros. Records album, *Never Say Die*, appeared in record stores. Unfortunately for Sabbath, Van Halen's newfound status as the label's darlings helped make Sabbath an afterthought in Burbank. Geezer Butler recalled, "Warner Bros. was losing interest in us as well. They were putting all this money into Van Halen and completely ignored us. Warner Bros. had this party for us for when *Never Say Die* was coming out. We got to the party, and nobody knows who we are. They weren't going to let us in at first. We got in, and they were playing Bob Marley, because nobody liked Sabbath." Ozzy summed things up by saying: "The record company didn't give a damn for us."[685]

Meanwhile, Van Halen built on their success by winning over audiences, night after night. Van Halen "supported" Sabbath by playing for as long as fifty-five minutes, which allowed them to perform most of *Van Halen*, along with a couple of tracks slated for their next album. All three instrumentalists took a turn in the spotlight by playing brief but intense solos: Anthony's bass notes rumbled out of the speaker like an avalanche, which he punctuated by stomping on a wah-wah pedal. Alex flailed away within a flashing strobe light before appearing to be playing in a ring of fire, courtesy of blazing drumsticks dipped in tiki-torch fluid. Edward, during his frenzied and mind-boggling renditions of "Eruption," wowed audiences by fucking his amps, Hendrix style, while feedback poured from the speakers.

Roth, too, had raised his game. While he'd started the tour wearing black leather biker pants and platforms onstage, by July he'd begun performing in tight striped pants and Capezios, all the better to allow him to conduct his death-defying aerial leaps and Russian toe-touches from the drum riser. In the last few minutes of the set, they'd launch into an extended jam during "You Really Got Me," which saw all the band members banging on Alex's drums. Roth then wrapped things up by spraying champagne into the crowd before dumping it over his own head.[686] Pete Angelus, who worked with Roth to script the show, comments, "Dave's intention was to throw a big party every night, and that's exactly what they did."

This kind of showmanship started to wear on Sabbath. Somewhere on tour, Iommi talked Osbourne into dressing down the Pasadena quartet for their over-the-top stage show. After a wasted Osbourne cornered them, they inquired, "Why are you yelling at us?" The addled Osbourne had no answer, since he couldn't recollect the conversation he'd just had with Iommi.[687]

The Van Halen camp, like the members of Sabbath, understood that the balance of power had shifted. Edward recalled, "That was our first tour. We were doing anything and everything we'd ever read about and then some. We were kind of a double-edged sword to them I guess. We forced them to have to rise to the occasion to follow us."[688] Berle's take is that by the fall, a spent Sabbath *couldn't* rise to the occasion. "The Sabbath tour was great. All those shows were just phenomenal. Eventually no band wanted Van Halen to open for them, because they couldn't follow Van Halen."

= =

A few weeks later, Sabbath and Van Halen found themselves trudging through the American South. Back at the hotel after the November 8 show in Birmingham, Roth and Ozzy stayed up all night in a fifteenth floor room, snorting enough cocaine to stop the hearts of a half-dozen men. The next morning, they were still at it, almost up to the moment they needed to leave to travel to Nashville. Roth and Ozzy declared an armistice in their "Krell War," as Roth dubbed it in his autobiography, around 9:30 a.m. and climbed aboard their respective buses.[689]

Once they'd arrived in the Music City, a red-eyed Ozzy staggered off Sabbath's bus with the key from the previous night's hotel room still in hand. After glancing at the tag, he headed for the fifteenth floor. Ozzy explained, "I'd been on a run for about three or four days of not sleeping . . . I put my hand in my pocket and I pulled out the key . . . I look at this number on the key ring, and the maid's just coming out. I go in."[690] Ozzy slammed the door and collapsed on the bed. Down on the sixth floor, Ozzy's actual hotel room remained unoccupied.

As the bands prepared for the night's performance, everyone began asking about Ozzy. "So we're supposed to do soundcheck," Edward recollected, "and nobody could find him."[691] Angelus says, "I actually remember seeing him get off the bus and wander across the street to the hotel. I thought, *He's going to get something to eat*, because everyone scatters when they get off the bus." No one else had seen him since.

In the meantime, a sold-out crowd of 9,800 fans began filing into the arena.[692] By now, Nashville police detectives had begun searching for Ozzy, fearing that he might have been kidnapped or become "the victim of some other form of foul play."[693] Angelus says, "What I remember is all the commotion. *Where is he? What are we going to do?* We were just in a holding pattern. *Did we find him? Are we going onstage?*" Eventually, Van Halen went on, not knowing if Sabbath would follow them.

When Van Halen finished, two members of Sabbath appeared in the dressing room, asking Roth if he might consider substituting for Osbourne. Roth demurred, saying that he didn't know Sabbath's lyrics.[694]

After an hour, some poor soul appeared onstage and announced that Sabbath wouldn't play and that the show would be rescheduled for the coming Sunday, November 12, which had been an off-day. Nathan Craddock, who was in the audience, recollects that this didn't go over well: "Needless to say, the place went fairly well apeshit. You must remember, this was not a canceled Pavarotti show. Somebody threw a fire extinguisher at one of the drum sets; people were chucking implements at the glass that surrounded the entire arena. I remember one guy kicking a trash can down the hallway, yelling and screaming, seriously pissed off."[695]

Early the next morning, Ozzy rejoined the living. "Next thing I know," he explained in 2010, "I wake up and I'm going, 'Wow, that was a good [sleep.]'"[696] When he finally reappeared, everyone breathed a sigh of relief. Angelus recollects, "I remember everyone saying, 'They found Ozzy! He's alive! He's *alive!*'"

═ ═

In the last few weeks of the tour, Van Halen shined as Sabbath faded away. Ozzy explained the effect this dynamic had on his band: "They did a whole world tour with us and we were very demoralized in ourselves because they were so good every night."[697] Butler's take was that his band was in the process of "just dying" after years of success.[698] Ozzy, to his credit, makes no excuses about how Sabbath's run with Van Halen actually played out: "They blew us off the stage every night. It was so embarrassing. We were having a lot of trouble with drugs and didn't have the fire anymore. Those guys were young and hungry. They kicked our asses, but it convinced me of two things: my days with Black Sabbath were over, and Van Halen was going to be a very successful band."[699]

= =

On December 3, Van Halen's nine-month tour in support of their debut album came to an end in San Diego. During that stretch of time they'd performed approximately 180 shows in eight different countries, in front of crowds as small as a few hundred people to as large as eighty-thousand-plus. They'd also seen their career fortunes radically transformed. On the first night of the tour back in March, almost nobody in Chicago had heard of Van Halen. When they got back to Pasadena in early December, they'd become international stars.

Perhaps the best indicator of that success came in the form of record sales. After peaking at No. 19 on the *Billboard* Top LP & Tape chart, *Van Halen* remained among the two hundred best-selling albums for an astounding 169 straight weeks. Along with earning platinum status in America, Van Halen had sold two million albums worldwide by November.[700]

While the cocky Roth may have had no doubts that Van Halen would succeed, Edward recalled his surprise at Van Halen's breakout, explaining to Steven Rosen that "with the first one" he "had no idea" that it would be a hit.[701] But as the album gained traction, Van Halen's whirlwind tour and growing commercial triumph made things a hell of a lot of fun. Edward told the *Dayton Daily*

Edward Van Halen visits the Velasco home in Pasadena, California, 1979.

News in 1995 that he remembered feeling "very excited" and "a lot of energy" as the band climbed the ladder of success. He summarized the course of events by saying, "Songs that we've been playing in the clubs for years — finally got 'em on a record, and had no idea what was gonna happen. Just went out and toured the world for eleven months, and came back and had a double-platinum record!"[702]

Still, not all the news was good. After looking over the band's books, the four musicians learned that they owed Warner Bros. Records a huge sum of money, this despite selling over two million records and gigging incessantly. Edward explained that Van Halen had "toured the world. We did twenty-five shows in twenty-six days in England and we were still owing Warner Brothers a million bucks."[703] What the band apparently didn't understand until after the tour was over was that Warner Bros. had been advancing the band money for tour support. However unfair the terms of the arrangement, Warner Bros. Records had bankrolled Van Halen's year of success, and now it was time for the band to start paying the company back.

= =

From the standpoint of history, of course, the liabilities Van Halen had accrued to their record label in support of their debut delivered a huge return to the band. They'd made millions of fans all over the world thanks to their explosive stage show. They'd also made the smart decision to hold on to the publishing rights for their songs, which would help to make them all rich down the road. Indeed, the royalties for *Van Halen* have been anything but insignificant, as the album has sold more than ten million copies since its release. In the final analysis, *Van Halen* — arguably the greatest debut in rock history — laid a foundation for success that would make David Lee Roth and Edward Van Halen household names and make their band one of the biggest in rock history. Who wouldn't take that in exchange for a 1.2-million-dollar loan?

AFTERWORD

After Van Halen returned to Los Angeles, there was no rest for the weary. Just a week after the last date of their 1978 tour, the Pasadena quartet once again entered Sunset Sound Studios to record their second album. With a 1.2-million-dollar debt in the balance, Warner Bros. Records now had the leverage to keep Van Halen on a relentless "album-tour" cycle, one that would continue for the original lineup through 1984.

Despite the band's abundance of original material, Edward worried about following up their platinum debut. "I was very scared at the end of 1978," he told *Circus*. "We were sitting in England near the end of the tour, and I'm saying, 'Hey guys, we've got another album to do when we get home.' And they're saying, 'Aww, don't worry about it.' And I'm sitting there, knowing that I've gotta write the goddamn music. I'm going, *Oh my God, how am I going to do it?*"[704]

= =

In the end, Edward and the others delivered. Spearheaded by the Top 20 pop-metal smash "Dance the Night Away," *Van Halen II* rocketed to gold status two weeks after its March 1979 release and went platinum by the end of May.[705] The band, eager to build on the momentum they'd generated on the road in 1978, supported the LP with another triumphant, barnstorming world tour.

Van Halen's success continued in the years that followed. The band's next three albums — *Women and Children First* (1980), *Fair Warning* (1981), and *Diver Down* (1982) — also went platinum, thanks in no small part to Van Halen's spectacular and successful arena tours.

But the apex of the original lineup's success came in 1984. *1984* topped out at No. 2 on the *Billboard* album chart. It sold four million copies by October of that year, and every date on the group's North American tour sold out.[706] Van Halen proved to be a band capable of writing a timeless pop hit as well, after the synth-driven "Jump" hit No. 1 in the spring of 1984. That album's success encouraged their new fans to seek out Van Halen's older releases, which propelled the band's debut back into the *Billboard* Top 200 albums six years after its release. In total, their album-catalog sales numbered twelve million by the time the year came to a close.[707]

The quartet had also hit their peak cultural influence. With Van Halen videos in heavy MTV rotation and Van Halen music topping the charts, David Lee Roth and Edward Van Halen achieved a level of fame that few rock musicians ever experience. Roth became rock's ultimate frontman, flamboyant and funny, athletic and charismatic. Likewise, Edward's virtuosity and creativity made him the world's most admired rock guitarist. After years of work, stretching back to their backyard party days, 1984 was Van Halen's moment.

= =

Van Halen's enormous success went far in guaranteeing that the band's influence on heavy metal would be deep and wide. The band's lead singer never tired of observing how Van Halen had changed the rules of the metal game in 1978. He said, "We were one of the first to pioneer the short song in heavy rock . . . At the time we started making records, everybody was blasting off on ten-minute guitar excursions, then sing another verse, then have your organ solo. That was your traditional heavy metal."[708] Roth's enthusiasm for revisiting this point, no doubt, grew out of his awareness that he was the driving force in shaping this aspect of the band's sound.

Still, what Roth referred to as traditional heavy metal, after being left for dead in the late 1970s, soon enjoyed a rebirth. Denim and leather, power and volume, and arena-sized spectacle, all powered by razor-sharp riffs and thunderous beats, came back into vogue by 1980.

Notably, bands that had fallen short of chart success in 1978 finally broke through. For example, AC/DC followed up the Top 20 *Highway to Hell* (1979) with the blockbuster *Back in Black* (1980), an album that would sell five million copies by the end of 1984.[709] The Scorpions, likewise, achieved gold and platinum success with *Blackout* (1982) and *Love at First Sting* (1984).[710] And after scoring a hit with *British Steel* in 1980, Judas Priest posted back-to-back Top 20 albums with *Screaming for Vengeance* (1982) and *Defenders of the Faith* (1984).[711]

As the genre's cultural power grew, Van Halen's guitarist and singer went to pains to argue that their band differed from these metal acts. "I don't consider us to be heavy metal," Edward noted. "The people who do obviously can't get beyond the trappings. They don't go beyond the volume and listen to what's really happening . . . when I think of heavy metal, I think of AC/DC and Judas Priest and Black Sabbath. I just can't see where we fit into that slot."[712] Roth, too, observed that while Van Halen's acrobatic guitar lines, pounding bottom end, and scream-punctuated vocals mirrored elements offered up by metal bands, Van Halen wasn't such an act. "If you have long hair and wear tight pants," he added, "you're qualified heavy metal."[713]

To be sure, Van Halen wasn't a traditional heavy metal band in this sense. But Van Halen's "big rock" formula, as laid out on the band's debut and the five LPs that followed, provided a roadmap to *pop-metal* success in the 1980s. Indeed, an entire generation of MTV-ready "glam rock" bands (Mötley Crüe, White Lion, Ratt, Poison, Autograph, Loudness, Warrant, Quiet Riot, BulletBoys, and Dokken, just to name a few) borrowed heavily from Van Halen in bids to top the *Billboard* charts and become video superstars. Whether it was Dokken's Van Halen–styled harmonies ("In My Dreams"), Ratt's recycled Edward-riffs ("Round and Round"), or Autograph's Van Halen–inspired lead vocal and lead guitar performances ("Turn Up the Radio"), Van Halen–animated songcraft proved to be the secret of success for these bands.

In an even starker demonstration of Van Halen's influence, even 1970s heavy metal pioneers — Roth's traditionalists — followed the Van Halen recipe to one degree or another in the 1980s. Consider Teutonic metal masters Accept. In an effort to break big in America, Accept offered up the radio-friendly *Metal Heart* in 1985. On the album's title track, guitarist Wolf Hoffmann paid tribute to "Eruption" via a storming, unaccompanied solo piece. Accept also gave listeners "Screaming for a Love Bite," a song with a hook that sounds straight out of the Edward Van Halen playbook.

Not to be outdone, in 1986 Judas Priest released *Turbo*, an album that saw the guitar-centric band follow in Van Halen's footsteps by adding synthesizers to their instrumental attack. Synths aside, listen to Priest's "Parental Guidance" with an ear for Van Halen. It's a song that shamelessly borrows Edward's pre-chorus and outro guitar riffs from "Jump."

Then there's KISS, which, in an effort to stay relevant, produced one of the decade's most egregious examples of Van Halen plagiarism (an accomplishment that should not be minimized) on 1987's *Crazy Nights*. On "No, No, No," Bruce Kulick introduces the track by mimicking "Eruption." His speedy licks segue into a "Hot for Teacher"–style shuffle, featuring a Gene Simmons vocal performance that's reminiscent of the distinctive style of a singer he'd "discovered" back in 1976.

In another sign of Van Halen's influence, Edward's innovative playing became an aspirational standard for guitar heroes in training. After his incredible fretwork sent shock waves through the guitar world, tens of thousands of players hunkered down with *Van Halen* on their turntables in an effort to bring their playing up to par, a sequence repeated with the release of each successive Van Halen album. By 1984, there was an army of rock guitarists wielding Edward Van Halen–styled guitars and playing Edward Van Halen–inspired riffs.

By the early 1980s, this type of adulation and inspiration manifested itself in shred guitar, a lead guitar style wholly centered upon the technical mastery of the instrument. Luminaries who attempted to take up Edward's gauntlet included L.A. guitarist Randy Rhoads (who was tragically killed in a plane crash in 1982 while playing in Ozzy Osbourne's band), Swedish neo-classicist Yngwie Malmsteen, and the Grammy-nominated Joe Satriani. Not surprisingly, David Lee Roth, the individual perhaps most aware of the scale of Edward's heroics, hired two of shred's most talented players, Steve Vai and Jason Becker, for some of his most successful post–Van Halen solo albums.

In fact, Edward's distinctive playing became so influential in the 1980s that it even caught the attention of musicians and producers working outside of the rock genre. This trend began in 1982 when R&B/pop megastar Michael Jackson and producer Quincy Jones invited Edward to lay down a guitar solo on Jackson's "Beat It." The song's massive success and significant crossover appeal encouraged other artists to follow the King of Pop's lead, and soon acrobatic guitar solos — formerly the sole province of heavy rock — came to be heard on tunes like Michael Sembello's 1983 hit "Maniac" and Janet Jackson's 1990 smash "Black Cat." In sum, "guitar solo" had become shorthand for "Edward Van Halen–style guitar solo," even on pop and R&B songs.

$$= =$$

Ultimately, Van Halen's place in rock history had been carved in stone long before the band entered its fifth decade of existence. Since 1978, Van Halen — in all its iterations — has sold more than 80 million records worldwide. This accomplishment includes two albums with Roth (*Van Halen* and *1984*) that have sold 10 million copies each in the US alone, a feat matched by only four other rock acts. And *A Different Kind of Truth*, which saw Roth sing for Van Halen once again, has sold more than half a million copies worldwide since its February 2012 release, a remarkably strong performance in an era when album sales have collapsed across the industry.[714]

Still, no one should forget that this monumental success and lasting influence grew from the band's unparalleled work ethic and growing self-confidence during its years as an unsigned act. In the face of smug dismissals of their talent and marketability, Van Halen persevered. Explaining how the band stayed self-assured in the face of criticism, Edward summarized: "Especially in our dues-paying days, when people would say we were undisciplined and had no commercial potential, a lot of club owners wouldn't touch us with a ten-foot pole. But our attitude was, 'Fuck you, we're good and we know it.'"[715]

But in the end, what made Van Halen not just good, but great, was the synergism that made the whole greater than the sum of its parts. Without David Lee Roth, Alex and Edward Van Halen might have become the world's most gifted heavy metal musicians, but then again, they might never have transcended the San Gabriel Valley music scene. Roth, too, might have become a great song-and-dance man, but without Edward's songwriting and virtuosity, it's unlikely that he would have become a rock legend. Without Michael Anthony's spectacular background vocals, it's difficult to imagine that Van Halen, in whatever form the band might have taken, would have developed the classic Van Halen sound, with its undeniable pop appeal.

In the final analysis, it's self-evident that the four original members gave rise to a band that by 1978 was capable of producing greatness both onstage and on vinyl. But the seeds of that greatness stem from a time long before the band played arenas and produced platinum records. They took root in places like Hamilton Park and John Muir High School, in backyards and biker bars, in improvised concert halls and Sunset Strip hotspots. They sprouted out of practice sessions filled with everything from Black Sabbath and James Brown covers to proto-metal originals and future Van Halen hit singles. They flourished in the face of spectacular audition failures and apparent career dead ends. And yet, Van Halen had grown into something magical long before anyone outside of Los Angeles had been let in on the secret. But today every rock fan knows: You can't get this stuff no more.

AUTHOR INTERVIEWS

Larry Abajian
Jeff Austin Addison
Art Agajanian
Mark Algorri
Tom Allen
Dana Anderson
Doug Anderson
Lorraine Anderson
Rusty Anderson
Pete Angelus
Michael Anthony
Gary Baca
Nicky Beat
Ric Bennewate
Marshall Berle
Joe Berman
Iris Berry
Lisa Berryman
Paul Blomeyer
Bobby Blotzer
Victor Bornia
Brian Box
Rob Broderick
Tom Broderick
Steve Bruen
Jim Burger
Peter Burke
Jeff Burkhardt
Carol Doupe' Canterbury
Patti Fujii Carberry
Vincent Carberry
Joe Carducci
Dennis Catron
Dean Chamberlain

Nancy Christensen
Lori Cifarelli
Billy Cioffi
Holly Clearman
Mike Cochrane
Dave Connor
Harry Conway
Hernando Courtright
George Courville, Jr.
Myles Crawley
John Crooymans
Mike Crowley
Renee Cummings
Beverly Daugherty
Rodney Davey
Martha Davis
Audie Desbrow
Dave DiMartino
Pete Dougherty
John Driscoll
Richard M. Ealy
Bruce Fernandez
Scott Finnell
Kim Fowley
Jackie Fox
Janice Pirre Francis
Taylor Freeland
Paul Fry
Kevin Gallagher
Richard Garbaccio
Mary Garson
Mike Gillin
Tommy Girvin
Lisa Christine Glave

Joni Gleason
Susan Schops Gliedman
Juliana Gondek
Tracy "G" Grijalva
Doug Guenther
Lee Gutenberg
Charlie Gwyn
Carl Haasis
Rob Haerr
Steve Hall
Greg Hardin
Mike Harker
Bobby Hatch
Leonard Haze
Eric Hensel
Tom Hensley
Bill Hermes
Dan Hernandez
Jeff Hershey
Chris Holmes
Sonny Hughes
Jose Hurtado
Denis Imler
Debbie Imler McDermott
Karen Imler
Cary Irwin
Bob James
Craig Jameson
Michael Jensen
Freddie Johnson
Randy Jones
Michael Kelley
Mark Kendall
David Kiles

Terry Kilgore
Bruce Kim
Shiloh Kleinschmit
Chris Koenig
Miles Komora
Richard Kymala
Jon Laidig
Donn Landee
Allen Lane
Scott Lasken
Roni Lee
Chris Legg
Greg Leon
Randy Linscott
Larry Logsdon
Debbie Hannaford Lorenz
Steve Loucks
George Lynch
Dana MacDuff
Dave Macias
Matt Marquisee
Rafael Marti
Bill Matsumoto
Bill Maxwell
Marsha Maxwell
Michael McCarthy
Forrest McDonald
Tim McGovern
Richard McKernan
Kim Miller
Mario Miranda
Loren Molinare
Ann Moorman
Ron Morgan
Doug Morris
Jim Mosley
Dennis Neugebauer
Mike Nichols
Gary Nissley
Valerie Evans Noel
John Nyman
Kevin O'Hagan

Susan Okuno
Wally Olney
Gary Ostby
Nicky Panicci
Maria Parkinson
George Perez
David Perry
Brent Pettit
Jim Pewsey
Matt Phillips
Steve Plunkett
Jim Poore
Mark Poynter
Gloria Prosper
Gary Putman
Joe Ramsey
Randy Rand
George Rangel
Scott Reese
Roger Renick
Joanne Resnick
Angelo Roman, Jr.
Don Ross
Janet Ross
Allison Roth
Scott McLean Rowe
Ben Rushing
Tim Ryerson
Werner Schuchner
Tony Scott
David Shelton
Drake Shining
Dan Simcox
Donny Simmons
Jeff Simons
Emmitt Siniard
Patti Smith Sutlick
Dana Spoonerow
Jim Steinwedell
Nancy Stout
Steve Sturgis
Danny Sullivan

David Swanson
David Swantek
Stanley Swantek
Mark Swenston
Fred Taccone
Brian Tannehill
Gary Taylor
Dan Teckenoff
Ted Templeman
Steven Tetsch
Steve Tortomasi
Jeff Touchie
Dennis Travis
Tim Tullio
Bill Urkopina
Jack Van Furche'
Dirk Van Tatenhove
Bill Velasco
Jan Velasco
Ross Velasco
Terry Vilsack
Robert Vogel
Chuck Wada
Scott Waller
Leslie Ward-Speers
John Warren
Dave Weiderman
Cheri Whitaker
Michael White
Fred Whittlesey
Liz Dollar Wiley
Joe Wilson
Peter Wilson
Dave Wittman
Mike Wolf
Alan Wood
Jim Wright
Taylor Yewell
Cindy Yrigollen
Neil Zlozower
Monte Zufelt

WORKS CITED

"41 Years Ago Today — Van Halen Hits the Sunset Strip." *Van Halen News Desk*. 4 April 2014. http://
www.vhnd.com/2014/04/04/40-years-ago-today-van-halen-hits-the-sunset-strip.
Albert, John. "Running with the Devil: A Lifetime of Van Halen." *Slake Los Angeles*. Accessed 22 June
2013. http://slake.la/features/running-with-the-devil-a-lifetime-of-van-halen.
"Alex Van Halen." *Drummerworld*. Accessed 16 May 2012. http://www.drummerworld.com/
drummers/Alex_Van_Halen.html.
Anthony, Michael. "Michael Anthony of Van Halen & Chickenfoot Shares His Favorite Songs." *AOL
Radio Blog*. 10 March 2010. http://aolradioblog.com/2010/03/10/michael-anthony-van-halen-
chickenfoot-shares-favorite-songs.
Aquilante, Dan. "Return of Diamond Dave." *New York Post*. 26 February 2012. http://nypost.com
/2012/02/26/return-of-diamond-dave/.
Atkinson, Terry. "Van Halen's Big Rock." *Rolling Stone*, 14 June 1979.
Baltin, Steve. "David Lee Roth Vents About Van Halen's Future." *Rolling Stone*. 12 February 2013.
http://www.rollingstone.com/music/news/q-a-david-lee-roth-vents-about-van-halens-
future-20130212.
—. "Eddie Van Halen Dismisses Jimi Hendrix Comparisons." *Spinner*. 16 March 2009. Accessed 9 July
2015. http://www.vhnd.com/2009/03/17/eddie-van-halen-dismisses-jimi-hendrix-comparisons/.
Bangs, Lester. "Heavy Metal: The Sinal Folution." *Hit Parader*, March 1978.
Bashe, Philip. *Heavy Metal Thunder: The Music, Its History, Its Heroes*. Garden City,
New York: Doubleday, 1985.
—. "Van Halen's Teen Hearts." *Circus*, 31 July 1981.
Bereskin, Laurie. "Van Halen's Invitation: Come Down and Party." *BAM*, July 1977.
"Bill Aucoin interview on 'The Rock and Roll Geek Show,' 11.8.2007." *YouTube*. 28 June 2013.
https://www.youtube.com/watch?v=bGj7p_o4lDM.
"Billboard Hot 100." *Billboard*, 11 March 1978.
"Blackout." *RIAA Searchable Database*. Accessed 14 October 2014. http://www.riaa.com/
goldandplatinumdata.php?table=SEARCH.
Blair, Iain. *Rock Video Superstars: Van Halen*, March 1985.
Blatt, Ruth. "When Compassion and Profit Go Together: The Case of Alice Cooper's Manager
Shep Gordon." *Forbes*. 13 June 2014. http://www.forbes.com/sites/ruthblatt/2014/06/13/when-
compassion-and-profit-go-together-the-case-of-alice-coopers-manager-shep-gordon/
Blush, Steven. "Runnin' with the Devil." *Seconds*, 1994.
Bonomo, Joe. *Highway to Hell*. London: Continuum International Publishing, 2010.

Bosso, Joe. "Michael Anthony: My 6 Career-Defining Records." *Music Radar*. 3 May 2010. http://www.musicradar.com/news/guitars/michael-anthony-my-6-career-defining-records-249695/7.

Buttner, Christopher. "Michael Anthony of Van Halen." *PRThatRocks*. Accessed 8 July 2015. http://www.prthatrocks.com/interviews/michael.html.

"Carlton Johnson, 52, Film Choreographer and Tap Dancer, Dies." *Los Angeles Times*. 31 December 1986. http://articles.latimes.com/1986-12-31/local/me-1211_1_carlton-johnson.

"Carmine Appice: Eddie Van Halen Seems to Be Out of His Tree Right Now." *Blabbermouth*. 6 October 2006. http://www.blabbermouth.net/news/carmine-appice-eddie-van-halen-seems-to-be-out-of-his-tree-right-now/.

Caves, Richard E. *Creative Industries: Contracts Between Art and Commerce*. Cambridge: Harvard University Press, 2001.

Christe, Ian. *Everybody Wants Some: The Van Halen Saga*. Hoboken, New Jersey: John Wiley & Sons, 2007.

Christgau, Robert. "Van Halen." *Robert Christgau*. http://robertchristgau.com/get_artist.php?id=1646&name=Van+Halen.

Cody, Randy. "Rocket Interviews George Lynch." *The Metal Den*. 15 March 2009. http://themetalden.com/index.php?p=198.

Cohen, Scott. "Heavy Metal Showdown." *Circus*, 10 October 1978.

Collins, Nancy. "David Lee Roth: The *Rolling Stone* Interview." *Rolling Stone*, 11 April 1985.

Considine, J. D. *Van Halen!* New York: Quill, 1985.

"CPI Inflation Calculator." *Bureau of Labor Statistics*. Accessed 1 February 2015. http://data.bls.gov/cgi-bin/cpicalc.pl.

Curcurito, David. "Eddie Van Halen: The Esquire Interview." *Esquire*. 17 April 2012. http://www.esquire.com/the-side/music/eddie-van-halen-interview-2012-8147775.

Dauphin, Edouard. "He Ain't Heavy! The Van Halen Boys Talk." *Creem Close Up: Van Halen*, summer 1984.

"David Lee Roth and Alex Van Halen." UK Radio interview. 7 June 1978.

"David Lee Roth TV interview with Martha Quinn, 1982." *YouTube*. 13 February 2012. https://www.youtube.com/watch?v=UkKwIm8M6D4.

"Defenders of the Faith." *Allmusic*. Accessed 18 October 2014. http://www.allmusic.com/album/defenders-of-the-faith-mw0000194425.

Dery, Mark. "David Lee Roth Takes Off His Warpaint." *Winner*, November 1986. Accessed 17 July 2014 (login required). http://www.rocksbackpages.com/Library/Article/david-lee-roth-takes-off-his-warpaint.

"A Different Kind of Truth." *Wikipedia*. Accessed 8 July 2015. https://en.wikipedia.org/wiki/A_Different_Kind_of_Truth.

Dodds, Kevin. *Edward Van Halen: A Definitive Biography*. Bloomington, Indiana: iUniverse.

Doerschuk, Andy. "Alex Van Halen." *Playing from the Heart: Great Musicians Talk About Their Craft*. Edited by Robert L. Doerschuk. San Francisco: Backbeat Books, 2002.

Driscoll, John. "Tales from Old Pasadena." *The Inside*, summer 1997.

Echols, Alice. *Hot Stuff: Disco and the Remaking of American Culture*. New York: W.W. Norton, 2010.

"Eddie on the Record." *Guitar World Presents Guitar Legends*, April 1992.

Edrei, Mary J., ed. *Top Rockers of the 80s*. Cresskill, New Jersey: Sharon Publications, 1985.

Elliott, Paul. "Born Again." *Classic Rock*, February 2010.

———. "Kiss Unmasked." *Classic Rock*, August 2013.

Ermilio, Brett, and Josh Levine. *Going Platinum: KISS, Donna Summer, and How Neil Bogart Built Casablanca Records*. London: Rowman & Littlefield, 2014.

Fee, Debi, and Linda Benjamin. "Van Halen's David Lee Roth." *Tiger Beat Super Special #3 Presents Rock*, June/July 1980.

Flans, Robyn. "Alex Van Halen." *Modern Drummer*, October 1983.

Flinker, Sue. "Black Sabbath." *Biography*. Directed by Barbara Kanowitz. Biography Channel. 15 July 2010.

Forte, Dan. "Van Halen's Stylish Raunch." *Record*, June 1982.

Fox, Doug. "15 Years On: Eddie Van Halen Interview Revisited." *Van Halen News Desk*. 8 July 2013. http://www.vhnd.com/2013/07/08/15-years-on-eddie-van-halen-interview-revisted/.

Freedland, Nat. "Punk Rock Due at L.A. Whisky." *Billboard*, 20 November 1976.

Fricke, David. "Van Halen Hosts Rock's Biggest Party of '79, and You're Invited." *Circus*, 24 July 1979.

———. "Why Are Rockers Going Disco?" *Circus*, 13 March 1979.

Ganaden, Gerry. "The Return of the Hot Rod Guitar." *Premier Guitar*, February 2009.

Gans, David. "Ted Templeman." *BAM*. 9 October 1981. Accessed 8 July 2015. http://dgans.com/writings/templeman/.

Gargano, Paul. "David Lee Roth: Past, Present & Future." *Metal Edge*, November 1998.

General Telephone Company of California. *City of Pomona, Street Address Directory for Pomona, Chino, Claremont, Diamond Bar, La Verne, San Dimas, Walnut, and Portions of Montclair*. Los Alamitos: GTE Directories Corp., 1975.

"Gene Simmons Comments on Van Halen Demos, 12.28.2001, Eddie Trunk." *YouTube*. 21 April 2012. https://www.youtube.com/watch?v=sgcVjurMwmo.

Gill, Chris. "Cast a Giant Shadow," *Guitar World*, anniversary issue 2010.
—. "A Different Kind of Trove." *Guitar Aficionado*, January/February 2013.
—. "Everybody Wants Some." *Guitar World*, November 2014.
—. "Home Improvement." *Guitar World*, February 2014.
Gilmore, Mikal. *Night Beat: A Shadow History of Rock & Roll*. New York: Doubleday, 1998.
Goddess. "David Lee Roth w/Steven Rosen in 1982." *Van Halen — The Band We Love*. 31 January 2012. http://vanhalen12.blogspot.com/2012/01/david-lee-roth-interview-w-steven-rosen.html.
Gold, Jude. "Ten Things You Gotta Do to Play like Eddie Van Halen." *Guitar Player*. 1 February 2009. http://www.guitarplayer.com/artist-lessons/1026/10-things-you-gotta-do-to-play-like-eddie-van-halen/16950.
Greenberg, Peter S. "Clockwork Rodney's." *Newsweek*, 7 January 1974.
Grein, Paul. "106 Multiple Platinums Kick Off RIAA Award." *Billboard*, 15 December 1984.
Guitar World Staff. "Prime Cuts: Eddie Van Halen Breaks Down 10 Van Halen Classics from 'Eruption' to 'Right Now.'" *Guitar World*. 13 November 2013. http://www.guitarworld.com/article/eddie_van_halen_prime_cuts.
Hamilton, Rusty, and Diana Clapton. "David Lee Roth and the Van Halen Gang: Preening Prophets of Post-Cube Punkpop." *Oui*, November 1981.
Hann, Michael. "David Lee Roth." *The Guardian*. 2 February 2012. www.guardian.co.uk/music/2012/feb/02/david-lee-roth-van-halen.
Hausman, Jeff. "Growing Up with the Van Halens." *The Inside*, spring 1995.
—. "*The Inside* Interviews Wally 'Cartoon' Olney." *The Inside*, summer 1997.
—. "New Kid on the Block." *The Inside*, spring 1999.
—. "Tom Broderick." *The Inside*, summer 1997.
Hedges, Dan. *Eddie Van Halen*. New York: Vintage Books, 1986.
Hiatt, Brian. "Secrets of the Guitar Heroes: Eddie Van Halen." *Rolling Stone*. 12 June 2008. Accessed 8 July 2015. http://web.archive.org/web/20080530133142/http://www.rollingstone.com/news/story/20979938/secrets_of_the_guitar_heroes_eddie_van_halen.
Hogan, Richard. "Van Halen: Best Group, Best Guitar, Best Year Ever." *Circus*, 28 February 1985.
Hoskyns, Barney. "The Rock's Backpages Flashback: David Lee Roth and the Secret of Van Halen's Excess." *Rock's BackPages Archives*. 3 January 2012. http://music.yahoo.com/blogs/rocks-backpages/rock-backpages-flashback-david-lee-roth-secret-van-162040845.html.
—. *Waiting for the Sun: A Rock and Roll History of Los Angeles*. New York: Backbeat Books, 2003.
Hunt, Ron. "Van Halen: Too Hot to Handle." *Hit Parader*, August 1984.
Ingham, Tim. "David Lee Roth." *Metro*. 27 October 2009. http://metro.co.uk/2009/10/27/david-lee-roth-636705/.
Johnson, Rick. "Is Heavy Metal Dead?" *Creem*, October 1979.
Kitts, Jeff. *Kisstory*. Los Angeles: Kisstory, 1994.
Kitts, Jeff, and Brad Tolinski, eds. *Guitar World Presents the 100 Greatest Guitarists of All Time*. Milwaukee: Hal Leonard, 2002.
Konow, David. *Bang Your Head: The Rise and Fall of Heavy Metal*. New York: Three Rivers Press, 2002.
Kubernik, Harvey. *Canyon of Dreams: The Magic and Music of Laurel Canyon*. New York: Sterling Publishing, 2009.
Kumar, Jay. "Exclusive: Recollections about EVH's Early Setup." *WoodyTone*. 24 June 2009. http://www.woodytone.com/2009/06/24/exclusive-recollections-about-evhs-early-setup/.
Ladd, Jim. "Van Halen." *Innerview*, KMET-FM, 1980.
Leaf, David, and Ken Sharp. *KISS Behind the Mask: The Official Authorized Biography*. New York: Warner Books, 2003.
Lendt, C. K. *Kiss and Sell: The Making of a Supergroup*. New York: Billboard Books, 1997.
"Love at First Sting." *RIAA Searchable Database*. Accessed 14 October 2014. http://www.riaa.com/goldandplatinumdata.php?table=SEARCH.
Lund, Ann Scheid. *Historic Pasadena: An Illustrated History*. San Antonio: Historical Publishing Network, 1999.
Masino, Susan. "Going Mad in Wisconsin." *The Inside*, spring 1999.
Matthews, Gordon. *Van Halen*. New York: Ballantine Books, 1984.
May, Kirse Granat. *Golden State, Golden Youth: The California Image in Popular Culture, 1955–1966*. Chapel Hill: University of North Carolina Press, 2002.
McGovern, Terry. "Van Halen." *Profiles in Rock*, 3 May 1980.
McLaughlin, Mark, and Ken Sharp. *The Van Halen Story: The Early Years*. DVD. Directed by Eduardo Eguia Dibildox. North Hollywood: Passport Video, 2003.
Mehler Mark. "The Crowds Are Wild." *Circus*, 10 October 1978.
—. "Will Disco Be the Death of Rock?" *Circus*, 16 January 1979.
Merrill, Kevin. "A Day in the Life of Kim Fowley." *Billboard*, 8 October 1977.
"Michael Anthony Biography." *Van Halen: The Official Website*. Accessed 8 July 2015. http://web.archive.org/web/20000826221013/http://www.van-halen.com/newsite/mikebio.html.
Miller, Debby. "Van Halen's Split Personality." *Rolling Stone*, 21 June 1984.
Obrecht, Jas. "An Appreciation." *Positively Van Halen*, winter 1986.

—. "Eddie Van Halen: The Complete 1978 Interviews." *Jas Obrecht Music Archives.* Accessed 8 July 2015. http://web.archive.org/web/20150216183941/http://jasobrecht.com/eddie-van-halen-complete-1978-interviews/

—. "The Van Halen Tapes: Early Eddie, 1978–1982." *Best of Guitar Player: Van Halen,* March 1993.

Obrecht, Jas, ed. *Masters of Heavy Metal.* New York: Quill, 1984.

"Our History." *Sunset Sound Recording Studio.* Accessed 8 July 2015. http://www.sunsetsound.com/?page_id=68.

Patterson, Rob. "Van Halen: In Search of the *Baaad* Chord." *Creem,* July 1978.

Phipps, Keith. "David Lee Roth." *A.V. Club.* 19 June 2002. http://www.avclub.com/article/david-lee-roth-13772.

"Platinum." *Billboard,* 30 September 1978.

"Powerage." *RIAA Searchable Database.* Accessed 14 October 2014. http://www.riaa.com/goldandplatinumdata.php?table=SEARCH.

"The Producers: Ted Templeman." *Rolling Stone's Continuous History of Rock and Roll Radio Show,* 26 June 1983.

Quick Draw. "Van Halen: Today L.A., Tomorrow the Galaxy." *Raw Power,* October/November 1977.

Redbeard. "In the Studio: 20th Anniversary of Van Halen." *In the Studio with Redbeard,* 1998.

—. "In the Studio for Van Halen II." *In the Studio with Redbeard.* Accessed 8 July 2015. http://www.inthestudio.net/redbeards-blog/van-halen-2-35th-anniversary.

Riegel, Richard. "Van Halen." *Creem,* June 1978.

Rocca, Jane. "What I Know About Women." *Brisbane Times.* 7 April 2013. http://www.brisbanetimes.com.au/lifestyle/what-iknow-about-women-20130403-2h66p.html.

"Rock and Roll Over." *Wikipedia.* Accessed 8 July 2015. http://en.wikipedia.org/wiki/Rock_and_Roll_Over.

"Rock and Roll Over Tour." *KISSMonster.* Accessed 8 July 2015. http://kissmonster.com/reference/inyourface7.php.

Rosen, Steven. "Ace of Bass." *Guitar World Presents Van Halen: 40 Years of the Great American Rock Band,* July 2012.

—. "California Dreamin'." *Guitar World Presents Van Halen: 40 Years of the Great American Rock Band,* July 2012.

—. "Diver Down Leaves No Sinking Feeling." *Record Review,* August 1982.

—. "On Fire." *Guitar World,* March 2003.

—. "The True Beginnings." *Classic Rock,* December 2005.

—. "Unchained Melodies." *Guitar World Presents Van Halen: 40 Years of the Great American Rock Band,* July 2012.

—. "Van Halen." *Record Review,* April 1979.

Roth, David Lee. *Crazy from the Heat.* New York: Hyperion, 1997.

Rowland, Mark. "Twilight of the Guitar Gods?" *Musician,* March 1995.

"Runnin' with Van Halen Radio Special," Warner Bros. Records, 1978.

Santoro, Gene. "Edward's Producer on the Brown Sound." *Guitar World,* July 1985.

Schneider, Wolf. "Don Airey Revealed." *The Highway Star.* 8 February 2004. http://thehighwaystar.com/interviews/airey/da-feb082004.html.

"Scorpions." *RIAA Searchable Database.* Accessed 14 October 2014. http://www.riaa.com/goldandplatinumdata.php?table=SEARCH.

"Screaming For Vengeance." *Allmusic.* Accessed 18 October 2014. http://www.allmusic.com/album/screaming-for-vengeance-mw0000194426/awards.

Secher, Andy. "Guitar Workshop with Gamma's Ronnie Montrose." *Hit Parader,* April 1981.

—. "The Wild Bunch." *Hit Parader,* September 1981.

Segell, Michael. "Van Halen's Party Gets a Whole Lot Better." *Rolling Stone,* 18 May 1978.

Sekuler, Eliot. "Van Halen Wild and Wonderful." *Hit Parader,* September 1982.

Shapiro, Peter. *Turn the Beat Around: The Secret History of Disco.* New York: Faber and Faber, 2005.

Sharp, Abel. *Van Halen 101.* Bloomington, Indiana: Author House, 2005.

Shearlaw, John. *Van Halen: Jumpin' for the Dollar.* Port Chester, New York: Cherry Lane Books, 1984.

Siegler, Joe. "Black Sabbath Concert Reviews." *Black Sabbath Online.* 1 December 2009. Accessed 8 July 2015. http://web.archive.org/web/20110323072905/http://www.black-sabbath.com/tourdates/1978/november_19_1978.html

Simmons, Gene. *Kiss and Make Up.* New York: Three Rivers Press, 2002.

Simmons, Sylvie. "The California Jam Festival." *Sounds.* 8 April 1978. Accessed 14 October 2014 (login required). http://www.rocksbackpages.com/Library/Article/the-california-jam-festival.

—. "Goodbye to Romance." *Mojo Classic: Ozzy: The Real Story,* April 2005.

—. "Van Halen." *Sounds.* 7 April 1979. Accessed 8 July 2015 (login required). http://www.rocksbackpages.com/Library/Article/van-halen-2.

Simons, Dave. "Tales from the Top." *BMI.* 5 September 2008. http://www.bmi.com/news/entry/Tales_From_the_Top_Van_Halens_Van_Halen_1978.

Sleazegrinder. "Desert Rats." *Classic Rock,* October 2006.

Smith, Robert. "Will Heavy Metal Survive the Seventies?" *Circus,* 11 May 1978.

361

"The Snake's Biography." *Harvey "The Snake" Mandel*. Accessed 8 July 2015. http://www.harveymandel.com/biography.html.

Spina, James. "Spin Addict." *Hit Parader*, 15 September 1978.

"Stained Class." *RIAA Searchable Database*. Accessed 14 October 2014. http://www.riaa.com/goldandplatinumdata.php?table=SEARCH.

Stanley, Paul. *Face the Music: A Life Exposed*. New York: Harper One, 2014.

Stark, Mike. *Black Sabbath: An Oral History*. Edited by Dave Marsh. New York: Harper Collins, 2002.

Starr, Kevin. *California: A History*. New York: Modern Library, 2007.

Stix, John. "Eddie Van Halen." *Guitar for the Practicing Musician*, April 1985.

—. "Eddie Van Halen Interviews Steve Lukather." *Guitar for the Practicing Musician*, September 1993.

—. "The Fountain." *Guitar Classics 8*, June 1994.

—. "George Lynch: Van Halen School Dropout." *Guitar for the Practicing Musician*, July 1986.

—. "In the Eye of the Storm." *Guitar for the Practicing Musician*, July 1991.

—. "Michael Anthony: The Last of the Pre–Van Halen Bands." *Guitar for the Practicing Musician*, December 1987.

Strigl, Mark, and John Ostronomy. "Episode 234: Bill Aucoin Special." *Talking Metal Podcast*, 18 October 2008. http://podbay.fm/show/78833595/e/1224313200.

"Talent in Action." *Billboard*, 19 February 1972.

Tangye, David, and Graham Wright. *How Black Was Our Sabbath: An Unauthorized View from the Crew*. London: Pan MacMillan UK, 2004.

Tolinski, Brad. "Iron Mike." *Guitar World*, September 1991.

—. "Whipper Snapper." *Guitar World*, September 1991.

Tolinski, Brad, ed. *Guitar World Presents Van Halen*. Milwaukee: Hal Leonard, 1997.

—. *Guitar World Presents Van Halen*. Milwaukee: Backbeat Books, 2010.

"Top LP & Tape." *Billboard*, 18 March 1978.

Traiman, Steven, and Robert Roth. "Wall Street: Mixed Music View." *Billboard*, 8 October 1977.

Tucker, Ken. "Van Halen." *High Fidelity*, May 1978.

Unterberger, Richie. *Music USA: The Rough Guide*. London: Rough Guides, 1999.

Van Der Leun, Gerard. "David Lee Roth." *Penthouse*, January 1987.

Van Halen. "The Van Halen Interview (Full Length)." *YouTube*. 8 March 2012. http://www.youtube.com/watch?v=UOTidtqG-Ko.

—. "Van Halen Interviews." *YouTube*. 9 May 2013. http://www.youtube.com/watch?v=YfW4OoIKM_U.

—. "Van Halen Interviews 4." *Vimeo*. 20 April 2012. http://vimeo.com/40734476.

—. "Van Halen Interviews 5." *Vimeo*. 30 May 2012. http://vimeo.com/42240360.

"Van Halen." *Allmusic*. Accessed 8 July 2015. http://www.allmusic.com/artist/van-halen-mn0000260206/awards.

"Van Halen: Discography." *45Cat*. Accessed 8 July 2015. http://www.45cat.com/artist/van-halen.

Van Halen, Eddie. "How Eddie Van Halen Hacks a Guitar." *Popular Mechanics*. 19 May 2015. http://www.popularmechanics.com/technology/a15615/how-eddie-van-halen-hacks-a-guitar/.

"Van Halen Hits the Big Time." *Circus*, 31 October 1984.

"Van Halen Rare Interview & First Radio Play 1976," *YouTube*. Accessed 14 July 2014, https://www.youtube.com/watch?v=cmz_yEkyaDA.

The Van Halen Scrapbook. Cresskill, New Jersey: Sharon Publications, 1984.

"Van Halen - Toronto - 2007 - Ice Cream Man." *YouTube*. 13 October 2007. http://www.youtube.com/watch?v=lQtijtfRoFM.

"Van Halen: Who Are These Guys and Why Are They So Famous?" *Hit Parader*, December 1980.

White, Emily. "Judas Priest Debut at No. 1 on Top Rock Albums." *Billboard*. 18 July 2014. http://www.billboard.com/articles/columns/chart-beat/6165345/judas-priest-debut-no-1-top-rock-albums.

Wild, David. "Balancing Act." *Rolling Stone*, 6 April 1995.

Wiley, Elizabeth. *Could This Be Magic: Van Halen before 1978*. Bloomington: Trafford Publishing, 2012.

Wilkinson, Paul. *Rat Salad: Black Sabbath, The Classic Years, 1969–1975*. New York: St. Martin's Press, 2007.

Wilton, Michael. "Van Halen's Babysitter." *L.A. Weekly*. 1 June 2012. Accessed 8 July 2015. http://www.laweekly.com/music/van-halens-babysitter-2175110.

Young, Charles M. "Van Halen." *Musician*, June 1984.

—. "Van Halen." *Rolling Stone*. 4 May 1978. http://www.rollingstone.com/music/albumreviews/van-halen-19780504.

Zanes, Warren. *Revolutions in Sound: Warner Bros. Records, The First Fifty Years*. San Francisco: Chronicle Books, 2008.

Zlozower, Neil. *Eddie Van Halen*. San Francisco: Chronicle Books, 2011.

—. *Van Halen*. San Francisco: Chronicle Books, 2008.

ENDNOTES

INTRODUCTION

1. Steven Traiman and Robert Roth, "Wall Street: Mixed Music View," *Billboard*, 8 October 1977, 8.
2. Richard Robinson, "Punk Rock at the Edge of Commercial Breakthrough," *Valley News (Van Nuys, CA)*, 20 November 1977.
3. Peter Shapiro, *Turn the Beat Around: The Secret History of Disco* (New York: Faber and Faber, 2005), 214; Alice Echols, *Hot Stuff: Disco and the Remaking of American Culture* (New York: W.W. Norton, 2010), 195–198.
4. Mark Mehler, "Will Disco Be the Death of Rock?" *Circus*, 16 January 1979, 34.
5. Brett Ermilio and Josh Levine, *Going Platinum: KISS, Donna Summer, and How Neil Bogart Built Casablanca Records* (London: Rowman & Littlefield, 2014), 139–140.
6. Rick Johnson, "Is Heavy Metal Dead?" *Creem*, October 1979, 42–46.
7. Robert Smith, "Will Heavy Metal Survive the Seventies?" *Circus*, 11 May 1978, 27–28; David Fricke, "Why Are Rockers Going Disco?" *Circus*, 13 March 1979, 31.
8. Sylvie Simmons, "The California Jam Festival," *Sounds*, 8 April 1978, accessed 14 October 2014 (login required), http://www.rocksbackpages.com/Library/Article/the-california-jam-festival.
9. Lester Bangs, "Heavy Metal: The Sinal Folution," *Hit Parader*, March 1978, 57.
10. John Shearlaw, *Van Halen: Jumpin' for the Dollar* (Port Chester, N.Y.: Cherry Lane Books, 1984), 17.
11. Robert Hilburn, "Homegrown Punk-Rock Blossoming," *Los Angeles Times*, 4 January 1977.
12. "Van Halen Has Enthusiasm," *Salina (Kansas) Journal*, 28 May 1978.
13. Robert Christgau, "Van Halen," *Robert Christgau*, accessed 16 October 2014, http://robert christgau.com/get_artist.php?id=1646&name=Van+Halen.
14. Richard Riegel, "Van Halen," *Creem*, June 1978, 61.
15. Steve Esmedina, "This Week's Concerts," *San Diego Reader*, 6 July 1978.
16. "Van Halen," *Allmusic*, accessed 8 July 2015, http://www.allmusic.com/artist/van-halen-mn0000260206/awards.
17. "Billboard Top LP & Tape," *Billboard*, 18 March 1978, 90–92.
18. Joe Bonomo, *Highway to Hell* (London: Continuum International Publishing, 2010), 4; "Powerage," *RIAA Searchable Database*, accessed 14 October 2014, http://www.riaa.com/goldandplatinumdata.php?table=SEARCH.
19. Emily White, "Judas Priest Debut at No. 1 on Top Rock Albums, *Billboard*, 18 July 2014, http://www.billboard.com/articles/columns/chart-beat/6165345/judas-priest-debut-no-1-top-rock-albums; "Stained Class," *RIAA Searchable Database*, accessed 14 October 2014, http://www.riaa.com/goldandplatinumdata.php?table=SEARCH.

20. "Scorpions," *RIAA Searchable Database*, accessed 14 October 2014, http://www.riaa.com/goldand platinumdata.php?table=SEARCH.
21. Richard E. Caves, *Creative Industries: Contracts Between Art and Commerce* (Cambridge: Harvard University Press, 2001), 61–62.

CHAPTER ONE: BEGINNINGS

22. John Albert, "Running with the Devil: A Lifetime of Van Halen," *Slake Los Angeles*, accessed 22 June 2013, http://slake.la/features/running-with-the-devil-a-lifetime-of-van-halen.
23. Jan Van Halen Certificate of Death, in author's possession; "Alex Van Halen," *Drummerworld*, accessed 16 May 2012, http://www.drummerworld.com/drummers/Alex_Van_Halen.html.
24. Debby Miller, "Van Halen's Split Personality," *Rolling Stone*, 21 June 1984, 28; Ian Christe, *Everybody Wants Some: The Van Halen Saga* (Hoboken, N.J., John Wiley & Sons, 2007), 7.
25. Jas Obrecht, "The Van Halen Tapes: Early Eddie, 1978–1982," *Best of Guitar Player: Van Halen*, March 1993, 8.
26. Van Halen, "Van Halen Interviews," *YouTube*, 8 July 2015, http://www.youtube.com/watch?v=YfW4OoIKM_U.
27. Obrecht, "The Van Halen Tapes," 8; Van Halen, "Van Halen Interviews."
28. Mike Boehm, "No Method to Their Madness," *Los Angeles Times*, 5 September 1991.
29. Mark Rowland, "Twilight of the Guitar Gods?" *Musician*, March 1995, 45.
30. Christe, *Everybody Wants Some*, 8.
31. Edward Van Halen quoted in Dan Hedges, *Eddie Van Halen* (New York: Vintage Books, 1986), 17.
32. Alex Van Halen quoted in Gordon Matthews, *Van Halen* (New York: Ballantine Books, 1984), 11.
33. "Alex Van Halen," *Drummerworld*; Chris Gill, "Cast a Giant Shadow," *Guitar World*, Anniversary Issue 2010, 50.
34. "Alex Van Halen," *Drummerworld*; Kevin Starr, *California: A History* (New York: Modern Library, 2007), 242; Kirse Granat May, *Golden State, Golden Youth: The California Image in Popular Culture, 1955–1966* (Chapel Hill: University of North Carolina Press, 2002), 12.
35. Hedges, *Eddie Van Halen*, 18.
36. Pasadena City Directories, 1962–1968, Pasadena Public Library, Pasadena, California, research courtesy of Michael Kelley; Peter B. King, "Eddie Van Halen is Obsessed With His Art," *Doylestown (Pennsylvania) Intelligencer*, 28 July 1988.
37. Pasadena City Directories, 1962–1968.
38. King, "Eddie Van Halen."
39. King, "Eddie Van Halen."
40. King, "Eddie Van Halen."
41. Hedges, *Eddie Van Halen*, 17.
42. Boehm, "No Method to Their Madness."
43. Pasadena City Directories, 1962 and 1963; Michael Kelley, email to author, 18 February 2010.
44. Boehm, "No Method to Their Madness."
45. Boehm, "No Method to Their Madness."
46. Edward Van Halen quoted in Kevin Dodds, *Edward Van Halen: A Definitive Biography* (Bloomington, Indiana: iUniverse), 9.
47. Jan and Eugenia Van Halen Joint Tenancy Grant Deed, in author's possession; Title Information, 1881 Las Lunas Street, in author's possession.
48. Brad Tolinski, ed., *Guitar World Presents Van Halen* (Milwaukee: Backbeat Books, 2010), 86.
49. Boehm, "No Method to Their Madness."
50. Jas Obrecht, ed., *Masters of Heavy Metal* (New York: Quill, 1984), 150.
51. F. C. Anderson, "People Talk," *Long Beach Independent*, 28 January 1976.
52. Carl Matthes, email to Michael Kelley, 15 February 2010.
53. Tolinski, ed., *Guitar World Presents Van Halen*, 87.
54. Alex Van Halen quoted in J. D. Considine, *Van Halen!* (New York: Quill, 1985), 22.
55. Steven Rosen, "The True Beginnings," *Classic Rock*, December 2005, 44.
56. Edward Van Halen quoted in Hedges, *Eddie Van Halen*, 18.
57. Alex Van Halen quoted in Philip Bashe, *Heavy Metal Thunder: The Music, Its History, Its Heroes* (Garden City, N.Y.: Doubleday, 1985), 131.
58. Alex Van Halen quoted in Considine, *Van Halen!*, 23.
59. Steve Baltin, "Eddie Van Halen Dismisses Jimi Hendrix Comparisons," *Spinner*, 16 March 2009, archived copy accessed 9 July 2015, http://www.vhnd.com/2009/03/17/eddie-van-halen-dismisses-jimi-hendrix-comparisons/.
60. Matthews, *Van Halen*, 12.
61. Edward Van Halen quoted in Considine, *Van Halen!*, 29.
62. Rudy Leiren, interview by Steven Rosen, in author's possession. Leiren recalled that the band he saw at Marshall was Genesis. But at the time, Leiren was in seventh grade. Edward, a year older than Leiren, was in eighth grade. Edward's eighth-grade year stretched from 1968 to 1969, approximately two years before Genesis formed.

63. Gill, "Cast a Giant Shadow," 50.
64. Miller, "Van Halen's Split Personality," 28.
65. Christe, *Everybody Wants Some*, 12.
66. David Lee Roth, *Crazy from the Heat* (New York: Hyperion, 1997), 27.
67. Nancy Collins, "David Lee Roth: The Rolling Stone Interview," *Rolling Stone*, 11 April 1985, 24.
68. Charles M. Young, "Van Halen," *Musician*, June 1984, 50.
69. Collins, "David Lee Roth," 24.
70. Van Halen, "The Van Halen Interview (Full Length)," *YouTube*, 8 March 2012, accessed 8 July 2015, http://www.youtube.com/watch?v=UOTidtqG-Ko; Fred Trietsch, "Van Halen, Short and Sweet," *The Drummer (Philadelphia)*, 4 April 1978.
71. Roth, *Crazy from the Heat*, 29.
72. David Lee Roth quoted in Christe, *Everybody Wants Some*, 14.
73. Matthews, *Van Halen*, 15; Redbeard, "In the Studio: 20th Anniversary of Van Halen," *In the Studio with Redbeard*, 1998, in author's possession; Tim Ingham, "David Lee Roth," *Metro*, 27 October 2009, accessed 8 July 2015, http://metro.co.uk/2009/10/27/david-lee-roth-636705/.
74. Jane Rocca, "What I Know About Women," *Brisbane Times*, 7 April 2013, accessed 8 July 2015, http://www.brisbanetimes.com.au/lifestyle/what-i-know-about-women-20130403-2h66p.html.
75. Rocca, "What I Know About Women."
76. Van Halen, "Van Halen Interviews."
77. Ann Scheid Lund, *Historic Pasadena: An Illustrated History* (San Antonio: Historical Publishing Network, 1999), 179; Carter Barber, "Pasadena Busing Improves," *(Pasadena) Star-News*, 15 September 1970; Vincent Carberry, email to author, 16 September 2014.
78. Considine, *Van Halen!*, 27–28.
79. Roth, *Crazy from the Heat*, 27.
80. Sandra Gurvis, "'Diamond Dave': Rock 'n' Roll's Jester," *Providence Journal*, 16 January 1987.
81. Dennis Travis, email to Michael Kelley, 26 July 2010.
82. Dennis Travis, email to Michael Kelley, 26 July 2010.
83. Jeff Hausman, "Growing Up with the Van Halens," *The Inside*, spring 1995, 10.
84. Dennis Travis, email to author, 12 September 2014.
85. For more on Jan's accident, see Eddie Van Halen, "How Eddie Van Halen Hacks a Guitar," *Popular Mechanics*, 19 May 2015, http://www.popularmechanics.com/technology/a15615/how-eddie-van-halen-hacks-a-guitar/.
86. Bill Maxwell, interview by author.
87. Music for Everyone receipt, 15 August 1969, in author's possession.
88. Dennis Travis, email to author, 12 September 2014.
89. Dennis Travis, email to Michael Kelley, 26 July 2010.
90. Dennis Travis, email to author, 12 September 2014.
91. Don Ross, emails to author, 11 January 2010 and 27 July 2011.
92. Sleazegrinder, "Desert Rats," *Classic Rock*, October 2006, 55.

CHAPTER TWO: THE GENESIS OF MAMMOTH

93. Tolinski, ed., *Guitar World Presents Van Halen*, 92.
94. Mark Stone, interview by Michael Kelley, 6 June 2010, in author's possession; Cheri Whitaker, interview by author; John Driscoll, email to author, 28 January 2010.
95. Mark Stone, interview by Michael Kelley, in author's possession.
96. Doug Fox, "15 Years On: Eddie Van Halen Interview Revisited," *Van Halen News Desk*, 8 July 2013, accessed 8 July 2015, http://www.vhnd.com/2013/07/08/15-years-on-eddie-van-halen-interview-revisited/.
97. Steven Rosen, "On Fire," *Guitar World*, March 2003, 60.
98. "Talent in Action," *Billboard*, 19 February 1972, 16; Paul Fry, interview by author.
99. John Driscoll, "Tales from Old Pasadena," *The Inside*, summer 1997, 8.
100. Paul Fry, interview by author.
101. Rudy Leiren, interview by Steven Rosen, in author's possession.

CHAPTER THREE: THE ADVENTURES OF RED BALL JET

102. David Wild, "Balancing Act," *Rolling Stone*, 6 April 1995, 46.
103. Wild, "Balancing Act," 46.
104. Rosen, "True Beginnings," 46.
105. Rosen, "True Beginnings," 46.
106. Dana Anderson, email to author, 22 February 2010.
107. Rosen, "True Beginnings," 46.
108. Andy Secher, "The Wild Bunch," *Hit Parader*, September 1981, 4.
109. Young, "Van Halen," 50.
110. Kristopher Doe, "Van Halen Announces Tour," You Know You Are from Old School Pasadena

When, *Facebook*, 31 December 2011, accessed 8 July 2015, https://facebook.com/groups/113883598
710531/180945635337660/?comment_id=1832468717742038&offset=0&total_comments=57#_=_.

111. David Fricke, "Van Halen Hosts Rock's Biggest Party of '79, and You're Invited," *Circus*, 24 July 1979, 32.
112. Gary Taylor, interview by author.
113. Miles Komora, email to author, 7 June 2012.
114. Jim Pewsey, interview by author.
115. George Perez, interview by author.
116. Mel Serrano, "You Know You're a Sierra Madre Kid When," Facebook, 27 November 2009, accessed 8 July 2015, https://www.facebook.com/groups/2204894695/permalink/101502178 30199696/?comment_id=10150217830574696&offset=0&total_comments=8&comment_track ing=%7B%22tn%22%3A%22R%22%7D.
117. Eliot Sekuler, "Van Halen Wild and Wonderful," *Hit Parader*, September 1982, 7.
118. Ron Hunt, "Van Halen: Too Hot to Handle," *Hit Parader*, August 1984, 16.
119. Philip Bashe, "Van Halen's Teen Hearts," *Circus*, 31 July 1981, 45.
120. Roth, *Crazy from the Heat*, 60–61.
121. Roth, *Crazy from the Heat*, 60.
122. Roth, *Crazy from the Heat*, 61.
123. Rudy Leiren, interview by Steven Rosen, in author's possession.
124. Fricke, "Van Halen Hosts Rock's Biggest Party," 32.
125. Sonny Hughes, interview by author.
126. Dan Hernandez, interview by author; Miles Komora, interview by author; Gary Taylor, interview by author.
127. Roth, who was an Alice Cooper fan, was likely inspired here by a spring 1972 publicity stunt cooked up by Cooper and his manager, Shep Gordon. During the run up to Cooper's June 30 show in London, a flatbed truck hauling a billboard of Cooper, naked except for a snake wrapped his torso, "broke down" in Piccadilly Circus. See Ruth Blatt, "When Compassion And Profit Go Together: The Case Of Alice Cooper's Manager Shep Gordon," *Forbes*, 13 June 2014, http://www. forbes.com/sites/ruthblatt/2014/06/13/when-compassion-and-profit-go-together-the-case-of-alice-coopers-manager-shep-gordon/.
128. Gary Taylor, interview by author.
129. Miles Komora, interview by author.
130. "Altadena Rock Fest Cancelled," *(Pasadena) Star-News*, 25 August 1972.
131. Bobby Hatch, interview by author.
132. "Van Halen — Toronto — 2007 — Ice Cream Man," *YouTube*, 13 October 2007, accessed 8 July 2015, http://www.youtube.com/watch?v=lQtijtfRoFM.
133. Elizabeth Wiley, email to author, 24 June 2012.
134. Dan Hernandez, interview by author.
135. "Carlton Johnson, 52, Film Choreographer and Tap Dancer, Dies," *Los Angeles Times*, 31 December 1986, accessed 8 July 2015, http://articles.latimes.com/1986-12-31/local/me-1211_1_carlton-johnson.
136. Gerard Van Der Leun, "David Lee Roth," *Penthouse*, January 1987, 66; Young, "Van Halen," 50; Elizabeth Wiley, *Could This Be Magic: Van Halen before 1978* (Bloomington: Ind.: Trafford Publishing, 2012), 38; Roth, *Crazy from the Heat*, 28.
137. Roth, *Crazy from the Heat*, 35.
138. Rudy Leiren, interview by Steven Rosen, in author's possession.
139. Barney Hoskyns, "The Rock's Backpages Flashback: David Lee Roth and the Secret of Van Halen's Excess," *Rock's BackPages Archives*, 3 January 2012, accessed 8 July 2015, http://music.yahoo.com/blogs/rocks-backpages/rock-backpages-flashback-david-lee-roth-secret-van-162040845.html.

CHAPTER FOUR: DAVID LEE ROTH JOINS VAN HALEN

140. Collins, "David Lee Roth," 24.
141. Wild, "Balancing Act," 46,
142. Rosen, "True Beginnings," 46.
143. Dan Aquilante, "Return of Diamond Dave," *New York Post*, 26 February 2012, accessed 8 July 2015, http://nypost.com/2012/02/26/return-of-diamond-dave/.
144. Prentiss Findlay, "Roth Barnstorming 'The Entire World,'" *Post and Courier (Charleston)*, 28 July 1994.
145. Tolinski, ed., *Guitar World Presents Van Halen*, 48.
146. Van Halen, "Van Halen Interviews 5," *Vimeo*, 19 June 2012, accessed 8 July 2015, http://vimeo .com/42240360.
147. Dodds, *Edward Van Halen*, 23.
148. Obrecht, "The Van Halen Tapes," 9.
149. Nicky Panicci, interview by author.
150. Brent Pettit, interview by author.

151. *The Van Halen Story: The Early Years*, directed by Eduardo Eguia Dibildox (North Hollywood: Passport Video, 2003), DVD; Wild, "Balancing Act," 46.
152. *The Van Halen Story: The Early Years*.
153. Wild, "Balancing Act," 46.
154. Eric Hensel, interview by author; Jim Pewsey, interview by author; Mark Stone, interview by Michael Kelley, in author's possession.
155. Lee Gutenberg, interview by author.
156. Mark Stone, interview by Michael Kelley, in author's possession; Jim Pewsey, interview by author.
157. Steven Rosen, "Diver Down Leaves No Sinking Feeling," *Record Review*, August 1982, 13.
158. Mark Stone, interview by Michael Kelley, in author's possession.
159. Roth, *Crazy from the Heat*, 68.
160. Roth, *Crazy from the Heat*, 68.
161. Rosen, "On Fire," 60–61.
162. Mark Stone, interview by Michael Kelley, in author's possession.
163. Rafael Marti, interview by author.
164. Chris Legg, interview by author.
165. Rafael Marti, interview by author.
166. Rafael Marti, interview by author.
167. Roth, *Crazy from the Heat*, 61.
168. Roth, *Crazy from the Heat*, 57, 63; Keith Phipps, "David Lee Roth," *A.V. Club*, 19 June 2002, accessed 8 July 2015, http://www.avclub.com/articles/david-lee-roth,13772; Michael Hann, "David Lee Roth," *The Guardian*, 2 February 2012, accessed 8 July 2015, http://www.guardian.co.uk/music/2012/feb/02/david-lee-roth-van-halen.
169. Wild, "Balancing Act," 46.
170. "Busing Controversy Unsettled," *Boca Raton News*, 12 March 1972.
171. Edward Van Halen quoted in Considine, *Van Halen!*, 28.
172. Jose Hurtado, email to author, 7 July 2012.
173. Roth, *Crazy from the Heat*, 75.
174. Roth, *Crazy from the* Heat, 73.
175. Roth, *Crazy from the Heat*, 73–75.
176. Mikal Gilmore, *Night Beat: A Shadow History of Rock & Roll* (New York: Doubleday, 1998), 201–202.
177. Roth, *Crazy from the Heat*, 66.
178. Jane Scott, "Van Halen: You Can Keep That Cosmic Stuff," *Cleveland Plain Dealer*, 16 March 1978.
179. Jeff Hausman, "Tom Broderick," *The Inside*, summer 1997, 14.
180. Rudy Leiren, interview by Steven Rosen, in author's possession.
181. Roth, *Crazy from the Heat*, 59–60.
182. Angelo Roman Jr., email to author, 25 January 2010.
183. Angelo Roman Jr., "Ebay Listing of Van Halen Recording from 1973," 15 October 2004, document in author's possession.
184. Gill, "Cast a Giant Shadow," 50.
185. Angelo Roman Jr., email to author, 25 January 2010.
186. Tolinski, ed., *Guitar World Presents Van Halen*, 185.
187. Gill, "Cast a Giant Shadow," 50.
188. Gill, "Cast a Giant Shadow," 50.
189. Gill, "Cast a Giant Shadow," 50.
190. Angelo Roman Jr., interview by author.
191. Michael Kelley, email to author, 22 November 2009; see ad in *Los Angeles Free Press*, 26 April 1974.
192. Rosen, "On Fire," 61.
193. Hedges, *Eddie Van Halen*, 35; Roth, *Crazy from the Heat*, 61.
194. Rosen, "On Fire," 61.
195. Tolinski, ed., *Guitar World Presents Van Halen*, 17.
196. Van Halen, "Van Halen Interviews 4," *Vimeo*, 20 April 2012, accessed 8 July 2015, http://vimeo.com/40734476.
197. Rosen, "Diver Down," 12.
198. Rosen, "Diver Down," 12.
199. David Curcurito, "Eddie Van Halen: The Esquire Interview," *Esquire*, 17 April 2012, accessed 8 July 2015, http://www.esquire.com/the-side/music/eddie-van-halen-interview-2012-8147775.
200. Obrecht, *Masters of Heavy Metal*, 161.
201. Obrecht, *Masters of Heavy Metal*, 146.
202. Considine, *Van Halen!*, 30.
203. Rosen, "Diver Down," 13.

CHAPTER FIVE: BREAKTHROUGH

204. Battle of the Bands research courtesy of Michael Kelley.
205. "41 Years Ago Today — Van Halen Hits the Sunset Strip," *Van Halen News Desk*, 4 April 2014,

accessed 8 July 2015, http://www.vhnd.com/2014/04/04/40-years-ago-today-van-halen-hits-the-sunset-strip.

206. Keith Murray, "Pasadena Party Erupts in Violence," *(Pasadena) Star-News*, 24 December 1973; "Shooting Suspect Arrested," *(Pasadena) Star-News*, 13 January 1974.
207. Tom Livingston, "One More Dance," *(Pasadena) Star-News*, 30 January 1974.
208. "Street Dance Highlights Pasadena's Centennial," *(Pasadena) Star-News*, 23 January 1974.
209. Livingston, "One More Dance."
210. Livingston, "One More Dance."
211. Wild, "Balancing Act," 46.
212. "Police Quiet Van Gathering in Pasadena," *San Marino Tribune*, 14 March 1974.
213. Janice Pirre Francis, interview by author.
214. "Copter Aids Police in Surveillance Role," *Courier (Pasadena City College)*, 4 May 1973.
215. "Police Quiet Van Gathering," *San Marino Tribune*.
216. "Police Quiet Van Gathering," *San Marino Tribune*.
217. Redbeard, "In the Studio: 20th Anniversary of Van Halen."
218. Redbeard, "In the Studio: 20th Anniversary of Van Halen."
219. Mark Algorri, interview by author.
220. Wiley, *Could This Be Magic*, 31.
221. Terry Kilgore, "Alex on His Original Ludwig Kit," *Facebook*, 7 July 2012, accessed 8 July 2015, https://www.facebook.com/photo.php?fbid=4171377133901&set=a.1531548979847.2076546 .1568434049&type=1&comment_id=2414580&offset=0&total_comments=5.
222. Wiley, *Could This Be Magic*, 35; Elizabeth Wiley, interview by author.
223. Wild, "Balancing Act," 48.
224. Tolinski, ed., *Guitar World Presents Van Halen*, 185.
225. Peter S. Greenberg, "Clockwork Rodney's," *Newsweek*, 7 January 1974, 48.
226. Mick Farren, "Rodney Bingenheimer's English Discotheque Revisited," *New Musical Express*, 28 December 1974.
227. Rosen, "Diver Down," 12.
228. Mark Algorri, interview by author.
229. Bill Urkopina, interview by author.
230. Bill Urkopina, interview by author.
231. Robyn McDonald, email to author, 10 August 2011.
232. Mark Stone, interview by Michael Kelley, in author's possession.
233. Mark Algorri, interview by author.
234. Mary J. Edrei, ed., *Top Rockers of the 80s* (Cresskill, N.J.: Sharon Publications, 1985), 186.
235. Wild, "Balancing Act," 46.
236. Proud Bird Advertisement, in author's possession.
237. Wiley, *Could This Be Magic*, 35.
238. Roth, *Crazy from the Heat*, 193–194.
239. Young, "Van Halen," 54.
240. "Michael Anthony Biography," *Van Halen: The Official Website*, accessed 8 July 2015, http://web.archive.org/web/*/http://van-halen.com/newsite/mikebio.html.
241. Joe Ramsey, "Garage Band," *Facebook*, 25 July 2009, accessed 8 July 2015, https://www.facebook.com/note.php?_rdr=p&note_id=112786957270.
242. Redbeard, "In the Studio: 20th Anniversary of Van Halen."
243. Considine, *Van Halen!*, 37; John Stix, "Michael Anthony: The Last of the Pre–Van Halen Bands," *Guitar for the Practicing Musician*, December 1987, 17.
244. Redbeard, "In the Studio: 20th Anniversary of Van Halen."
245. Brad Tolinski, "Iron Mike," *Guitar World*, September 1991, 99.
246. Obrecht, "The Van Halen Tapes," 9.
247. Richard Garbaccio, "Van Halen Rocks Students," *Pasadena (High School) Chronicle*, 10 May 1974.
248. Christopher Buttner, "Michael Anthony of Van Halen," *PRThatRocks*, 2004, http://www.prthatrocks.com/interviews/michael.html.
249. Considine, *Van Halen!*, 37.
250. "Carmine Appice: Eddie Van Halen Seems to Be Out of His Tree Right Now," *Blabbermouth*, 6 October 2006, accessed 8 July 2015, http://www.blabbermouth.net/news/carmine-appice-eddie-van-halen-seems-to-be-out-of-his-tree-right-now/.
251. Mark Algorri, interview by author.
252. Buttner, "Michael Anthony of Van Halen"; Redbeard, "In the Studio: 20th Anniversary of Van Halen."
253. Stix, "Michael Anthony: The Last of the Pre–Van Halen Bands," 17.
254. Jonathan Laidig, interview by author.
255. Steven Rosen, "Ace of Bass," *Guitar World Presents Van Halen: 40 Years of the Great American Rock Band*, July 2012, 63.
256. Redbeard, "In the Studio: 20th Anniversary of Van Halen"; Considine, *Van Halen!*, 37.
257. Rosen, "Ace of Bass," 63.

258. Rosen, "Ace of Bass," 63.
259. Tolinski, "Iron Mike," 99; Stix, "Michael Anthony: The Last of the Pre–Van Halen Bands," 17.
260. Rosen, "Ace of Bass," 63.
261. *The Van Halen Story: The Early Years.*
262. *The Van Halen Story: The Early Years.*
263. Rudy Leiren, interview by Steven Rosen, in author's possession.
264. Christe, *Everybody Wants Some*, 25; *The Van Halen Story: The Early Years.*

CHAPTER SIX: THE BATTLE OF PASADENA

265. Debbie Imler McDermott, interview by author.
266. Andy Secher, "Van Halen Blasts Apart Myth of Mellow California Sound," *(Omaha) Sunday World Herald Magazine*, 17 August 1980.
267. Jeff Touchie, interview by author.
268. Hausman, "Tom Broderick," 22; Miller, "Van Halen's Split Personality," 77.
269. Michael Anthony, interview by author; Miller, "Van Halen's Split Personality," 77.
270. Debbie Imler McDermott, interview by author.
271. Roth, *Crazy from the Heat*, 79.
272. Debbie Imler McDermott, email to author, 11 June 2014.
273. Rudy Leiren, interview by Steven Rosen, in author's possession.
274. Roth, *Crazy from the Heat*, 82.
275. Tim Tullio, "TT . . . tell us what you think," *Vintage Amps Forum*, 29 April 2003, accessed 8 July 2015, http:// www.vintageamps.com/plexiboard/viewtopic.php?p=148352&sid=05c2d070c7bf a4ec2c674a93ea3dd98e#p148352.
276. Jeff Touchie, interview by author.
277. Ross Velasco, interview by author.
278. Roth, *Crazy from the Heat*, 76.
279. "21 Arrested in Pasadena Party Melee," *(Pasadena) Star-News*, 11 November 1974.
280. "21 Arrested in Pasadena Party Melee."
281. Debbie Imler McDermott, interview by author.
282. Jeff Touchie, interview by author.
283. Hausman, "Tom Broderick," 14.
284. Roth, *Crazy from the Heat*, 75.
285. Roth, *Crazy from the Heat*, 76.
286. Debbie Imler McDermott, interview by author.
287. Roth, *Crazy from the Heat*, 76–77.
288. "21 Arrested in Pasadena Party Melee."
289. "21 Arrested in Pasadena Party Melee."
290. Debbie Imler McDermott, interview by author.
291. "Van Halen Has Enthusiasm."
292. Van der Leun, "David Lee Roth," 188.

CHAPTER SEVEN: THE CONTEST

293. Dan Warfield, "Van Halen: From the Starwood to Offenbach," *European Stars and Stripes*, 24 October 1978.
294. Considine, *Van Halen!*, 39.
295. Pete Oppel, "Van Halen's 'Big Rock' Ready To Sweep Across the Land," *Dallas Morning News*, 25 November 1978.
296. Rudy Leiren, interview by Steven Rosen, in author's possession.
297. Dan Forte, "Van Halen's Stylish Raunch," *Record*, June 1982, 14.
298. Robert Hilburn, "Pasadena's Van Halen: Slow Start, Strong Finish," *Los Angeles Times*, 11 July 1978; Art Fein, "Club Notes," *Los Angeles Free Press*, 12 March 1976.
299. Shearlaw, *Van Halen*, 18.
300. Terry Atkinson, "Van Halen's Big Rock," *Rolling Stone*, 14 June 1979, 14.
301. Andy Doerschuk, "Alex Van Halen," in *Playing from the Heart: Great Musicians Talk About Their Craft*, ed. Robert L. Doerschuk (San Francisco: Backbeat Books, 2002), 258.
302. Goddess, "David Lee Roth w/Steven Rosen in 1982," *Van Halen — The Band We Love*, 31 January 2012, accessed 8 July 2015, http://vanhalen12.blogspot.com/2012/01/david-lee-roth-interview-w-steven-rosen.html.
303. "David Lee Roth and Alex Van Halen," UK radio interview, 7 June 1978, in author's possession.
304. Jeff Simons, interview by author.
305. Fein, "Club Notes."
306. Kim Miller, email to author, 22 July 2014.
307. Chris Gill, "Everybody Wants Some," *Guitar World*, November 2014, 74.
308. Gill, "Everybody Wants Some," 74.

309. "The Snake's Biography," *Harvey "The Snake" Mandel*, accessed 29 September 2014, www.harvey mandel.com/biography.html.
310. Abel Sharp, *Van Halen 101* (Bloomington, Indiana: Author House, 2005), 200.
311. Rosen, "Ace of Bass," 65.
312. Tolinski, ed., *Guitar World Presents Van Halen*, 92.
313. Curcurito, "Eddie Van Halen: The Esquire Interview."
314. Jay Kumar, "Exclusive: Recollections about EVH's Early Setup," *WoodyTone*, 24 June 2009, accessed 8 July 2015, www.woodytone.com/2009/06/24/exclusive-recollections-about-evhs -early-setup/.
315. Obrecht, *Masters of Heavy Metal*, 156; Obrecht, "Van Halen Tapes," 10.
316. Roth, *Crazy from the Heat*, 85.
317. Tom Broderick, email to author, 13 February 2010.
318. General Telephone Company of California, *City of Pomona, Street Address Directory for Pomona, Chino, Claremont, Diamond Bar, La Verne, San Dimas, Walnut, and Portions of Montclair* (Los Alamitos: GTE Directories Corp, 1975), 73, Special Collections, Pomona Public Library, Pomona, California.
319. Rudy Leiren, interview by Steven Rosen, in author's possession.
320. Charlie Gwyn, email to author, 17 February 2010; Charlie Gwyn, email to author, 20 February 2010.
321. John Stix, "The Fountain," *Guitar Classics 8*, June 1994, 100.
322. Roth, *Crazy from the Heat*, 85.
323. Laurie Bereskin, "Van Halen's Invitation: Come Down and Party," *BAM*, July 1977, 52.
324. "Running with Van Halen," radio show, circa fall 1978, in author's possession.
325. Robyn Flans, "Alex Van Halen," *Modern Drummer*, October 1983, 11.
326. Hilburn, "Pasadena's Van Halen."
327. Alex Van Halen quoted in Christe, *Everybody Wants Some*, 26.
328. John Stix, "In the Eye of the Storm," *Guitar for the Practicing Musician*, July 1991, 90.
329. Roth, *Crazy from the Heat*, 85.
330. Terry Atkinson, "Breaking Out of Bar-Band Gigs," *Los Angeles Times*, 27 December 1977.
331. Rusty Hamilton and Diana Clapton, "David Lee Roth and the Van Halen Gang: Preening Prophets of Post-Cube Punkpop," *Oui*, November 1981, 20.
332. Hamilton and Clapton, "David Lee Roth," 20.
333. "Rock Scene," *(Van Nuys) Valley News*, 3 September 1976; Jeff Simons, interview by author.
334. Richard Cromelin, "Van Halen: From Tahiti to the 7-11," *Los Angeles Times*, 10 September 1982.
335. "David Lee Roth TV interview with Martha Quinn, 1982," YouTube, 13 February 2012, accessed 8 July 2015, https://www.youtube.com/watch?v=UkKwIm8M6D4.

CHAPTER EIGHT: THE GOLDEN WEST

336. This account is based on author interviews with Jeff Burkhardt, Steve Hall, Janice Pirre Francis, Dan Teckenoff, Rodney Davey, and Steven Rosen's interview with Rudy Leiren.
337. Richie Unterberger, *Music USA: The Rough Guide* (London: Rough Guides, 1999), 395–398.
338. Bereskin, "Van Halen's Invitation," 52.
339. Ken Tucker quoted in Considine, *Van Halen!*, 33.
340. Atkinson, "Breaking Out of Bar-Band Gigs."
341. Golden West Ballroom Ledger, 11 April 1976, in author's possession. Special thanks to Janice Pirre Francis for this source.
342. Barney Hoskyns, *Waiting for the Sun: A Rock and Roll History of Los Angeles* (1996; reprint, New York: Backbeat Books, 2003), 268–271; Harvey Kubernik, *Canyon of Dreams: The Magic and Music of Laurel Canyon* (New York: Sterling Publishing, 2009), 298–303.
343. Considine, *Van Halen!*, 35.
344. Mike Cochrane, interview by author.
345. Gary Putman, interview by author.
346. Victor Bornia, interview by author.
347. John Nyman, interview by author.
348. Neil Zlozower, *Van Halen* (San Francisco: Chronicle Books, 2008), 17.
349. Zlozower, *Van Halen*, 17.
350. Rosen, "On Fire," 64; Rosen, "True Beginnings," 48.
351. Rosen, "On Fire," 63–64.
352. "House History," Pasadena Showcase House of Design Brochure, circa 1984, in author's possession; Kim Miller, email to author, 27 July 2014.
353. Roth, *Crazy from the Heat*, 88.
354. "Film & Rock Concert," *Los Angeles Free Press*, 20 June 1975.
355. Bereskin, "Van Halen's Invitation," 52.
356. Hilburn, "Pasadena's Van Halen."
357. Michael Kelley, email to author, 7 December 2009.

358. Golden West Ballroom receipt for UFO/Van Halen gig, in author's possession. Special thanks to Janice Pirre Francis for this source.
359. Dennis Catron, "Review of the UFO/Van Halen Golden West Show," in author's possession.
360. Catron, "Review," in author's possession.
361. Dennis Catron, "Excerpt from an interview with the late, great Rick Gagnon/Mentone Music Month regarding The Golden West," in author's possession.
362. *The Van Halen Story: The Early Years.*
363. Rudy Leiren, interview by Steven Rosen, in author's possession.
364. Catron, "Excerpt," in author's possession.
365. Catron, "Review," in author's possession.
366. Catron, "Review," in author's possession.
367. Rudy Leiren, interview by Steven Rosen, in author's possession.
368. Rudy Leiren, interview by Steven Rosen, in author's possession.
369. Edward Van Halen quoted in Christe, *Everybody Wants Some*, 23. Edward recalls that he overdosed in 1972, but all eyewitnesses agree it took place years later.
370. Rudy Leiren, interview by Steven Rosen, in author's possession.

CHAPTER NINE: NO COMMERCIAL POTENTIAL

371. C. K. Lendt, *Kiss and Sell: The Making of a Supergroup* (New York: Billboard Books, 1997), 153.
372. Roth, *Crazy from the Heat*, 91; Steven Blush, "Runnin' with the Devil," *Seconds*, 1994, 36.
373. Hilburn, "Homegrown Punk-Rock Blossoming."
374. Paul Elliott, "Kiss Unmasked," *Classic Rock*, August 2013, 64.
375. Hedges, *Eddie Van Halen*, 39.
376. "Gazzarri's," *(Pasadena City College) Courier*, 22 October 1976.
377. Jackie Fox, interview by author.
378. Michael Kelley, interview by author, 16 June 2014.
379. John Stix, "George Lynch: Van Halen School Dropout," *Guitar for the Practicing Musician*, July 1986, 48.
380. Michael Kelley, email to author, 16 June 2014.
381. Michael Kelley, email to author, 22 November 2009.
382. Michael Kelley, email to author, 16 June 2014.
383. Hedges, *Eddie Van Halen*, 39.
384. Rosen, "True Beginnings," 48–49.
385. Elliott, "Kiss Unmasked," 64.
386. Hedges, *Eddie Van Halen*, 41–42.
387. Wayne Robins, "David Lee Roth and the Pursuit of Happiness," *Newsday*, 16 February 1986.
388. Hedges, *Eddie Van Halen*, 40–41.
389. Paul Stanley, *Face the Music: A Life Exposed* (New York: Harper One, 2014), 221.
390. Rosen, "True Beginnings," 48–49.
391. Steven Rosen, "California Dreamin'," *Guitar World Presents Van Halen: 40 Years of the Great American Rock Band*, July 2012, 20.
392. Gene Simmons, *Kiss and Make Up* (New York: Three Rivers Press, 2002), 131–132.
393. John Stix, "Eddie Van Halen," *Guitar for the Practicing Musician*, April 1985, 75.
394. Tolinski, "Iron Mike," 103.
395. Stix, "Eddie Van Halen," 74–75.
396. Hedges, *Van Halen*, 42–43.
397. Rosen, "True Beginnings," 48–49.
398. Hedges, *Van Halen*, 48.
399. John Stix, "The Fountain," *Guitar Classics 8*, June 1994, 100.
400. Mark Strigl and John Ostronomy, "Episode 234: Bill Aucoin Special," *Talking Metal Podcast*, 18 October 2008, accessed 15 July 2014, http://podbay.fm/show/78833595/e/1224313200.
401. Strigl and Ostronomy, *Talking Metal Podcast*, episode 234.
402. Strigl and Ostronomy, *Talking Metal Podcast*, episode 234.
403. "Rock and Roll Over," *Wikipedia*, accessed 1 October 2014, http://en.wikipedia.org/wiki/Rock_and_Roll_Over.
404. "'Rock and Roll Over' Tour," *KISSMonster*, accessed 1 October 2014, http://kissmonster.com/reference/inyourface7.php.
405. Stix, "The Fountain," 100.
406. Stix, "The Fountain," 100.
407. Hedges, *Eddie Van Halen*, 43.
408. Stix, "The Fountain," 100.
409. "Eddie on the Record," *Guitar World Presents Guitar Legends*, April 1992, 39.
410. Guitar World Staff, "Prime Cuts: Eddie Van Halen Breaks Down 10 Van Halen Classics from 'Eruption' to 'Right Now,'" *Guitar World*, 13 November 2013, accessed 8 July 2015, http://www.guitarworld.com/article/eddie_van_halen_prime_cuts.

411.   "Eddie on the Record," 39.
412.   Stix, "The Fountain," 100.
413.   Stix, "The Fountain," 100.
414.   Stix, "The Fountain," 100.
415.   Guitar World Staff, "Prime Cuts."
416.   Stix, "The Fountain," 101.
417.   Stix, "The Fountain," 100–101.
418.   Rosen, "True Beginnings," 48–49.
419.   Rosen, "True Beginnings," 48–49.
420.   Rudy Leiren, interview by Steven Rosen, in author's possession.
421.   Stix, "The Fountain," 101.
422.   Stix, "Eddie Van Halen," 75.
423.   Stix, "The Fountain," 101.
424.   Stix, "Eddie Van Halen," 75.
425.   Strigl and Ostronomy, *Talking Metal Podcast*, episode 234.
426.   "Bill Aucoin interview on 'The Rock and Roll Geek Show,' 11.8.2007," *YouTube*, accessed 8 July 2015, https://www.youtube.com/watch?v=bGj7p_04lDM.
427.   Stanley, *Face the Music*, 221–222.
428.   Stanley, *Face the Music*, 223.
429.   Guitar World Staff, "Prime Cuts."
430.   Roth, *Crazy from the Heat*, 92.
431.   Hedges, *Eddie Van Halen*, 44.
432.   Simmons, *Kiss and Make Up*, 132.
433.   "Gene Simmons Comments on Van Halen Demos, 12.28.2001, Eddie Trunk," *YouTube*, 21 April 2012, accessed 8 July 2015, https://www.youtube.com/watch?v=sgcVjurMwmo.
434.   Simmons, *Kiss and Make Up*, 44.
435.   Hedges, *Eddie Van Halen*, 45.
436.   Elliott, "Kiss Unmasked," 64.
437.   Stix, "The Fountain," 101.
438.   Roth, *Crazy from the Heat*, 92.
439.   Simmons, *Kiss and Make Up*, 131–132.
440.   Hedges, *Eddie Van Halen*, 39–45.
441.   Guitar World Staff, "Prime Cuts."
442.   Guitar World Staff, "Prime Cuts."
443.   Tolinski, ed., *Guitar World Presents Van Halen*, 37.
444.   "Van Halen Rare Interview & First Radio Play 1976," *YouTube*, 2 July 2013, accessed 8 July 2015, https://www.youtube.com/watch?v=cmz_yEkyaDA.
445.   David Leaf and Ken Sharp, *Kiss Behind the Mask: The Official Authorized Biography* (New York: Warner Books, 2003), 287; Jeff Kitts, *Kisstory* (Los Angeles: Kisstory, 1994), 223. Thanks to Nik Browning for tracking down the latter source.
446.   Roth, *Crazy from the Heat*, 92.
447.   Rudy Leiren, interview by Steven Rosen, in author's possession.
448.   Jeff Hausman, "*The Inside* Interviews Wally 'Cartoon' Olney," *The Inside*, summer 1997, 24.
449.   Roth, *Crazy from the Heat*, 92.
450.   Rudy Leiren, interview by Steven Rosen, in author's possession.
451.   Hedges, *Eddie Van Halen*, 54–55.
452.   Rudy Leiren, interview by Steven Rosen, in author's possession.
453.   Rudy Leiren, interview by Steven Rosen, in author's possession.
454.   Kitts, *Kisstory*, 223.
455.   Rudy Leiren, interview by Steven Rosen, in author's possession.
456.   Kim Miller, email to the author, 22 July 2014.
457.   Roth, *Crazy from the Heat*, 92–93.
458.   Rudy Leiren, interview by Steven Rosen, in author's possession.
459.   Rudy Leiren, interview by Steven Rosen, in author's possession.

CHAPTER TEN: RIGHT OUT OF THE MOVIES

460.   Steve Gett, "Get Van Halenized," *Record Mirror*, 3 June 1978.
461.   Jas Obrecht, "Eddie Van Halen: The Complete 1978 Interviews," *Jas Obrecht Music Archives*, accessed 29 June 2015, http://web.archive.org/web/20150216183941/http://jasobrecht.com/eddie-van-halen-complete-1978-interviews/.
462.   Michael Segell, "Van Halen's Party Gets a Whole Lot Better," *Rolling Stone*, 18 May 1978, 20; Atkinson, "Breaking Out of Bar-Band Gigs."
463.   "Van Halen Warner Bros. media information," November 1977, in author's possession.
464.   Kevin Merrill, "A Day in the Life of Kim Fowley," *Billboard*, 8 October 1977, 64–65.

465. Rosen, "On Fire," 62; Kim Fowley, interview by author.
466. Rosen, "On Fire," 62; Kim Fowley, interview by author.
467. Brian Hiatt, "Secrets of the Guitar Heroes: Eddie Van Halen," *Rolling Stone*, 12 June 2008, accessed 8 July 2015, http://web.archive.org/web/20080602005114/http://www.rollingstone .com/news/story/20979938/secrets_of_the_guitar_heroes_eddie_van_halen?.
468. Dennis Hunt, "Whisky, on the Rocks, to Become Disco," *Los Angeles Times*, 23 March 1975; Hilburn, "Homegrown Punk-Rock Blossoming."
469. Nat Freedland, "Punk Rock Due at L.A. Whisky," *Billboard*, 20 November 1976, 32.
470. Kim Fowley, interview by author.
471. Neil Zlozower, *Eddie Van Halen* (San Francisco: Chronicle Books, 2011), 21; Kim Fowley, interview by author.
472. Zlozower, *Eddie Van Halen*, 21.
473. Hausman, "Tom Broderick," 22.
474. Dave Meniketti, "Y&T/VH at the Starwood," *Y&T/Meniketti Forums*, 16 June 2008, transcript in author's possession.
475. Richard Cromelin, "Spreading Out from Punk Rock," *Los Angeles Times*, 24 December 1976.
476. Richard Cromelin, "Van Halen Keeps Asserting Itself," *Los Angeles Times*, 29 January 1977.
477. Hilburn, "Homegrown Punk-Rock Blossoming."
478. Buttner, "Michael Anthony of Van Halen"; Rob Broderick, interview by author.
479. Tim Grobaty, "Santana Older, But No Better," *Long Beach Independent-Press Telegram*, 1 February 1977.
480. Considine, *Van Halen!*, 41–42.
481. Marshall Berle, interview by author.
482. Robins, "David Lee Roth."
483. Warren Zanes, *Revolutions in Sound: Warner Bros. Records, The First Fifty Years* (San Francisco: Chronicle Books, 2008), 185.
484. Considine, *Van Halen!*, 41.
485. Iain Blair, *Rock Video Superstars: Van Halen*, March 1985, 10.
486. Paul Grein, "Pop Eye," *Los Angeles Times*, 27 August 1989.
487. Jas Obrecht, "Eddie Van Halen: The Complete 1978 Interviews."
488. Rudy Leiren, interview by Steven Rosen, in author's possession.
489. Rosen, "Ace of Bass," 66.
490. Rosen, "Ace of Bass," 66.
491. Rosen, "California Dreamin'," 21
492. Blair, *Rock Video Superstars*, 4
493. Marshall Berle, interview by author.
494. Rudy Leiren, interview by Steven Rosen, in author's possession.
495. Rosen, "Ace of Bass," 66.
496. Blair, *Rock Video Superstars*, 4
497. Warfield, "Van Halen: From the Starwood to Offenbach."
498. Considine, *Van Halen!*, 41.
499. Rudy Leiren, interview by Steven Rosen, in author's possession.
500. Rudy Leiren, interview by Steven Rosen, in author's possession.
501. Marshall Berle, interview by author.
502. Michael Anthony, "Michael Anthony of Van Halen & Chickenfoot Shares His Favorite Songs," *AOL Radio Blog*, 10 March 2010, accessed 8 July 2015, http://aolradioblog.com/2010/03/10/ michael-anthony-van-halen-chickenfoot-shares-favorite-songs.
503. Zanes, *Revolutions in Sound*, 129.
504. Tolinski, ed., *Guitar World Presents Van Halen*, 38.
505. "The Hunter," *Los Angeles Free Press*, 11 February 1977.
506. Tolinski, ed., *Guitar World Presents Van Halen*, 99.
507. "Our History," *Sunset Sound Recording Studio*, accessed 4 October 2014, http://www.sunsetsound .com/?page_id=68.
508. Dave Simons, "Tales From the Top," *BMI*, 5 September 2008, accessed 8 July 2015, http://www.bmi.com/news/entry/Tales_From_the_Top_Van_Halens_Van_Halen_1978.
509. Gary Nissley, interview by author.
510. Donn Landee, interview by author; Simons, "Tales from the Top."
511. Tolinski, ed., *Guitar World Presents Van Halen*, 98.
512. Richard McKernan, interview by author.
513. Rosen, "Ace of Bass," 66.
514. Howard Pearson, "Paul Williams — He's Tall on Talent," *Deseret News (Salt Lake City, Utah)*, 29 July 1982; "Majors, Fawcett File for Divorce," *Victoria (Texas) Advocate*, 30 May 1980.
515. Young, "Van Halen," 54.
516. George Courville, interview by author.
517. George Courville, email to author, 22 August 2013.

518. Rosen, "Ace of Bass," 66.
519. David Gans, "Ted Templeman," *BAM*, 9 October 1981, accessed 8 July 2015, http://dgans.com/writings/templeman/.
520. Mark Dery, "David Lee Roth Takes Off His Warpaint," *Winner*, November 1986, accessed 17 July 2014 (login required), http://www.rocksbackpages.com/Library/Article/david-lee-roth-takes-off-his-warpaint.
521. Gloria Prosper, interview by author.
522. Redbeard, "In the Studio for Van Halen II," *In the Studio with Redbeard*, accessed 4 October 2014, http://www.inthestudio.net/redbeards-blog/van-halen-2-35th-anniversary.
523. Gett, "Get Van Halenized"; Obrecht, *Masters of Heavy Metal*, 155; Steven Rosen, "Unchained Melodies," *Guitar World Presents Van Halen: 40 Years of the Great American Rock Band*, July 2012, 106; Tolinski, ed., *Guitar World Presents Van Halen*, 97.
524. David Gans, "Ted Templeman."
525. Redbeard, "In the Studio: 20th Anniversary of Van Halen."
526. Brad Tolinski, "Whipper Snapper," *Guitar World*, September 1991, 92.
527. Gene Santoro, "Edward's Producer on the Brown Sound," *Guitar World*, July 1985, 57.
528. Buttner, "Michael Anthony of Van Halen."
529. Gerry Ganaden, "The Return of the Hot Rod Guitar," *Premier Guitar*, February 2009, 119.
530. Jas Obrecht, "An Appreciation," *Positively Van Halen*, winter 1986, 4.
531. Edward and George met on this night in December 1976 because Van Halen was gigging on the other nights Canned Heat played the Starwood.
532. The Starwood advertisement for this date specifically notes that Mandel would be guesting with Canned Heat. See "Starwood," *Los Angeles Times*, 19 December 1976.
533. Randy Cody, "Rocket Interviews George Lynch," *The Metal Den*, 15 March 2009, accessed 8 July 2015, http://themetalden.com/index.php?p=198; George Lynch, interview by author.
534. Hedges, *Van Halen*, 52.
535. Terry Kilgore, "The Last Word on the Ed clone thing," *Vintage Amps Bulletin Board*, 28 April 2004, accessed 8 July 2015, http://vintageamps.com/plexiboard/viewtopic.php?f=5&t=17153&p=163983#p163983.
536. Anthony, "Michael Anthony of Van Halen & Chickenfoot Shares His Favorite Songs."
537. Chris Gill, "Home Improvement," *Guitar World*, February 2014, 67.
538. Joe Bosso, "Michael Anthony: My 6 Career-Defining Records," *Music Radar*, 3 May 2010, accessed 8 July 2015, http://www.musicradar.com/news/guitars/michael-anthony-my-6-career-defining-records-249695/7.
539. Obrecht, *Masters of Heavy Metal*, 146.
540. Peggy McCreary, email to author, 12 September 2012.
541. Zanes, *Revolutions in Sound*, 185.
542. Edward Van Halen quoted in Considine, *Van Halen!*, 42.
543. Tolinski, ed., *Guitar World Presents Van Halen*, 30–31; Jeff Hausman, "New Kid on the Block," *The Inside*, spring 1999, 28–29.
544. Santoro, "Edward's Producer," 57.
545. Stix, "In the Eye of the Storm," 95.
546. Rosen, "True Beginnings," 50; Rosen, "On Fire," 68; Rosen, "Ace of Bass," 67–68.
547. Obrecht, *Masters of Heavy Metal*, 158; Sunset Sound tape boxes and track sheets for *Van Halen*, in author's possession, courtesy of Warner Music Group.
548. Scott, "Van Halen: You Can Keep That Cosmic Stuff."
549. Atkinson, "Van Halen's Big Rock," 12.
550. Scott, "Van Halen: You Can Keep that Cosmic Stuff."
551. Gans, "Ted Templeman"; Santoro, "Edward's Producer," 57; Richard McKernan, interview by author.
552. Rosen, "True Beginnings," 50.
553. "High Energy Rockers," *St. Louis Post-Dispatch*, 26 April 1979.
554. Rosen, "True Beginnings," 50.
555. "The Producers: Ted Templeman," *Rolling Stone's Continuous History of Rock and Roll Radio Show*, 26 June 1983, in author's possession.
556. Chris Gill, "A Different Kind of Trove," *Guitar Aficionado*, January/February 2013, 60.
557. Rosen, "On Fire," 164.
558. "The Producers: Ted Templeman"; Ted Templeman, interview by author.
559. Bruce Westbrook, "Rock Around the Clock," *Sunday Oklahoman*, 6 August 1978.
560. Tolinski, ed., *Guitar World Presents Van Halen*, 50.
561. Thank you to Bill Flanagan for his assistance with this paragraph.
562. Redbeard, "In the Studio: 20th Anniversary of Van Halen."
563. Zlozower, *Van Halen*, 33.
564. Rosen, "Ace of Bass," 66–67; Rosen, "On Fire," 68.

565. Rosen, "On Fire," 68.
566. Steven Baltin, "David Lee Roth Vents About Van Halen's Future," *Rolling Stone*, 12 February 2013, accessed 8 July 2015, http://www.rollingstone.com/music/news/q-a-david-lee-roth-vents-about-van-halens-future-20130212.
567. Matthews, *Van Halen*, 31.
568. Dennis Hunt, "Van Halen's Roth Likes Rock Rough," *Los Angeles Times*, 1 April 1979.
569. Sylvie Simmons, "Van Halen," *Sounds*, 7 April 1979, accessed 8 July 2015 (login required), http://www.rocksbackpages.com/Library/Article/van-halen-2.
570. Hann, "David Lee Roth."
571. Roth, *Crazy from the Heat*, 115.
572. Scott, "Van Halen: You Can Keep That Cosmic Stuff."
573. Edward Van Halen quoted in Jeff Kitts and Brad Tolinski, eds., *Guitar World Presents the 100 Greatest Guitarists of All Time* (Milwaukee: Hal Leonard, 2002), 121.
574. Rosen, "Unchained Melodies," 107.
575. Tolinski, ed., *Guitar World Presents Van Halen*, 97.
576. Tolinski, ed., *Guitar World Presents Van Halen*, 97.
577. Edward Van Halen quoted in Kitts and Tolinski, eds., *Guitar World Presents the 100 Greatest Guitarists of All Time*, 121.
578. Tolinski, ed., *Guitar World Presents Van Halen*, 97.
579. Robert Vosgien, email to author, 25 July 2014. Thanks to Robert for explaining this process to me.
580. Simons, "Tales from the Top."
581. Tolinski, ed., *Guitar World Presents Van Halen*, 96–97.
582. Tolinski, ed., *Guitar World Presents Van Halen*, 34–35.
583. Harold Bronson, "This Man," *Penn State Daily Collegian*, 5 October 1978; *CPI Inflation Calculator*, accessed 1 February 2015, http://data.bls.gov/cgi-bin/cpicalc.pl.
584. Guitar World Staff, "Prime Cuts."
585. Segell, "Van Halen's Party," 20.
586. Matthews, *Van Halen*, 32.

CHAPTER TWELVE: CALM BEFORE THE STORM

587. Quick Draw, "Van Halen: Today L.A., Tomorrow the Galaxy," *Raw Power*, October–November 1977, 35.
588. Paul Gargano, "David Lee Roth: Past, Present & Future," *Metal Edge*, November 1998, 12.
589. Stix, "In the Eye of the Storm," 90.
590. Debi Fee and Linda Benjamin, "Van Halen's David Lee Roth," *Tiger Beat Super Special #3 Presents Rock!*, June/July 1980, 18.
591. Stix, "In the Eye of the Storm," 90.
592. Ted Templeman, interview by author; Tom Broderick, interview by author; Roth, *Crazy from the Heat*, 84.
593. Roth, *Crazy from the Heat*, 83–84.
594. Rosen, "Unchained Melodies," 107–108.
595. Michael Wilton, "Van Halen's Babysitter," *L.A. Weekly*, 1 June 2012, accessed 8 July 2015, http://www.laweekly.com/music/van-halens-babysitter-2175110.
596. Stix, "In the Eye of the Storm," 90.
597. Rosen, "Unchained Melodies," 107–108.
598. Considine, *Van Halen!*, 43.
599. Rosen, "True Beginnings," 51.
600. Robert Hilburn, "Under the Rock, an Exciting Crop of Newcomers," *Los Angeles Times*, 27 November 1977.
601. Atkinson, "Breaking Out of Bar Band Gigs."
602. Gargano, "David Lee Roth," 110.
603. Hausman, "Tom Broderick," 21.
604. Hausman, "Tom Broderick," 21.

CHAPTER THIRTEEN: UNLEASHED

605. Wolf Schneider, "Don Airey Revealed," *The Highway Star*, 8 February 2004, accessed 8 July 2015, http://thehighwaystar.com/interviews/airey/da-feb082004.html.
606. Rosen, "Diver Down," 11.
607. Rosen, "Diver Down," 11.
608. "Billboard Hot 100," *Billboard*, 11 March 1978, 96.
609. Hausman, "Tom Broderick," 16.
610. Michael St. John, "Runnin' with Van Halen," *(Madison) Emerald City Chronicle*, 21 March 1978, 4.
611. David Konow, *Bang Your Head: The Rise and Fall of Heavy Metal* (New York: Three Rivers Press, 2002), 93–94.

612. Susan Masino, "Going Mad in Wisconsin," *The Inside*, spring 1999, 27.
613. *The Van Halen Scrapbook* (Cresskill, NJ: Sharon Publications, 1984), 51–52.
614. "Van Halen: Who Are These Guys and Why Are They So Famous," *Hit Parader*, December 1980, 10.
615. Hedges, *Eddie Van Halen*, 52.
616. Edouard Dauphin, "He Ain't Heavy! The Van Halen Boys Talk," *Creem Close Up: Van Halen*, summer 1984, 22.
617. Kim Miller, email to author, 5 August 2014.
618. Trietsch, "Van Halen: Short and Sweet."
619. Rosen, "Diver Down," 11.
620. Rob Patterson, "Van Halen: In Search of the *Baaad* Chord," *Creem*, July 1978, 22.
621. Stix, "In the Eye of the Storm," 90.
622. Michael Oldfield, "Van Halen," *Melody Maker*, 3 June 1978; "Van Halen Hits the Big Time," *Circus*, 31 October 1984, 57. For a listing of Van Halen's singles from *Van Halen*, see "Van Halen - Discography," *45Cat*, accessed 8 July 2015, http://www.45cat.com/artist/van-halen.
623. Shearlaw, *Van Halen*, 29.
624. Elizabeth Reich, "Van Halen Album Hard Rock Jewel," *Orange County Register*, 2 March 1978.
625. Neil Peters, "Van Halen," *New Musical Express*, 27 May 1978.
626. James Spina, "Spin Addict," *Hit Parader*, September 1978, 15.
627. Terry Atkinson, "Riffs Run Rampant in Van Halen Debut," *Los Angeles Times*, 5 March 1978.
628. Charles M. Young, "Van Halen," *Rolling Stone*, 4 May 1978, accessed 8 July 2015, http://www.rollingstone.com/music/albumreviews/van-halen-19780504.
629. Margaret Moser, "Hard, and I Mean HARD, Rock," *Austin Sun*, 21 April 1978.
630. John Bryant, "Rock Band Crams in Quality," *Austin American-Statesman*, 14 April 1978.
631. Stix, "The Last of the Pre–Van Halen Bands," 19.
632. Jude Gold, "Ten Things You Gotta Do To Play Like Eddie Van Halen," *Guitar Player*, 1 February 2009, accessed 8 July 2015, http://www.guitarplayer.com/artist-lessons/1026/10-things-you-gotta-do-to-play-like-eddie-van-halen/16950.
633. Andy Secher, "Guitar Workshop with Gamma's Ronnie Montrose," *Hit Parader*, April 1981, 38.
634. Rudy Leiren, interview by Steven Rosen, in author's possession.
635. Paul Wilkinson, *Rat Salad: Black Sabbath, The Classic Years, 1969–1975* (New York: St. Martin's Press, 2007), 224–225.
636. Tom Noble, "Black Sabbath Van Halen," *New Musical Express*, 3 June 1978.
637. Steve Gett, "Van Halen: Colston Hall, Bristol," *Record Mirror*, 3 June 1978.
638. Terry McGovern, "Van Halen," *Profiles in Rock*, 3 May 1980, in author's possession.
639. "Van Halen Has Enthusiasm," *Salina (Kansas) Journal*, 28 May 1978.
640. Mike Simmons, "'Texas Jam' Provides Hot Times," *Deer Park (Texas) Progress*, 13 July 1978.
641. Rudy Leiren, interview by Steven Rosen, in author's possession.
642. McGovern, "Van Halen."
643. Simmons, "'Texas Jam' Provides Hot Times."
644. McGovern, "Van Halen."
645. Zlozower, *Eddie Van Halen*, 22.
646. Simmons, "'Texas Jam' Provides Hot Times."
647. Rudy Leiren, interview by Steven Rosen, in author's possession.
648. Hilburn, "Pasadena's Van Halen."
649. Hilburn, "Pasadena's Van Halen."
650. Hilburn, "Pasadena's Van Halen."
651. Charlie Crespo, "Everynight Charley," *Aquarian*, 13 September 1978.
652. Frank Donze, "Stones Mob Rolls in Early for Rock Show," *(New Orleans) Times-Picayune*, 14 July 1978.
653. Alan Citron, "80,173 Fill Dome for Stones Show," *(New Orleans) Times-Picayune*, 14 July 1978.
654. "Runnin' with Van Halen Radio Special," Warner Bros. Records, 1978, in author's possession.
655. Crespo, "Everynight Charley."
656. Jim Ladd, "Van Halen," *Innerview*, KMET-FM, 1980, in author's possession.
657. Ken Tucker, "Van Halen," *High Fidelity*, May 1978, 138.
658. Heidi Siegmund, "For Van Halen It's about Balance Right Now," *(Pasadena) Star-News*, 31 March 1995.
659. Ellis Widner, "Van Halen Overnight Success," *Tulsa Tribune*, 15 July 1978.
660. Bob Claypool, "Big Rock," *Houston Post*, 17 November 1978.
661. Oppel, "Van Halen's Big Rock."
662. Hilburn, "Pasadena's Van Halen."
663. Scott Noecker and Craig Nienaber, "Sizzling Crowd Waits, Rocks, Waits," *Quad-City Times (Iowa)*, 17 July 1978.
664. Douglas Guenther, email to author, 13 January 2014.
665. Noecker and Nienaber, "Sizzling Crowd."
666. Rosen, "Unchained Melodies," 108; Brad Tolinski, ed., *Guitar World Presents Van Halen* (Milwaukee: Hal Leonard, 1997), 198.

667. Zlozower, *Van Halen*, 48; Rosen, "Unchained Melodies," 108.
668. *San Francisco Chronicle* clipping, July 1978, in author's possession.
669. Jennefer Hirshberg, "The Ted Nugent Sellout," *Washington Post*, 14 August 1978.
670. Henry Rollins quoted in Sanchez, *Van Halen* 101, 360–361.
671. Henry Rollins, "Henry Rollins — Van Halen," *YouTube*, 12 May 2012, accessed 8 July 2015, https://www.youtube.com/watch?v=O5mGVjcStiM.
672. Henry Rollins quoted in Sanchez, *Van Halen* 101, 360–361.
673. Shearlaw, *Van Halen*, 61.
674. Crespo, "Everynight Charley."
675. Mark Mehler, "The Crowds Are Wild," *Circus*, 10 October 1978, 31.
676. Scott Cohen, "Heavy Metal Showdown," *Circus*, 10 October 1978, 26.
677. David Tangye and Graham Wright, *How Black Was Our Sabbath: An Unauthorized View from the Crew* (London: Pan MacMillan UK, 2004), 212–213.
678. Rudy Leiren, interview by Steven Rosen, in author's possession.
679. Sue Flinker, "Black Sabbath," directed by Barbara Kanowitz, *Biography*, Biography Channel, 15 July 2010.
680. Sylvie Simmons, "Goodbye to Romance," *Mojo Classic: Ozzy: The Real Story*, April 2005, 48.
681. Zanes, *Revolutions in Sound*, 185.
682. Robert Hilburn, "Jumping at the Big A," *Los Angeles Times*, 25 September 1978.
683. Sharon Gazin, "Lots of Life in Old Band Yet," *Utica (New York) Daily Press*, 8 September 1978.
684. "Platinum," *Billboard*, 30 September 1978, 94.
685. Flinker, "Black Sabbath."
686. Pete Oppel, "Black Sabbath Plods Through Heavy Evening," *Dallas Morning News*, 27 November 1978.
687. Konow, *Bang Your Head*, 111.
688. Flinker, "Black Sabbath."
689. Roth, *Crazy from the Heat*, 249–251.
690. Flinker, "Black Sabbath."
691. Flinker, "Black Sabbath."
692. "Lead Singer Gets Lost," *(Huntingdon and Mount Union, Pennsylvania) Daily News*, 13 November 1978.
693. "He Slept in the Wrong Room, Missed Show," *Sarasota Herald-Tribune*, 11 November 1978.
694. Roth, *Crazy from the Heat*, 249–251.
695. Joe Siegler, "Black Sabbath Concert Reviews," *Black Sabbath Online*, 1 December 2009, accessed 8 July 2015, http://web.archive.org/web/20110323072905/http://www.black-sabbath.com/tourdates/1978/november_19_1978.html.
696. Flinker, "Black Sabbath."
697. Mike Stark, *Black Sabbath: An Oral History*, ed. Dave Marsh (New York: Harper Collins, 2002), 38.
698. Paul Elliott, "Born Again," *Classic Rock*, February 2010, 49.
699. Hedges, *Eddie Van Halen*, 53.
700. Claypool, "Big Rock"; Christe, *Everybody Wants Some*, 50.
701. Steven Rosen, "Van Halen," *Record Review*, April 1979, 5.
702. Dave Larsen, "Eddie Van Halen Finds His Balance," *Dayton Daily News*, 21 April 1995.
703. John Stix, "Eddie Van Halen Interviews Steve Lukather," *Guitar for the Practicing Musician*, September 1993, 102.

AFTERWORD

704. Richard Hogan, "Van Halen: Best Group, Best Guitar, Best Year Ever," *Circus*, 28 February 1985, 60.
705. Considine, *Van Halen!*, 59; Dodds, *Edward Van Halen*, 55.
706. Christe, *Everybody Wants Some*, 100; Dodds, *Edward Van Halen*, 103–104.
707. Christe, *Everybody Wants Some*, 112.
708. Hedges, *Eddie Van Halen*, 123.
709. Paul Grein, "106 Multiple Platinums Kick Off RIAA Award," *Billboard*, 15 December 1984, 79, 81.
710. "Blackout" and "Love at First Sting," *RIAA Searchable Database*, accessed 14 October 2014, http://www.riaa.com/goldandplatinumdata.php?table=SEARCH; Grein, "106 Multiple Platinums Kick Off RIAA Award," 79, 81.
711. "Screaming for Vengeance," *Allmusic*, accessed 18 October 2014, http://www.allmusic.com/album/screaming-for-vengeance-mw0000194426/awards; "Defenders of the Faith," *Allmusic*, accessed 18 October 2014, http://www.allmusic.com/album/defenders-of-the-faith-mw0000194425/awards.
712. "A Different Kind of Truth," *Wikipedia*, accessed 8 July 2015, https://en.wikipedia.org/wiki/A_Different_Kind_of_Truth
713. Hedges, *Eddie Van Halen*, 66–67.
714. Hedges, *Eddie Van Halen*, 67.
715. Hedges, *Eddie Van Halen*, 133.

Published by ECW Press
665 Gerrard Street East
Toronto, ON M4M 1Y2
416-694-3348 / info@ecwpress.com

Printing: Marquis   7   8
Printed and bound in Canada

LIBRARY AND ARCHIVES CANADA
CATALOGUING IN PUBLICATION

Renoff, Gregory J., 1969–, author

Van Halen rising : how a Southern
California backyard party band saved
heavy metal / written by Greg Renoff.

Issued in print and electronic formats.
ISBN 978-1-77041-263-7 (pbk)
978-1-77090-790-4 (pdf)
978-1-77090-791-1 (epub)

1. Van Halen (Musical group).
2. Rock groups—United States—
Biography. 3. Rock musicians—
United States—Biography. I. Title.

ML421.V36R42 2015   782.42166092'2
C2015-902819-1   C2015-902820-5

Editor for the press: Michael Holmes
Cover design: VAiN Eudes
Cover images: Mary Garson/Hot Shotz
and Elizabeth Wiley
Author photo: Leslie Hoyt